Media in
SOCIETY
Readings in
Mass Communication

Caren J. Deming
The University of Arizona

Samuel L. Becker
The University of Iowa

Scott, Foresman/Little, Brown College Division
SCOTT, FORESMAN AND COMPANY
Glenview, Illinois *Boston London*

Acknowledgments are listed on p. 432, which constitutes a legal extension of the copyright page.

Library of Congress Cataloging-in-Publication Data

Media in society: readings in mass communication/[edited by] Caren
    J. Deming, Samuel L. Becker.
        p. cm.
    ISBN 0-673-15820-9 (soft)
    1. Mass media—United States.   2.   Mass media—Social aspects—
United States.   I.   Deming, Caren J.,   II.   Becker, Samuel
L.
    P92.U5M427   1988
302.2'34'0973—dc19   88-730
                        CIP

Preface

In virtually every country in the world today, national debates on the role of mass media occur frequently. Leaders in developed and emerging nations alike recognize that the operations and content of the media are too important to ignore. In some countries, such as the United States, these debates are confined largely to agencies and individuals in government and to groups with financial interests in the media industries. In other countries, citizens, concerned about the future of their society and recognizing that neither government nor industry adequately represents them, also are deeply involved in the debate. A major purpose of this collection of readings is to stimulate such involvement by those whose futures will be affected most by the outcomes—the young, educated citizens of this country.

No one collection can adequately cover all of the important issues related to phenomena so complex, varied, and far-reaching in their implications as the mass media. What we have tried to do in this collection is to provide a range of articles that students will find interesting and challenging, that will provoke them to think about the media in ways they have not done before, and that will get them involved in debate. Inside and outside the classroom, students should consider the roles the media are and should be playing in our society and, equally important, the roles audience members are and should be playing in the mass communication process.

Although the authors represented here look at the media from a variety of perspectives, the dominant approach is interpretive. That is, they see the functions and effects of the media as greatly dependent on the ways audience members, as well as journalists and other media creators, *process* or *interpret* the "realities" with which they are confronted. Collectively, these authors believe that Walter Lippmann's insights about "the world out there and the pictures in our heads" apply equally to reporters, editors, entertainers, and producers on one side and readers, viewers, and listeners on the other. Therefore, when students read about the ethical dilemmas of editors or about mass media stereotyping, they should be encouraged to think about the analogous issues involving all of the participants in the mass communication process, including audience members. They should be forced to confront the issue of the audience's influence on the choices editors and other gatekeepers make, as well as the ways in which audiences stereotype and create other "realities" from the media they experience. The more students get away from conceiving of audience members as "receivers" and begin thinking of them as "participants" in the communication process, the more sophisticated and insightful will be their understandings of mass media and the more they will be able to contribute to the national debate on the topic.

As you will see, some of the articles in this collection are not easy to understand on first reading. Some, such as McLuhan's essay, may even be confusing to students—at least we hope so. We believe it is from being forced to struggle with difficult material, to make sense from material that at first glance seems confusing, that students learn. Few things that are worth learning come easily. Thus we hope that students will not only gain useful knowledge about mass media from studying the readings in this book, but that they also will increase substantially their skills at interpretation and analysis. In this way, both the content and the process of your course will help students become better citizens.

The articles in *Media in Society: Readings in Mass Communication* are organized, roughly, according to eight major functions of mass communication: informing, entertaining, expressing, selling, shaping perceptions, shaping behavior, shaping institutions, and shaping our future. However, this is not necessarily the best organization for every class. The order in which the readings are assigned should depend on the goals of the particular course and the other material being covered. A topical table of contents is provided for those who wish to follow the sequence of an introductory textbook such as Becker's *Discovering Mass Communication,* Second Edition (Glenview, Illinois: Scott, Foresman and Company, 1987). The essays in *Media in Society* may be used as counterpoints for sections of any textbook, as supplements where issues are ignored or too lightly treated, and as stimulators for discussion and student papers. They can serve to remind students that no one has all of the right answers to the questions raised by mass media in our society, that in many cases we are not yet agreed even on what the right questions are, and that in all cases it is important that they—the students—develop their own questions and their own answers about these mass media that are so much a part of their lives.

Our thanks to the professionals at Scott, Foresman who have contributed much to the development and production of this work. Although we have not always agreed with them, or with each other, their questions, suggestions, and general support have made this a better book than it otherwise would have been. We acknowledge especially the help of Barbara Muller, Louise Howe, and Kay Bartolo.

Caren J. Deming and Samuel L. Becker

Table of Contents

Topical Table of Contents

INTRODUCTION

Americans inhabit a mediated world: our lives are saturated with information and images delivered by a wealth of media technologies. Because the media are so prominent in contemporary life, they inevitably arouse questions about how well they serve different individuals and societies, why they operate as they do, and how they might be structured or regulated to serve people better. The debate is multitudinous, both in the sense that the issues are numerous and varied and in the sense that many people have a stake in the outcomes. As an educated citizen, it is important that you participate in this debate.

Communication media are such integral parts of our world that it is easy to take them and their present modes of operation for granted. To do so is a serious mistake. Their proper operation is too vital to our lives to be disregarded. It is essential that all who care about the kind of society we inhabit become as knowledgeable as possible about the media. This knowledge will help us to influence their operation and, hence, their usefulness to us and their impact upon us. Toward that end, we need to become aware of the questions we ought to address and to acquire analytical skills for answering those questions intelligently.

The readings in this book set before you a range of viewpoints on a variety of issues pertinent to today's media. The purpose of the book is to help you sharpen your analytical skills as you weigh the various authors' arguments on behalf of their viewpoints. At the same time, the editors hope to increase substantially your awareness of the various questions about the media that you, as a citizen in the world of mediated communication, should be able to answer.

Those questions tend to fall into three general categories. There are questions relating to the functions that television, newspapers, radio, books, motion pictures, magazines, and the rest serve in our private lives and in the public life of our society. Examples of questions about function are: *Why do Americans watch so much television? Which media do we rely upon most for news? What role do media play in elections?* Questions about function lead immediately to questions about impact or influence: *Does watching violent television or movies make people more violent? Has an increase in televangelism contributed to a decline in church attendance?* Third, there are questions of policy: *Should sexually explicit material be banned from the media? Should advertising aimed at children be controlled? Should projections of election winners be printed or broadcast before all of the polls have closed?*

The way people answer such questions—indeed, the very questions raised or not raised—depends upon people's values. In other words, valid answers to questions about the media depend ultimately upon your beliefs and ideals, upon your vision of the kind of world in which you want to live. *Are the media providing the kinds of information and entertainment that Americans ought to have? Is it good or bad that the media stimulate consumption?* Empirical research, such as surveys of people's habits of media use and experiments designed to test the influence of advertising on individuals' buying decisions, may be helpful in answering these questions. Ultimately, however, your answers must depend on your analysis of the issues in terms of the values you hold.

No single book can cover adequately a topic as vast and complex as media in society. The articles in this collection were selected to provide you with diverse opinions on some important current issues. A few of the essays first were published a long time ago. They are included because they provide historical perspective on these issues. Because change occurs so rapidly in the media, even some of the articles published recently may contain details that are no longer current; but this fact does not hamper materially the articles' usefulness. Indeed, the questions raised by the authors represented in this volume are all the more striking for this reason: despite all of the recent changes in the media and in our society, these important questions remain unanswered.

Although selected for their diversity and, in many cases, for the controversial opinions they contain, the articles in this book are not as representative of interested constituencies as the editors would like them to be. We would have preferred more articles by representatives of minority groups and by women, for example. Just as the media have not manifested the heterogeneity of the American population, white men have been overrepresented in published writing about the media.

The language used by the contributors to this book is sometimes controversial as well. Although patently offensive material was avoided, the Scott, Foresman guidelines for references to gender and ethnicity were not applied to the reprinted material as stringently as they normally are applied to original material. In this case, our interest in diversity took precedence over our interest in gender- and bias-free language. As you read this collection of essays by media practitioners, academics, regulators, and others, you should consider how authors representative of other constituencies might talk about the issues raised here or how they might even raise other issues altogether.

Some articles in this book were selected because they reveal sophisticated or profound understandings of media and society. Thus, you will find challenging reading here. Some of the vocabulary and abstract ideas you encounter will require effort to comprehend. Your effort will be rewarded, though, with new depths of understanding and enhanced ability to describe and evaluate your media world.

The book is organized around some basic functions and effects of communication media. The first half focuses on functions. Sections 1 and 2 are about the roles media play in providing information and entertainment to audiences. Section 3 highlights ways in which media provide avenues of expression for people and ideas. Section 4 provides analysis of the roles that media play in our economic system.

The second half of the book focuses on different kinds of effects the media probably have. Section 5 focuses on the most basic of these—media influences on our perceptions. Section 6 is about various kinds of behavior influenced by the media, from teenage drinking to rape. Section 7 contains articles on institutions influenced by communication media, including politics, religion, and sports. Unlike the first seven sections, which emphasize the present and the recent past, Section 8 deals directly with the future and the options that new and existing communications media offer to us.

The articles in each section should cause you to think about various aspects of each function or effect and about various points of view. Those ideas will be the jumping off points for your own analyses and the development of your personal points of view. To help you in this endeavor, the editors have provided you with an introduction to each section containing an overview of the readings and a set of issues or questions pertaining to the entire section. As the sections progress, these general questions get tougher, asking you to think more deeply and more carefully as you increase your knowledge of the media.

Each reading is preceded by an additional series of questions. These questions are designed to guide your study, to help you see relationships between each author's ideas and the more general questions raised in the section introductions. You should read the questions before you read each article and then return to the questions and formulate your answers. Among the study questions you will find many ideas for papers your instructor may assign.

As you read this book the question you should be asking constantly is *why . . . ? Why do these authors and other people believe what they do about the media and their proper role in society? Why do* you *believe what you do?* To the extent that you read carefully and answer these questions and the ones in the book thoughtfully, your class discussion will be stimulating and—more importantly—you will increase your power to exercise your rights and responsibilities as a citizen in the mediated world.

Section 1

MEDIA AS PROVIDERS OF INFORMATION

Since Revolutionary times, Americans have assumed that a well-informed electorate is vital to a democracy such as ours. Citizens are unable to vote intelligently or adequately control their government and the other major forces that affect their lives if they lack the relevant knowledge. If these assumptions are valid, as we believe they are, the quality of sources of information and the way people use them must be among the society's central concerns. Thus, they must be among the central concerns of anyone examining the media. For this reason, it is appropriate that our first set of readings in this book focus on the issues related to the media as providers of information.

Do the media make available to people the kinds of information they need in order to be effective citizens? If not, why not? Are Americans taking sufficient advantage of that information? Are they using the media as they should? What should the media do to better serve the public? What should readers, listeners, and viewers do to fulfill their responsibilities to become well-informed citizens? Does concern about the impact of news coverage on those who are the subjects of the stories increase or decrease the chances that the public will be adequately informed? And underlying all of these questions are four fundamental issues: *What is news? What is the relationship of "news" to "truth"? What kinds of news are needed in our society? How should news be presented in order to best fulfill its purposes?* These four questions must be answered before we can assess whether present-day news media are doing a good job and whether Americans are taking adequate advantage of these sources of information. These questions also are important as we consider what, if any, government regulation of the media we should have. Although the papers in this section do not directly address all of these questions, they provide a basis for development of your own answers. Keep them in mind as you study this first group of papers and, at the end, return to these questions and construct your answers.

Most of the views expressed in this section are those of men. As you read these papers, consider whether the authors' gender affects the way they perceive the news world. For example, women and black men are mentioned only occasionally in these essays. Oppel's case studies include one female rape victim and one female hostage. Schorr's discussion of *The Atlanta Child Murders* brings a black criminal to the scene. As you read these pages, think about what probably would be said, or said differently, if the news world and the newsworthy world were dominated by blacks, by women, or by any other identifiable group. How would the issues be addressed then? Would the examples cited be different? Would there be different issues under discussion?

Some other general questions these authors should help you address include the following:

Where do Americans get their information about the world? Evan Witt's analysis would lead us to believe that we know far less about audiences' information consumption habits than we thought. Witt's sobering message suggests that our exposure and attention to information are subject to a wide array of influences.

Next, in "Can the Press Tell the Truth?" a panel of journalists debates the issues surrounding the demand that reporters be objective. Through the panelists' discussion, we learn that the age-old journalistic value of objectivity is actually a highly controversial matter.

The outright clash between society's need for information and an individual's right to privacy is Nat Hentoff's focus. *Where should journalists draw the line between their own right to free speech and their subjects' right to a private life?* Just how difficult it can be to draw that line becomes clear from Hentoff's analysis. More ethical dilemmas facing reporters and editors are confronted in the articles by Richard Oppel and Arthur Caplan. Conflict of interest, sensationalism, when to run a story, when not to, and when to suppress information—all are addressed in five case studies in editorial gatekeeping.

This first group of readings ends with the subject of television docudrama. Daniel Schorr wrestles with the ethics of dramatically portraying newsworthy people and events. His discussion shows how the ethics of information encoding seem to change according to whether a person is writing or being written about. Schorr's article also reveals how network guidelines for program content emerge.

---

*S*tudy *Q*uestions: *W*itt

? *Witt asks, "What is news?" How would you answer that question?*

What conclusions about American's news habits do you draw from this article? Why is the question of where Americans get most of their news important? Why is it important to the media? To our society? To you?

Is it possible that where people get most of their news and where they think they get most of it are different? On what evidence would you base your answer to the question of which medium people "rely on most" for news? Which medium do you rely on most? Does your response differ for different kinds of news—local, national, world, sports? If so, how do you explain that difference?

Witt reports a study finding that 78 percent of adults read at least part of a newspaper every day, while 24 percent watch a network newscast on an average day. What do you conclude from those figures? When people read part of a newspaper, are they necessarily reading news stories? When people

> *are not watching news on television, are they necessarily* not *getting news or information? How would you ask people to describe their news viewing and reading habits so as to get more valid responses?*
>
> *Witt talks about "the different needs and motivations of adults" that news serves. What do you think those different needs and motivations are? For example, what are your needs or motivations for reading newspapers? Listening to radio news? Watching television news?*

Evans Witt

HERE, THERE, AND EVERYWHERE: WHERE AMERICANS GET THEIR NEWS

It seemed like such a simple question twenty-four years ago. Needing an easy, nonthreatening way to open a questionnaire, researchers at the Roper Organization hit upon a straightforward little query asking where people get most of their news. But that innocuous question has helped spawn a two-decades-old controversy that pits the giants of the media—television and newspapers—against one another.

The answers to Roper's question (asked yearly since 1959) are often cited as proof that television is now the dominant source of news and information for the American public, overshadowing newspapers, radio, and magazines. The results have been sweepingly interpreted as forecasting the extinction of newspapers and the creation of a nation solely dependent on news from the TV networks.

At stake in this controversy, on one level, are boasting rights—which medium is entitled to call itself the premier source of news for the American people? On another level, the fight entails much more.

The answer to Roper's question helps determine where billions of dollars in advertising are channeled every year. It helps shape how people in the news business think of themselves, their competition, and the news itself. And it has a significant influence on how political debate and election campaigns are structured.

In addition, the controversy helps highlight the strengths and weaknesses of survey research. It suggests that limited survey results can all too easily be exploded into overwhelming declarations of the way the world is.

As one might expect, the public's sources and uses of news have been the focus of thousands of research projects. The issues are too important to the multibillion dollar media industry for it to settle for any single answer; and the issues are too interesting for academic researchers to ignore.

Some of the research remains locked up in the vaults of industry, but a great deal has been published in popular and academic journals. A substantial fraction of this published research has been funded by a newspaper chain, a television association, or other industry groups. The Roper studies, for example, were conducted for the Television Information Office, an arm of the National Association of Broadcasters, and some work that calls Roper's results into question has been paid for by the American Newspaper Publishers Association (ANPA). This does not, of course, suggest that the results have been swayed by the sources of funding, but it serves as a reminder that stakes in this argument have been found well worth defending.

TURNING ON TO TELEVISION

Where *do* Americans get their news? When the printed word—meaning largely newspapers—was the only significant daily news outlet, it was easy to tell. But then came the miracle of radio; it could bring Franklin D. Roosevelt into the living room for a chat and could put Chicago's listeners on a rooftop in London alongside Edward R. Murrow as German planes dropped bombs. The news and drama—previously confined to black and white print and locked into production schedules that put hours or days between the event and the reader—were suddenly right there for the radio listener.

The advent of television added pictures to radio's innovations—the scenes of the events as they happened. And as the television set became a fixture in the American living room, the controversy took shape.

In 1959, the television industry was reeling from the quiz show scandals. Broadcasters wanted to know whether the revelation of rigged games had tarnished the medium's image, and whether it had damaged the credibility of the networks' still-brief news shows.

The Television Information Office (TIO) went to the Roper Organization for survey research to address these questions. If the results were negative for the industry, Bud Roper says, the TIO would have distributed them to the broadcasters for their own edification: If the results were positive, the NAB wanted Elmo Roper—Bud's father and then head of the firm—to testify before the Federal Communications Commission. And so he did.

The question which began the survey wasn't too substantive, but seemed a good way to introduce the topic to the respondent:

"First, I'd like to ask you where you usually get most of your news about what's going on in the world today—from the newspapers or radio or television or magazines or talking to people or where?"

Though the question asked for only one source of news, people could mention as many as they liked. The responses didn't add up to anything startling in 1959: Newspapers were the major source, cited by 59 percent of the adults. Television, still sporting its 15-minute national newscasts, was second, not far behind with 51 percent. Radio got the nod from 34 percent.

When Roper repeated the questions in 1961, not a great deal had changed. But by 1963, things were different. When the November 1963 results were tallied, television had overtaken newspapers, with 55 percent naming TV as their top source for news, 53 percent mentioning newspapers, and radio hanging in with 34 percent.

That the results had changed should have been no surprise, for TV news was changing dramatically. On September 2, 1963, CBS expanded its evening newscast from 15 minutes to half an hour. NBC followed suit within days, while ABC would wait several years to expand its shows. Even as the networks were giving the public more news, technological improvements were adding other dimensions—videotape allowed stories to be fed over telephone lines to New York rather than requiring the film to be flown in, and Telstar gave the networks a video link to Europe, opening the way for more foreign coverage.

Late November 1963 also brought an event that was a watershed for many Americans and certainly for television news—the assassination of President John F. Kennedy. For long and tragic days, the nation watched the scene unfold live on the television screens. Millions saw Lee Harvey Oswald shot and killed, and much of the nation joined the funeral march to Arlington Cemetery via the TV screen.

Since 1963 in the Roper surveys, television news has held its lead over newspapers. The most recent poll, conducted last December, found 65 percent naming television as the source for most of their news, while only 44 percent mentioned newspapers. That 21-point edge was the largest Roper had found.

IS SEEING BELIEVING?

Adding to the newspapers' concerns, Roper's surveys also find people saying they tend to believe TV news over what they see in the papers. Since 1961, television has come out on top in the polls when people are asked which source they would believe if the media offered conflicting versions of the same event. In 1982, 53 percent said they would believe the TV news story, compared to only 22 percent accepting the newspaper's rendition.

Another set of studies over the last two decades—these by Robert Bower, now at the Bureau of Social Science Research—helps flesh out the Roper surveys. Bower finds that television is overwhelmingly the public's choice as the most entertaining medium. Given the predominance of entertainment as the major fare of television, this is not surprising. Perhaps, then, TV news wins part of its lead in the Roper studies as a result of the important role television—not just TV news—plays in many people's lives. Bud Roper has suggested that some sort of "halo effect" might be at work.

Bower's studies also found that, by a big margin, television is viewed as getting the news most quickly. But he did find in 1970 that TV news and newspapers came out even in the public's view of which medium gave the most complete news coverage; each was mentioned by about two-fifths of the people.

Television's role as a provider of news has been a major source of concern to the nation's newspaper industry for years, and not just because of the Roper surveys. Newspaper circulation rose less than 4 million copies a day from 1960 through 1982, while the nation's population expanded by 51 million. Publishers reported readers cancelling their subscriptions because they "already got the news on TV." And television looms as an important competitor for advertising dollars, both locally and nationally.

As worries accumulated, the volume of research grew, and the complexity of the controversy became more apparent. A 1979 report in an ANPA publication listed 120 published studies on television and newspapers as sources of news. And this collection included only those published in academic journals.

The results of the studies have not always been consistent. But their main points can be stated simply: 1. Where people say they get their news and where they do are often different; 2. People's news habits are more complicated than one might suspect.

FALSE ASSUMPTIONS

Finding out exactly what media Americans read, watch, and listen to is the goal of the massive annual surveys conducted by the Simmons Market Research Bureau. These surveys seek to measure the audience for all the major media. Using a variety of techniques—including diaries which ask the respondent to detail TV watching by the quarter-hour segment—Simmons gathers information from a large sample, more than 15,000 in 1981.

In 1971, John Robinson used Simmons data to call the Roper results into question in an article in *Public Opinion Quarterly*. Robinson found that 78 percent of the adult population read at least part of a newspaper every day, while only 24 percent reported watching a network newscast on an average day in 1969. And Robinson, then at the Survey Research Center at the University of Michigan, said 53 percent reported *not* seeing a single national news show on any day over the two-week period covered by the diaries.

The Simmons data also provided the foundation for the latest outbreak of the news source controversy. Lawrence Lichty, a communications professor at the University of Maryland, took an updated look at the 1981 Simmons data and reported his findings in the *Wilson Quarterly* last November.

Lichty wrote that 68 percent reported reading part of a newspaper every day.

And then he wrote: "Fewer than one-third of U.S. adults watch TV news, local or national, on a given day."

If you interpret that sentence as meaning less than 33.3 percent of the public watches TV news on an average day, you would have a lot of company.

But that is not what the Simmons data show. Nor is it what Lichty now says he meant. The Simmons data say 56 percent of the public watched a local or national TV news show on an average day. Lichty now says his analysis showed less than a third watched local news, less than a third watched national news, and that—taken together with those who watched both, counted only once—56 percent watched one or the other.

Thus, Lichty argues that while people may *think* they get most of their news from television, "this is almost certainly not true, even though presidents, senators, and other politicians (to say nothing of TV journalists and TV critics) have come to act on the assumption that it *is* true."

One must be careful here not to assume that mere exposure to a newspaper—even as carefully measured by Simmons—means reading and absorbing that day's news. When people say they have "read or looked into" a day's edition of a newspaper, this can mean a quick scan of the front-page headlines, detailed perusal of the sports section, a good laugh from a "Peanuts" cartoon, or even a swipe at the crossword puzzle.

A NEWS-HUNGRY PUBLIC

While the conflicts between people's claims about sources of news and their behavior raise serious doubts, most of the research presents an even more important confounding reality: Newspaper readership and TV news viewership overlap to a substantial degree. One simply cannot speak of the TV news audience and newspaper readers as if they were discrete groups.

Even the Roper surveys have always shown a substantial number of people mentioning both newspapers and television as the sources for most of their news. In the 1982 survey, 20 percent mentioned both; 41 percent named television alone; and 21 percent singled out newspapers.

Another study—this one also by John Robinson, who is now at the University of Maryland—found an even larger audience for both TV news and newspapers. In this 1975-1976 study, Robinson found fully 39 percent of those responding saying they had both read a newspaper and watched a TV news show on the previous day. And more than half of those over age fifty-five reported both activities.

This study's findings on overall news sources are quite similar to those found by Simmons several years later. Sixty-eight percent read a newspaper the previous day, while only 52 percent watched a TV news show, local or national, in the mid-1970s. This particular study by Robinson was partially funded by the ANPA.

Another survey, conducted by Syracuse University's Thomas Patterson for his book *The Mass Media Election,* suggests that TV news doesn't expand the news audience by much. He concludes that TV expands the news audience by only about one-fourth of what it is, based just on newspaper readership.

Still another experiment suggested that hearing a news story on television or radio actually increases the likelihood that a person will read about that event in a newspaper.

Thus, the research shows there is a substantial news-hungry segment of the American public. For whatever reason, this group of adults has multiple sources for news. And Robinson's work suggests as well that the TV news audience is also one that reads a newspaper every day. This strongly suggests that Roper's results substantially overstate any kind of single-source dependency on TV news for the majority of the public.

COMPLEX INTERACTIONS

This is not to say that the Robinson work is full of only good news for the print side. Newspapers may be leading TV news, but the margin is shrinking.

Comparing data from his 1965-1966 work to the similar subsample of the 1975-1976 study, Robinson found that the percentage of those reading a newspaper every day fell 11 percentage points, from 78 percent to 67 percent. In the same decade and among the same subgroup, TV news viewership rose from 46 percent on an average day to 52 percent. What had been a 32-point margin for the newspapers in 1965 had withered to a 15-point edge a decade later. Robinson also reported a drop in the average amount of time spent reading a newspaper over the period.

Lest TV's partisans become too certain of an inexorable tide in their favor, a study for the NAB by the consulting firm of McHugh and Hoffman reported on surveys that found sharply lower satisfaction with local and national TV news. While in 1977 about half of those questioned were very satisfied with local news and with national news, the survey earlier this year found only about a third of the public expressing that level of satisfaction.

And there are other studies which raise questions about just how much attention people are paying to TV news when the set is on during the newcast. Some of Robinson's work suggests that TV is often only one of several activities under way in the home. For example, many people apparently eat dinner while watching the evening news. One study based on the 1974 Simmons surveys estimates that fewer than one out of four adults gives full attention to the network news on three or more nights every two weeks.

Since television does not necessarily demand the concentration that a newspaper does, those people who are watching the news may not be acquiring as much information as they might from spending a shorter time reading the news.

It has also been shown repeatedly that Americans have different expectations of the various news media. TV news—particularly the network shows—is viewed as the source for national and international news. Newspapers are viewed as better sources for local information.

Asked in a 1981 *Los Angeles Times* poll where they get most of their news about "what is going on in the world," 55 percent said television and 22 percent newspapers. But, asked where they go for news about "what's happening around here," 42 percent said newspapers and 30 percent TV news—a reversal from the previous question.

Thus, the question "Where do Americans get their news?" is really too simple to convey the complex interactions between the public and its sources of information.

Yes, Americans pick up those 62.4 million newspapers that are sold every day and read them—for news, for sports, for the comics, for Ann Landers' column, for a whole variety of reasons. And even that circulation figure may drastically understate readership; one study of 37 major markets put the average number of readers per paper at 2.7. And yes, perhaps 50 million Americans tune in the three networks' evening news shows on a given weeknight—for the news, for sports, for the weather, or even for background noise. But the audience for news is clearly not a unit; it is several different audiences that vary in how much they want and how they wish to obtain it.

MAY WE HAVE YOUR ATTENTION?

A key research problem for this whole debate revolves around the question "What is news?" and how one would measure it. What would be the unit of news—a minute on the network news shows, ten column inches on the front page, or forty seconds on the radio? Without the definition of a unit of news, trying to develop a logically rigorous answer to the question of where one gets *most* of one's news is difficult or impossible.

Despite all the criticisms and the conflicting evidence, the Roper surveys do show that Americans increasingly *believe* that they are getting most of their news from television. This should not be surprising in a society where the television is a fixture in more homes than the telephone, and when that TV set is turned on for more than six hours every day in the average home, according to some research.

Television is indisputably bringing more news to Americans. The news is now available around the clock on certain cable networks and virtually so on the commercial networks—early morning shows, noon newscasts, local news at 4:00 P.M., *Nightline, Overnight,* and *Late Night.* Just watching prime time programming in some major cities from 8:00 P.M. until 11:00 P.M. can expose a viewer to as many as six short "news breaks" from the networks and local stations.

Television, with its minicams and satellite relays, also can now bring the big story live any time the news breaks. For many people, the major spot news event that television brings live in color to them—the assassination, plane crash, earthquake, political convention, presidential election—may be "the news" in an important sense, while the more routine, more predictable contents of the morning front page may not be linked to that concept with quite the same strength.

What does all of this research and argument add up to? Is television the dominant news medium or, as Lichty writes, are presidents, senators, and TV journalists wrong in assuming such a thing?

One point that should be made about the relationship of politicians and others seeking national exposure to television is network news' efficiency. By appearing in a story on the CBS Evening News, a politician can be seen by 15 million people or more. Not one of the 1,170 daily newspapers in the country has such a massive primary audience. Depending on the politician's goals, it might be wiser to try to be quoted on the front page of *The New York Times* or *The Washington Post* than to be the featured speaker in a network news story. Or it might be much wiser to be on the front page of the largest circulation daily in his district. But, for national exposure, network news has its advantages. Of course, politicians try to get those precious seconds of air time.

To argue that television is the dominant source of news for most Americans, however, is to make a leap that logic and the available information do not support. Given the different needs and motivations of adults, given the variation in the news sources from city to city, it should be no surprise that media habits are an untidy collection of variables. It seems clear that most Americans get their news from a variety of sources and that many regularly rely on both television and newspapers.

So, we come back to the question: What is Americans' number one news source? That was the simple question in 1959 and it remains that today. And in today's multimedia society it is a question without real meaning, giving answers that try to simplify one of the complexities of modern life into an overly neat column of numbers.

Study Questions: Lapham et al.

This selection is excerpted from a discussion of press freedom by journalists Tom Wicker, Walter Karp, Sidney Zion, and Frances Fitzgerald; public relations expert Herbert Schmertz; and attorney Charles Rembar. Editor Lewis H. Lapham moderated the discussion.

[?] *What is your answer to the question, "Can the press tell the truth?"*

Members of the panel offer different definitions of a free press. What definition do you believe is most useful for a democratic society?

Overall, do you agree more with Schmertz or Wicker?

Do you agree with Schmertz that the marketplace is an adequate regulator of the media, or is there a need for some government regulation? If the marketplace is an adequate regulator, why do you think Schmertz approves of libel laws?

Do you think the press generally presents American government and business leaders fairly or unfairly?

Is there conflict between the responsibility of the media to serve the needs of individuals and society and the need of most media to make a profit? Rembar asks, "Should the government control the press or should people with enough money (that is, those who own the media) control the press?" What is your answer?

Can media avoid influencing government policies when they report on those policies?

Do current journalistic methods of being "objective" reduce objectivity? Is it possible to write a news story that is completely objective, as Schmertz suggests? Or do you agree with Wicker and Fitzgerald that it is not? What, if anything, can journalists do to increase objectivity in their reporting?

Is there a role for subjectivity in news reporting? If so, what is that role?

From your reading of this discussion, and your own analysis of the news media, what do you conclude are the contemporary journalistic practices that lead to biased or misleading stories? At the end of this article, Wicker asserts that the press will get better only if more press workers try sincerely to do a better job. He believes that nothing else will help. Do you agree with his argument? If not, why not?

Finally, how would a "better" press be different from today's press?

Lewis Lapham, Tom Wicker, Walter Karp, Herbert Schmertz, Sidney Zion, Frances Fitzgerald, and Charles Rembar

CAN THE PRESS TELL THE TRUTH?

WICKER: ... Before I was a columnist I worked as a news reporter for more than twenty years for many different newspapers. I learned very well from that experience that a reporter can't avoid influencing policy. Suppose I write a news story about the Geneva arms-control negotiations from the point of view of, say, Paul Warnke, President Carter's SALT negotiator, because he has explained the negotiations to me. That influences policy in one direction. If I write the piece from the point of view of Richard Perle, the current assistant secretary of defense, after *he* has explained what's happening, that influences policy in a different direction. And if I write my story as if I worked for the Associated Press— which is to say, with the least possible interpretation—then that influences policy in still another direction. No matter how a journalist reports news stories, no matter how much he tries to be neutral, what he writes tends to influence policy.

REMBAR: But isn't there a difference, Tom, between a reporter's necessarily having an effect on policy, whether or not he intends to, and the deliberate distortion of the news that Herb was referring to?

WICKER: Not in the final analysis, because it comes down to basic choices a reporter has to make in writing his story—what to include and what to leave out, for example. Suppose it's the early fifties and I am reporting on one of Joseph McCarthy's speeches. After my lead paragraph—"Senator McCarthy declared today that he has found forty-two communists in the State Department," or whatever—I write a paragraph explaining that no one else in the country has any evidence to support McCarthy's assertion and no one else believes it. Now, including that paragraph is a deliberate effort on my part to influence policy—to tell readers how to interpret the news I've just given them. But is including that information more iniquitous than omitting it?

FITZGERALD: It seems to me absolutely naive to believe otherwise than what Tom is saying. Putting a sentence on a piece of paper is necessarily a subjective act. There is no such thing as objectivity in writing. When people talk about ethical standards in journalism—"objectivity," and so on—they are really talking about a set of conventions that have been created in this country over the past fifty years or so. These conventions tell the journalist how to write, and the reader how to read, a news story in an American newspaper. They set out what sort of information should go in the lead, who should be quoted in reference to what, and so on. As newspaper readers, we are so accustomed to these conventions that we barely notice them anymore. But their effect is to allow the reporter and the reader to share certain markers. You as the reader cannot be certain that what you are reading is "the truth"; you cannot be certain that it is "objective" in any real sense. But you can be sure that the reporter will interview certain people and ask certain questions, that he will go about constructing the written account in a certain way, and that certain standards of accuracy and, if you like, fairness will be observed.

SCHMERTZ: I disagree. A reporter can approach his story intending to write it as objectively as he possibly can, giving us the facts as he sees them. Or he can bend the facts to suit his own political agenda. When too many reporters let their politics dictate their reporting, the news columns become filled with what I call advocacy journalism.

WICKER: But I am asserting that *all* journalism is in fact advocacy journalism. There is no way for a reporter to be neutral; to report an event is to select what is important and significant about it. Of course, if I were an editor sending out reporters, I would prefer that they approached the government or whatever they're covering with an open mind. If a reporter comes to an event with a fixed conviction, he is much less likely to be evenhanded—and evenhandedness is, it seems to me, the desired consequence. But in the final analysis, as to whether the story influences policy—it doesn't matter whether the reporter is advocating a particular position deliberately or not.

SCHMERTZ: I think there's a big difference, Tom.

FITZGERALD: Any writer knows the truth of what Tom is saying: from the first sentence he sets down on paper, from the simple subjective act of choosing what the lead of the story will be, a writer influences the way in which the story he is telling will be interpreted.

WICKER: Here's another problem. Most people would agree that a reporter who deliberately prints a lie is violating ethical standards. Now, suppose that in following the conventions of journalism the reporter does not dispute a statement he knows to be a lie.

SCHMERTZ: That's just as bad.

WICKER: Exactly. But under the conventions of journalism prevailing today, there is sometimes no alternative to doing just that. It is impossible, under those conventions, for a reporter to step in and refute a false statement in his own voice.

ZION:

There were countless examples of that during the Vietnam War. The State Department's official White Papers were full of lies, and every reporter knew it. But if a reporter described what one of those statements said without disputing anything in it, that was called "objective" reporting.

KARP:

I want to return to Mr. Schmertz's statement about a reporter giving us the objective facts as he sees them—a reporter giving us the truth. Or perhaps "truth" is too lofty a word; after all, the Founding Fathers themselves spoke only of "information" as in James Madison's statement that "a popular government without popular information or the means of acquiring it is but a prologue to a farce or a tragedy, or perhaps both." So, ideally the press should provide the public with "popular information." I'd like to cite an occasion when providing the public with the "truth" of an event would not have involved bias or advocacy reporting but merely *facts*. Do you remember the elections in El Salvador in 1982 and 1984? In the months before those elections, the American press, which I won't call entirely "free" but which certainly has a formal freedom, published hundreds of articles about their significance. According to the President of the United States, according to House majority leader Jim Wright, according to the State Department and all the trusted experts, the chief measure of the significance of those elections was voter turnout. If there was a high turnout at the polls, we would know that something positive and encouraging had occurred. But what was scarcely mentioned in *The New York Times* or *The Washington Post* in those days and weeks and months of articles that preceded the elections was that voting is *compulsory* in El Salvador: every adult, by law, must vote.

So here we have a perfect example of an objective news event—let's say a statement by the President of the United States on the significance of voter turnout in El Salvador. Reports say that the turnout was 75 percent, and the President declares that this is an example of unparalleled heroism by the Salvadoran people and, not incidentally, proves the success of his policies. Now, to puncture this story, a reporter didn't need to practice advocacy journalism or smuggle his own opinions into the news columns. All he needed was a fact.

SCHMERTZ:

But you're making my point, Walter. If the reporter knowingly omitted that fact, then it is advocacy journalism.

KARP:

No, Herb, I think I've just given an example, a very rich example, of completely *objective* journalism as practiced in the United States. It's unreasonable to expect to gain a full understanding of public life in America from the daily newspaper, but the citizen ought not to be deprived of information the reporter has. Yet because of our rules of journalism, this often happens. . . .

Study Questions: Hentoff

?

Does the First Amendment give journalists the right to invade people's privacy? Would you respond to that question differently if the person whose privacy is being invaded is a United States senator? A movie star? A professional basketball player? A college basketball player? A teacher who committed a crime? A carpenter?

How do Hentoff's views in this essay fit with those of the discussants in the preceding paper? Does he agree or disagree with them?

Nat Hentoff argues that the arrest records of people should be kept from the press. Do you agree? If you do, does that mean that if someone is arrested for theft or sexual abuse in your home town, that fact should be kept secret from the public?

How would you balance the right of privacy against freedom of the press? Or do you agree with Hentoff that they cannot be balanced? If so, which one should take precedence?

Nat Hentoff

PRIVACY AND THE PRESS

Is nothing sacred?

Defenders of the personal information industry are fond of pointing out that the press is no more solicitous of privacy rights than they are. And they're right. More journalists, feeling that all privacy rights tumble before

Nat Hentoff is a staff writer for the *Village Voice* and *The New Yorker*. His new book, *The First Freedom: A Tumultuous History of Free Speech in America* (Delacorte Press) is due in September.

the First Amendment, feel no compunction about adopting pretexts for interviews, or printing intimate information of dubious value.

For several years, I have taught a course on investigative reporting at New York's New School for Social Research. Many of the students and nearly all the guest experts are journalists. I ask each guest if there is anything he or she would *not* do to get a story. Most react as if they had never even thought of the question before. They have simply taken it for granted that a diligent journalist may—and indeed, must—get the news by whatever means are necessary.

I ask these reporters if they would bug and wiretap an uncooperative subject. Would they disguise their identities and infiltrate the subject's business or even family? The answer usually is affirmative, proudly so. After all, in order to satisfy "the people's right to know"—the basic credo of our calling—a reporter has to be uncommonly resourceful, daringly inventive.

Outside of class, other journalists tell me of secret grand jury minutes that they have somehow obtained and printed. This, mind you, before the person being investigated by the grand jury has been indicted. What about the presumption of his innocence? Because he has been brought before the grand jury, I am told, he is news and that's all that ultimately counts.

My own maverick view is that journalists are second only to the state in their imperiling of individual privacy. They often act like undercover cops and sometimes like righteously aggressive prosecutors. It is a citizen's right, for example, not to speak to the press; but a "no comment" almost invariably leads the reporter to assume guilt. That assumption having been made, the reporter feels free to "get" the silent citizen. If I were recruiting for the FBI these days, I would surely canvass the press for prospects.

What most disturbs me is that exceedingly few journalists see anything wrong with this way of doing their job. They apparently forget, for one thing, that the First Amendment is a shield, increasingly battered, against state interference with the press's functions. It was not intended to be a blunt instrument against individual citizens who would be strewn about in the wake of journalists gathering news. But most reporters think only of getting the story. The notion that they should be sensitive to individual's privacy rights strikes them as a dangerous form of outside meddling with their special status. (Again, they react like cops.)

This is not to say that privacy should always be inviolate. Then we'd have nothing to read but press releases and shopping news. The privacy of Richard Nixon's White House was legitimately invaded because crimes were being committed there. Similarly, I have printed information about private meetings in and outside of municipal agencies because public lies were being concocted there.

On the other hand, years ago I did not print a tip from a cop that a legislator had been swept up in a dragnet raid of a homosexual bar. I knew his public record, and I saw no relevant relationship between that apparent aspect of his private life and what he did as a lawmaker. Conversely, I do think the Washington press has been remiss through the years in not naming those members of Congress who are manifestly drunk during the course of legislative business. That is news their constituents should surely have. But what about extramarital affairs? It depends on whether the liaison affects the public figure's public life. If the inamorata is on the payroll of, let's say, the Chilean government, and her friend is on the Foreign Relations Committee, that's legitimate news. And if a President is an active satyr, the electorate ought to be told, if only on grounds of national security.

No clear line of judgment can be drawn in these matters, but reporters must at least be continually aware of a conflict between the colliding interests of privacy and the free flow of information. Instead the trend has been toward publishing just about anything that can be obtained, by whatever means. I am not, however, particularly concerned with the steamy proliferation of gossip in the nation's press, since no one gets into those columns unless they're renowned or notorious and indeed have worked at achieving such visibility. Accordingly, they have voluntarily given up much of their privacy.

What does greatly concern me are those private citizens who can be severely injured by needless press attention. Consider the printing of arrest records. News organizations have been fighting for years to get at that information. Their opponents, including the American Civil Liberties Union, maintain that there is no public need to know if someone has been arrested if the arrest has not resulted in a conviction. The vast majority of arrests do not. Why, then, if someone has been found innocent, subject him to public obloquy by publishing the fact that he was arrested? Yet in many states the press has won this dubious right.

In New York State, for instance, the law says that no employer, public or private, and no agency, can ask anyone if he's ever been arrested. Furthermore, anyone exonerated of a criminal charge can have his fingerprints expunged from all official records. The privacy of such individuals is thus safeguarded—except from the press, which can search out the arrest records and print them.

As an illustration of the press's zeal in these matters, there was a triumphant tour of Maine last October by a task force of 100 reporters testing the state's "right-to-know" law. Marching into local police stations, they demanded to see the complete records of the most recent arrests. (Not convictions, arrests.) Out of 111 police stations, 99 complied entirely. One of the tiny minority of officers defending privacy rights was the sole cop in the town of New Gloucester. He told the posse that he hadn't arrested anybody during the past four years, but if he had, those records would be out-of-bounds to reporters. As they should be.

Similarly, there have been moves in some states to seal juvenile records and accounts of certain misdemeanors committed by adults. If the once and former defendants don't get into any more trouble, the slate is wiped clean. This too offends the press, which insists that every record should be open and publishable. Otherwise, how can vigilant reporters keep a check on the criminal justice system?

Arthur Miller, an expert on privacy and a professor at Harvard Law School, states:

> Vigorous and diligent reporters can effectively monitor the criminal justice system without examining the records of those who have paid their debt to society, who have met the stringent conditions of the statutes, and who deserve a second chance. If we believe in rehabilitation . . . then we must tolerate some risks. We should permit some people to reenter the mainstream of society by eliminating the social and vocational ostracism associated with an ancient record that does not reflect their present worth. How can you quarrel with the principle of sealing the record of a youthful peccadillo which has never been repeated?

Much of the press eagerly does quarrel with that principle, as with the principle that the names of people on welfare should not be published. But what is the point of doing that, except to embarrass those on the rolls? The public is entitled to know the cost of welfare and the percentage of the population being aided. But not the individual names.

The press's mania for going after just about everything is not unlike the sleuthing habits of the FBI, other government agencies, and insurance companies—all of whom are criticized by much of the press for invading privacy. Now, however, as *the press* is being recognized as one of the more fearsome enemies of privacy, there is some movement toward trying to legislate journalists into becoming "responsible." Professor Arthur Miller, for instance, speaks darkly, if unspecifically, of "a reexamination of the favored position currently enjoyed by the press."

Wherever that "corrective" route might lead would be worse than the disease, for it would necessarily involve weakening the First Amendment even further than has the present Supreme Court. Although Justice William O. Douglas said in the tradition of Louis Brandeis that "the right to be let alone is indeed the beginning of all freedom," he also persistently maintained that the First Amendment cannot be balanced. I am also largely of that view. Even if I were not, I cannot conceive of any "privacy" strictures on what the press can print—or additions to present punishments for what is published—that would not be subject to crippling abuse by the state. To make the press "responsible" in this way is to paralyze it.

In terms, however, of *how* privacy is sometimes invaded by journalists, there are already laws that can be applied without violating the First Amendment. If, without cover of law, a journalist breaks into an apartment to snatch diaries or other such material, he can and ought to be charged, just like an errant FBI agent, with breaking and entering. If he unlawfully wiretaps, he should be punished for breaking the relevant law.

But what of those invasions of privacy that occur without crimes being committed? Visiting notoriety, for instance, upon a public official's son for living with another man. Is all privacy to be lost to the families of newsworthy figures? And what of the continuing, quasireligious crusade of the press to be allowed to poke into all kinds of dossiers, from everyone's arrest records to reckless driving charges (later dismissed) against a public official?

I have no confident answer. The press as a whole is no more likely to become more humane on its own, than bill-collecting agencies. When I most despair of the majority of journalists ever growing less reckless about the privacy of everyone else, I think that it might be grandly therapeutic—though contrary to the spirit of this article—if one paper in a city would subject reporters and editors at another paper to exactly this kind of privacy-shredding. That is, headlining the extramarital affairs and ancient arrest records of some of these journalists. The experience could greatly concentrate the victims' minds on privacy when next they went on assignment.

Study Questions: Oppel/Caplan

[?] *If you were a newspaper editor in the city in which each of the events described in the Oppel essay occurred, how would you answer the questions that follow each case description? How would you justify your publication decision in each case?*

How do you explain the strong disagreement between readers and editors in Case 5? Does this disagreement have anything to do with the issues raised by Hentoff in the previous essay?

Oppel quotes one reader of these cases who said he could think of no consistent principle upon which to answer all of the questions following the case descriptions. Can you devise a general principle or set of principles that underlies your answers to these cases?

Would you handle all of these cases the same way if they were from another city and came in as stories on the news wire than if they were written by a local reporter about events in your home town?

When journalists and editors protect the privacy of people involved in newsworthy events, is it more likely or less likely that the public will be adequately informed? Does it make any difference?

Richard A. Oppel

READERS "IN THE EDITOR'S CHAIR" SQUIRM OVER ETHICAL DILEMMAS

But they tend to opt for privacy and compassion more often than professionals do

T. C. Price Zimmermann is a brainy fellow. He knifes through ambiguity in pursuit of meaning with the determination of a gray shark sniffing a dead mackerel in muddy seas.

Zimmermann has degrees from Williams, Oxford, and Harvard, and is vice-president for academic affairs at Davidson College, a "Southern Ivy" with tough academic standards, situated 20 miles north of Charlotte, N.C.

So I was amused to read Zimmermann's comment after he—along with nearly 300 other readers of the *Charlotte Observer*—wrestled with five hypothetical cases of journalistic ethics.

"I must confess I have to cry uncle!" he wrote. "You have me with your hypothetical cases. I can't think of any infallibly consistent principle upon which I would answer each of the questions . . . You have sensitized me to your dilemmas."

Score one.

Zimmermann's comment suggested we had achieved one objective of three we had sought in luring readers into an exercise called "Put Yourself in the Editor's Chair." Staffers of the *Observer* and the *Charlotte News* also participated in the exercise.

I don't want to exaggerate the results, but I think it accomplished the following:

- It nudged news staffers into addressing the tension in our society between press freedoms versus privacy and fairness considerations from new perspectives. Age-old shibboleths repeatedly were dragged out and hooted down.
- Readers discovered how difficult it is for editors to produce simple, consistent, clear-cut resolutions of the ethical questions of journalism, and perhaps a few saw how the stumbling denizens of the newsroom were often choosing between gray and darker gray, instead of black and white.
- Although the in-newspaper questionnaire was utterly lacking a scientific base, the exercise hinted of the gap between readers and editors. (Better news than Burgoon, I might add.)

Rich Oppel is editor of the *Charlotte* (N.C.) *Observer* and *News*.

Here is how "Put Yourself in the Editor's Chair" worked:

On July 29, 1984, I devoted my column to the conflicts in which a newspaper often finds itself in deciding whether to publish information. I included a questionnaire of five hypothetical cases that tested ethics, with possible responses, and invited readers to return the quiz to me.

We received 285 responses.

Sixty-nine *Observer* and *News* staffers also completed the questionnaire. We did not compel staff participation.

On August 20, we held a two-hour staff meeting where the hypothetical cases were discussed. The text of each case was projected on a movie screen.

With apologies to Harvard's Arthur Miller, assistant managing editor Gil Thelen and I moved about the auditorium, leading questioning, pitting staffer against staffer, and provoking some of the most intense debate we've had in a staff meeting.

There were moments of drama, and even my own indecision.

While discussing Case No. 1 (all five appear with this article), a female editor in her late 20s acknowledged she had been raped several years earlier and argued with feeling for not publishing the names of rape victims—no matter whom.

While discussing Case No. 2, someone asked whether we would publish a story if my son, who is 15, were arrested for possession of a small amount of marijuana. Since I would not publish a story on the arrest of the mayor's son on the same charge, I would be consistent in saying no. We routinely do not publish stories of minor drug arrests.

But before I could answer, someone noted that a previous editor of the *Observer* had published—on the front page—a story about his son being arrested for reckless driving. Now where is consistency?

Like most of us who edit newspapers, I resolved long ago that if I were ever nailed on a drunken driving charge, the story would go in the paper. But how many of us have thought about thrusting our children into the front-page caldron on a minor charge?

The "Put Yourself in the Editor's Chair" exercise was not original with the *Observer*. Variants have been used across the nation.

Michael Davies, editor and publisher of the *Hartford Courant*, has done something similar.

Robert Ingle, executive editor of the *San Jose* (Calif.) *Mercury-News*, earlier this year published a set of hypotheticals and elicited 75 reader responses, then conducted staff discussions.

The five hypothetical cases I used were borrowed from *The Miami Herald* and *The St. Paul* (Minn.) *Pioneer Press*. Heath Meriwether, executive editor of the *Herald*, who first published the cases (except for No. 5, which was written in St. Paul), received 690 reader responses when they were published. The *Herald's* managing editor, Pete Weitzel, later conducted 24 seminars with small groups of staffers.

"It opened a tremendous dialogue among staffers," said Weitzel. "It showed me how truly staffers do care about what they are doing and the decisions we make."

John Finnegan, editor of the *Pioneer Press,* followed Miami, and compared readers' and staffers' responses in St. Paul with those in Miami. St. Paul received 294 responses from readers.

Deborah Howell, St. Paul executive editor, said, "From the standpoint of readers, it was just great. They got a chance to participate as editors. I heard enough comments on the street that I was convinced it was a great exercise to do."

In Charlotte, we compared our results with those of Miami and St. Paul. We found remarkable similarities among readers from city to city. There was greater variation among editors in the three cities. Generally, readers were more conservative than editors in what they would publish.

CASE NO. 1

A woman county commissioner is raped. The afternoon newspaper reports she was hospitalized following an assault but does not indicate it was a sexual attack. A conservative and antifeminist, she has blocked the expenditure of funds for a rape crisis center at the local hospital. This has been a much publicized local controversy for the past six months. But now she tells you that she plans to rethink her position on the crisis center. She also makes clear the deep personal trauma she is suffering as a result of the assault and asks that you not say she was raped.

The survey results:
▪ *Do you go ahead with the full story, including her change of mind, recognizing that the shift is a significant public policy development?*

Charlotte:

Readers	Yes	31	No 69
Editors	Yes	8	No 92

St. Paul:

Readers	Yes	33	No 67
Editors	Yes	22	No 78

Miami:

Readers	Yes	35	No 65
Editors	Yes	39	No 61

■ *Do you say no more than the afternoon paper did?*

Charlotte:
Readers	Yes 30	No 70
Editors	Yes 75	No 25

St. Paul:
Readers	Yes 54	No 46
Editors	Yes 41	No 59

Miami:
Readers	Yes 22	No 78
Editors	Yes 18	No 82

■ *Do you refer to the attack simply as an assault but report that the convalescing board member is rethinking her position on the crisis center, thus suggesting the nature of the attack?*

Charlotte:
Readers	Yes 32	No 68
Editors	Yes 13	No 87

St. Paul:
Readers	Yes 35	No 65
Editors	Yes 30	No 70

Miami:
Readers	Yes 30	No 70
Editors	Yes 14	No 86

■ *Do you report the assault and say nothing about the rape now, but decide that when she actually votes for the rape crisis center you will report the reasons for her change of mind whether or not she wants to talk about it?*

Charlotte:
Readers	Yes 5	No 95
Editors	Yes 4	No 96

St. Paul:
Readers	Yes 16	No 84
Editors	Yes 12	No 88

Miami:

Readers	Yes 18	No 82
Editors	Yes 29	No 71

"I would go ahead with the full story. Elected public officials by their own choice have put themselves in a very special category. Since she was a victim, there is no shame to her. I share her anguish at the trauma of it, but my sympathy is lessened by the fact that she had been insensitive herself to the trauma of others."

—T. C. Price Zimmermann

CASE NO. 2

A mayor is a hard-liner on crime. He has made drug enforcement a major issue. You learn that his 19-year-old son, who lives at home and attends junior college, has been arrested for possession of a small quantity of marijuana, a misdemeanor if convicted.

The survey results:
- *Would you run the story on his arrest?*

Charlotte:

Readers	Yes 61	No 39
Editors	Yes 42	No 58

St. Paul:

Readers	Yes 58	No 42
Editors	Yes 48	No 52

Miami:

Readers	Yes 64	No 36
Editors	Yes 75	No 25

- *Would you run the story if the arrest were for selling a pound of marijuana?*

Charlotte:

Readers	Yes 83	No 17
Editors	Yes 75	No 25

St. Paul:

Readers	Yes 50	No 50
Editors	Yes 89	No 11

Miami:
| Readers | Yes 92 | No 8 |
| Editors | Yes 100 | No 0 |

- *Would you run the story if the arrest were for using cocaine?*

Charlotte:
| Readers | Yes 70 | No 30 |
| Editors | Yes 54 | No 46 |

St. Paul:
| Readers | Yes 72 | No 28 |
| Editors | Yes 74 | No 26 |

Miami:
| Readers | Yes 78 | No 22 |
| Editors | Yes 86 | No 14 |

- *Would you run the story if the arrest were for selling cocaine?*

Charlotte:
| Readers | Yes 83 | No 17 |
| Editors | Yes 83 | No 17 |

St. Paul:
| Readers | Yes 93 | No 7 |
| Editors | Yes 96 | No 4 |

Miami:
| Readers | Yes 94 | No 6 |
| Editors | Yes 100 | No 0 |

"I think anyone that has been voted into an office to represent the people is and should be someone that has enough interest in the people of the city that an incident such as this should not hurt him. To report a crime by a child of the mayor would only show to the public that he too is human and, as others, can't always control those close to him."

—Jay F. Clontz, Charlotte

But that wasn't always true. The responses showed that particularly in St. Paul and Charlotte, and to a lesser extent in Miami, readers were sometimes more inclined to decide in favor of publication and against privacy.

Again, the questionnaires were not scientific samples. Miami's Weitzel speculates that the reader respondents "could be more in the category of newspaper junkies—genuine newspaper readers, information junkies, and thus more inclined than a true sample of our readership to argue in favor of publication.

In any event, readers in Charlotte and elsewhere dug fiercely into the debate.

CASE NO. 3

A prominent businessman identified with United Way and many other charitable causes is discovered to have embezzled $25,000 from one of the charities he heads. There is no question about his guilt, although charges have not yet been filed. The story is yours alone. When your reporter contacts him for comment, the man says there are extenuating circumstances he cannot go into and that he will make full restitution if given a chance. He pleads that no story be written, saying his wife suffered a serious heart attack, is in critical condition in the hospital and he fears that public disclosure of what he has done would kill her.

The survey results:
- *Would you run the story?*

Charlotte:

Readers	Yes 25	No 75
Editors	Yes 42	No 58

St. Paul:

Readers	Yes 39	No 61
Editors	Yes 26	No 74

Miami:

Readers	Yes 33	No 67
Editors	Yes 61	No 39

- *Would you wait until you had an opportunity to talk with the hospital's doctors and are confident the woman is out of immediate danger, then run the story?*

Charlotte:

Readers	Yes 54	No 46
Editors	Yes 46	No 54

St. Paul:

Readers	Yes 51	No 49
Editors	Yes 33	No 67

Miami:
Readers	Yes 50	No 50
Editors	Yes 39	No 61

▪ *Would you give him time to make restitution and, if this is done, write nothing?*

Charlotte:
Readers	Yes 15	No 85
Editors	Yes 4	No 96

St. Paul:
Readers	Yes 27	No 73
Editors	Yes 5	No 95

Miami:
Readers	Yes 17	No 83
Editors	Yes 0	No 100

"I would give the businessman about 30 minutes to get to his wife first and then proceed with the first choice (print the story)."

—John G. Leggoe, Pineville

"Who says there is no question of guilt—the newspaper? Until charges are filed there should be no story."

—Jim Singleton, Matthews

CASE NO. 4

A businessman donated $5 million to UNC to expand Kenan Stadium. Checking his background, you learn the man was arrested at age 18 for armed robbery and avoided prison only by volunteering for military duty in World War II. His record, as far as you can discover, has been spotless since. He refuses to talk about the incident, says he has never even told his closest friends and threatens to withdraw the contribution to the university if you print the story. UNC officials are shocked and urge that you write nothing.

The survey results:
▪ *Do you print the information on the arrest as an element in an overall profile of the man and who he is?*

Charlotte:
Readers	Yes 7	No 83
Editors	Yes 21	No 79

St. Paul:

Readers	Yes 13	No 87
Editors	Yes 11	No 89

Miami:

Readers	Yes 14	No 86
Editors	Yes 57	No 43

■ *Do you take the position that the information is not relevant and discard it?*

Charlotte:

Readers	Yes 92	No 8
Editors	Yes 67	No 33

St. Paul:

Readers	Yes 88	No 12
Editors	Yes 80	No 20

Miami:

Readers	Yes 84	No 16
Editors	Yes 43	No 57

"To report (his past) would serve only to fuel the fires of gossip. Stay away from gossip and sensationalism."

—Debbie Helms, Charlotte

CASE NO. 5

A man wanted for armed robbery and with a long list of prior convictions for assault and robbery is trapped by police at the house of his former girlfriend. He takes the woman and her two children hostage, forces them into his car and makes a dash for freedom. He is chased by police, finally stopped at a roadblock. Before he surrenders to police, he shoots and kills the woman. Your photographer is at the scene and takes a series of photographs, including one of the murder victim in the car with the children crying over her body. He also has shots of the man being handcuffed by police.

The survey results:
■ *Do you fully identify the woman victim and her children with names, addresses?*

Charlotte:

Readers	Yes 25	No 75
Editors	Yes 71	No 29

St. Paul:

Readers	Yes 32	No 68
Editors	Yes 88	No 12

■ *Do you use the photograph of the victim and the children?*

Charlotte:

Readers	Yes 12	No 88
Editors	Yes 25	No 75

St. Paul:

Readers	Yes 15	No 85
Editors	Yes 42	No 58

■ *Do you use the photograph of the man being arrested?*

Charlotte:

Readers	Yes 76	No 24
Editors	Yes 92	No 8

St. Paul:

Readers	Yes 97	No 3
Editors	Yes 92	No 8

■ *Do you publish the list of the suspect's prior convictions in the story about the car chase and murder?*

Charlotte:

Readers	Yes 75	No 25
Editors	Yes 84	No 16

St. Paul:

Readers	Yes 84	No 16
Editors	Yes 74	No 26

■ *Would you get as much information on the woman and her relationship with the suspect as possible and publish it?*

Charlotte:

Readers	Yes 18	No 82
Editors	Yes 36	No 64

St. Paul:

Readers	Yes 19	No 81
Editors	Yes 60	No 40

"We don't need all the titillating details. Innocent victims' privacy should be zealously guarded. Leave the exposes to the National Enquirer."

—Sarah Wilson, Huntersville

"I think the editor, photographer, or the person doing the story has a job to do. So go for it all the way."

—Gary L. Spencer, Charlotte

"I hate to see close-up shots of someone else's grief. People crying over dead loved ones is personal—leave it that way!"

Nina Outlaw, Charlotte

In the rape case:

Mrs. Walter Boone of Valdese, N.C., implored, "The choice is fairly clear that you must report this important shift in position of a public official. The story can be written with compassion, and the headline could be tasteful and not focus on the rape."

But L. S. Shepherd of Clover, S.C., said, "The raped are victims whose private feelings should be respectfully kept private."

In the United Way embezzling case:

A. W. Cowan of Matthews, N.C., said, "Run the story. Public confidence must be maintained in the allocation of monies given to charities. The newspaper's discretion is on the 'splash' they make with the story and whether you imply guilt, which is the court's responsibility."

Mike Rains of Charlotte argued, "No story should be run until an indictment is delivered. At such time the article should be written without concern for the man's wife."

And on and on. . . .

My view is that the exercise, which consumed at least 100 hours of the time of two editors and one secretary, was enormously valuable in attuning the staff to questions of fairness.

Arthur L. Caplan

EDITORS SHOULDN'T FEAR ETHICAL THINKING —THEY DO IT NATURALLY ALL THE TIME

Few things produce as much anxiety for some journalists as the discussion of newspaper ethics. Ethics smacks of censorship, either imposed by a

Arthur Caplan is an associate for the humanities at The Hastings Center, Hastings-on-Hudson, N.Y. This article is reprinted from the ASNE book, *Drawing the Line.*

government agency or by peers. Neither form goes over well in a field whose practitioners pride themselves on being independent, autonomous and beholden to no one.

Speak of ethics and the journalist envisions an ethereal system full of rigid rules, unbreakable prescriptions and abstract codes. Journalists are more likely to put their moral faith in intuition and gut feelings rather than in the ornate theoretical constructions of moral philosophers or theologians.

Nevertheless, just like the character in Molière's play who was delighted to learn that she had been speaking prose all her life, it may come as a surprise to those who read these cases to learn that, whether they are aware of it or not, journalists engage in ethical thinking throughout their professional lives.

Value judgments are at the heart of the practice of journalism. While it may seem grandiose to label decisions about how many inches a story will receive or whether someone's name will be omitted from a particular item as ethical, they are certainly no less so than the agonizing decisions about weightier matters of fairness, balance and objectivity. Only the familiarity of these everyday choices within the world of journalism disguises their ethical content.

The discussions in the various cases (in *Drawing the Line*) reveal another and more important fact about ethics and journalism. Each case is both difficult and unique. No simple moral rule of thumb satisfactorily handles all of them. But those who read these cases should not lose sight of the ethical forest for all of the many moral trees that are described.

A number of prescriptions, considerations and indeed, moral rules form a constant background for the case discussions. In each case the contributors reveal that moral responsibility in journalism extends beyond a simple duty to tell the truth or get the "facts" straight. The contributors try to balance the obligations they feel to provide the public with accurate information against the oftentimes conflicting obligations to protect personal privacy, to show compassion toward society's weakest or most vulnerable sources as well as the subjects of stories, and, to avoid surreptitiously imposing their own values upon their readers.

Those who say out of fear or ignorance or both that ethical rules and principles play no role in journalism have simply not read these cases carefully. The rules and core values of the field appear on every page.

No single rule can solve every problem whether it be a matter of ethics or anything else. To think otherwise is to misunderstand the role rules play in ethics. Ethical rules in themselves are of no practical use to anyone. They must always be fleshed out and supplemented with information as to the specifics of a situation or case. Without facts moral rules are blind. With facts moral rules can be properly and appropriately applied.

As the cases show, it is not always easy to know how to give proper weight to privacy, dignity, and compassion in the process of trying to present a story. Nor is it easy to know when conflicts of interest exist that may impugn the credibility of a newspaper in the eyes of its readers. Nonetheless, each case reveals that the ethically sensitive journalist must often agonize over which value ought to take priority when conflicts arise.

It is more than likely that the reader will differ with the conclusions reached by the author of one or more of these cases. But disagreement is not incompatible with objectivity in ethics any more than it is in journalism.

As citizens in a democratic society we are all properly leery of anyone who claims to have a patent on moral truth. But, as the cases plainly reveal, our society expects all of its citizens to adhere to a core set of ethical rules and values that constitute a democracy. We may not all agree, as the contributors surely do not, as to what constitutes the right decision in a tough case. But there appears to be no disagreement among the authors of these cases as to the nature of the values that belong in the quiver of the ethically responsible journalist.

---

*S*tudy *Q*uestions: *S*chorr

⟦?⟧ *What is a docudrama? How is it different from traditional historical drama? From a news story?*

Since all drama must be based, to some extent, on life, why does Schorr raise questions about docudramas that he probably would not raise about other dramas?

By what criteria should docudramas be evaluated—the criteria of journalism or the criteria of art and/or entertainment? Which of these kinds of criteria is Schorr using when he selects the docudramas that offend him most?

Do you think a story "acted out" is more real to viewers than a news story? Why or why not? Should the answer to this question affect whether we apply news criteria or artistic criteria to the evaluation of docudramas?

Do you think that either a news story or a drama can contain the "the real truth" about people or events?

Schorr says that "a real issue is whether the entertainment divisions' authentic-looking docudramas affect the credibility of news programs shown on the same channels." Do you agree with Schorr that programs should be altered if it appears that they might reduce the credibility of network news programs?

> *Schorr also says the docudrama replaces the genuine with the ersatz. Is there such a thing as a "genuine" story about Murrow? Is the "genuine" story Murrow experienced the same Murrow story that the head of the network or the reporters who worked under Murrow experienced? If not, how many "genuine" stories about Murrow are there? As a media consumer and critic, how do you know when you are seeing a "genuine" story and when you are not?*

Daniel Schorr

HARVEST OF SHAM

"**D**ramas based on fact are part of literature and the theater, and we think if television is to be a vital and contemporary medium, they have to be a part of television."

Thus, with some spirit, did Donald Wear, vice-president of the CBS Broadcast Group, respond to critics who say docudrama represents entertainment's unprovoked aggression against the shrinking world of reality. Wear was defending docudramas while CBS was under attack for the most controversial show of the 1985 season, *The Atlanta Child Murders*, which outraged many by suggesting a conspiratorial miscarriage of justice.

But CBS had a markedly different view of another controversial docudrama, *Murrow*, whose setting was CBS itself and which appeared on Home Box Office in January. The network has left it mainly to its news stars to register outrage at the docudrama's treatment of William S. Paley, former CBS chairman, and Frank Stanton, former president. Walter Cronkite called the dramatization "a docudrama of the worst type."

My own opinion is that *Murrow* is far from being the worst, or the best, of that genre of entertainment that shreds, compacts, and reprocesses real lives and events to make them more exciting. It goes wrong in ways many docudramas do. It is depressing, for instance, to see men of stature, such as Paley and Stanton, diminished both by the script and the actors chosen to portray them. They appear not only as villains, but as rather uninteresting villains. The production also manages to diminish Edward R. Murrow as it seeks to canonize him. The well-researched dialogue given to his impersonator, Daniel J. Travanti, seems authentic enough, and the actor cleverly imitates the newsman's cigarette-dangling mannerisms—but he

---

Daniel Schorr, a CBS News correspondent for 25 years, was probably the last of the network's team hired by Edward R. Murrow. He is now senior news analyst at National Public Radio.

totally lacks Murrow's style and force of personality, and the bold lines ring hollow.

Distortion of a man's personality, however, is the least of *Murrow's* faults. More serious is what happens when, to meet show-biz requirements, a large and complex conflict is reduced to a brawl. Presenting the Murrow–CBS conflict of the late 1950s as a struggle between good guys and bad guys, between crusading journalist and corporate greed, not only distorts the truth but misses the real drama of Murrow's *Götterdämmerung.*

The real conflict—which the television industry still has not resolved—was between a journalistic conception of responsibility to the public and a corporate conception of responsibility to stockholders in a vast and chronically insecure entertainment enterprise to which, after all, journalism is a relatively small and often irritating appendage. There was a better story than the one told on HBO. The real drama in the open Murrow–Stanton feud, and the less visible Murrow–Paley conflict, was a tragedy in the Greek manner: honorable men propelled on a collision course no intermediary could change. Murrow and Stanton warred over whether the newsman's public statements that criticized television's underachievement were undermining Stanton's desperate efforts to repair CBS's credibility after the 1959 quiz-show scandals. Murrow, who was on sabbatical at the time, never really returned to work in the news organization he virtually founded.

In real life, Murrow admitted to friends, "If I were in charge of CBS, I am sure it would go broke." And Stanton, long after he and Murrow had exchanged their last civil words, warmly endorsed him to President-elect Kennedy to head the U.S. Information Agency.

Murrow, who demanded "information, unslanted, untarnished, and undistorted," would have hated *Murrow*. Docudramas epitomize the manipulation he abhorred in television. CBS, however, has less reason to complain, because it pioneered programming on the frontier between reality and fantasy.

In the 1950s, and then later in a Saturday-morning version in the 1970s, the network assigned Walter Cronkite to host *You Are There!* (the original radio version had been titled *CBS Is There!*). The series put news correspondents, CBS's guardians of reality, on stage sets with professional actors reenacting events of pretelevision history.

I once played (voluntarily and for a fee, let me admit) a television correspondent on the scene in Berlin during World War I for an episode titled "The Zimmermann Telegram." Surrounded by actors playing German diplomats, I reported "live" from the Wilhelmstrasse on the developing crisis in German–U.S. relations—an anachronism that may have confused viewers who had seen me reporting from Berlin only a few years earlier. That was precisely the point of the gimmick.

From such seeds the docudrama grew. Indeed, this convergence of reality and fantasy was only the logical result of the magnetic pull between them. While Jason Robards was learning to play Ben Bradlee and President Nixon in two major docudramas, actual news correspondents were learning make-up and camera angles for their own broadcasts, as well as techniques of the rehearsed ad lib, the reflective nod of the "reaction shot," and the adept use of TelePrompTers to simulate feats of memory. Journalism borrowed from the theater, highlighting personality clashes to heighten the excitement of events, and theater borrowed journalism's documentary techniques. Reality became increasingly fantastic, and fantasy increasingly realistic.

Docudramas have removed the last remaining inhibitions against the assault on reality. At best they simplify reality, at worst they pervert it. Many of those dealing with such figures of the past as Marco Polo, Christopher Columbus, and General Custer took some license with history but seemed relatively harmless, and many historical dramas have had redeeming qualities. *Holocaust* on NBC and Herman Wouk's *The Winds of War* on ABC, despite their over-personalization of cataclysmic events, were based on serious research and brought important subjects to a mass audience. Alex Haley's *Roots* on ABC was a powerful morality play.

But program executives also preyed on unauthenticated rumors, about Franklin and Eleanor Roosevelt, Marilyn Monroe, and the Kennedy brothers—Joseph Jr., John, and Robert. And some docudramas have distorted what journalists and historians were honestly able to discern and write about real events. ABC's *Attica*, in 1980, altered Tom Wicker's ambiguous account of a prison uprising to suggest that the authorities attacked the prisoners after, not before, the prisoners threatened the lives of hostages they were holding—a key element in judging the case. More recently, *A Hero's Story* on NBC distorted for the sake of titillation the relationship between the Swedish diplomat Raoul Wallenberg and a Hungarian noblewoman who was helping him save the lives of thousands of Jews during World War II.

Of the docudramas I have seen over the years, I have found three particularly offensive, because they have exploited—and compounded—Americans' uncertainty about traumatic episodes of the recent past.

- ABC's *Washington: Behind Closed Doors* (1977) created the impression that President Nixon, covering up Watergate, and CIA director Richard Helms, covering up a political assassination, may have blackmailed each other into silence in a meeting at Camp David. The mischievous script came from a novel by John Ehrlichman, a disaffected former Nixon aide. Along with *Blind Ambition*, the less outrageous but still tendentious dramatization of a book by John Dean, another disaffected aide, *Behind Closed Doors* gave millions of Americans a perverted view of Watergate's real drama and tragedy.
- ABC's *The Trial of Lee Harvey Oswald* (1977) suggested that if Oswald had survived to be tried for killing President Kennedy, he would have

emerged as the innocent scapegoat for Mafia or CIA assassins. The script hinted at President Johnson's complicity when the prosecutor asserted that he would press his investigation, "no matter how many Presidents call me from Washington to tell me to stop digging."

- *The Atlanta Child Murders* led viewers toward the conclusion that Wayne B. Williams, convicted of two murders and linked to 23 others in one of the most agonizing episodes of any American city's history, was actually innocent. The Abby Mann script indicated that Williams had been railroaded by city officials anxious to restore Atlanta's reputation.

Following the broadcast, Donald Wear of CBS responded to Atlanta's civic outrage by pontificating about television's need to be "vital and contemporary." But shortly thereafter the network published guidelines for docudramas, stating that "factual elements should be accurate and cannot be changed merely to enhance dramatic value." George Busbee, former governor of Georgia, commented that had those guidelines been applied earlier, *Child Murders* would never have reached the screen.

ABC has guidelines, too. They require that "the overall presentation impart authenticity regardless of whether or not dramatic license has been exercised for portrayals of characters or composites of persons or events." Would ABC really claim "authenticity" for *Oswald* or *Behind Closed Doors*?

A real issue is whether the entertainment divisions' authentic-looking docudramas affect the credibility of news programs shown on the same channels. Lawrence K. Grossman, president of NBC News, had trouble with that question when interviewed by *The Christian Science Monitor* recently. "That's a complicated question," he said. "I'm not sure I know my own mind about that." He went on to say that "news should be fact and reality, and nobody should reenact anything," but as to drama, "I would not like to restrict anything. There's good drama and there's bad drama."

Does that make everything clear?

David W. Rintels, one of the most prolific and talented of Hollywood docudrama writers, and co-author of *Behind Closed Doors*, has confessed to being troubled by criticism, and faced up to it forthrightly in a 1979 article in *The New York Times*. "We are at the mercy of incomplete and biased sources," he said. "We have to guess at what was said in the bedroom. But we are not liars, and no one should imagine that we change characters or events whimsically or maliciously or—perhaps worst of all—thoughtlessly." Yet, Rintels said, "I do worry that make-believe makes belief," and he pointed to the networks as the source of the problem. "They want the advantages both of exploitation and of sober responsibility," Rintels said. "They give conflicting messages to the creative community about the kinds of shows they are looking for and the treatment of those shows they require. Sometimes they sound publicly like *The New York Times* and privately like *The National Enquirer*."

But television's make-believe makes belief in a way that words on the printed page cannot. It tends to loosen the viewer's grip on reality. For those who find real-life ambiguity too much to contend with, it provides a quick fix. Its messages are seen as easy answers to difficult problems. It substitutes a world of heroes and villains for the world of contending political, economic, and social forces.

Relying on emotional manipulation and sensory experience rather than understanding, while exploiting real persons and events, the docudrama replaces the genuine with the ersatz. In 1938 E. B. White, after seeing his first demonstration of television, predicted a race "between the things that are and the things that seem to be."

Last time I looked, the things that seem to be were pulling ahead. And Ed Murrow, who always hated their masquerading as things that are, had been made into the hero of a seem-to-be docudrama.

Section 2

MEDIA AS PROVIDERS OF PLEASURE AND ENJOYMENT

Although most discussion and criticism of media centers upon news, other media content also is tremendously important. Most people use the media far more for enjoyment than for enlightenment, more to relax than to learn. Entertainment content also produces the greatest portion of the media's income. To understand the role of the media in our society, it is essential that we give some attention to entertainment.

The articles in Section 2 concern popular, mediated forms of entertainment in relation to American culture. Despite differences in subject matter and analytical approach, the authors of the articles in this section believe that entertainment is highly important for our society and that we need to understand its operation and functions far better than we do. Most of us take entertainment too much for granted; we seldom think seriously about it.

Richard Goldstein's essay is concerned with music videos—"tube rock"—and why they should be taken seriously. He also asserts that music videos are important because they are entertaining. He demonstrates the way an analysis of politics, theoretical economics, and aesthetics can expand our understanding and appreciation of a public art form such as tube rock.

Unlike the authors who precede and follow him in this section, Victor Lidz claims that popular entertainments are "inhospitable" to aesthetic analysis. He argues that television is best understood as the bearer of American secular morality, or, more precisely, middle-class morality characterized by Puritan and democratic themes. Lidz shows how these themes operate in dramatic series and concludes with an extended discussion of M*A*S*H.

In contrast to Lidz's emphasis on the sober moralizing of dramatic series, David Marc's focus is television comedy. Characterizing television as America's despised jester, he shows how presentational and representational comedic forms parody our cultural preoccupations. Marc sees tangible signs that contemporary Americans are knowing and critical actors in a demographic drama, not "couch potatoes" at all.

Like Marc, Michael Pollan gives evidence that television program creators know viewers are awake. Pollan's subject is the game show *Wheel of Fortune*. He analyzes the reasons for the show's success; that is, the way it appeals to dominant strains in American culture and the reasons it attracts so many advertising dollars. He demonstrates how the game show can be as ironic as comedy, poking wry fun at the very values that lie at its core.

The sophisticated attitude toward viewers that Marc and Pollan find in television is matched by Robert P. Snow's description of a parasocial relationship involving radio and its listeners. He argues that radio's individual listener finds companionship—a replacement for interpersonal communication—in radio personalities. He analyzes the role-taking behaviors of radio performers in the context of a contemporary radio station's systematically-constructed sound.

As you read the articles in this section, we hope you will be persuaded to think more about the various kinds of entertainment you and your friends enjoy. There are risks in such thought, but we believe the potential gains far outweigh the risks. Critically analyzing your favorite pastimes may take the fun out of them. That is the risk and the challenge of giving serious thought to the popular arts and to the other activities you now find enjoyable. On the other hand, we believe you are more likely to find your appreciation for entertainments enhanced by a better understanding of their form and meaning and a deeper understanding of their role in your life. In either event, the result will be better than complacency. Either way, you liberate yourself. You can't lose.

Study Questions: Goldstein

? *How does Goldstein describe the relationship between rock and music video? How does he distinguish between rock video and advertising? Do you think the distinctions he makes are justified?*

In what ways has tube rock brought traditional distinctions among media into question?

Goldstein claims music videos are not narratives. Do you accept his argument? What does he say they are?

In what ways are rock music and rock music videos sexist?

The author of this article quotes Theodore Adorno, who wrote, "Nothing may exist which is not like the world as it is." Are music videos evidence for or against Adorno's generalization? Would Goldstein agree with your position?

What historical, aesthetic, and social factors does Goldstein claim affected or continue to affect music videos?

Do you agree with him that tube rock should be studied seriously? Why or why not?

How do the tone and language of this article reflect the author's age? His reading audience?

Richard Goldstein

TUBE ROCK: HOW MUSIC VIDEO IS CHANGING MUSIC

You'd think we were our parents' generation bitching about rock'n'roll. From the venom Our Crowd propels toward music video and its main squeeze, MTV, you'd think we were talking about the decline of Counter-cultural Civ. "Rock'n'roll has been replaced by commercials," bleats *Rolling Stone,* and *Film Comment* chimes in, "It is not possible to speculate on the future of [this form], locked as it is in a frozen visual rhetoric of posture and display."

Even so remote a quarter as *The New York Times Book Review* has heard the news that music video represents yet another invasion of the vulgarians, a reduction upon the reduction that is rock'n'roll. A new novel is called by its reviewer "a literary equivalent of rock video, in which technical adroitness in manipulating an image and sensuous pleasure in what can be done with it rather preclude questions about why."

"Shitty little movies" is how Robert Cristgau described the genre in these pages last year, though he hastened to add, "I like some and even learn from a few." Dave Hickey was less charitable: "May be the most heartless, sociopathic idiom in the history of the known world." The consensus among these hard-driving literary proles is that music video "asphyxiates the imagination," as Chuck Morris put it. "They have never enhanced my appreciation of a song," Mark Moses confesses; and Larry Katz proclaims, in a more cosmological vein (he's from Boston): "Music . . . is all about using our ears, not our eyes."

So much for opera. Or ballet. So much for all that silly Wagnerian striving to merge music and theater, and those experiments in color-coordinated sound by the likes of Scriabin. So much for psychedelic light-shows. Rock'n'roll should be savored in a dimly lit room, over gourmet coffee. Seems like only yesterday we couldn't even pronounce the word "gourmet."

As the first rock generation ages, we've inherited the power to define quality in culture, even as we slip from the edge of cultural change. Along with that power comes the right to invest the shlock of our childhood with retrospective worth. We get to reinvent that epoch of high hustlers and cheap shooters as the Golden Age of Rock'n'Roll. We get to rehabilitate the sleazeballs who marketed the music as Hegelian princes. In the process of assembling this hagiography, we lose sight of how utterly traditional the music video environment is.

Television has always promoted rock'n'roll, and the music's greatest stars have been those who knew how to communicate on the tube. Elvis Presley and the Beatles have this much in common with Michael Jackson: they crossed over (Presley from rockabilly, the Beatles from Euro-r&b, Jackson from the Motown stable) because they knew how to manipulate emblems—hairstyles, body parts, a single glove. These are signifiers of heightened individuality, crucial to the star-making process, and they have little to do with music. I wasn't drawn to Elvis, as a 12-year-old in 1956, for his orientation in the delta blues tradition. Elvis was able to suggest a connection between his music and our sexual awakening because of television.

Rock and video have greased each other's palms since both were technologically feasible. The fear seems to be that MTV and its legion of imitators are subsuming rock'n'roll and adulterating its values. "In the pre-MTV world," Steven Levy writes in *Rolling Stone,* "we used to construct our own fantasies to music, provide our own images rich in personal meaning. Now, mass images are provided for us. And the primary criterion for choosing these images is not artistic validity, or even what the songwriter had in mind, but what might sell the song." Levy sees the best minds of his generation "lost in the funhouse environment of MTV, [spending] idle hours in a dull stereo stupor."

Now, that's the kind of thing the Quality folks used to say about rock'n'roll. They were right—it *did* put you in a kind of grateful trance. Jazz fans warned that chronic exposure to electric instruments would destroy the discriminating ear—and they were right, too, up to a point. Some people think every technical innovation flattens the aesthetic field. One thing's for sure: the more you knew about music, the less likely you were to appreciate the reductive energy of rock'n'roll; and the more you know about rock music, the less you like MTV.

But the success of MTV (it's the only format on cable to make a profit) suggests that kids no longer approach their music in a state of undivided attention. Rock'n'roll ushered in the youth market, but in the eighties, it must compete with movies, sports, fashion, and other leisure time pursuits for a more hotly contested teenage buck. Tube rock makes it more likely that music will compete, by linking its eroticism to the heightened sensuality video can provide. The result has been an outpouring of big, bright video anthems—from Van Halen's "Jump" to Springsteen's "Born in the U.S.A."—and a surge in record sales. The pursuit of happiness has returned to music in the eighties, and music video is one reason why. The "stereo stupor" Levy envisions is actually a realization of the old multimedia ideal—rock as personal pleasure dome.

Seems like a contradiction to suggest that rock'n'roll before the birth of MTV was *not* delightful, but in fact, the dominant mood of music in the seventies was agony over ecstasy. The confrontational stance of modernism collided with a reverence for rockabilly to produce music only a hebephrenic could dance to. Dancing itself fell into disrepair, and melody fell into disrepute; harmonics of the sort black music championed existed only in disco—that music of greasers and queers—and the only emotion with any integrity was "aggro," the thinking man's brutality. A generation of musicians was burdened by what, in academic circles, is called "the anxiety of influence." They were too self-conscious to be authentic rockers and, for the most part, too banal to be authentic modernists. But they sure knew how to get beyond the pleasure principle. Whatever gratification may be gleaned from a punk classic like "Oh Bondage, Up Yours," no one who recalls that song would call it fun.

David Lee Roth is fun. Traipsing through an unlikely medley, he's the lounge singer in a whorehouse, the jock in top hat and tails. In video, he's the all-around good-time guy, immune to herpes and self-doubt. When he leers into the bubble lens, like the proverbial one-eyed cat in a seafood store, you forget that he's shoving the word "girls" down your throat.

Cyndi Lauper is fun. She reconciles Teresa Brewer with the Shangri-las and makes you understand something about the continuum of styles that is rock'n'roll. In her artfully constructed audiovisual pastiche, she is Betty Boop as waif, arms and legs hilariously akimbo. But her critique of Pure Beauty carries an edge of vulnerability so affecting you want to reach out and cradle her, outsized earrings and all.

Madonna and Prince are fun, both of them sending up the notion of a sex symbol while simultaneously claiming the title. Tina Turner, the incarnation of Bessie Smith as a mud wrestler, is hot fun. Duran Duran may be a singing fashion show, a group that was born to play the theme song in a James Bond flick, but hey, they've got a good beat and you can watch to it.

The triumph of hedonism in rock'n'roll today is some sort of return of the repressed—or so it must seem to the "disco sucks" contingent. But there's a fundamental difference between Barry White's opulent oeuvre and the mainstream that tube rock has spawned, a distinction that comes down to demographics. At least in this country, disco was the sound of late-night, urban outgroups, but the new mainstream is suburban, majoritarian, and high noon.

I'd argue with anyone who claims this market consists of nothing but Reaganites—its political loyalties, as Springsteen's emergence suggests, are still up for grabs. But the tube rock generation does believe in Self, and it loves the spectacle of selves wrought larger than life. Disco urged its devotees to strive for tribalism through rhythm—what one writer called "the democracy of the dance"—but music video promotes the oligarchy of image; it augments the authority of stars.

Tube rock forces musicians to act. Not that they haven't been acting since Jerry Lee Lewis learned to stomp on a piano and Chuck Berry essayed his first duckwalk; but on MTV, musicians have to emote the way matinee idols once did if they're to establish the kind of contact tube rockers covet— the heightened typology of a classic movie star. What once made a rock performer powerful—the ability to move an arena with broad gesture and precision timing—has been supplanted by a new strategy: the performer must project in close-up.

The implications of this shift for rock'n'roll are already being felt in the new crop of stars whose self-image seems to supplant their material. Boy George would have been just another fey Smokey Robinson were it not for his ability to suggest a new basis for male allure on MTV, where makeup counts for a great deal. George Thorogood would have been just another pretender to the throne of whiteboy blues were it not for his ability to stroke a pool cue. Michael Jackson would not have emerged as the premier performer of post-Beatles music were it not for the aching ambiguity of his body strained in dance, an emotional complexity that can only be sustained in the dialectic between camera and star.

Tube rock makes every performer of a certain magnitude a potential box-office attraction: Tina Turner, Grace Jones, Sting, and Prince. We await the multiplex debut of David Lee Roth, now embarked on a feature film with Peter Angelus, the director of his videos. The title is taken from Roth's first solo album, *Crazy from the Heat*; so which is the spinoff and which the original work? The question suggests one reason tube rock makes so many critics nervous: If a song can be expanded into a movie, then compressed into a video clip, where does rock'n'roll begin and end?

Add to this the frequent appearances of rock stars in commercials and you've got a heresy of Albigensian proportions. Rock is losing its adversarial stance; it can be—yearns to be—used to move products, and vice versa: Does Grace Jones hawk Hondas, or Honda hawk Grace Jones?

Compression, personification, dissociation: these are time-tested Mad. Ave. techniques, and in music video they emerge for the first time as an entertainment form. Critics who complain that tube rock intrudes upon the listener's capacity to "imagine" a song miss the point: it's not narrative these clips promote, but self-image. Music video strives to build a campaign in which individual hits are less important than an ongoing identity. Lighting, costume, setting, pace—all are used to sustain an emotional response, so that the Material Girl is the virginoid of yore, and the Private Dancer is the mama from "Better Be Good to Me." If product identification works for Pepsi, why shouldn't persona identification work for Prince?

Ominous as this equation may seem, it would be a mistake to assume from the connection between music video and advertising that music video *is* advertising. It's programming, and as such, it has a greater potential to foster meaning and a broader range of aesthetic options than commercials do. The proof is in the offensiveness: When was the last time an ad stirred the wrath of fundamentalists and feminists alike? The reason music videos inspire such outrage is their content, and content is the basis on which they must be judged.

Is tube rock sexist? Maybe the question should be, Is rock sexist? The themes of music video are rooted in the music; its obsession with torment and lust is a reminder that rock'n'roll has been an adolescent male adventure. And the look of music video is an *hommage* to cinematic chic: when it comes to mayhem and misogyny played out on a surface of lurid luminosity, Billy Idol pales before Brian De Palma. Yet it's music video, the renegade form, that takes the rap for "selling hate."

But the medium is not the message. Tube rock can encompass enlightened politics and vanguard sensibilities alongside retro and rape. There are no rules to this game—it's too new. There's only a voracious ingestion of styles and attitudes, and their rapid degeneration into cliché. But if the half-life of an image on MTV is pitifully brief, the demand for innovation is so strong that sometimes art can break through, unmediated and unannounced.

Consider Julian Temple's "Jazzin' for Blue Jean" (the long version), an essay in the ironies of mystique, in which Bowie the actor is upstaged by Bowie the performer, and then returns as Bowie the executive to hector the director of his video. Consider Godley and Creme's "Every Breath You Take," in which the starkly framed face of Sting emerges from a chiaroscuro worthy of Orson Welles to deliver a monologue in *noir*. Consider Bob Rafelson's "All Night Long," in which tropicalist color and costume transform an ordinary street, and in the process, an ordinary party anthem, into the incarnation of the American dream. Is it extravagant to suggest that these songs have been enhanced by their settings as video? Is it grandiose to suggest that each of these videos is, in some sense, progressive?

Consider what this malicious medium has done for Bruce Springsteen. It's expanded not only his audience, but his range as an actor. In director John Sayles's empathetic hands, this master of arena rock projects such passion on the tube that one can sense his potential to reinvent the dramatic musical. How can it be that a progressive performer captures the hearts of so many material girls? The answer is that Springsteen reconciles conscience with pleasure. He respects desire and knows how to arouse it in an intimate encounter; and in tube rock, that's entertainment!

You can argue that the sense of community is missing, that Live Aid is no Woodstock and Martha Quinn no Allen Freed. You can argue that the vigor of mainstream music is also its tyranny, pushing experiment to the periphery, relegating New Wave to the status of bebop. You can argue that MTV reinforces the marginal status of black music. Yes folks, this is not the world as it should be. But as Theodore Adorno wrote about the impact of popular culture on art, "Nothing may exist which is not like the world as it is." Tube rock is the world as it is. It's eclectic, expansive, and, like rock'n'roll itself, less a set of rhythms and attitudes than a representation of reality. It must be engaged, in all its nascent treachery, by the best minds of our generation, or its power will slip into other hands.

Study Questions: Lidz

[?] *What is Lidz's explanation for Americans' attraction to television despite what he sees as its artistic shortcomings? Do you agree with him that American popular culture is inhospitable to aesthetic cultural forms?*

What does Lidz mean by the "secular moral order"? Do other mass media share television's adherence to the secular moral order?

Do you think it is appropriate to judge television on moral criteria? Why or why not?

Take a recent news event with which you are familiar and that you believe exemplifies Lidz's argument that the television presentations of secular events "are subtly saturated with themes of mission, portent, destiny, and fulfillment that are religious in origin." Justify your choice, explaining how these themes saturated the stories about that event. Are there other conventions of televisual portrayal that convey the middle-class morality Lidz describes?

What does Lidz mean when he says television is "sensuous"?

What does Lidz seem to mean by "middle-class morality"? Do the television programs with which you are most familiar espouse such a morality? Can you identify television programs on the air today that contradict Lidz's claims about the morality that dominates the medium?

What does television drama's focus on strong and vivid characters, such as Hawkeye Pierce in M*A*S*H, *have to do with the Puritan tradition or the Puritan ethic?*

In his analysis of M*A*S*H *as an example of television's adherence to middle-class morality, does Lidz fail to consider any aspects of the show that are contrary to middle-class morality? Are there aspects of other series on television that seem to run counter to middle-class morality? If you think of any, does their existence mean that Lidz's analysis is wrong?*

Do you see any signs that television's morality is changing?

Do you think television should play a central role in the moral education of Americans? Why or why not?

Victor Lidz

TELEVISION AND MORAL ORDER IN A SECULAR AGE

The denunciations of television as an artistic wasteland leave the social scientist with a puzzle: How has television grown to such prominence in American cultural life? If television shows are so lacking in aesthetic worth, how have they captured so large a place in the life of the American imagination? The intent of this essay is to outline a partial solution to the puzzle. The solution is not an answer to the aesthetic attacks on television, for it presupposes them to be in key respects valid. But it does seek to understand how and why a vast American audience finds meaning in television shows despite their artistic shortcomings. My argument will be that television shows participate deeply in American *moral* culture. They are saturated with moral themes of individualism, strength of character, energetic activism, and commitment to freedom. However, in a manner that has descended from Puritan times, our popular moral culture tends to be inhospitable to frankly aesthetic cultural forms. The artistic possibilities of television are often overwhelmed by a deeply fixed emphasis on moral beliefs.

SECULAR MORALITY

Television has arisen in an age of secularized moral culture. In speaking of secularization, we need not presume that religious life is certainly and

AUTHOR'S NOTE: An earlier incarnation of this chapter was presented at a conference, "Toward a Public Philosophy of Communication," convened by Trinity Institute of New York. I am indebted to Durstan McDonald and William Fore for an invitation to that conference, and to Dunbar Moodie, James Carey, and Gregor Goethals for insightful comments on and criticisms of my talk there. Barry Schwartz and Harold Bershady have also given me helpful critiques of the earlier paper.

finally waning in our time or that, if yet active, it must be inauthentic, without spirit, or radically maladapted to the broader society (Parsons, 1979). The secularity of modern civilization is simply this: there has grown up since the Enlightenment a framework of secular moral culture that is independent of religion (functionally differentiated, in the lingo of sociologists) and that serves as the primary body of beliefs legitimating social institutions (Lidz, 1979). The same body of beliefs also provides ethical restraint over individuals who act with moral authority under the cover of the legitimate social order. The secular moral order encompasses our beliefs about the foundations of constitutional and legal order, economic ethics and practices, civil freedoms and duties, educational ideals, personal, familial, and community morals, and so forth. On these many matters, Americans share both agreements and certain patterns of disagreement, such as that between political liberals and conservatives, that are structured independently of religious commitments. Most issues of public deliberation, whether controversial or not, are broached primarily within the frameworks of secular moral belief. These frameworks were constructed largely at the founding of the republic and have evolved as common understandings about how public deliberations should be conducted ever since. If public discussion is to result in legitimate convictions about a need for change in policies or institutions, the secular moral order provides the necessary terms of conscientious judgment.

The secular order is a differentiated and specialized sphere of the moral life. It is therefore not fully self-sufficient, but related in various ways to religious institutions and spiritual life. The major concern of the secular moral order is with the world of practical affairs and with the legitimation of our principal social institutions. It appeals to the individual in terms of conscientious duty and the reciprocation of duty. To religious life it leaves the underpinnings of duty in the realm of faith. It leaves to religion questions of ultimate principles and identities, the sustenance of the spirit, and the resolution of existential dilemmas (Bellah, 1968). The secular order maintains a variety of civil rituals, but few that answer to the needs of the person or provide celebration of the life-course. Its ethics do not concentrate on dilemmas and problems of the individual life-world. Nor do they answer directly to the "problem of meaning" (Weber, 1963) generated by illness, poverty, failure, disappointment, loneliness, and sin, except insofar as they foster practical hopes or assign duties for meliorating undesirable conditions. In these respects, secular beliefs do not preclude a religious life—social action addressed to the sacred rather than the profane world—and perhaps they even leave individuals dependent upon it.

Television, however, has been aligned mainly with the claims of the secular order. The network audience during prime time is addressed in terms provided almost entirely by the secular culture. The God who is occasionally invoked is the curiously abstract figure conceived as a foundation of the "entire Judeo-Christian tradition" in the now conventional phrase. He is called upon through a precise etiquette only to frame a statement of moral commitment and underscore the good faith with which it is intended. The overt action of primetime, network television is enclosed within worldly concerns that focus on job, family, health, safety, neighborhood, law-and-order, skill, achievements, material well-being, success, fellowship, and loyalty to nation and way-of-life. Whether a drama is placed out in space and in the future, in the frontier of the Old West, in the dangerous streets of today's cities, in the offices of doctors, lawyers, private investigators, or journalists, or in one or another type of comic family situation, the overt concerns of the action remain secular and mundane. Life is depicted as largely enclosed within the realities of the secular order, as even comprehensible only within its prosaic terms.

And yet there is also a deeper, somewhat more covert aspect to the action of television. There is a mystification of character and motive, a dwelling on unseen ways in which mundane persons come to serve high callings, worldly conduct assumes qualities of a larger mission, or individual sacrifice becomes heroic devotion to duty—in short, in which activities in the everyday world figure the workings of a transcendental reality. On this plane of implied deeper meaning, television drama reflects the dependence of the secular order on certain modes of religious belief and symbolism. To understand penetratingly the events and characters of American television dramas, we must apprehend them against a background of long-established, essentially Puritan traditions of order, calling, duty, and motive. The secular order, prominent as it stands in the American view of values, concerns, and energizing interests in the make-up of civil society, is also a screen on which a characterology deriving from the Puritan sense of self and conscience is still projected (see Bercovitch, 1975).

The use of television to convey ritual and ceremony to the nation at large, one of its most vivid uses, confirms its strong relation to the secular morality. Most of the ceremonial occasions that have engrossed and sentimentally united large audiences have turned on secular events, for example, State of the Union Addresses, Presidential Inaugurals, the return of prisoners of war from North Vietnam, the landing on the moon and other space "missions." Certain recurrent secular celebrations are ritualized on television in palpable connection to themes central to American moral culture, for example, the Super Bowl and World Series, the Academy Award Presentations, even the Miss America contests. A number of complicated political events have been realized largely through television and its special capacity to dramatize their portents for the American destiny before the public as a whole, for example, the Army-McCarthy Hearings, events in the Vietnam War, especially the denouement of the Tet Offensive, the Watergate Hearings of the Senate Judiciary Committee, and the impeachment proceedings of the House Judiciary Committee. Television presentations such as these are concerned with secular events and framed in terms of secular beliefs, but are subtly saturated with themes of mission, portent, destiny, and fulfillment that are religious in origin. They show the American secular morality, despite its functional autonomy as a belief system, to be vitally connected to traditions of civil religion (Bellah, 1970). The continuing importance of religious thematics and attitudes within the context of American secular morality was especially apparent during the weekend of national mourning for President Kennedy, surely the most memorable of all televised rituals (Parsons and Lidz, 1967).

Were it to project its qualities of vivid presence centrally into the affairs of denominational religions, television would potentially be caught up with forces of social division. The growth of television as a civil institution has thus precluded denominational religion from a prominent role. Television, like radio, follows a model developed in the public print media, newspapers in particular, during the nineteenth century. Although many newspapers and journals directed to special religious readerships prosper, the central media of mass circulation address the public at large without denominational concern. Similarly, religious shows appear on cable television and on television stations unaffiliated with a major network, but infrequently address a large part of the primetime audience. . . .

MIDDLE-CLASS MORALITY

. . . Television dramatizes moral themes that are old and well established. Two sets of themes appear to be especially strongly emphasized, which I will call the Puritan and the democratic. Together they comprise what I speak of as the "middle-class morality": our conventional, mundane, eminently practical, sternly disciplined, yet sentimentally expansive moral sensibility.

The middle-class morality can already be recognized in de Tocqueville's account of the pragmatic mediocrity of American social standards in the 1830s (de Tocqueville, 1948). As de Tocqueville understood, it is intimately connected with the relative absence of fixed—ascriptive—grounds of association in American society. Indeed, many kinds of association in the world of practical affairs are commonly established on quite impersonal grounds. Individuals and groups often must decide whether or not to trust one another and establish ties of common association even though they cannot assess each other through relations of mutual familiarity. Americans frequently have to calculate the degrees to which they can depend on others whose origins, background, and character they cannot know reliably and in circumstantial detail. Reciprocally, they often face the task of having to show themselves to be trustworthy in settings where others cannot know their qualities of character. Not only are situations requiring impersonal judgments of character and reliability a practical reality with which Americans have to cope without leaving their interests open to exploitation, but they are also valued and idealized. They are commonly viewed as fair arrangements that extend opportunities to all who wish to improve their status in society. The middle-class morality, then, affirms the ideology of universalistic opportunity while providing standards for the subtle interplay by which citizens warrant their own characters while assessing the characters of others. Specific standards of characterological assessment vary considerably from situation to situation. They are different in the academic world as compared with the industrial world, in the financial world as compared with the world of marketing and advertising, in the snobbish world of country clubs as compared with the world of community service associations, and so forth. Yet, the middle-class morality also has a unity of common emphasis on honesty, hard work, development of skill, self-improvement, performance of duty, and the trustworthiness of promises.

Given the importance that American society attaches to judgments of character based on the middle-class morality, it should not surprise us that television exhibits a veritable cult of character. Heavy emphasis falls on depicting the practical benefits, for the individual and for society, to be derived from principled character. The viewer is drawn sentimentally into relations of respect for characters who maintain authentic integrity in situations that tempt and test them severely. Dramatic emphasis may also be placed on matters of inherent abilities, skills, training, or knowledge, but usually in ways that give priority to the moral commitment to develop and use one's personal talents methodically. Exceptional ability can thus be portrayed as in essence a manifestation of strong character. A tendency to heroize admirable abilities as signs of disciplined character is probably the most persistent moral "argument" of American television. It pervades the broadcasts of sports events of all kinds, but especially of the sports most engrained in American culture—baseball, football, and basketball. It is highlighted on shows that portray the socialization and education of youth, for example, *Fame,* with its elaborations on themes of personal promise for the future. Shows focusing on physicians, especially surgeons, and on scientists dwell on the long, disciplined hours of education and training and on virtuosities of knowledge and skill that must be displayed. Even shows with more humble settings, detective shows, westerns, even shows depicting office work, underscore uses of exceptional abilities. Given the widespread conviction that the "work ethic" is no longer respected in America, it is noteworthy that popular television stresses that ethic so relentlessly to an audience so large.

The dramatization of character on television also emphasizes the importance of association with others and capacity for teamwork. Character is made evident through reliability and trustworthiness and through dependable devotion to collective ends. The praiseworthy athlete is not only skilled but reliable in doing his or her part on a team, will be cooperative and selfless in devotion to teamwork, and will make the sacrifice of playing with pain. Telecasts of football games are tireless in reiterating these moral points and in self-consciously emphasizing their relevance to other spheres of life. But the same lessons are dramatized in the surgery of *M*A*S*H*, the detective work of *Hill Street Blues,* or the stages and studios of *Fame.* More deeply, the involvement of individuals in cooperative teamwork tends to be portrayed as having larger purposes. Cooperation in the laboratory follows from a devotion to science. Physicians are depicted as ideal paradigms of cooperation because lives depend on their teamwork. Television shows that portray conflicts on hospital staffs quickly become dramas of life-and-death; and documentaries on doctors and hospitals take care to show the absence of conflict or deny its importance. Patriotism and civic spirit are depicted as the grounds of teamwork in shows about spies, diplomats, the military, or political leaders.

American dramas rarely portray groups, teams, or associations as indissoluble wholes—as, for example, they are shown in Japanese films such as *The Magnificent Seven* or *High and Low.* American television dwells on the prominent characters who make up a group and assume responsibilities for spheres of the collective action. Sports teams are televised with concentration on their stars and on the ways in which the stars do or do not accept the discipline of teamwork. The surgery of *M*A*S*H* is similarly a cooperative field for the action of vivid figures, as are the courtrooms of *Perry Mason,* the laboratory of *Quincy,* the New York streets as shown in *Kojak,* and the newspaper cityroom of *Lou Grant.* For American television, collective action provides occasions for examining the conscientious conduct of autonomous individuals as they commit themselves to shared purposes and procedures. If members of a group are not suitable for dramatization as vivid and usually heroic individuals, television is unlikely to take an interest.

The tenuous portrayal of the reality of groups has a complement in television's emphasis on self-reliance. The westerns and private-eye shows, which so often culminate in life-and-death confrontations between a single hero and a villain or group of villains, are the genres most consistent in depicting individuals as ultimately alone and dependent on their own resources. Many kinds of adventure story typically arrive at denouements that turn on tests of individuals who must confront their difficulties by themselves, however. Spy stories tend to heighten the issue of self-reliance by placing the hero quite alone or with support of doubtful reliability in a setting dominated by enemies. Dramas placed in everyday situations may also rest on the theme of self-reliance. When emphasis falls on the qualities

of character needed to develop successful careers, times and situations that
test a central figure are likely to be shown in ways that highlight the value
of self-reliance. The time of test must follow the death of a mentor, a
divorce, or betrayal by a colleague. Figures in positions of high authority
or on whom many others may depend for their well-being are especially
likely to be portrayed as essentially alone when difficult responsibilities must
be discharged. Historical and documentary television is emphatic on depicting presidents and generals in this fashion, as are political advertisements.

The Puritan sources of television portrayals of character become more
evident when we look into the nature of the obligation on individuals to
live up to high standards or withstand demanding trials. Television often
highlights a duty to perfect oneself as an instrument of higher principles
or purposes. Given the secular temper of our times, entertainments addressed to the public at large rarely highlight divine inspirations or ordainments of valued conduct, although they do portray religious people.
The final source of moral obligation is usually left implicit, rather myste-
riously taken for granted. Yet, the principles of our secular moral order
may be treated as ineffably transcendent, genuine grounds of action that
establish categorical rather than contingent imperatives. Secular principles
that are transcendental in this fashion may take on certain religious col-
orations. Thus, American television shows are preoccupied with secular
"missions," as are news reports. The American way of life as a whole, with
its devotion to freedom of the conscience and political liberty, is regarded
as a grand mission (Bellah, 1970). Stories about the protection of that way
of life, especially from Nazi or Communist armies or agents, become saturated with senses of mission. Advancing the qualities of American civilization in sciences or the arts, perfecting the principles of popular democracy, or contributing to the material welfare of the citizenry may be portrayed as forms of mission. Matters as worldly as conspicuous success in
business or even athletics are commonly interpreted on television shows as
favorable outcomes of missions. Thus, the human condition as dramatized
on television is shown to be filled with higher principles, missions, and
ordainments in a fashion that remains Puritan-like. However secularized
contemporary American world-views, life would seem flat, purposeless,
lacking in fascination and marvel were its portrayals empty of implications
of mission. In this respect, the tradition of Puritanism has passed through
the process of secularization without succumbing to the utter disenchant-
ment of the world that Max Weber feared (Weber, 1963).

The Puritan tradition has also contributed to television's culture of
character a tendency to treat the individualistic presuppositions of its moralism as ontological. In almost any setting of action, television selects out
the involvements of focal individuals as the ultimate matters of concern.

The dramatic fascination with missions comes to dwell on the dilemmas of conscience that individuals must confront in order to fulfill higher duties. The outcomes of stories are presented as reportage on the fates of the individuals whose efforts at conscientious conduct have been dramatized. The drama of episodic shows is dominated by particularly vivid individuals who are elevated above the others with whom they interact. As the episodic formats have evolved over the past few decades, the drama has focused ever more completely around vividly highlighted persons—Marshal Dillon, Elliot Ness, Marcus Welby, Hawkeye Pierce, Archie Bunker, Kojak, Lou Grant, and so forth. As Puritan conduct reduced culturally to dilemmas of the conscience, so the action dramatized on television reduces to stories of vivid characters.

The democratic element in the middle-class morality shows up on television in the variety of situations that are dramatized and in their modes of symbolic connection to American society. The settings of television shows often reflect ordinary features of American life, although they may do so through idealized typifications. The customs and routines of television characters may be presented as depicting common practices in American communities. Shows that focus on occupational roles often dramatize work that has a firm status in practically every locality. Thus, television often dramatizes situations that will be familiar to us in outlines, at least. We see homes, schools, hospitals, fire stations, town halls, shops, offices, and so forth that are like ones in our own communities, even if they appear newer, better equipped, and better cared for. We see teachers, firemen, policemen, doctors, politicians, lawyers, shopowners, and bureaucrats who seem to be typified after and intended as comments upon people we commonly encounter.

Sometimes we are shown figures who are "representative" in another sense, not as typical but as approximating what is the "best" in America— dutiful, able youth, tenaciously honest public servants, teachers devoted to the futures of their students, surgeons who are bold, yet calm, and virtuosos of the scalpel. Figures who represent excellence are connected to a popular audience by the values that their exemplary performances may reinforce. Viewers who appreciate their special qualities have been moved to respect their principles of conduct. Where the action of television occurs in exotic settings that cannot be portrayed as representative, it is often dramatized from a standpoint that is very ordinarily American. Dramas of World War II, even when they relate exceptionally harrowing and heroic experience, tend to be peopled with a set of "types" that together represent America— the Texas cowboy, the Brooklyn Jew, the WASP New Englander with Ivy League education, the Iowa corn farmer, and so forth. A story of the German concentration camps is likely to be related by a subsequent immigrant who gives it a location in American experience. The crew of a space rocket set centuries in the future, as on *Star Trek* or *Battlestar Galactica*, will on television consist of several recognizably American types whose reactions to their experiences confirm our conventional judgment.

Beyond these basic ways of democratizing their moral import, television shows use some special devices for broadening their sentimental appeals to a mass audience. One common device is the designed use of a humble setting. It is employed most consistently in comedy shows, where much of the humor turns on a familiar relation between the dramatis personae and viewers. It has been used in many episodic shows situated in families, from *Ozzie and Harriet* to *All in the Family* or *The Jeffersons*. It has also been used on many comedies located in ordinary workplaces, from *Duffy's Tavern* to *Barney Miller* or *Alice*.

A notable example, *The Honeymooners*, dates back as long as 25 years, but continues to be popular in many parts of the country through reruns. Its focal character, played in the vaudeville tradition of exaggerated gestures by Jackie Gleason, was a bus driver frustratingly trapped in a life of poverty despite harboring fantasies of wealth and success. Most of the action was set in Ralph Kramden's sparsely and poorly furnished, cramped and seedy New York apartment. The show's set for the apartment was designed in the naturalistic tradition to convey the emptiness of poverty more graphically than, to my knowledge, it has otherwise ever been portrayed on television. Typically, the action involved the bus driver's relations with his loyal, though outspoken, wife Alice—the couple had no children—and his closest friend Ed Norton, a sewer worker, and Norton's wife. Many episodes turned on the appeals of a get-rich-quick opportunity or scheme, not always an honest one, which would stimulate the hopes of Ralph and his friend despite the misgivings of common sense voiced by their wives. After the men invested effort and savings as well as hopes, the scheme would turn sour and leave them more hopelessly trapped in poverty and dependent on their tiresome jobs. While loud recriminations usually ensued, the resolutions of the stories generally involved the husbands and wives reaffirming mutual love and the two men renewing their friendship.

The Honeymooners episodes and especially their endings were as lavishly sentimental as the setting of action was materially austere. The sentiment projected to the audience a moral that poverty and ill-rewarded, unappreciated work were difficult to endure in America, the land of successes, but also that, with love, they could be endured and were best endured through responsible involvement in one's calling and family life. The moral was thoroughly in line with respectable middle-class convention. Yet, it was given a setting so humble and stories so melodramatic that the sentimental appeal could hardly "pass over" any class within the active television audience. The bus driver's and sewer worker's circumstances may have been depicted as so poor and their conduct as so childish to assure that members of the working class, while identifying with the characters, could also feel themselves, by comparison, superior in conscience and more successful in material condition.

Another form of appeal to democratic sentiment involves dramatizing matters of current moral concern. In recent years, many shows have presented episodes that moralize on problems of drug use among youth. Kojak, the officers of *Hill Street Blues,* Lou Grant and his colleagues, Quincy, Dr. Welby, the teachers and kids of *Fame,* and many other television worthies have tried to assist with the much publicized "drug crisis." Devoting episodes to what are regarded as real problems in American society—whether the drug crisis (see Lidz and Walker, 1980), the crime on the streets crisis, the mental health crisis, the "warehousing" of the elderly crisis, the child abuse crisis, the police corruption crisis, the mediocre schools crisis, or the shoddy work on the assembly line crisis—is presented as marking the show's authenticity. Such episodes give viewers the assurance that the characters of the show, police, journalists, doctors, or whatever, are engaged with American society in all of its actuality and with all of its serious problems. Although episodes dealing with "touchy" problems, mental illness, rape, or child-molestation, tend to be self-conscious about being venturesome, they are typically cautious in conveying only the moral conclusions currently being voiced by authoritative experts (or people deemed to be such). Television can be profuse with sympathy for individuals and families caught up in serious problems, such as drug use, but it tends to be firm in prescribing the kinds of conduct deemed "right" as solutions. Often the problems are portrayed as having their sources in underlying difficulties in family life and as having remedies in action that can be taken by ordinary citizens. In the context of an "entertaining" show, then, a problem may be depicted as typically existing within the neighborhoods of viewers and its solution as resting largely on viewers' having the consciences to act. The democratic element in this moralistic stance lies in the universalism of the conscientious appeal addressed to the audience as a whole.

A third means of democratizing a moral appeal is to dramatize kinds of action with which members of the audience can be presumed to identify. Some of the identities taken as a basis of dramatic involvement are fairly concrete and familiar. Patriotic sentiments are involved in the depictions of GIs fighting in World War II that continue to be popular. Given the controversies over the Vietnam War, television producers have needed a number of years to devise dramatizations of it that do not offend viewers by their treatments of patriotic sentiments. Presentations of most scientific or medical work can also presume widespread identification with their underlying missions, usually treated as betterment of the human condition in a material fashion. Yet, there is also a genre, presented at times on television though more popular in movies, of Frankenstein-like science fiction depicting mad or evil scientists plotting harm against humankind. It tells us that there is enough ambivalence that large audiences can identify negatively toward science. Human missions are also projected into fantasies of a future where conflicts between good and evil, often between the American way and a Communist-like threat to it, can be depicted as cosmic and cataclysmic.

Many shows have been set in an expressional midground between the domains of the familiar and the domains of fantasy. Most spy stories, especially ones about Free World-Communist World conflicts, take place in a frame constructed out of special literary, movie, and television genres that mix references to real characters, events, and locations with quite fantastic matters and eschatology. Stories set in the Old West, whether emphasizing conflicts between settlers and Indians, homesteaders and ranchers, hard working townspeople and bands of outlaws, or sheriffs and gunslingers, also take on a semblance of actuality largely from long-evolving popular genres. Shows of these types, for example, the durable *Gunsmoke*, also act on viewers' identifications with valued endeavors of the past—civilizing new territory, making the land productive, ridding towns of vice, upholding law and order. Popular in their sentimental frames, they reinforce old moral understandings about the legitimation of venturesome and risky conduct. By dramatizing that moral principles are worth the devotion of a life's work or the risk or even sacrifice of a life, they support conventional American beliefs. The moralization flows less from the daring adventures, the challenges few of us will ever experience, than from the ordinary ideals to which we presume one another to be committed and which are shown to be served by true heroism. Heroic or fantastic missions are thereby related in sentiment to the routine lives of viewers.

Through the Puritan focus on character and the democratic embrace of the commonplaces of American life, the middle-class morality is projected over television to a vast audience that it exhorts and integrates. To be sure, network television has been set up primarily to entertain. However, given the ethical traditions of America, not least its venerable distrust of the expressionally immediate and sensuous, entertainments must be thoroughly moralized if they are to be culturally acceptable. Moreover, they must be popularly moralized. Television is thus the heir of Puritan sermonizing, of the revival mentality, of popular self-improvement literature, of mass readership newspapers, of the radio shows that devised the weekly episode, and of the Hollywood film industry with which it is now so closely joined.

THE EXAMPLE OF *M*A*S*H*

The extraordinary success of *M*A*S*H* as a television show highlights some rather interesting ways in which the middle-class morality shapes an episodic series and its reception by a mass audience. An exceptionally well-

sustained commercial success, *M*A*S*H* has also become a celebrated part
of contemporary American popular culture. Its characters (and the actors
portraying them) are widely known and talked about. Critics of television
and popular culture have been nearly unanimous in their enthusiasm for
the show. Self-consciously bizarre in its humor, although more restrained
than the novel and movie it followed, it has not lacked courage to delve
into matters involving intense moral sentiments for an American audience.

The setting for *M*A*S*H* seems at first an improbable scene for comedy
and too removed from present-day concerns to be made popular. *M*A*S*H*
is set in a small military surgical hospital, a hospital of tents, just behind
the front lines of the Korean War. Its main characters are two young
surgeons whose presenting qualities are dislike for the war and alienation
from military discipline. They are in many respects dramatized as modern
anti-heroes, being comic in dress, personal manners, and characteristic
motives. However, these qualities are given more serious texture by their
imaginative efforts to dissociate themselves from the war and army in which
they are caught up. The plots of most episodes turn on events that transform the comic anti-heroes into true heroes displaying exceptional integrity
and fortitude under duress. They show uncommon skill as surgeons, ideal
physicianly compassion for the wounded, fellow-feeling for a member of
the hospital staff in personal difficulty or, beneath their anger toward the
military, a finer patriotism. Their attitudes toward war and the military are
never undermined (even if stated more moderately in the late episodes),
but are connected to personal virtues widely admired in American culture:
willingness to work hard, creatively, and selflessly; devotion to duty, com-
rades, and nation; technical skill, personal integrity, and compassion.

Portrayals of other characters in the series serve to accentuate the
qualities shown by the two young surgeons. Initially, they are set off against
another surgeon who covers over his professional incompetence and lack
of commitment to patients with a veneer of aggressive, intolerant, self-
serving patriotism; a commanding officer who is bumbling as a leader and
unwilling to accept the responsibilities of authority, yet ambitious to please
superiors; a sexy but capable chief nurse whose strongest concern is to
advance her army career; a compassionate and dedicated company clerk
whose inexperience and naivete makes him dependent on the hero-
surgeons for guidance; a well-intended, cooperative, though other-worldly
and often ineffective, Catholic chaplain; an orderly who resorts to transves-
tism in a desperate effort to win discharge from the army; and, more
occasionally, a paranoid intelligence officer who finds Communist plots in
everyday events, a psychiatrist whose expressions of sympathy by psycho-
therapeutic formula offer meager relief from the burdens of wartime, and
various generals whose vanity makes them easily gulled and ineffective. In
later episodes, the incompetent colleague is replaced by a surgeon of exceptional skill, but whose upper-class snobbery and professional ambition

strain the fellowship of the hospital staff. The commanding officer in the late episodes is a career colonel who represents military discipline more favorably, but who wisely tempers it out of respect for the personal needs of his staff, especially the surgeons, whose skill and devotion he appreciates.

The cast of characters is a parody of the "e pluribus unum" variety of figures that commonly appear in American dramas about national causes. These characters exhibit variety, but largely as a variety of personal failings. They are often seriously divided against themselves, caught up in egocentric jealousies, peeves, and competitive ambitions that break down the cooperation necessary in a hospital. The humor developed in the antic playing on human weaknesses highlights characteristically American deficiencies: ambition, self-centeredness, intolerance of the unfamiliar, self-interested abuse of higher principles, vanity, and so forth. When the surgeon heroes galvanize this morally fragmented group into effective cooperation and mutual respect, the surpassing nature of their qualities is dramatized strongly. The comedy of *M*A*S*H* is exploited methodically for didactic moralism. As self-consciously innovative as its humor may be, it retains a footing in the familiar middle-class culture of character and calling.

The popularity of *M*A*S*H* has yet another key source. The widespread conviction that it was an especially meaningful show rested on a crucial symbolic device: its setting in Korea was a moderately transparent substitute for the war of its own times in Vietnam. By using an apparent setting in the Korean War, *M*A*S*H* could become a popular vehicle for the antiwar, antimilitary, antinationalistic attitudes of the opposition to the Vietnam War. Moreover, it could dramatize these attitudes in ways that reassuringly connected them with traditionally recognized virtues of character. The critique of war, the military, and fervent nationalism was united with traditional social criticism of ambition, egocentrism, incompetence, and lack of feeling. Had *M*A*S*H* been set overtly in Vietnam, such morally and sentimentally serious matters could not have been addressed. The affront to Americans who served in Vietnam and/or backed the war policies would have been too direct. Only a storm of disapproval could have resulted. However, the temperate effort to show the grounding of war-criticism in traditional moral culture, giving it broader legitimacy in American life, could not have been undertaken either. It would have seemed overly compromising and lacking in integrity. Yet, the audience for *M*A*S*H* could not miss the point that Korea was a tasteful stand-in for Vietnam. Much of the culture, not least the style of humor and the slang, but at times material objects and even items of medical technology, was taken from the era of the Vietnam War, not the Korean War. The events of *M*A*S*H* existed in their own world with typical features of their own. They could not have happened in Korea or Vietnam. But by matters of cultural style they commented with only slight ambiguity on Vietnam.

*M*A*S*H* can provide an occasion for considering the relevance of routine television forms to more serious sources of order and common commitment. *M*A*S*H* was presented to its audience as an "entertainment," not as a didactic treatment of an ideology or religion. Its success was realized through its ability to "entertain" an audience embodying most of the ideological and spiritual diversity of the nation. In experiencing an "entertainment," its audience was engaged with a form of popular art that ordinarily maintains an attitudinal distance from serious dilemmas and controversies. The satire of *M*A*S*H* often had serious themes or overtones, but viewers were allowed to remain in the experimental frame of enjoying entertainment. Had the audience felt that the satire amounted to ideological proselytization, it would likely have rejected *M*A*S*H* as an inappropriate exploitation of the television format of a "show." At least, the success of *M*A*S*H* as a show of general appeal would have been jeopardized. We may also speculate that more diffuse and overtly critical satire could not have been sustained at a high level for the long run of *M*A*S*H*, at least not within its episodic formulae.

Many of the themes in *M*A*S*H* are utterly typical of the way in which the secular entertainments of American television participate in the middle-class morality. *M*A*S*H* presents us with vivid heroes who display skill, dedication, compassion, bravery, conscientiousness, and so forth. Their missions and activities reverberate in our senses of national identity. They are surrounded by figures who represent a wide range of the types that compose the American community. The show's persistent concern with the horrors of war dramatizes what may be America's greatest social problem. More deeply, *M*A*S*H* gave its huge audience a healing mediation between the antiwar culture of the Vietnam War years and many long-established values of the middle-class morality. In doing so, it served American civilization more penetratingly and venturesomely than most television has dared to attempt. It endeavored to provide a culture of reconciliation to resolve strongly felt social and cultural divisions. Here, *M*A*S*H* took up a higher calling than just continuing to dramatize conventional moralism. It adopted a stance of respectful criticism as well as a stance of affirmation. By uniting these stances in a continuing drama, *M*A*S*H* reached a moral and spiritual fulfillment to which television has not often aspired.

CONCLUSION

The American middle-class morality, ever since it crystallized as a major force through early nineteenth century nondenominational evangelism, has been an ethic of social integration (Miller, 1965; Ryan, 1982). In styles varying from Tom Sawyer's Aunt Polly to the bus driver's wife in *The Honeymooners,* it has upheld the values of a trustworthy way of life that can unite a diverse and mobile people. However different Americans are from one another and however unknown they may be to one another, they hold a basis of mutual trust in their common displays of conformity to an elaborate ethic of conventional behavior. From early in American history, mass media preaching conformity to conventional standards have complemented our traditions of individualism.

The sensuous, captivating, even hypnotic qualities of television would appear to clash with the ascetic emphases of American culture. However, the television industry has developed the cultural forms—particularly in the episodic shows focusing on character and on situations of popular concern—that bring its vast expressional capacities into concord with the middle-class morality. Television today has become—implicitly, yet relentlessly—a national medium of expression for middle-class moral conventionalism. Day and night it addresses diverse sectors of its national audience with one or another mode of expression of the common ethic. The audience addressed by television is essentially the social whole, Americans, conceived as ethically and conventionally alike as subjects of morality. Pluralism of ethnic background, region of the country, job or calling, and socioeconomic circumstance may be ritually acknowledged, but generally as additional means of dramatizing the claim of the common ethic over all and its appeal to all who are essentially conscientious. The controversies over the ways in which Blacks, Hispanic-Americans, Native Americans, women, homosexuals, and other disadvantaged groups are shown on television have turned mainly on the right to be portrayed as equally respectworthy in the terms of middle-class morality. The legitimacy of its conventional claims have been largely presupposed. In this respect, the controversies may themselves be evidence of the integrative efficacy of the American middle-class ethic.

To be emphasizing the respects in which television has remade a vast and diverse country into a "national village" may seem to be belaboring a cliche of television criticism. The cliche, however, has portrayed the national village as growing out of the lavish deployment of television's technology. I emphasize rather the middle-class morality as a factor controlling the expressional use of television, especially its dramatic formats. I argue that it has been television's standing as an agent of conventional moralism that has made it so meaningful within the routines of daily life as well as integrative of popular social experience as a whole. Its efficacy in contemporary social life cannot be grasped unless its role as scion of a moral tradition stemming from the popular strains of Puritanism is understood. The vitality of television in American popular culture must be seen as a historical derivation, for secularized society, of the mass-oriented, moralistic religious movements that flourished in the early decades of the Republic.

REFERENCES

Bellah, Robert N. "Religion, the Sociology of." *International Encyclopedia of the Social Sciences.* New York: Macmillan, 1968.

Bellah, Robert N. "Civil Religion in America." In *Beyond Belief.* New York: Harper & Row, 1970.

Bercovitch, Sacvan. *The Puritan Origins of the American Self.* New Haven, Conn.: Yale University Press, 1975.

de Tocqueville, Alexis. *Democracy in America.* New York: Alfred A. Knopf, 1948.

Lidz, Charles and Andrew Walker. *Heroin, Deviance, and Morality.* Beverly Hills, Calif.: Sage, 1980.

Lidz, Victor. "Secularization, Ethical Life, and Religion in Modern Societies." In *Religious Change and Continuity,* edited by H.M. Johnson. San Francisco: Jossey-Bass, 1979.

Miller, Perry. *The Life of the Mind in America.* New York: Harcourt Brace Jovanovich, 1965.

Parsons, Talcott. "Religion in Postindustrial America: The Problem of Secularization." In *Action Theory and the Human Condition.* New York: Free Press, 1979.

Parsons, Talcott and Victor Lidz. "Death in American Society." In *Essays in Self-Destruction,* edited by E. Schneidman. New York: Science House, 1967.

Ryan, Mary. *The Cradle of the Middle Class.* New York: Cambridge University Press, 1982.

Weber, Max. *The Protestant Ethic and the Spirit of Capitalism.* New York: Scribner, 1930.

Weber, Max. *The Sociology of Religion.* Boston: Beacon, 1963.

Study Questions: Marc

[?] *How do Marc's and Lidz's views of television differ?*

What does Marc mean when he talks about television as a "flow of dreams"? Is his view of television essentially positive or negative? On what do you base that judgment?

Why does Marc say that television is America's jester? How do you explain the phenomenon he is talking about; that is, why does television function that way?

If the individual episodes of television's situation comedies are as trivial and predictable as Marc claims, why are they so popular? For example, how would Marc account for the popularity of The Bill Cosby Show or M*A*S*H? How would you account for it?

What reasons does Marc offer for his assertion that comedy is the most important element of television content? Why does he believe presentational comedy no longer can succeed on television? Do you agree with his argument?

How can marketing factors explain the pressures for television producers to deal with current issues in situation comedies?

What does Marc believe is the most important impact of television on its viewers?

What is demographic research? What is Marc's attitude toward it? When he says that "the technique of television arts is not democratic but demographic," what does he mean? Is his point valid? Are there some demographic groups that do not watch and enjoy television?

Is Marc's evidence for the validity of the "Least Objectionable Program" theory persuasive? What other evidence can you think of that supports the theory? What evidence contradicts it?

What do you believe Marc would say about the rock videos that Goldstein discusses? What would Lidz say about them? That is, does MTV fit Marc's characterization of television? Does it fit Lidz's characterization?

How does Marc's position differ from other ways of thinking about television with which you are familiar?

David Marc

UNDERSTANDING TELEVISION

In one of the few famous speeches given on the subject of television, Federal Communications Commission chairman Newton N. Minow shocked the 1961 convention of the National Association of Broadcasters by summarily categorizing the membership's handiwork as "a vast wasteland." The degree to which Minow's metaphor has been accepted is outstripped only by the appeal of television itself. Americans look askance at television, but look at it nonetheless. Owners of thousand-dollar sets think nothing of calling them "idiot boxes." The home stereo system, regardless of what plays on it, is

David Marc, who teaches in the American Civilization program at Brown University, is the author of *Demographic Vistas*, a book about television which was published recently by the University of Pennsylvania Press.

by comparison holy. Even as millions of dollars change hands daily on the assumption that 98 percent of American homes are equipped with sets and that these sets play an average of more than six and a half hours each day, a well-pronounced distaste for TV has become a prerequisite for claims of intellectual and even of ethical legitimacy. "Value-free" social scientists, perhaps less concerned with these matters than others are, have rushed to fill the critical gap left by status-conscious literati. Denying the mysteries of teller, tale, and told, they have reduced the significance of this American storytelling medium to clinical studies of the effects of stimuli on the millions, producing volumes of data that in turn justify each season's network schedules. Jerry Mander, a disillusioned advertising executive, his fortune presumably socked away, has even written a book titled *Four Arguments for the Elimination of Television.* Hans Magnus Enzensberger anticipated such criticism as early as 1962, when he wrote,

> The process is irreversible. Therefore, all criticism of the mind industry which is abolitionist in its essence is inept and beside the point, since the idea of arresting and liquidating industrialization itself (which such criticism implies) is suicidal. There is a macabre irony to any such proposal, for it is indeed no longer a technical problem for our civilization to abolish itself.

Though Mander, the abolitionist critic, dutifully listed Enzensberger's *The Consciousness Industry* in his bibliography, his zealous piety—the piety of the convert—could not be restrained. Television viewers (who else would read such a book?) scooped up copies at $6.95 each (paperback). As Enzensberger pointed out, everyone works for the consciousness industry.

Despite the efforts of a few television historians and critics, like Erik Barnouw and Horace Newcomb, the fact is that the most effective purveyor of language, image, and narrative in American culture has failed to become a subject of lively humanistic discourse. It is laughed at, reviled, feared, and generally treated as persona non grata by university humanities departments and the "serious" journals they patronize. Whether this is the cause or merely a symptom of the precipitous decline of the influence of the humanities during recent years is difficult to say. In either case, it is unfortunate that the scholars and teachers of *The Waste Land* have found "the vast wasteland" unworthy of their attention. Edward Shils spoke for many literary critics when he chastised those who know better but who still give their attention to works of mass culture, for indulging in "a continuation of childish pleasures." Forgoing a defense of childish pleasures, I cannot imagine an attitude more destructive to the future of both humanistic inquiry and television. If the imagination is to play an epistemological role in a scientific age, it cannot be restricted to "safe" media. Shils teased pop-culture critics for trying to be "folksy"; unfortunately, it is literature that is in danger of becoming a precious antique.

As the transcontinental industrial plant built since the Civil War was furiously at work meeting the new production quotas encouraged by modern advertising techniques, President Calvin Coolidge observed that "the business of America is business." Since that time television has become the art of business. The intensive specialization of skills called for by collaborative production technologies has forced most Americans into the marketplace to consume an exceptional range of goods and services. "Do-it-yourself" is itself something to buy. Necessities and trifles blur to indistinction. Everything is for sale to everybody. As James M. Cain wrote, the "whole goddamn country lives selling hot dogs to each other." Choice, however, is greatly restricted. Mass-marketing theory has formalized taste into a multiple-choice question. Like the menu at McDonald's and the suits on the racks, the choices on the dial—and, thus far, the cable converter— are limited and guided. Yet even if the material in each TV show single-mindedly aims at increasing consumption of its sponsors' products, the medium leaves behind a body of dreams that is, to a large extent, the culture we live in. If, as Enzensberger claimed, we are stuck with television and nothing short of nuclear Armageddon will deliver us, then there is little choice but increased consciousness of how television is shaping our environment. Scripts are written. Sets, costumes, and camera angles are imagined and designed. Performances are rendered. No drama, not even melodrama, can be born of a void. Myths are recuperated, legends conjured. These acts are not yet carried out by computers, although network executives might prefer a system in which they were.

Beneath the reams of audience-research reports stockpiled during decades of agency billings is the living work of scores of TV-makers who accepted the marketable formats, found ways to satisfy both censors and the popular id, hawked the Alka-Seltzer beyond the limits of indigestion, and still managed to leave behind images that demand a place in collective memory. The life of this work in American culture is dependent upon public taste, not market research. A fantastic, wavy, glowing procession of images hovers over the American antennascape, filling the air and millions of screens and minds with endless reruns. To accept a long-term relationship with a television program is to allow a vision to enter one's life. That vision is peopled with characters who speak a familiar idiosyncratic language, dress to purpose, worship God, fall in love, show élan and naiveté, become neurotic and psychotic, revenge themselves, and take it easy. While individual episodes—their plots and climaxes—are rarely memorable (though often remembered), cosmologies cannot fail to be rich for those viewers who have shared so many hours in their construction. The salient impact of television comes not from "special events," like the coverage of the Kennedy assassinations or of men on the moon playing golf, but from day-to-day exposure. Show and viewer may share the same living room for years before developing a relationship. If a show is a hit, if the Nielsen families go for it, it is likely to become a Monday-through-Friday "strip." The weekly series in strip syndication is television's most potent oracle. Because of a sitcom's half-hour format, two or even three of its episodes may be aired in a day by local stations. Months become weeks, and years become months. Mary accelerates through hairdos and hem lengths; Phyllis and Rhoda disappear as Mary moves to her high-rise swinging-singles apartment. Mere plot suspense or identification with characters yields to the subtler nuances of cohabitation. The threshold of expectation becomes fixed, as daily viewing becomes an established procedure or ritual. The ultimate suspension of disbelief occurs when the drama—the realm of heightened artifice—becomes normal.

The aim of television is to be normal. The industry is obsessed with the problem of norms, and this manifests itself in both process and product. Whole new logics, usually accepted under the general classification "demographics," have been imagined, to create models that explain the perimeters of objectionability and attraction. A network sales executive would not dare ask hundreds of thousands of dollars for a prime-time ad on the basis of his high opinion of the show that surrounds it. The sponsor is paying for "heads" (that is, viewers). What guarantees, he demands, can be given for delivery? Personal assurances—opinions—are not enough. The network must show scientific evidence in the form of results of demographic experiments. Each pilot episode is prescreened for test audiences who then fill out multiple-choice questionnaires to describe their reactions. Data are processed by age, income, race, religion, or whatever cultural determinants the tester deems relevant. Thus the dull annual autumn dialogue of popular-television criticism:

Why the same old junk every year? ask the smug, ironic television critics after running down their witty lists of the season's "winners and losers."

We know nothing of junk, cry the "value-free" social scientists of the industry research factories. The people have voted with their number 2 pencils and black boxes. We are merely the board of elections in a modern cultural democracy.

But no one ever asked me what I thought, mumbles the viewer in a random burst from stupefaction.

Not to worry, the chart-and-graph crowd replies. We have taken a biopsy from the body politic, and as you would know if this were your job, if you've seen one cell—or 1,200—you've seen them all.

But is demography democracy?

Fortunately, TV is capable of inspiring at least as much cynicism as docility. The viewer who can transform that cynicism into critical energy can declare the war with television over and instead savor the oracular quality of the medium. As Roland Barthes, Jean-Luc Godard, and the French devotees of Jerry Lewis have realized for years, television is American Dada, Charles Dickens on LSD, the greatest parody of European culture since *The Dunciad*. Yahoos and Houyhnhnms battling it out nightly with submachine guns. Sex objects stored in a box. Art or not art? This is largely a lexicographical quibble for the culturally insecure. Interesting? Only the hopelessly genteel could find such a phantasmagoria flat. Yesterday's trashy Hollywood movies have become recognized as the unheralded work of auteurs; they are screened at the ritziest art houses for connoisseurs of *le cinéma*. Shall we need the French once again to tell us what we have?

TELEVISION IS FUNNY

Though network executives reserve public pride for the achievements of their news divisions and their dramatic specials, comedy has always been an essential, even the dominant, ingredient of American commercial-television programming. As Gilbert Seldes wrote, in *The Public Arts*, "Comedy is the axis on which broadcasting revolves." The little box, with its oblong screen egregiously set in a piece of overpriced woodgrained furniture or cheap industrial plastic, has provoked a share of titters in its own right from a viewing public that casually calls it the "boob tube." Television is America's jester. It has assumed the guise of an idiot while actually accruing power and authority behind the smoke screen of its self-degradation. The Fool, of course, gets a kind word from no one: "Knee-jerk liberalism," cry the offended conservatives. "Corporate mass manipulation," scream the resentful liberals. Neo-Comstockians are aghast, righteously indignant at the orgiastic decay of morality invading their split-level homes. The avant-garde strikes a pose of smug terror before the empty, sterile images. Like the abused jester in Edgar Allan Poe's "Hop-Frog," however, the moguls of Television Row make monkeys out of their tormentors. Profits are their only consolation; the show must go on.

In 1927 Philo T. Farnsworth, one of TV's many inventors, presented a dollar sign on a television screen in the first demonstration of his television system. By the late 1940s baggy-pants vaudevillians, stand-up comedians, sketch comics, and game show hosts had all become familiar video images. No television genre has ever been without what Robert Warshow called "the euphoria [that] spreads over the culture like the broad smile of an idiot." Police shows, family dramas, adventure series, and made-for-TV movies all rely heavily on humor to mitigate their bathos. Even the news is not immune, as evidenced by the spread of "happy-talk" formats in TV journalism in recent years. While the industry experiments with new ways to package humor, television's most hilarious moments are often unintentional, or at least incidental. Reruns of ancient dramatic series display plot devices, dialogue, and camera techniques that are obviously dated. Styles materialize and vanish with astonishing speed. Series like *Dragnet*, *The Mod Squad*, and *Ironside* surrender their credibility as "serious" police mysteries after only a few years in syndication. They self-destruct into ridiculous stereotypes and clichés, betraying their slick production values and affording heights of comic ecstasy that dwarf their "original" intentions. This is an intense comedy of obsolescence that grows richer with each passing television season. Starsky and Hutch render Jack Webb's Sergeant Joe Friday a messianic madman. *Hill Street Blues* returns the favor to *Starsky and Hutch*. The distinction between taking television on one's own terms and taking it the way it presents itself is of critical importance. It is the difference between activity and passivity. It is what saves TV from becoming the homogenizing, monolithic, authoritarian tool that the doomsday critics claim it is. The self-proclaimed champions of "high art" who dismiss TV shows as barren imitations of the real article simply do not know how to watch. They are like freshmen thrust into survey courses and forced to read Fielding and Sterne; they lack both the background and the tough-skinned skepticism that can make the experience meaningful. In 1953 Dwight Macdonald was apparently not embarrassed to condemn all "mass culture" (including the new chief villain, TV) without offering any evidence that he had watched television. Not a single show was mentioned in his famous essay "A Theory of Mass Culture." Twenty-five years later it is possible to find English professors who will admit to watching *Masterpiece Theatre*. But American commercial shows? How could they possibly measure up to drama produced in Britain and tied in form and sensibility to the nineteenth-century novel? To this widespread English Department line there is an important reply: TV is culture. The more one watches, the more relationships develop among the shows and between the shows and the world. To rip the shows out of their context and judge them against the standards of other media and other cultural traditions is to ignore their American origins and misplace their identities. . . .

THE THEATER COLLAPSES

The television industry is at the heart of a vast entertainment complex that oversees the coordination of consumption and culture. "Entertainment" has been established as a buzz word for narrative and other imaginative presentations that make money. It is used as a rhetorical ploy to specialize popular arts and isolate them from the aesthetic and political scrutiny reserved for "art." An important implication of the definition of *entertain* is the intimate social relationship it implies between the entertainer and the entertained. In 1956 Gunther Anders wrote that the "television viewer, although living in an alienated world, is made to believe that he is on a footing of the greatest intimacy with everything and everybody." The technological means to produce this illusion have since been significantly enhanced. Anders described this illusion as "chumminess." Television offers itself to the viewer as a hospitable friend: Welcome to *The Wonderful World of Disney*. Good evening, folks. We'll be right back. See you next week. Y'all come back, now. As technology synthesizes more and more previously human functions, there is a proliferation of anthropomorphic metaphor: automated teller machines ask us how much money we need. Computers send us bills. Channel 7 is predicting snow. The car won't start. It is in this context that television entertains. There is an odd sensation of titillation in all this service. Whitman and other nineteenth-century optimists foresaw an elevation of the common man to a proud master in the technoworld. Machines would take care of life's dirty work—slavery without guilt. Television enthusiastically smiles and shuffles for the viewer's favor. Even television programs we do not like contribute to the illusion (that is, "We are not amused"). Success in tele-American life is measured largely by the quantity of machines at one's disposal. Are all the household chores mechanized? Do you have HBO? Work is minimized. Leisure is maximized. There is more time to watch television—to live like a king.

Backstage of this public drama a quite different set of relationships is at work. In a demography the marketing apparatus becomes synonymous with the state. As the quality of goods takes a back seat to the quantity of services, the most valued commodity of all—the measure of truth— becomes information on the consuming preferences of the hundreds of millions of consumer-kings. Every ticket to the movies, every book, every tube of toothpaste purchased is a vote. The shelves of the supermarkets are stocked with referenda. Watching television is an act of citizenship, participation in culture. The networks entertain the viewer; in return, the viewer entertains thousands of notions on what to buy (that is, how to live). The democrat Whitman wrote that the most important person in any society is the "average man." The demographer Nielsen cannot agree more:

> While the average household viewed over 49 hours of television per week in the fall of 1980, certain types viewed considerably more hours. Households with 3 or more people and those with non-adults watched over 60 hours a week. Cable subscribing households viewed about 7 hours a week more than non-cable households.

Paul Klein, the chief programmer at NBC in the late seventies, built his programming philosophy upon what he called the Least Objectionable Program (LOP) theory. This theory, expounded by Klein, plays down the importance of viewer loyalty to specific programs. It asserts that the viewer turns on the set not so much to view this or that program as to fulfill a desire to "watch television." R. D. Percy and Company, an audience-research firm, has found some evidence to support Klein's thesis. *TV Guide*, summarizing Percy's two-year experiment with 200 Seattle families, reported: "Most of us simply snap on the set rather than select a show. The first five minutes are spent *prospecting* channels, looking for gripping images." After giving in to the impulse (compulsion?) to watch TV the viewer is faced with the secondary consideration of choosing a program. In evolved cable markets this can mean confronting dozens of possibilities. The low social prestige of TV watching, even among heavy viewers, coupled with the remarkably narrow range of what is usually available, inhibits the viewer from expressing enthusiasm for any given show. The viewer or viewers (watching TV, it must not be forgotten, is one of the chief social activities of the culture) must therefore "LOP" about, looking for the least bad, least embarrassing, or otherwise least objectionable program. While I am ill prepared to speculate on the demographic truth of this picture of the "average man," two things are worth noting: anyone who watches television has surely experienced the LOP phenomenon; and NBC fell into last place in the ratings under Klein's stewardship.

I cite Klein (and Nielsen) to demonstrate the character of demographic thought, the ideology that ultimately produces most television programs and that is always employed to authorize or censor their exhibition on the distribution system. The optimistic, democratic view of man as a self-perfecting individual, limited only by superimposed circumstance, is turned on its head. Man is defined as a prisoner of limitations who takes the path of least resistance. This is an industrial nightmare, the gray dream of Fritz Lang's *Metropolis* reshot in glossy Technicolor. Workers return from their multicollared tasks drained of all taste and personality. They seek nothing more than merciful release from the day's production pressures, or as certain critics tell us, they want only to "escape."

"Escapism" is a much-used but puzzling term. Its ambiguities illustrate the overall bankruptcy of the television criticism that uses it as a flag. The television industry is only too happy to accept "escapism" as the definition of its work; the idea constitutes a carte-blanche release from responsibility for what is presented. Escapism critics seem to believe that the value of art should be measured only by rigorously naturalistic standards. Television programs are viewed as worthless or destructive because they divert consciousness from "reality" to fantasy. However, all art, even social realism, does this. Brecht was certainly mindful of this fact when he found it necessary to attach intrusive Marxist sermons to the fringes of social-realist stage plays. Is metaphor possible at all without "escapism"? Presumably, the mechanism of metaphor is to call a thing something it is not in order to demonstrate emphatically what it is. When the network voice of control says, "NBC is proud as a peacock," it is asking the recipient of this message to "escape" from all realistic data about the corporate institution NBC into a fantastic image of a bird displaying its colorful feathers in a grand and striking manner. The request is made on the assumption that the recipient will be able to sort the shared features of the two entities from the irrelevant features and "return" to a clearer picture of the corporation. Representational television programs work in much the same way. If there were no recognizable features of family life in *The Waltons*, if there were no shared features of life-style in *Three's Company*, if there were no credible features of urban paranoia in *Baretta*, then watching these shows would truly be "escapism." But if those features are there, the viewer is engaging in an act that does not differ in essence from reading a Zola novel. The anti-escapist argument makes a better point about the structure of narrative in the television series. In the world of the series problems are not only solvable but usually solved. To accept this as "realistic" is indeed an escape from the planet Earth. But how many viewers accept a TV series as realistic in this sense? Interestingly, it is the soap opera—the one genre of series television that is committed to an anticlimactic, existential narrative structure—that has created the most compelling illusion of realism for the viewing audience. The survival and triumphs of an action-series hero are neither convincing nor surprising but merely a convention of the medium. Like the theater audience that attends *The Tragedy of Hamlet*, the TV audience knows what the outcome will be before the curtain goes up. The seduction is not What? but How?

Thus far, I have limited my discussion to traditional ways of looking at television. However, the television industry has made a commitment to relentless technological innovation of the medium. The cable converter has already made the traditional tuner obsolete. From a comfortable vantage point anywhere in the room the viewer can scan dozens of channels with a fingertip. From the decadent splendor of a divan the viewer is less committed to the inertia of program choice. It is possible to watch half a dozen shows more or less simultaneously, fixing on an image for the duration of its allure, dismissing it as its force disintegrates, and returning to the scan mode. Unscheduled programming emerges as the viewer assumes control of montage. It is also clear that program choice is expanding. The grass-roots public-access movement is still in its infancy, but the network *mise en scène* has been somewhat augmented by new corporate players such as the superstations and the premium services. Cheap home recording and editing equipment may turn the television receiver into a bottomless pit of "footage" for any artist who dares use it.

Michael Smith, a Chicago-born New York grantee/comedian, is among those pointing the way in this respect. Whether dancing with *Donny and Marie*, in front of a giant video screen, at the Museum of Contemporary Art, in Chicago, or performing rap songs at the Institute of Contemporary Art, in Boston, Smith offers an unabashed display of embarrassments and highlights in the day of a life with television. Mike (Smith's master persona) is the star of his own videotapes (that is, TV shows). In "It Starts at Home" Mike gets cable and learns the true meaning of public access. In "Secret Horror" reception is plagued by ghosts. The passive viewer—that well-known zombie who has been blamed for every American problem from the Vietnam War to Japanese technological hegemony—becomes a do-it-yourself artist in Smith. If, as Susan Sontag writes, "interpretation is the revenge of the intellect upon art," parody is the special revenge of the viewer upon TV.

Whatever the so-called blue-sky technologies bring, there can be no doubt that the enormous body of video text generated during the decades of the network era will make itself felt in what will follow. The shows and commercials and systems of signs and gestures that the networks have presented for the past thirty-five years constitute the television we know how to watch. There won't be a future without a past.

In *Popular Culture and High Culture* Herbert Gans took the position that all human beings have aesthetic urges and are receptive to symbolic expression of their wishes and fears. As simple and obvious as Gans's assertion seems, it is the wild card in the otherwise stacked deck of demographic culture. Paul Buhle and Daniel Czitrom have written,

> We believe that the population at large shares a definite history in modern popular culture and is, on some levels, increasingly aware of that history. We do not think that the masses of television viewers, radio listeners, moviegoers, and magazine readers are numbed and insensible, incapable of understanding their fate or historical condition until a group of "advanced revolutionaries" explains it to them.

Evidence of this shared, definite history, in the form of self-referential parody, is already finding its way to the air. The television babies are beginning to make television shows. In the signature montage that introduces each week's episode of *SCTV,* there is a shot of a large apartment house with dozens of televisions flying out the windows and crashing to the ground. As the viewer learns, this does not mean the end of TV in Jerry Mander's sense but signifies the end of television as it has traditionally been experienced. *SCTV* is television beginning to begin again. The familiar theatrical notions of representation and presentation that have guided the development of programming genres are ground to fine dust in the crucible of a satire that draws its inspiration directly from the experience of watching television. *SCTV* has been the first television program absolutely to demand of its viewers a knowledge of the traditions of TV, a self-conscious awareness of cultural history. In such a context viewing at last becomes an active process. Without a well-developed knowledge of and sensitivity to the taxonomy and individual texts of the first thirty-five years of TV, *SCTV* is meaningless—and probably not even funny. In 1953 Dwight Macdonald described "Mass Culture" as "a parasitic, a cancerous growth on High Culture." By this, I take it, he meant that mass-consumed cultural items such as television programs "steal" the forms of "High Culture," reduce their complexity, and replace their content with infantile or worthless substitutes.

The relationship of mass culture to high culture, Macdonald told us, "is not that of the leaf and the branch but rather that of the caterpillar and the leaf." *SCTV* bears no such relationship to any so-called high culture. It is a work that emerges out of the culture of television itself, a fully realized work in which history and art synthesize the conditions for a new consciousness of both. Other media—theater, film, radio, music—do not bend the show to televised renderings of their own forms but instead are forced to become television. The viewer is not pandered to with the apologetic overdefining of linear development that denies much of television its potential force. Presentation and representation merge into a seamless whole. The ersatz proscenium theater used by the networks to create marketing genres is smashed; the true montage beaming into the television home refuses to cover itself with superficial framing devices. The pseudo-Marxist supposition that *SCTV* is still guilty of selling the products is boring—the show is not.

SCTV is among the first tangible signs of a critical relationship to TV viewing that is more widespread than a reading of the TV critics would indicate. American TV was born a bastard art of mass-marketing theory and recognizable forms of popular culture. Thirty-five years later a generation finds in this dubious pedigree its identity and heritage. The poverty of TV drama in all traditional senses is not as important as the richness of the montage. For the TV-lifer, a rerun of *Leave It to Beaver* or *I Love Lucy* or *The Twilight Zone* offers the sensation of traveling through time in one's own life and cultural history. The recognizable, formulaic narrative releases the viewer from what becomes the superficial concerns of suspense and character development. The greater imaginative adventures of movement through time, space, and culture take precedence over the flimsy mimesis that seems to be the intention of the scripts. The whole fast-food smorgasbord of American culture is laid out for consumption. This is not merely kitsch. Clement Greenberg wrote that "the precondition for kitsch [the German word for mass culture], a condition without which kitsch would be impossible, is the availability close at hand of a fully matured cultural tradition, whose discoveries, acquisitions, and perfected self-consciousness kitsch can take advantage of for its own ends." In fact, this process is reversed in television appreciation. The referent culture has become the mass, or kitsch, culture. Instead of masscult ripping off highcult, we have art being fashioned from the junk pile. The banal hysteria of the supermarket is capable of elegant clarity in Andy Warhol's *Campbell's Soup Can*. Experience is re-formed and recontextualized, reclaimed from chaos. Television offers many opportunities of this kind.

The networks and ad agencies care little about these particulars of culture and criticism. The networks promise to deliver heads in front of sets and no more. But, as we will find in any hierarchical or "downstream" system, there is a personal stance that will at least allow the subject of institutional power to maintain personal dignity. In the television demography this stance gains its power from the act of recontextualization. If there is no exit from the demographic theater, each viewer will have to pull down the rafters from within. What will remote-control "SOUND: OFF" buttons mean to the future of marketing? What images are filling the imaginations of people as they "listen" to television on the TV bands of transistor radios, wearing headphones while walking the streets of the cities? Why are silent TV screens playing at social gatherings? When will the average "Household Using TV" (HUT) be equipped with split-screen, multichannel capability? What is interesting about a game show? The suspense as to who will win, or the spectacle of people brought frothing to the point of hysteria at the prospect of a new microwave oven? What is interesting about a cop show? The "catharsis" of witnessing the punishment of the criminal for his misdeeds, or the attitude of the cop toward evil? What is interesting about a sitcom? The funniness of the jokes, or the underlining of the jokes on the laugh track? The plausibility of the plot, or the portrayal of a particular style of living as "normal"? What is interesting about Suzanne Somers and Erik Estrada? Their acting, or their bodies? Television is made to sell products but is used for quite different purposes by lonely, alienated people, families, marijuana smokers, born-again Christians, alcoholics, Hasidic Jews, destitute people, millionaires, jocks, shut-ins, illiterates, hanggliding enthusiasts, intellectuals, and the vast, heterogeneous procession that continues to be American culture in spite of all demographic odds. If demography is an attack on the individual, then the resilience of the human spirit must welcome the test.

"To be a voter with the rest is not so much," Whitman warned in his *Democratic Vistas* of 1871. The shopper/citizen of the demography ought to know this only too well. Whitman recognized that no political system could ever summarily grant its citizens freedom. Government is a system of power; freedom is a function of personality. "What have we here [in America]," he asked, "if not, towering above all talk and argument, the plentifully-supplied, last-needed proof of democracy, in its personalities?" Television is the Rorschach test of the American personality. I hope the social psychologists will not find our responses lacking.

*S*tudy *Q*uestions: *P*ollan

[?] *Can any, or all, of the analyses in the three preceding articles (Goldstein, Lidz, and Marc) help to account for the phenomenal success of* Wheel of Fortune? *If so, how? If not, what does account for it?*

> *How does Pollan account for the success of the show with viewers?*
>
> *What sort of morality is communicated by* Wheel of Fortune? *Is it the secular, middle-class morality described by Lidz? If you think so, what in the program led you to that conclusion? If you do not think so, what sort of morality do you think the show seems to legitimate?*
>
> *In what ways do the successful elements of the show "open a small window on the national consciousness"?*
>
> *What elements of the show are ironic? Do you think the show's ironic tone is unique? Can you cite examples of irony in other game shows?*
>
> *How do the elements of* Wheel of Fortune *relate to television's role as America's jester?*
>
> *Pollan concludes that* Wheel of Fortune *can be conceived validly by some viewers as nostalgia or parody, or that it may be taken at face value. Can you think of other ways the show might be taken?*
>
> *What market factors make scheduling this program just after the early-evening local news and just before prime time a wise decision?*

Michael Pollan

JACKPOT!

The biggest, shrewdest, moneymakingest little show on earth

Game shows have had their ups and downs, their scandals and excesses, but they've never lost their hold on the American audience. This salient fact of television history was not lost on Mike Levinton early in 1983, when he was looking over the new shows that syndicators were pitching to stations for that fall. As head of programming for Blair Television, largest of the national rep firms that sell advertising time for local stations, Levinton advises clients on choosing shows for their all-important "prime-time access" slot—the half hour preceding network programming. In 1983, Lev-

Michael Pollan is executive editor of *Harper's Magazine* and a contributing editor of *Channels*.

inton noticed that audiences for several popular game shows—*Family Feud, Tic Tac Dough* and *Joker's Wild*—had peaked or were beginning to slip, particularly among women 25 to 54, a key demographic target for advertisers. At the same time, new forms of syndicated programming such as *Entertainment Tonight* were starting to draw off the game show's traditional audience.

Many interpreted these developments as signs that the game show's days in access time were numbered. But Levinton's faith in the form could not be so easily shaken. He liked game shows so much that he once appeared as a contestant on *Jeopardy!*, doing quite respectably until the final round. Levinton thought the access period merely needed a fresh game show, one with "all the classic elements—simplicity, a clear focus and a high degree of audience involvement," as he puts it.

Levinton found what he was looking for in a game show that Merv Griffin Enterprises had been producing for NBC's daytime schedule since 1973, and that King World Productions was syndicating for the first time that fall. The show was called *Wheel of Fortune* and Levinton recommended it to many of his stations. Blair was the only major rep firm to do so, and roughly a third of the 59 stations that bought *Wheel of Fortune* in its first season were Blair clients. Without them the show might never have gotten off the ground.

Today, station executives who heeded Levinton's advice have reason to gloat. *Wheel of Fortune* will surely become the most successful show in the history of syndication, and the game show is once again king. Now in 193 markets (reaching 99 percent of all homes with television), *Wheel of Fortune* consistently achieves a national rating of 20 or better. It is as popular as one of the top 15 shows in prime time, which is unheard of for a syndicated program. Aired five times a week in syndication, usually in the access period (as well as weekday mornings on NBC), *Wheel of Fortune* lights up more screens each week than any other program on television, and it should earn its producers and syndicators well over $100 million this year alone. But *Wheel* is much more than a money machine. Its business success is built on the abiding appeal of a well-crafted game show to the American audience. *Wheel* is one of those rare programs that, in becoming a national obsession, opens up a small window on the national consciousness.

The value to a local station of a show like *Wheel* is almost incalculable. Not only do spots in the show bring premium prices, but because they are generally sold to advertisers as part of a larger schedule, *Wheel* helps a station move its entire advertising inventory. Then there are the promotional opportunities and the visibility that a hot show gives a broadcaster. But surely *Wheel's* greatest value is as a lead-in and lead-out. Besides winning its own time period for the great majority of its stations, *Wheel* has significantly boosted the ratings of the programs that precede and follow it.

A local station's profitability depends less on its ratings during prime time than on the two hours that precede it—the "early fringe" period, the local news and then prime-time access—and *Wheel's* impact on this block of time has been powerful enough to turn a number of stations around. Since December 1983 when the NBC affiliate in St. Louis, KSDK, replaced *Entertainment Tonight* with *Wheel of Fortune* (and installed *Jeopardy!*, another King World-Griffin hit, in early fringe), it has seen the ratings of its local news programs jump 60 percent. In New York, WCBS was languishing in fifth place during the access period with the locally produced *Two on the Town*. The station bought *Wheel* in March 1984 and soon was first, soundly defeating both *Family Feud* on WNBC and *Entertainment Tonight* on WABC.

WLS, ABC's Chicago outlet, was third in its market in 1984 when it bought *Wheel*—the first network-owned station to do so. General manager Dennis Swanson (now president of ABC Sports) put the show in access, replacing the last half hour of an extended newscast. By the next year, for a variety of reasons including *Wheel's* value as a lead-out, the station had increased its local news ratings by half, putting it on top of the market. One reason *Wheel* has such a powerful lineup of stations today is that, in many cases, the program made them powerful.

If *Wheel* has been a boon to its local stations, it's been nothing short of El Dorado for King World and Merv Griffin Enterprises, its syndicator and producer. The program has showered King World and Griffin with the kind of instant winnings that one associates with . . . game shows. Before *Wheel*, King World was an obscure, family-run program distributor in Summit, N.J. For most of its two decades in business, the company's principal revenue source was its library of 101 episodes of *The Little Rascals*. The company was so small that during a low period it operated out of the King family kitchen. In 1982, the King brothers (who took over the company after their father's death in 1973) approached Griffin and bought the rights to syndicate *Wheel* for $50,000. On the strength of that investment, King's revenues shot up from $8 million to $80 million in two years. In December 1984, the company went public, and its over-the-counter stock became one of the hottest on Wall Street, jumping from $10 to $50 a share within a few months. (It then split two-for-one and is now trading around 40.)

Before *Wheel of Fortune*, most people assumed that Merv Griffin's contributions to American culture were limited to his long-running syndicated talk show and his recording of "I've Got a Lovely Bunch of Coconuts." But it was Griffin himself who dreamed up *Wheel*, and *Jeopardy!* before that. In operation since 1962, Merv Griffin Enterprises currently has five syndicated shows in production: *Wheel, Jeopardy!, Headline Chasers, Dance Fever* and the talk show. With *Wheel's* success, its fortunes have soared, and this spring Griffin sold the production company to the Coca-Cola Company for $250 million.

"If you're going to have a hit, there's nothing better than a game show," says Stuart Hersh, King World's chief operating officer. A hit game show's economics are better than those of virtually any other business, except perhaps the cocaine trade. "Once you've done a successful game, unlike a sitcom or an adventure, it's almost like a cookie cutter," Hersh explains. "New shows can be produced in mass using the same set, so the costs are much lower."

Griffin produced an episode of *Wheel* for around $25,000, often shooting five a day, and this year, according to industry estimates, each new show will earn Coke's Griffin subsidiary and King World more than $650,000. (The Griffin operation takes about 65 percent and King World about 35 percent.) For the 195 episodes produced each year (another 65 shows are repeated to fill out the 260 episodes a station needs to strip *Wheel* for 52 weeks), that comes to more than $125 million—for a show that costs about $5 million a year to produce.

To a national advertiser, the syndicated *Wheel of Fortune* offers what amounts to a powerful fourth network, half an hour each weekday. That's because the two national 30-second spots King World sells in every episode represent an efficient alternative to expensive network time. Indeed, during its half hour, *Wheel* is actually a stronger network than NBC, CBS or ABC: It has more number-one stations in its lineup and its average weekly rating (21.6) is higher than that of the NBC prime-time schedule (17.7). Since syndicators typically sell their advertising time at a lower cost-per-thousand than the networks, the show is a boon to many national advertisers, who, at about $70,000 a spot, will spend a total of more than $40 million to advertise on the program this year.

All very impressive, but how long can *Wheel* keep it up? Probably quite a while. In the television jungle, game shows are the elephants. According to King World, the average life span of a game show that has survived its first three years on the air is seven years. Also, the curve of a game show's popularity is, according to Mike Levinton, usually a gentle one: Once *Wheel of Fortune* finally peaks (the February ratings indicate that hasn't happened yet), its decline will be gradual.

Clearly a hit game show is one of the great prizes in television, and one wonders if the success of *Wheel* and many of its imitators won't inspire one of the networks to try a game show of its own in prime time, where the genre once thrived. For a network struggling at 8 o'clock (like CBS) and willing to aim for the oldish audience that game shows usually attract, it could represent smart counterprogramming. The return of *What's My Line?* or *To Tell the Truth* to CBS's prime-time schedule may not be quite as farfetched as it first sounds.

"Frankly," Mike Levinton admits today, "we thought *Wheel* would be good, not great. I don't think anybody foresaw what a phenomenon it would become." Indeed, even with the benefit of hindsight, it's hard to see what the big deal is. On first viewing, *Wheel* looks like pretty generic television: Tacky set. Plastic host. Canned music. Overstimulated studio audience. A garden-variety game show, circa 1965. Timing might account for *Wheel's* doing reasonably well, even winning its time period. But how does a modest show like this get wired into the national consciousness?

To begin with, *Wheel* is remarkably well crafted. It incorporates the wisdom of 30 years of game show experience; though hardly innovative, *Wheel* is nevertheless state of the art. The first principle of that art is simplicity, and this show could scarcely be easier to learn. In inventing *Wheel*, Griffin says he was inspired by the traditional game of Hangman, which he and his sister played as children during long family car trips. Players guess the letters in a hidden word or phrase and "earn" money for each letter correctly guessed, the amount determined by a spin of the wheel. The puzzles consist chiefly of clichés known to everyone, with the possible exception of poorly briefed space aliens. (In a perfect illustration of television's ecological self-sufficiency, Griffin comes up with many of the puzzles himself by watching TV and jotting down linguistic flotsam as it drifts by.) Are you familiar with the expressions "red carpet treatment," "over 40," "better luck next time" or even "wheel of fortune"? Then you're ready to play.

According to Levinton, the single most important factor in a game show's success is the degree of participation it offers the home viewer. This viewer found he could guess the solutions a moment or two before the contestants did, and that this intellectual feat felt pretty good. At least until you realize that the contestants have been chosen to obtain precisely that effect. They are not so slow that you get bored screaming "You can't teach an old dog new tricks" at the screen, or so swift that you feel inadequate. The producers of *Wheel* have accurately taken the nation's mental measure, and they're making 40 million Americans feel good about their intelligence every day.

Whoever solves the puzzle first wins the right to spend the money he or she has "earned" at the exceptionally well-stocked *Wheel of Fortune* "store." Here too the show offers viewers vicarious kicks. Since we at home actually solved the puzzle first and, were it not for a mere accident of space and time, would be up there shopping right now, we find ourselves deliberating whether the cat lithograph or the backyard grill makes more sense. *Wheel* has brought the pleasures of window shopping to television.

Supposedly, greed is the dirty little secret of game shows, but Levinton doubts that it's the key to *Wheel's* popularity. One of the show's most welcome attributes is its relative decorum. Nobody screams, jumps up and down or otherwise visibly lusts after inanimate objects. Yet the prizes themselves offer an important clue to *Wheel's* appeal. Traditionally, the game show gift has been fairly practical: the bedroom set, the washer-dryer, the American Tourister luggage—all the accouterments of the suburban middle-class lifestyle. By contrast, *Wheel* prizes are always the stuff of conspicuous consumption. The brand names come from Fifth Avenue and Rodeo Drive: Cartier, Tiffany, Van Cleef & Arpels. Contestants win gift certificates from Gucci instead of from the Spiegel catalog. Many of the prizes are strictly for show: $5,000 grandfather clocks and sets of gold-plated golf clubs "guaranteed to make an impression on the links." What contestants on *Wheel of Fortune* vie for are not so much valuable commodities as the outward symbols of contemporary success.

Each night, the show stages a cartoon version of President Reagan's "opportunity society" (which sounds a lot like a game show to begin with). Three contestants drawn from every conceivable walk of life "take their shot" in this exaggerated land of fabulous wealth, overnight success and, of course, equal opportunity. "Whose life will it change tonight?" intones the announcer in the promotional spot.

Of course, all game shows enact some such fantasy of making it, but none holds out a version of society quite as benign as the one conjured on *Wheel of Fortune*. On *Jeopardy!* or *Headline Chasers*, for example, you actually have to know something about the world in order to win, and some game shows—like the *$25,000 Pyramid*—actually test your mental and verbal agility. Still others (*The New Price Is Right*, or *The $1,000,000 Chance of a Lifetime*, where a table heaped with currency and guarded by two Pinkertons is a permanent part of the set) are Darwinian nightmares of self-interest and greed. These shows are harsh meritocracies—and much more elitist than *Wheel*. Then there are the shows where luck rules—*Card Sharks* and the raft of bingo-based extravaganzas coming this fall. But how meaningful is success if it depends strictly on a throw of the dice? Doesn't hard work count for anything?

In an era that sanctions greed and rewards speculation, it's not surprising that all these shows have found an audience. Yet none approaches *Wheel of Fortune*'s. That's probably because the social and economic rules that govern *Wheel* approximate most closely what most of us consider proper and just. As Horatio Alger knew, the American race did not go to the swiftest, but to the average fellow who was diligent and deserving. He also knew it wasn't really a race at all—according to the American dream, success does not depend on beating the other guy so much as making your own way. And in fact, *Wheel* is surprisingly noncompetitive. There are no clocks or buzzers, and no head-to-head competition. Everyone politely roots for whoever is "up" and each contestant gets to take his or her turn unmolested by host, clock or opponent. Nothing, however, is handed to you, as the *Wheel of Fortune* vocabulary makes it clear: You don't win, but "earn the right to buy a prize . . . at the actual retail prices." *Wheel* is the only game show on television to strike the proper balance between skill and luck, accomplishment and good fortune, or, in the Puritan vocabulary, between works and faith.

How seriously do audiences take all this? *Wheel's* following by now is so large that, in addition to the dedicated game show fan, there must be a significant number of viewers for whom watching the show is at least partly an exercise in camp. Certainly hostess Vanna White's extraordinary popularity involves elements of irony and nostalgia. She's a throwback to *Let's Make a Deal's* Carol Merrill, and to a time when men were men and women were girls. The whole show, in fact, is a throwback to sixties television. As game shows go, it's neoclassical, eschewing the baroque excesses of the seventies and the hightech flourishes of most eighties games in favor of simplicity and decorum. This is a game show designed for people who grew up with television and spent days home sick from school being ministered to by Hugh Downs, Allen Ludden and Art Fleming.

Like much of television in the eighties, *Wheel of Fortune* can be taken many ways—as nostalgia, as parody, as well as at face value. Pat Sajak's self-deprecating humor—the mild sense of absurdity he confides to us from time to time—and the studio audience's exaggerated oohs and aahs suggest that the whole experience is something less than entirely sincere. By dropping such hints of irony here and there, *Wheel of Fortune* gives its vast audience license to indulge in something many would otherwise consider beneath them. You don't have to admit you're getting off on the crude fantasies of success, or on Vanna White, this ridiculous antefeminist cheerleader. For you, it's camp. *Wheel of Fortune* lets you have it both ways.

Study Questions: Snow

[?] *Why were the 1930s and 1940s called the "golden age of radio"? Are there any reasons for calling today an even more "golden age" for radio?*

What is radio's "interpersonal dimension"? Do you agree with Snow's claim that radio serves functions of interpersonal communication for some listeners? Cite examples from your personal experience or the experience of others you know. For example, have you ever felt that sense of closeness to a disc jockey or radio performer that Snow describes? How do you explain it? What effect do you think the increasing automation of radio stations has on radio's companionability?

In what way is radio a "specialized medium"? What is the relationship of format radio to subcultural norms and values in America? Use a format other than rock to explain and support your response.

What does Snow mean by role making and altercasting? What do these concepts have to do with radio? What are the various roles that disc jockeys play (such as the mood facilitation role)? What are the things they do to play each role? Try to think of possible roles that Snow did not mention. What roles have you heard radio personalities construct?

Are the appeals of a rock video program, such as those described by Goldstein, the same as the appeals Snow describes for a radio station with a rock format? Why or why not?

What does Snow mean by the syntax, inflection, and vocabulary of radio? What is the "grammar" of your favorite radio station?

What does listeners' use of radio to combat loneliness say about our society?

What are the other functions Snow says radio serves? Which of these does it serve for you? Explain the conditions under which it has done so. Are there other functions it serves for you that Snow did not mention? Explain.

Why does Snow label radio and magazines the most "demassified" of the major media?

Robert P. Snow

RADIO

The companion medium

With more radios in America than television sets and telephones combined, this is the most ubiquitous and the most taken for granted of all mass media. People rarely reflect on how often they listen, how many activities they carry on to the accompaniment of radio, how significant radio is for some of their subcultural involvements, or simply how much they rely on radio for contact with the outside world. Newspapers are praised for defending freedom and attacked for ideological bias. Film is applauded for artistic achievements and disdained for its unrealistic fantasy. Television is acclaimed for its educational value and vilified for its violence. But the best thing people say about radio is that it's always there and the worst thing is that it sometimes is too noisy. Why is it that radio is rarely given critical attention even by people who study mass communication? Scan the pages of most survey texts on mass media, and you will notice that radio usually receives the least amount of space and analysis. But consider the reaction if radio suddenly vanished.

As with other major media, radio began as a toy or hobby for a few electronic eccentrics at the turn of the century. It was not until 1920 that a station (KDKA–Westinghouse, Inc.) began regularly scheduled broadcasts. During the affluent twenties, radio grew rapidly through the competitive efforts of RCA, which formed a dual coast-to-coast system (the NBC Red and Blue networks); CBS, founded by William Paley out of profits from his cigar empire; and the Mutual Network, which pioneered entertainment serials including *The Lone Ranger.* Throughout the thirties these three companies developed the mass entertainment formats of situation comedy *(Amos 'n' Andy),* drama through such favorites as Orson Welles's *Mercury Theatre,* deejay remotes from famous ballrooms, detective thrillers (*Ellery Queen* and *The Fat Man*), day-time soap operas (*Our Gal Sunday* and *The Romance of Helen Trent*), quiz shows, talk shows, news, sportscasts, and religious programs. In fact, radio, during its "golden" mass age of the thirties and forties, served as the prototype for television entertainment. It was a creative, free-wheeling period governed only by the licensing regulations of the Federal Communications Commission (FCC), established in 1934.

Today, all that remains of these giant radio systems are several news networks that serve a loose system of affiliated stations. Radio has changed significantly from the mass entertainment age of the depression and war years, but it is still a vital and significant part of American culture and an essential medium in the daily lives of a great many people. Despite the entertainment power of television, radio has not suffered the collapse predicted by so many. With an average of five sets per home and over 8600 stations on the air, radio is more popular and profitable today than at any time in its history. With inexpensive battery-operated transistors, radio goes everywhere. It turns on and off automatically, listeners develop loyalties to stations and broadcasters, and it is used routinely to accompany many activities. Periods in a person's life, such as adolescence, can be recalled through reference to a station's call letters or the name of a disc jockey. We wake up to the clock radio, enjoy its companionship while driving to work, use it as background for a variety of activities from housework to tinkering with the car, and we fall asleep to its mellow sound. If radio suddenly disappeared, most people would quickly discover how significant, perhaps even essential, radio is in their daily lives.

In the early 1960s Harold Mendelsohn (1964) completed what is considered by some media analysts to be the most important study of how listeners use radio. He found that radio provides listeners with much more than practical information and general entertainment. People use radio as a tension release, an accompaniment for various moods, and as a companion. These points are significant particularly in light of the fact that many people listen to radio when they are alone. As a companion, radio keeps people in touch with the outside world and brings that world into the listener's realm of activity. As a housewife reported in Mendelsohn's study: "To me when the radio is off, the house is empty. There is no life without the radio being on. As soon as I get up at 6:30, the first thing I do is turn it on" (1964:91).

In this capacity, radio provides some of the same satisfactions that people obtain from normal face-to-face conversation. In providing some assurance that you are still part of an on-going world, radio is a means for being alone without feeling alone. Unlike most television programs, which are taped and rerun, or a newspaper, which is history, radio is a "live" companion and an activity that involves a listener in a present-oriented social endeavor. It is this personal or, more accurately, interpersonal dimension that gives radio its special appeal. While music can be a background companion, listeners also know that a broadcaster can augment that music with a personal touch. Advertisements tell prospective listeners that stations and announcers create moods and other experiences just for them, and, since radio is communication directed at a specific audience in a specific locality, listeners can personalize the experience in a manner similar to face-to-face encounters. While Mendelsohn emphasized that radio gratifies certain listener needs, it seems legitimate to consider the extent to which the process of communication through radio is similar to interpersonal interaction.

Mendelsohn hinted at the interpersonal dimension of radio when he remarked that radio serves as a "social lubricant." In making this observation he claimed that radio binds people together through common shared experiences and provides subjects to talk about with others. While he restricts radio to the category of a catalyst for face-to-face interaction, evidence will be presented that demonstrates that listeners actually interact with broadcasters in a fashion very much like interpersonal conversation. Radio may facilitate social activity outside the immediate listening experience, but broadcasters and listeners also create the image of communicating with each other. This point will be examined in some detail throughout the chapter.

Another point that orients our analysis of radio is that it is a specialized medium delivering specialized subjects to specific listener interests. Specialized radio has become so successful that it is not uncommon for a large city to offer over thirty stations catering to interests from popular music to education and news. Even the large middle-of-the-road (MOR) stations maintain a degree of homogeneity in music with either country, soft rock, or standards.

Since radio functions much like highly specialized magazines, listeners with these interests come to depend on particular stations for the content of their subcultures. As a result, a radio station becomes symbolic of a particular identity for the listener. In contrast to television, in which viewers form attachments to particular programs, radio listeners are more likely to identify with a particular station, as exemplified by bumper stickers announcing the driver as a KDKB listener and T-shirts emblazoned with WXRT. For these listeners a radio station is much more than a channel of communication or a source of information—it is a dimension of self. Stations even add this factor to their cash-call contests such as, "What is your favorite country?—KNIX."

Assuming that a definition of radio as a personal companion and a subculture medium is correct, the first phase of our analysis will be to describe the communication strategies employed by stations and broadcasters. The next step is to examine the meanings listeners make of their listening experience. Finally, we shall compare the strategies used by stations and broadcasters to listener experience with attention to some of the implications on how radio is part of the media culture of our age.

RADIO FORMAT: PERSPECTIVES AND GRAMMAR

Communication strategy in radio, as with other media, may largely be described under the heading of *format*. Format is simply a shorthand term that describes the perspectives and grammar used in presenting programmed material. . . . [P]erspective is a way of "seeing" or defining various phenomena, such as the entertainment perspective used in television to present everything from news to sports. Radio also uses entertainment, but it is designed to appeal to a more narrow range of interests, such as folk music subculture. Every subculture has a set of norms and values that orient its members and provide a framework for evaluating life within the subculture. For example, rock fans value youth and have a rebellious yet playful attitude toward most traditional institutional practices. Rock subculture includes a style of dress, a brashness in personal demeanor, and high volume on the stereo; rock fans are robust in their listening and dancing behavior. These values and norms become the general orienting perspective for a station in every phase of its strategy. When stations advertise through slogans such as "It's what FM ought to be," "The no-disco kick-ass rock of K — — —," or "The rhythm of Phoenix K Q Fusion," the explicit message is that your music subculture is served by this station.

The grammar of syntax, inflection, and vocabulary in radio is part of the strategy used in making a subculture come alive to its members. It is commonly understood that each radio subculture has a specific grammar. It takes an experienced listener no more than a few seconds to identify that grammar and the particular subculture when dialing across frequencies. Certainly knowing the difference between classical and country music is evidence for instant recognition, but in cases where musical selections are used in more than one format or where music is absent, such as on all-news stations, listeners rely on subtle aspects of grammar to decide quickly whether the station they have dialed is all news, or just a news segment on a rock, beautiful music, or country station. Listeners also know instantly whether they have tuned-in a hard rock or a bubblegum station, an uptown or more traditional country station, or a gospel compared to a modern evangelist religion station. The grammatical differences among some sub-culture formats may be subtle to the untutored ear, but experienced listeners instantly recognize the differences.

The scheduling or *syntax* part of radio grammar is based on following listeners' activity through their typical daily routines. We take it as common sense that most people follow particular behavior patterns that are appropriate for particular times of the day and days of the week. Waking in the morning, driving to work, doing household chores, relaxing in the afternoon, or informal evening activity may be facilitated by specific information available from radio. From the simple reporting of time and temperature and news briefs to household tips, lost pets, and closing stock market reports, listeners obtain information that is generally relevant for what they are doing at a particular time of day. With this organization radio aids in bracketing or breaking the day into meaningful periods. A listener in Phoenix once commented, "When Haywood's show [early morning—KOY] is over, I know the work-day has begun." Similarly, another person stated, "When 'All Things Considered' [National Public Radio] comes on I feel the job part of my day is over." In this fashion, radio not only brackets specific routines but serves as a signal for changing from one routine to another. Just as twelve noon signals the lunch hour, a radio station provides signals for a wide variety of routine behavior. In turn, personal interests vary during each day of the week from mellow Sundays to TGIF and seasonally from winter holidays to summer vacation.

In addition to the bracketing of routines, a primary characteristic of radio grammar is the familiar organization of music selections according to prescribed subculture formulas. In fact, the organization of music selections is what radio professionals specifically refer to as format. In 1961, Bill Drake, a bright young broadcaster in Los Angeles, designed a simple and very successful formula for rock music that took the guesswork out of music selection. The formula consists of time segments, such as a quarter or half-hour period, in which a specific pattern of popular tunes is logged and played. A segment may begin with a current hit, followed by a recent hit, a golden oldie, a newcomer, and so on. Often these selections are color-coded as red, blue, yellow, and so on so the disc jockey can't go wrong. At many stations the format is so precise that each record is logged by a program or music director on a log sheet and timed along with commercials and announcements.

While this rigid, formalistic procedure eliminates much of the deejay's creativity, it ensures a definite "sound" for the station. Basically, this procedure is a formalization of informal practices used by broadcasters for many years, such as the tradition of following an up-tempo selection with a ballad and a lyric rendition with an instrumental. What program and music directors discovered was that listeners wanted a degree of predictability (when and how often the hits would be played), and also a particular *rhythm* (inflection) of musical selections, which in turn aid in maintaining the style of a particular music subculture.

On the last point, music subcultures have particular rhythms that vary from frantic beat to an easy swing. Even beautiful music, or Muzak, all-news, and MOR radio are programmed according to specific formulas that correspond to listeners' lifestyles. The matching of music format to listener lifestyle is so common in radio that most professionals believe that rating points are gained or lost primarily on the basis of these formulas. As one program director remarked, "It's the format [syntax and inflection formula] that gets me the points, not the disc jockey."

In addition, variations in music rhythm match the tempo changes in listener routines from the rush of early morning activity to the midday slowdown, the evening race to get home, the relaxing early evening, and the mixed bag of late-night listeners.

Broadcasters' delivery is consistent with the tempo and rhythm of music as exemplified by the length of time they are allowed to talk between records, the pace of delivery, the apparent volume of their voices, and a high or low pitch. Top-40 stations typically reduce the amount of talk between records to a minimum of giving station ID, time, temperature, and the deejay's name while one record ends and the next begins. An MOR station allows broadcasters more time to establish their personalities, while beautiful music and adult rock stations play three or more selections before any words are spoken. Knowing these unstated grammatical norms, listeners easily identify the rockjock's familiar rapid-fire, high-pitched, compact style of talk, the beautiful music announcer's somnambulent, pear-shaped tones; the adult rock and folk station announcer's normal room conversation manner; and the soul deejay's hip style. When the king of rock radio in Los Angeles (KHJ) changed to a country format in 1980, *Los Angeles Times* radio critic James Brown commented that the deejays were still using the "accelerated, overly modulated banter of Top 40 chatter." He advised them that for a country format, "They'll get a lot more accomplished by slowing down . . . way down."

Finally, there are specific aspects of radio talk *(vocabulary)* that set radio apart from other media. Broadcasters in all major markets demonstrate great facility in clear, crisp enunciation and speech devoid of embarrassing pauses or slow-witted phrasing. In fact, listeners have come to expect and demand an articulation and polish in radio talk that far exceeds what is expected in normal face-to-face conversation (Goffman, 1981). Listeners also expect a broadcaster's vocabulary and jargon to be consistent with the subculture the station represents. Broadcasters must talk to their listeners in words that are not only understood but also remind the listener that this is indeed the world of rock, jazz, classics, country, or mainstream Americana.

Combining these facets of radio grammar results in radio having a high degree of clarity that is seldom confusing to the audience. Music is distinctive, speech is clear, the content is aimed at the cognitive and emotional desires of a specific audience, and material is presented at a tempo that is consistent with a typical listener's routine. In short, radio grammar is designed to produce a fairly low degree of ambiguity for the intended audience.

How Broadcasters Communicate

To communicate with listeners, disc jockeys or "communicators" (as they prefer to be called) must follow the prescribed format designed by the radio station. Disc jockeys generally rely on the fact that listeners will find the program acceptable if they follow the station's format. However, attracting listeners by following the format is not sufficient for most radio communicators. Since they talk to an unseen audience, there is a desire to discover whether listeners relate to them personally or are listening simply matter-of-factly to the station. (In everyday life there are few situations in which a person wants to be an impersonal voice or nonperson.) In fact, the term "communicator" implies something distinctive about the abilities and special talents of an individual over and above the more formalistic criteria of station format. Simply put, disc jockeys want to become radio personalities; to accomplish this they engage in role making and altercasting.

Role making is an activity in which an individual develops and acts out a particular behavioral strategy designed to elicit particular responses from others. But to make a role, an actor (individual) must cast the other (the person to whom one speaks) in a reciprocal role—i.e., he or she casts an alter role for the other. For example, a disc jockey may wish to be known as a satirical wit among listeners. To achieve this the broadcaster casts the listener in the reciprocal role of entertainment spectator and attempts to elicit a favorable response from the listener.

There is nothing complicated or mysterious about this process, as everyone engages in both role making and altercasting in their daily life. We establish roles (identities) with friends, family, and co-workers and elicit responses from these people that will support our identity intentions and claims. From single activities around the home to making a point with the boss, role making and altercasting are part of the normal, everyday interaction process.

But how does a radio broadcaster know whether his or her role-making activity with the unseen listener is successful? One source of evidence is found in the previous discussion of listener routines. Since the organization or scheduling of program content is designed to be consistent with listener routines, a communicator can anticipate the type of role or identity that is relevant for the listener at that moment. Literally, the communicator projects images of typical listeners and their activities, such as driving to work, doing housework, or relaxing on the patio.

This projection enables the broadcaster to create a role that will be relevant to the listener's concerns. The constructed role may follow strict conformity to the listener's expectations or be a creative endeavor, making a slight variation to what the listener might normally expect. An example of the latter point is the deejay who becomes a comedian or repertoire actor in addition to announcing records and reporting news. In this case the radio communicator has constructed a role and cast the listener in a particular relationship, one that the broadcaster anticipates is acceptable within broad entertainment parameters for an audience.

In addition to a general knowledge of listener routines, a broadcaster has contact with listeners through the telephone and letters, as well as public settings. Through these interactions a broadcaster may form specific images of the type of people who listen and how they evaluate the broadcast performance. This facilitates the broadcaster's ability to develop a more personal and even intimate relationship with the listener. In describing this process, most broadcasters claim they attempt to speak "one-on-one" to the listener. Specifically, they project an image of a listener or group of people and talk directly to that visualized image. When a significant other is not present in a situation we may construct an image that enables a vicarious acting-out of a conversation even to the point of creating the responses the imagined other might give. This is precisely what occurs in radio communication; by speaking one on one to an imagined listener, a broadcaster is able to personalize the communication beyond the limits of the station format.

The functions of radio discussed by Mendelsohn provide additional evidence of how broadcasters develop strategies and evaluate their role-making performances. In addition to knowing typical listener routines, broadcasters understand the desire among many listeners to enhance moods and obtain a sense of companionship. For example, radio professionals are aware that listener moods will change as they go through various routines during the day and week. Getting to and from work, midday work schedules, and evening relaxation involve an emotional experience as well as cognitive-rational activity. Broadcasters facilitate typical changes in listener moods mainly through techniques such as variations in the tone of their voice, the length of pauses, inflection, and selected comments. Many broadcasters believe that it is not precisely what one says but how it is communicated that enhances a mood or feeling. One disc jockey remarked, "I try to understand how a listener might feel and then deal with that." This empathy, followed by various affective expressions, enables a broadcaster to create and meet a listener's emotional desires as they change throughout the day and from day to day.

A period of the broadcast day in which listener mood takes precedence over utilitarian concerns is evening and late night. Via the request line broadcasters become quite sensitive to the desires of the lonely, the romantic, and the nighthawks. In my research on radio broadcasters, some of whom specialized in late-night programs, disc jockeys claimed vehemently that communication during late-night hours requires a greater sensitivity to the emotional or affective desires of listeners. During the late-night hours deejays imagined listeners on dates, at parties, or doing a variety of solitary work tasks, and callers during these hours confirmed the accuracy of those images.

Listener comments such as "play the blues," "make it mellow," or "get me out of this funk" were typical. One broadcaster stated, "It's a real kick to think you're playing a part in making love or chasing the blues." A graveyard shift broadcaster was more egotistical in stating: "I orchestrate and swing moods for my people. But I won't take requests when I feel it's going right. You see, I have an intuitive sense of the right flow for night action. It's what I do best." In a similar sense, a night talk show host said, "I sense the mood of the caller and try to flow with their mood. When someone talks loud and fast so do I. If their voice is soft and slow I become very calm." Some of these broadcasters were so successful at playing to the moods of night owls that they became entrenched or typecast as nighttime broadcasters. One familiar example is Franklin Hobbs, whose low, sandy voice drew a national audience during the night hours from clear-channel WCCO in Minneapolis for many years.

Consistent with the role of mood facilitation is the role of companion. Developing a friendship or companion relation with listeners is for most broadcasters the best strategy for eliciting loyalty and commitment from listeners, and developing commitment through companionship is no different through a mass medium than it is in face-to-face situations. Usually, commitment and loyalty are given in response to a feeling of security and trust established in a relationship. Since broadcasters understand that a continued expression of friendliness is what many listeners desire, it becomes part of their delivery. From my research, some broadcasters claimed that they actually practiced smiling through their voices but were quick to add that listeners could easily hear when the attempt was "put on" or phoney. Stations even adopt friendship as a focal point of their public relations campaigns. In Phoenix, Bill Haywood (morning personality of KOY) was pictured with five different friendly facial expressions in a recent billboard campaign. In a 1980 interview the station manager of KABC in

Los Angeles stated, "Trust, warmth, honesty, communication. They all have to be there. Our personalities become friends to the listeners, somebody they feel they can turn to." While achieving companionship with listeners is still a matter of acceptance by the listener, the point is that promoting friendship is an important concern in radio strategy.

Research data also indicate that radio broadcasters have a special sensitivity to loneliness, which in part is due to their working conditions. Many of these individuals work in the solitude of a soundproof booth with little opportunity to see or hear other people, a circumstance that is particularly acute for the late-night disc jockey, who may work up to six hours alone. Common sense suggests that in experiencing isolation during these periods, broadcasters develop empathy for the plight of the lonely listener. Almost everyone has experienced lonely periods when they have obtained a degree of comfort through radio. Common examples are the social isolation of driving long distance, especially at night; coming home to an empty house or apartment; and the emotional isolation after a lost love or weekend without friends. As mentioned previously, radio can normalize these situations or at least reduce the anxiety.

For some listeners in these situations the companionship of radio is not just chatter and musical rhythms; it is the personal touch provided by a surrogate friend—the radio broadcaster. In interviewing several late-night deejays, I had the opportunity to talk with listeners who phoned the station. When asked why they listened and called during the early morning hours, several candidly admitted they were simply lonely. Responses such as these indicate that a kindred spirit exists between some broadcasters and listeners, both empathically understanding the other's situation.

To promote friendship with listeners, broadcasters claim to use three role-making strategies: an expression of sincerity, a spontaneous and relaxed delivery, and an avoidance of talking down to the listener. Most broadcasters state that sincerity is not easy to express to listeners on rigid format stations that require the hard sell or rock or urban country. Others offer the rationalization that you either have sincerity or you do not. However, many radio communicators, especially those on MOR stations, admit to working hard at conveying sincerity through such techniques as the use of personal pronouns, references to ideals of honesty and fairness, concern for listener safety on the road, and the ever-popular "hope you're having a good day." Regardless of their ability to express sincerity, the point is that it is considered an important quality for successful radio communication.

Spontaneity and a relaxed voice quality are the speech characteristics that enable the broadcaster to appear as the typical nextdoor neighbor. As one deejay remarked, "The biggest compliment you could pay me is to say I sound off-the-cuff." While a relaxed voice quality is not found in formats such as rock or disco, even broadcasters at these stations will occasionally attempt to create the impression of spontaneity, usually through prepared ad libs. Ex-disc jockey Dan O'Day developed a lucrative business by putting out a monthly newsletter, "O'Liners," which supplied humorous stories, anecdotes, and one-liners to disc jockeys throughout the country. Yet it takes a special ability to make prepared material sound spontaneous. As Fred (Dr. Voice) Lewis, a veteran of over twenty years in radio, stated in a recent interview, "Good voices are nice, but what I'm trying to convince my students is that naturalness and believability are the really important ingredients in speech."

Finally, friendship strategy involves the conscious attempt to avoid talking down to the listener. On the practical side, broadcasters believe they cannot sell products to listeners who feel that a condescending attitude is being expressed. The same logic holds for establishing a friendship and companion role; friends simply do not establish superiority over one another. While listeners demand a superior level in speech characteristics from radio broadcasters, they will not tolerate being "lorded-over" or conceit from these same broadcasters.

In being attuned to listener routines, attempting to communicate one on one, enhancing listener moods, and in striving for a companionship with listeners, broadcasters seek to go beyond the boundaries of format and achieve a sense of personal interaction with listeners. When they sense this has been achieved, they feel they have earned the right to think of themselves as communicators and perhaps as radio personalities.

To be considered a radio personality is the highest status anyone can achieve in commercial radio, and with it comes stardom, a lucrative salary, talent fees, and prime-time broadcast slots. Radio personalities from Arthur Godfrey to Wolfman Jack, Cousin Brucie, Larry King, and many others obtained their success in at least two ways: they became supreme entertainers, and they created a sense of intimacy with their listeners. As entertainers, disc jockeys such as Murray the K (often called the Fifth Beatle) or Wolfman Jack can enhance a particular type of music, elevate the fame of performers, and develop a subculture to the point that it is impossible to separate the performer, broadcaster, and music; each is interdependent with the other.

Listeners are as loyal to these broadcasters as they are to musical performers. Loyal followers of Bill Haywood's morning show (KOY) are so addicted to him that they feel a sense of loss if they miss his show. Talk show host Larry King commands a nation-wide audience who would rather miss some sleep than miss his show. These personalities may even become cultural heroes, as was the case among rock fans with Wolfman Jack. At one time broadcasters Al Collins and Symphony Sid were as important to jazz fans as were the musicians featured on their programs. There is little doubt that a few radio personalities have and will continue to achieve the status attributed to Hollywood film stars and recording artists.

A significant feature of success in entertainment is the sense of intimacy that fans feel toward a performer. While songs are significant for their lyrics, a fan may feel the performer is singing directly to them and about their joys and sorrows. From Frank Sinatra to Elvis Presley, there is a closeness that fans believe exists between themselves and their idols. Although a person must have the talent and skills to perform, an essential part of talent is charisma. In part, charisma translates into the ability to captivate and influence people through emotional rather than rational appeal. This definition also describes the bond between intimate friends. It follows then that a sense of intimacy is an important factor in measuring the relationship between performers and spectators.

As evidence to support this claim, consider how anyone explains why they like a particular performer. Along with admiring or respecting a performer's talent, the spectator will usually mention a feeling of closeness or identification they have with that performer (this is especially acute with singers). How else does one explain the reaction of fans to Elvis, John Lennon, Willie Nelson, Odetta, and the like? Therefore, it seems reasonable to suggest that charisma and the attending intimacy are necessary ingredients to becoming a radio personality such as Arthur Godfrey in his radio days, Murry the K during the Beatlemania days, Wolfman Jack during the sixties, or Larry King as the master of the talk show. Radio broadcasters understand the necessity for intimacy, and successful personalities are constantly aware of the need to project and achieve it with their listeners. As one of the more successful radio personalities in Phoenix said, "I want you to feel I'm there in the room or car talking with, not at, you, and that you know that I care . . . and that you can trust me. And that's why radio is a personal medium." . . .

Comparing Radio Strategy and Listener Experience

In comparing the strategies of radio stations and broadcasters with reasons for listening there is a striking compatibility. When radio serves the subculture interests of listeners, complaints are rare. Listeners accept radio because it meets their specialized desires whether for rational, utilitarian concerns or emotional satisfaction. Similar to specialized print media, people usually do not listen to stations outside the boundary of their lifestyles, except for curiosity, occasional mood changes, and when someone else controls the dial. Even when a person is forced to listen, the experience may be tolerated rather than perceived as a threat, as sometimes occurs with the limited alternatives on television and newspapers. Even parents who find their teenager's rock station irritating may tolerate it as a passing phase. Consequently, radio usually makes a well-calculated attempt to meet the desires of listeners within a monetarily profitable framework.

However, if the profit orientation expands to the point at which stations attempt to enlarge their audience to near mass proportions, they run the risk of destroying the compatibility that initially led to their success. Since radio has achieved success by catering to subcultural interests, it may easily lose its appeal by diluting its approach. Indeed, this has recently occurred in large urban markets where formerly esoteric FM stations decided to become all things to all people or jumped from one format to another in search of the magic number one rating. The old formula of "play it safe," meaning hit the middle or top of the bell-shaped curve, is risky business, especially when the radio audience may not be characterized by a normal statistical distribution. As long as radio caters to specific rather than general interests, its success is, in part, assured.

But radio communication is more than a compatibility of interests as found in a music subculture or a sports talk show; at times it is a personal interaction between listener and broadcaster. While many people listen routinely at specific times of the day to particular broadcasters, this action is more than a ritual; it is a stable relationship with a consistent form and content. This consistency is achieved through the same procedures found in everyday, face-to-face interaction. Both broadcaster and listener form images of each other, imagine each other in a social setting, and speak or listen to each other in terms of those images. Once this role-taking process is routinized, both parties can predict the concerns of the other and how the other will act with a fair degree of accuracy. Listeners can depend on the fact that a broadcaster's emotional demeanor will remain consistent each day. They can anticipate without fear of disappointment that unique features of a broadcaster's program, humorous vignettes, anecdotes, quips, or serious features, will occur. Broadcasters can also predict with accuracy the profile of a typical listener and the social context in which listening occurs.

In other words, both broadcaster and listener can depend on the form and content of the relationship in much the same manner as occurs between friends. Therefore, compatibility between broadcaster and listener may occur on a personal level, providing a sense of stability to life. Surprisingly, this occurs in a communication context that appears at first glance to be fraught with ambiguity. In a setting in which neither party has visual contact with each other, and in which only one party, the listener, can form a somewhat specific image of the other, radio interaction can take on many of the characteristics of a compatible friendship, even to a level of intimacy. . . .

MEDIA AS MEANS OF EXPRESSION

Two major issues underlie the essays in this section: (1) balance among the rights and interests of the varied individuals, groups, and institutions involved in mass communication and (2) the roles of government, industry, pressure groups, and the individual media consumer in seeking that balance.

The First Amendment protection of freedom of speech is one of the most sacred principles of our democracy. Yet freedom of speech is far from unlimited—and perhaps further from uncontroversial—in our society. The articles in this section address First Amendment issues that occur in media. They demonstrate that restrictions of various kinds limit free speech and that some Americans insist that there ought to be more limitations. Others insist with equal fervor that free speech ought to be virtually unlimited. As is the case in Section 1, which stand individuals take often depends on whether their own rights or the rights of others are at issue.

The first two selections in this section discuss limitations to free speech imposed by media through self-regulatory mechanisms. Edward D. Miller and Michael Gartner, both newspaper editors, debate whether a paper has the right to refuse to print advertisements its editors find objectionable or to refuse ads from firms whose business the editors judge to be immoral. The authors take opposing stands on whether papers should accept ads for X-rated movies, among other products and services.

Herminio Traviesas reflects upon the job of a television network censor. Traviesas, chief censor at NBC for a number of years, describes the struggles between the network and creative personnel (for example, performers, writers, and production companies) over content issues. He shows how the networks have responded to changes in the social mores that regulate such things as language use and the portrayal of nudity. Traviesas also explains how the context of potentially offensive material can influence a censor's judgment, suggesting that there are persuasive artistic justifications for using otherwise objectionable material.

Reo Christenson takes a far less moderate stance on the issue. He insists that explicitly sexual content is not protected by the First Amendment at all. He argues, on moral grounds, that obscene and pornographic materials should not be allowed to appear in the media.

The next three articles address means by which people have used media to express themselves without restriction (in public access cable television) and despite limitations (in music videos). Michael I. Meyerson offers a description of various "obnoxious" materials that appear on cable television. His article contains a historical review of the differential treatment of books, movies, and television in the law and in the courts. He shows how in some cities cable television has brought about a radical change from the traditionally restrained content of television. John Schwartz describes the very colorful programs—"something to offend just about anyone"—that appear on the public access channel in Austin, Texas, providing an illustration of the developments Meyerson discusses. Schwartz tells how both advocates and opponents of censorship are using Austin's public access channels as the forum of debate.

Jeremy Weir Alderson takes up the defense of public access in the face of efforts to drive it off cable television. He maintains that public access cable is the one place where anyone can speak with total freedom and that it should be preserved for that reason. He describes how it has been used by blacks and women in New York City to voice their messages to the community. He concludes by urging more people to watch and to appear on public access as a defense against its abolition.

To conclude the section, Lisa A. Lewis's article returns to the subject of music video, this time for a discussion of the ways performers—particularly Tina Turner and Cyndi Lauper—use music videos to negotiate gender inequality. She shows how these vocalists assert a female authorial voice and address their messages to female audiences even while working in a medium notorious for its hostility to female points of view.

Thus this section closes by directing these unresolved issues to you for evaluation. *Are there differences among media that justify differential treatment before the law? Should television be more restricted than books or movies? Should broadcast television be more restricted than cable television? What lines, if any, would you draw around anyone's free speech via the media? Is there any middle ground on these questions, or must you be on one side or the other? How can we maximize the freedom of people who prefer ideas or experiences that others find obnoxious without endangering or infringing on the rights of those others?* Civil liberties should never be taken for granted, lest they be undermined or even lost altogether. *How will you protect and nurture your precious freedom of speech?*

Study Questions: Miller and Gartner

? *With which of these editors do you agree? Why? If the advertiser were a political candidate instead of the owner of a movie theater, would that change your answer? Does it make a difference whether publishers refuse an ad because of its language and illustration or refuse it because they disapprove of the product being advertised?*

Should editors or publishers have the right to determine who can advertise in their newspapers? If you think they should, do you believe any limitations in the exercise of that right should be placed on them? If so, what should those limitations be? That is, under what circumstances could a publisher reject an advertisement? Under what circumstances, if any, would you forbid a publisher from rejecting an advertisement?

Should newspaper owners have greater freedom to refuse their services to an advertiser than restaurant owners or barbers have to refuse their services? Why? What about owners of television stations?

If a newspaper owner also owned a chain of movie theaters, should that affect your decision on whether he or she could refuse advertising from other movie theaters?

What is the probable impact on a local business that cannot advertise in a local paper?

Is the First Amendment relevant to the issue discussed by Miller and Gartner?

Edward D. Miller and Michael Gartner

PUBLISH ADS FOR X-MOVIES AND SUCH?

NO
Edward D. Miller

It's ironic and annoying how often language gets in the way of communication. Words become devalued by misuse, complicated concepts are stuffed into simple code words, clarity succumbs to the pressures of camouflage.

Editors familiar with these dangers ought to recognize all three in the verb "censor." It is a blasting cap designed to trigger explosions of alarm and indignation. Into one neat six-letter word are stuffed all the foes of our profession, from Peter Zenger's trial judge to Richard Nixon.

But life is not that simple. It is not "good guys and bad guys," "cowboys

This debate on the publishing of advertisements for products or services many people find objectionable appeared in the Bulletin of the American Society of Newspaper Editors. Edward D. Miller is executive editor of the Allentown (Pa.) *Call-Chronicle;* Michael Gartner is editor of *The Register and Tribune.*

and Indians," "cops and robbers." Differences are measured by degree, often with only the minutest subtleties separating degrees.

Our use of the language should be equally sensitive. To label all judgment over advertising as "censorship" is to ignore the subtleties.

There's a significant difference between applying standards of advertising and exercising what most would accept to be "censorship." Screening ad copy is no more censorship than editing reporters' copy. You set standards, and you apply judgments based on those standards.

Frankly, I wish newspapers did more of it, for our credibility is reduced as quickly by tasteless or misleading ad copy as it is by poor news copy.

Another subtlety usually lost in the debate is the distinction between a film producer's right to make the movie and my obligation to help him make a profit.

The same First Amendment that stirs pledges of allegiance from editors protects the right of a film producer to make and distribute a movie, an act of art and commerce independent of anyone else's First Amendment expressiveness.

Why am I obligated to help him make a profit? I have not said he can't show the movie. I have even said I would fight for his right to do so. But why must I take his money and help him take yours?

My answer is simple: I don't have to, any more than I have to take a release from a government agency or a house ad from a competitor.

Each year during election campaigns I screen political ads as a service to my ad department. My devotion to the First Amendment being deep, I offer wide latitude of expression, yet I invariably block or force rewrite on ads containing information I know to be false or misleading. Is this censorship or common sense?

Our advertising executives are constantly on the lookout for ads that make false claims. Consequently, each year they turn down a lot of business because some ads do not meet a variety of ethical and commercial standards. Is this censorship or common sense?

Finally, standards needn't be monolithic or inflexible. Occasionally our movie reviewer will write (even favorably) about a movie our ad department will not accept copy for, an amusing irony that reveals something is going on other than censorship. To be consistent should I tell my reporters to adopt the standards of the ad department? Should I tell the ad department to let the general desk set policy throughout the paper? Can there not exist two standards without having a "double standard"?

To me the issue is simple. That a person has a right to operate a legal business does not obligate me to help him make a profit by sharing the credibility of my newspaper. Obviously, this is a freedom with great potential for abuse, but that potential is not reason enough to erode the freedom.

YES
Michael Gartner

There is a bank in my town that is reluctant to give mortgages on houses in certain areas of the city.

There is a grocer who I suspect encourages the poor to use their food stamps foolishly on fad foods that are priced outlandishly high.

There is a car dealer who I think gives terrible—but costly—service to the wealthy people who buy his very expensive automobiles.

And there are some X-rated movie houses that show films that offend a good deal of my readership.

All advertise regularly in *The Register and Tribune*. And that is as it should be.

But it is not that way everywhere. Increasingly, newspapers are censoring the type of advertising they will accept, limiting or eliminating ads for purveyors of dirty books and movies. Every few weeks, it seems, *Editor & Publisher* prints a little article on how some paper has restricted its policy. The stories have become routine.

It is not a matter to be dealt with routinely, however. The newspaper is supposed to be a chronicle, a mirror, an informer and an entertainer. And perhaps much more. But it is not supposed to be a censor.

If *The New York Times* limits its ads for X-rated movies, why shouldn't I limit my ads from that banker? If the *Los Angeles Times* restricts X-rated movie ads, why shouldn't I tell that automobile dealer that he can't advertise with me any more? By restricting ads, newspapers are, in effect, determining who can do business in their town and who can't. This is not the role of the newspaper.

Three years ago, there was a great hue and cry in Des Moines because of all the massage parlors that had sprung up in town. It was the general feeling that the newspaper was responsible (whenever anything "bad" happens, it is the general feeling that the newspaper is responsible), and the letters poured in urging us to stop taking the ads for those terrible places.

At that point, my friend and predecessor, Kenneth MacDonald, wrote an editorial. He wrote:

> . . . It is easy to understand why many persons have strong feelings about massage parlors. They assume the parlors are immoral and illegal. They want the newspaper to put the parlors out of business by refusing to accept their advertising.
>
> Perhaps some of them should be put out of business. Perhaps all of them should be. The important question, however, is how this should be done. We don't think newspapers should decide who is permitted to operate a business in this community and who is forbidden to operate. In a democratic society, that is a function of the community's elected officials, the police and the courts.

As MacDonald told the readers, our policy is to accept advertising for any product or service that may legally be offered for sale, reserving always the right to pass judgment on the copy printed in the ad.

It should be no other way. Suppose, for instance, that the Coca-Cola company purchased your newspaper—a not-too-farfetched supposition in these days of acquisitions by conglomerates. Would you stand for an advertising ban on Pepsi or 7-Up?

Or suppose that the government determined that cigarettes should not be advertised in your paper, even though it remained quite legal to buy and smoke cigarettes. Would you stand for such an advertising ban?

Of course not. Editors would rise up in wrath and righteousness in both these instances. They would fume on the editorial page, and their reporters would fulminate (in a balanced way, of course) in the news pages.

Yet why is no one rising up to attack the decisions on smut? Are dirty books any worse than discriminatory bankers? Are dirty movies worse than unscrupulous grocers? Is it worse to advertise Linda Lovelace than it is to run ads for guns? (In Des Moines last year, more than a score of people were shot dead. No one was even maimed by a dirty movie.)

And who is to say what is good and what is bad? Does a publisher or advertising director have some divine guidance that the rest of us lack? Is it in the public interest for newspapers to decide who can survive and who can't?

Finally, hasn't anyone ever heard of free expression?

Study Questions: Traviesas

? *Do you think television's tolerance for "blue" language or explicitly sexual content is greater or lesser than the American public's? What is the basis for your answer? Traviesas says that the standards of NBC have changed as public norms have changed. Do you think that is appropriate, or should the networks stick to "proper" language and behavior no matter how the public's norms change?*

Assuming you believe, with Traviesas, that the network should consider public norms in deciding what to say and show, should television lead the change in public norms, stay even with the changing public norms, or follow behind those changes? What is Traviesas' opinion on this question? What is your opinion?

Why does Traviesas think it is all right for standards to be lower for certain times of day and for certain programs than for others? Do you agree with him?

Why do you think NBC gets more protests over jokes about religion than about other subjects?

Should a network be able to show provocative material if the audience is warned beforehand that some people might find the program offensive? What is Traviesas' position on this?

Which do you think is the best way to handle material that some audience members are likely to find objectionable: edit it out, warn the audience ahead of time, or something else? Why?

Why should the artistry with which a show is done affect whether nudity, sexual behavior, or sacrilegious comments are permitted on the air?

Do you agree with Traviesas that television networks must have censors? Why or why not?

Herminio Traviesas

THEY NEVER TOLD ME ABOUT "LAUGH-IN"

How have things changed since you came on board?
First of all, there was the breakthrough in bold types of humor, as reflected in *Laugh-In* and the *Smothers Brothers,* especially, and there has been an evolution of storytelling. In the past two or three years we were sort of criticized for suddenly going into sex, especially when they said that now that violence is over, we've got to have sex.

I always denied that it was a sudden thing. We had been telling much more provocative stories for some time. I go back to *Silent Night, Lonely Night,* with its black-white relationship theme, and that was about 1969. Ever since then, we have been doing more provocative stories—although still controlling the language, the overt nudity, and many times turning down something thematically that you just can't live with.

Herminio Traviesas was for 13 years in charge of NBC's "broadcast standards," and probably the most visible of all the so-called network censors—the people with the final cut on sex, violence and other sensitivities in television (and sometimes radio) programming and commercials. Traviesas, now retired, was NBC's vice president, broadcast standards, from 1969 to 1977, when he became vice president for broadcast standards policy.

What are the things that exercise people most?
There are two things: nudity and religion. They complained about the slit skirts on the Dean Martin gals, the Golddiggers, thinking that that was lascivious or something, but it wasn't in my judgment.

It's not as bad as it used to be. I remember the first time that one of our stars appeared on the *Johnny Carson Show* without a bra, and my staff was wondering what I was going to do about it—and even then it had already been a part of society. And we just allowed it to happen—but at the same time making certain that the cameraman wasn't focusing on it. Now the braless look is there all the time.

You see, one of the things that has influenced television is the tremendous strides forward in other media, including feature films and some very conservative magazines for women. Not only are they showing the braless look, but they're showing see-through, which we do not allow.

Do you have any arguments among your staff about the range of taste, and do you find that you represent a different generational taste than other people on your staff?
That's a good question, and it has hit me in a different way—mainly from the younger people because the younger people think that we should have younger people on our staff.

We have very little turnover on our staff—I sometimes wonder about it, because it's such dedication. Now in general, I think they're a little tougher than I am, and there's a good reason: If they're not, they don't last long. Let *me* make the mistakes, because I'm at a level that . . . you know, in my job, you're only remembered by your mistakes.

Whenever you get called up on something, it's because somebody wrote too many letters and why did it happen? And nobody remembers that we had taken out hundreds of bedroom scenes and low-cut gowns and language and we even still cut down on "hells" and "damns" if there are too many of them. So, all of a sudden, you allow a legitimate use of the word "bastard," and we're dirty.

The first time I allowed "bastard" was on *Bonanza*. Very legit. But unfortunately, the press got hold of it beforehand, and the headlines said, "NBC allows dirty word on *Bonanza*."

What are the mistakes they will remember you for?
The one I always remember, because it was in my early days on *Laugh-In*, was when we did a very provocative joke on the pill, and when Dan and Dick were talking about 20 years ahead of time, I knew instinctively I shouldn't have done it, but I finally allowed it by telling them to constantly say "20 years from now." But the public never heard the "20 years from now." The story was something about a reporter going to Rome and finding the Pope wasn't there, but his wife was. And it ended up that they thought of the pill as St. Joseph's aspirin for children. Well, it was beautifully written and very, very funny. But it was a mistake; there were just too many people

who didn't think that it was as funny as I thought it was. And so that was a mistake.

There were certain things that happened on *Saturday Night Live* which provoked me more.

Provoked you or provoked the public?
Well, maybe it was because I'm too old. I allow them to do it because they're not trying to go for my Edwardians—they're going for a younger audience, and the young people that I talk with, certainly based on the mail reaction, find it very, very funny and provocative, while I sometimes find it strange that they're laughing.

But do you hear audience protests?
Again, the audience protests are always on religion—if you make fun of or if you satirize religion. The most recent was the one we did at Easter on *Saturday Night Live,* which was a legitimate satire because there are so many feature films and television shows based on the life of Christ. These two 12-year-olds are looking at "Jesus of Nazareth" and they're each telling each other which star they liked as Jesus. You know, it could have been the competition between Paul Newman and Bob Redford. And that was the satire.

I would say if we get 400 or 500 phone calls overnight, that's a major protest. This one only had about 160 or 170.

Do you have a typical audience in mind as you consider what you're going to allow and what you're not going to?
Lots of time I am accused of using double or different standards, because I consider what the *audience expectations* are, based on the time of the day and the show's personality.

There's no doubt that *Saturday Night Live* watches *Johnny Carson* and Johnny Carson's staff watches *Saturday Night Live.* And I get the phone calls the next week, if I allow something for them that I won't allow the other to do. And my defense has always been that it's a different audience. Johnny Carson's audience has been with him a long time; he has very good control of himself. The *Saturday Night Live* audience is a very special audience, too. It's a younger audience, not necessarily young in terms of the 17–21 age bracket. It's sinking into young married couples and to the 35's and it's spreading a little toward the high school age which I guess has some parents a little concerned. But we cannot control the set.

We at NBC have always felt concern about the 8 o'clock time period. For instance, we will review a script right now, a comedy script, and if it's a little provocative, we'll note: "We are approving this if it's after 9 o'clock."

Well, there still is the family hour concept.

At NBC we have always felt there was a family hour concept, and we continue to feel that way.

Another thing that has developed in the industry which has been very successful as we went into more provocative storytelling is what we call the "advisory legend," to let the public know that tonight, if you're going out or if you want to sit around with your family, maybe this is the time to be careful of what you're watching.

Now that isn't because we think it's not acceptable. It is probably the most important responsibility that ends in my lap, because if you do not use it with tremendous caution, you can be accused of titillating just to get the audience. And if you use it too often, it's ignored.

So that when you have a story like the feature film, "Coming Home," which thematically was an emotional problem—we took care of the sex problem in it, to the regret of some people who remembered the original— but the story was emotional and we put up a legend to advise the public.

What next tool of that sort have you got up your sleeve? Is there a way that you can enlarge the range of acceptability, and get away with it?
No. I tell you, the best tool that I know of—and you can't put a figure to it—is being certain that you do the story with tremendous artistry. When you do *Skag* or even *United States*—when you think of the subject matter that's discussed in *United States*—we had no complaints. It was so well done.

But artistry is not your final arbiter, I take it.
I am in the hands of God, because I cannot . . . well, except for one thing. We do recognize who the more responsible and experienced producers are, and while all producers obviously say that they are responsible, there are degrees of responsibility. And if I see a provocative show come in, from the thematic point of view, I usually ask who is going to do it. And if it's a certain three or four types of guys that we know well, I find I'm relaxed more.

One show that I'm so proud of having at least participated in is *Shogun.* If you've ever read the book you'll know that the problems *Shogun* has, per se, in terms of sex and violence, are such that you'd say you couldn't put it on television.

I happened to be on the West Coast when I found, to my delight, that I was going to meet with James Clavell himself, the original author, who had taken over the show. It was an interesting meeting; I remember it so well because he came in with his dark glasses and a little stiff, because he was familiar with the "censors." So anyway, we sat down and we said, "Well, why don't we just go over the things that concern us?" and we started to read scenes from the first draft, and he turned around to me and said, "Where are you getting that stuff from?" And I said, "Well, it's here, so we have to tell you." He said, "I wouldn't touch that with a 10-foot pole! I just won't do it that way."

And as we went along, talking to him, suddenly the dark glasses came off, and suddenly he relaxed, and suddenly we were friends, and what he has done in working with us is one of the most outstanding television programs that I have ever seen in my entire career. It is a fabulous show, and in terms of taste, just magnificent.

It's great when you have quality. That was why I was always proud of being a part of "The Godfather." A lot of people said I was wrong because it was so violent, but that was a work of art, and to work with Francis Ford Coppola was a tremendous experience for me personally.

I'm wondering what television could do to get rid of your job.
Well, I don't think they can. I think you're always going to have somebody. It's a responsibility that is inherent in your license for stations. The network is not licensed, as we all know, but somebody has to take over that responsibility and defend it. . . .

Study Questions: Christenson

[?] *What kinds of restrictions are placed on free speech and press in the United States today? Do you agree with Christenson that, if these kinds of expression can be restricted without violating the First Amendment, so can pornography? Why or why not?*

Is pornography different in some essential way from the kinds of news, information, and art that the First Amendment traditionally has protected?

Why is it difficult to define obscenity *precisely? Do you agree with Christenson's arguments that difficulty in defining obscenity should not be a deterrent to regulating it? How would you define* obscenity *or* pornography? *Who should decide what materials in the mass media are obscene or pornographic?*

In what ways are some groups in our society victimized by pornography, according to Christenson? Based on whatever experiences you have had with pornography, directly or indirectly, do Christenson's claims about its effect seem valid to you? Why or why not?

Has Christenson persuaded you that explicitly sexual material is not, and should not be, protected by the First Amendment? What are his strongest and weakest arguments?

Assuming we should agree on the need to reduce some of the extremely pornographic material now being distributed in this country, are Christenson's suggestions for doing so likely to be effective? Are there other approaches that you believe are preferable?

What should be done when a publisher, filmmaker, or broadcaster makes pornographic materials available to the public? If you believe something should be done, who should do it?

Reo Christenson

IT'S TIME TO EXCISE THE PORNOGRAPHIC CANCER

Is pornography protected by the First Amendment—or is it properly subject to legal restraint? Does it have damaging effects—or is it relatively harmless? Do Christians have a moral and civic obligation to be involved in the dispute?

This author, who has lectured on pornography before university audiences for 20 years and has testified as an expert witness for the prosecution in federal pornography cases, is convinced that pornography is an even graver menace than most Christians are aware. I believe that it is not protected by the First Amendment and that it is urgently important to curb this abomination. And I believe, moreover, that the intellectuals who oppose censorship can be refuted on every front.

Is pornography a form of expression protected by the free-speech, free-press provision of the First Amendment? The answer is—absolutely not. The Constitution has always permitted certain restrictions of freedom of speech and press. For example, laws properly forbid incitement to violence, libel, slander, partisan campaign speeches by federal civil servants, misleading and fraudulent advertising, the divulgence of military secrets,

Reo Christenson is professor of political science at Miami University in Oxford, Ohio. He is the author of several books; the most recent is *American Politics* (Harper and Row, 1979).

verbal interference with court proceedings, picketing in a context of violence, and a score of other restraints.

Reasonable restrictions on *marginal* aspects of speech and press are not only constitutional but essential to the functioning of an orderly and self-respecting society. Among those restraints are long-standing curbs on obscene materials, curbs that were never rebuked by our constitutional fathers or by any court. Specific obscenity laws have been found wanting—but the principle that the state may proscribe the distribution of obscene materials has never been successfully challenged in any court.

What the First Amendment does do, however, is protect the expression of all heretical opinions, however subversive or obnoxious they may appear to others. Thus dissenters have the right to attack any sexual code, to recommend polygamy, or to agitate for abolition of marriage and the family. So long as people have this sweeping freedom to challenge any cherished idea or institution, and to recommend any religious, political, economic, or social policy, the First Amendment is adequately protected.

Chief Justice Burger put it well: "To equate the free and robust exchange of ideas and political debate with the commercial exploitation of obscene material . . . demeans the First Amendment and its high purposes in the historic struggle for freedom."

Much is made of the lack of precision in defining what is obscene, and in the difficulties of meeting due process standards because of the vagueness involved. But if obscenity is impossible to define, why do opponents of censorship concede that society can legitimately protect children from it? If we can't define it, what do we keep from our kids?

While the lack of precision in defining obscenity is worrisome, the problem is by no means unique to this area. In most criminal or regulatory laws, behavior relating to those laws is clearly forbidden at one end of the continuum and clearly permissible at the other. But as we approach the center of the continuum, a zone of uncertainty is reached which yields much of our litigation. Pornography laws share this zone of uncertainty with a host of other laws. (I have yet to hear liberals deplore the unreasonable search and seizure provision of the Constitution because it is too vague.)

Pornographers merit precious little sympathy when they are uncertain about what is legally obscene and what is not. If they choose to operate in the danger zone, it is because that is where the profits are greatest. If they want to play for these kinds of stakes in this kind of game, let them take the risks that go with their wretched business.

Having established the fact that obscene materials can be curbed constitutionally, are they a sufficiently serious evil to merit major attention by Christians?

Defenders of the $4 billion pornography racket contend that the production and distribution of pornography is a relatively innocuous enterprise. They cite findings by the President's Commission on Obscenity and Pornography in 1971 that no measurable damage to consumers of pornography could be found.

But the commission report has been subjected to more withering criticism than almost any commission report in modern times. Half a dozen reputable social scientists have either pointed out serious flaws in the scientific character of the commission's work or have rejected its conclusions as inadequately supported by the evidence.

Nonetheless, the notion persists that pornography involves a "victimless crime," an assumption that leads law enforcement officers to give antipornography law enforcement a very low priority. A cogent case can be made, however, that four groups *are* victimized by pornography.

Women

The image of women so relentlessly propagated by pornography is that they are creatures whose hypnotic anatomical features proclaim their role and their relationships to men. They are a gender ordained for the sexual pleasure of men, and are principally distinguished by their possession of genitalia offering rich possibilities for male gratification. Much contemporary pornography highlights the joys of sadomasochistic sex, since sexual experience allegedly acquires a special flavor when women are physically abused.

Even if one cannot follow cause and effect with scientific verity, common sense tells us that millions of men cannot consume quantities of these products year after year without being affected by them.

For those who believe pornography relieves rather than intensifies unhealthy sexual urges, it should be noted that psychologists are now largely convinced that violent entertainment stimulates rather than reduces violent impulses. Only the willfully dogmatic can believe that the reverse effect takes place in pornography.

Adolescents

Teenagers who read pornography are the second category of victims. There is no way that pornography can freely circulate around this country, as it is doing today, without falling into the hands of millions of teenagers.

But does this really matter? To answer this question we must ask what is pornography's subliminal "message" to its viewers—what impression emerges from the totality of its pictures and narrative?

In addition to portraying a demeaning picture of women, pornography tells adolescents (and others) that sexual activity need not be related to love, morality, commitment, or responsibility. For people, as for animals, sex is designed to satisfy a purely physical desire.

Thus if sex is nothing but fun and games, to be indulged without shame as impulses dictate, why be faithful to one's spouse if someone more attractive—and willing—is at hand? Why not follow your lust wherever it leads? And why not have sex with whatever 14-year-old is willing to copulate with you?

Pornography denies that sexual experience is essentially a private matter. Group sex—why not? Wife-swapping—why not? Invite the kids to witness the fun when Mom and Pop are having sex—why not? What's so private about sex? And what's so wrong with voyeurism?

Pornography tells adolescents that aberrational sex is the most exciting and appealing form of sex. *Hustler* magazine, for example, has presented bestiality as an unrivalled form of sexual gratification—the supreme sexual experience.

Pornography encourages impulsive sex, careless sex, daring sex, irresponsible sex, and implies that there are no adverse consequences. You would never guess from viewing pornography that irresponsible sex leads to teenage pregnancies, premature marriages, abortions, illegitimate children, venereal disease, or psychic traumas. Nor would you suspect that extramarital sex had any unhappy consequences.

Pornography's message may not do much harm to adolescents from good homes who are taught sound values and whose parents set a good example of moral behavior. The question rather is what it will do to adolescents from the millions of homes in which little moral instruction is given, and where poor moral example is set. Such is their lot, moreover, when they are in a rebellious mood and inclined to challenge societal standards.

Does this concern for adolescents run athwart the Supreme Court's ruling in *Butler v. Michigan* (1957) that no state should quarantine "the general reading public against books not too rugged for grown men and women in order to shield juvenile innocence . . ."? It does not. It is not being suggested that any books should be banned; pornographic magazines, movies, and peep shows are the target.

Children

Youngsters who pose for pornographers are obvious victims. Thousands of children are photographed after being seduced into various forms of explicit sexual behavior. The pornographers make obscene profits peddling such wares to the sick souls who feast on them. These children would not be caught up in this vicious business if the pornography merchants weren't confident they could sell this stuff with relative impunity.

Society in General and the Family in Particular

Both groups are victimized by pornography.

Pornography is a direct challenge to the family because it encourages attitudes that are destructive of it. We have a right to be concerned about material that undermines the family, not by an open and reasoned attack (which would be protected by the First Amendment), but by inference, implication, and subliminal messages that infiltrate the mind while numbing the rational zone. Family stability lies at the heart of a stable society, and a healthy attitude toward sexual behavior is central to a sound, general moral code.

It cannot be reasonably denied that today's pornography scene is making a contribution toward the decline of moral standards. True, pornography has been around for centuries. But the pornography of the past does not remotely compare in volume to that which exists today. In previous eras, most people saw it infrequently, furtively, with an aura of social disapproval surrounding it. Because it is viewed with greater social tolerance today, its subversive impact is bound to increase. Its prevalence partially explains why material of increasing raunchiness is invading television and motion pictures. Five years ago we would not have tolerated scenes that now appear on television and in the theater; each year both media offer more daring material than the year before. Pornography leads the way; it is the cutting edge of our future.

Recent news reports indicate that videotape cassettes featuring both soft- and hard-core pornography are selling like hot cakes in some of our larger cities. Along with cable TV pornographic offerings, the spectacular growth of this field foreshadows America's future—if we let it happen. We could become a nation of vicarious voyeurs, with growing numbers of men huddled around TV sets after 11:30 P.M. watching performers engage in every form of explicit sexual behavior that commercial ingenuity can invent. How could one evaluate that scene as anything but evidence of a decadent culture?

The French nobility, before the French Revolution, used to amuse themselves by watching people have sexual intercourse. The Fascist African despot Idi Amin would order condemned prisoners to "make love before him" while he sipped wine and enjoyed the spectacle. The implications and parallels are worth reflecting upon.

Some will say that as adult citizens of a free society we should have the privilege of reading or watching whatever we wish. What's wrong with this view? In the first place, laws forbid the distribution and exhibition of obscene material, whatever people's tastes may be. Second, if the libertarian assumption is correct, why shouldn't enterpreneurs sell tickets to live sex shows? Why not give the customers live exhibitions of women having relations with animals? And why not give the interested public the opportunity to watch women being sexually abused and humiliated by men, in demonstration of the pornographic theory that sexual pain can become pleasure if we approach it with the right attitude? If some want to see these things, why shouldn't they be free to do so? If others dislike them, they can stay away.

I find it hard to believe that intelligent people would solemnly argue that society has no right to intervene in matters like these. But does society have no right to establish minimum standards of decency, whatever a minority may think? Has it no right to say, This goes beyond the bounds of the minimally civilized, this we will not tolerate?

The attitude that "I want to see what I want to see," without regard for the larger and long-run interests of society, is a posture common to our times. But it is a narcissistic, self-indulgent, and socially irresponsible view. In Maoist China, the interests of the state were almost everything, the interests of the individual, almost nothing. In America we have moved toward the opposite extreme, with the claims of individual freedom often transcending society's needs. A point somewhere between the anthill mentality of Mao's China and the individualist primacy of America represents a greater wisdom than either society has recognized.

Some will ask, why censor pornography and not the violence that abounds in movies and TV? Excessive violence in the entertainment world *is* an important social problem with which we should be concerned. But as entertainment, illegal violence is normally presented as an evil to be punished while pornography presents heedless, irresponsible sex as a good to be sought. That difference is a quantum leap, and one which warrants giving priority to pornography control.

Does history warn us that effective enforcement is impossible? As in every area of crime, perfect enforcement is, of course, unattainable. But those who believe we cannot stem the pornographic tide overlook the probability that a few stiff jail sentences (not just fines) would go a long way toward diminishing the supply of pornography. If major publishers or distributors were obliged to spend years in jail for their criminal activities, pornography would rapidly revert to its former underground status. And that is where it belongs.

Isn't *any* censorship terribly dangerous, since it may spread to other and wholly legitimate publishing enterprises? Won't censorship spread to the newspapers, to the political journals, and elsewhere?

Such questions provide more of the solemn malarkey the anticensorship forces have peddled so long—and so successfully. We have had obscenity laws throughout our history and they have never led to a creeping repression of press freedom. There is not a shred of empirical evidence to support the notion that censorship of obscenity threatens free expression of heretical political, social, or religious ideas. What sensible person really believes that if we enforce the antipornographic laws we would start censoring *The New York Times?*

What, then, should conservative Christians (and others who share their concern) do about all this?

Antipornography laws currently are not being enforced. Just why state laws should be enforced against the rest of us but not against pornographers is unclear. Why should they be privileged characters? Unhappily, experience makes it clear that the laws will not be enforced unless concerned citizens demand it—and hold the proper officials responsible if they fail to do so.

An appropriate course of action would seem to be first to ask your librarian to help you locate the provision of your state law that deals with obscenity. Then obtain copies of several of the more flagrantly obscene publications sold in your community—publications that deal primarily with explicit sexual activity in pornographic fashion. Take those offensive publications to your local prosecutor, invite his attention to the law, remind him of the "community standards" provision of *Miller v. California* (413 U.S. 15 [1973], pp. 23–24) and request that the local dealers (or publisher, if the magazine originates in your city) be prosecuted. If the prosecutor is uncooperative, ask members of your church to write a staggered succession of individually composed letters to local newspapers, courteously but firmly demanding that the obscenity laws be enforced, and briefly explaining why. If the prosecutor is an appointed officer, let the elected official who appointed him know that failure to enforce obscenity laws will seriously affect his political future. If the prosecutor is locally elected, the warning should go directly to him.

The same general procedure should apply to "adult films" that feature explicit sexual behavior. Someone must undergo the disagreeable task of viewing some of these films in order knowledgeably to protest their showing, but that is not an insuperable barrier.

To be most effective, such a campaign should be conducted by those more temperate, rather than those more strident, members of the religious community—and by those who have the interpersonal skills that successful community action requires. It is possible to be resolute and persistent without being shrill and obnoxious.

Finally, the Attorney General of the U.S. should become the recipient of a blizzard of mail requesting the enforcement of the federal law that prohibits obscene materials from moving in interstate commerce. Wave after wave of local prosecutions in every state, along with prosecutions in federal district courts, could deal the pornographers the staggering blow they so richly deserve—and which social responsibility requires.

With morality, logic, and the law all on their side, it is imperative for concerned Christians to organize at the community level and channel their indignation into effective action. If they lose this battle by default—by refusing to do what they can—their consciences will have a heavy burden to bear. It is their children—and everyone's children—whose future is involved.

Study Questions: Meyerson / Schwartz

[?] As Meyerson points out, books, magazines, and videocassettes today are relatively free of censorship. Why have these media enjoyed greater freedom from censorship than radio and television have enjoyed?

Is cable more like magazines, books, and videocassettes in this respect, or more like radio and television? What, if anything, should be banned from cable?

Is the imposition of different standards for different media justifiable? How do you rationalize your position in terms of the First Amendment and the Supreme Court's standard for obscenity?

Why do many cable operators want to run soft-core pornography that cannot be shown on broadcast television?

In what way do members of the general public who want to speak (or produce programs) have greater freedom of speech with cable than they did with pre-cable radio and television? Is this a good or bad situation? Should groups such as the Ku Klux Klan have freedom to argue for their ideas on cable? On broadcast radio and television? Do you believe that the Klan can be barred from access channels without violating the First Amendment?

If you were the manager of the Austin, Texas, cable system, how would you handle the "Hymns for Heathens" case described by Schwartz?

Michael I. Meyerson

CABLE'S "NEW OBNOXIOUSNESS" TESTS THE FIRST AMENDMENT

Throw the deadbolt! Pull down the blinds! Bad words and dirty pictures are invading the American home . . . thanks to cable television.

There's plenty to enjoy on cable, to be sure. But there's also enough to offend everyone you know: sex acts (which may or may not be simulated), foul language, militant harangues from the left and right, and all other manner of provocation.

Until recently television has been quite tame. The sexual innuendo on the average sitcom and the worst treacheries of Joan Collins aren't likely to upset many viewers. The strongest commentaries by George Will or Bill

Moyers won't provoke rage throughout a community. Both government and private forces have labored to ensure that offensive or even particularly controversial programming is not sent into viewers' living rooms.

Now, however, coaxial cable is bringing into the home troublesome kinds of programs never before seen on television. On one cable channel, the film *Wanda Whips Wall Street* presents a view of the world of stocks and bondage you're not likely to get from Louis Rukeyser. On a public access channel, spokesmen for the Ku Klux Klan glorify the white race. Suddenly that old 19-inch family friend is showing salacious pictures and espousing hateful ideology.

The result: public outcry in many communities. In Memphis more than 6,000 demonstrated to force the local cable operator to drop the Playboy Channel. In Austin black and white people alike are agitating to get the Klan off the public access channel. Anti-cableporn laws were enacted (only to be ruled unconstitutional) in Utah and Miami.

The battles over the new obnoxiousness on cable television mark the end of a First Amendment standoff, established by the courts, between the forces of free speech and those of censorship. While broadcasting has been protected from indecency, the courts have allowed Americans to voluntarily bring books, magazines, and video cassettes of unprecedented sexual explicitness into their own homes. What has been forbidden over the airwaves has been permitted in print and other media. The question now in heated dispute is what will be permitted over cable.

The Supreme Court has protected the interests of both the want-to-sees and the don't-want-to-sees in recent years through the application of a basic principle: the "ancient concept that a man's home is his castle," as the Court put it.

For the don't-want-to-sees, the Court defended people's right "to be let alone." In 1970 it upheld a law enabling individuals to prevent advertisers from mailing them unsolicited sexually provocative material. The Court said that every American, at least in the home, has "the right to be free from sights, sounds, and tangible material" he does not want.

For the want-to-sees, the court ruled the previous year that the mere possession of obscene material in a home could not be made illegal. That issue arose in an unusual manner. In Georgia the police were investigating one Robert Stanley on suspicion of bookmaking. They obtained a search warrant, went through Stanley's house, and failed to find evidence of gambling–but did find three reels of 8mm film. He was arrested and tried, not for bookmaking but for knowingly possessing obscene material. The court found the films obscene and convicted Stanley.

On appeal the Supreme Court reversed the conviction. Citing Stanley's right to receive information and ideas "regardless of their social worth," the Court ruled that criminalizing the possession of such material would be akin to giving the government the power to control the moral content of a person's thoughts. "If the First Amendment means anything," the Court held, "it means that a state has no business telling a man, sitting alone in his own house, what books he may read, or what films he may watch." Once you get the material past your front door you are, so to speak, home free.

But the government can still try to keep you from obtaining "obscene" material by outlawing its sale, importation, and mailing.

That leaves the courts with the vexing responsibility of defining obscenity, a task that has, in the words of one Supreme Court justice, "produced a variety of views among the members of the Court unmatched in any other course of Constitutional adjudication."

In 1973 Warren Burger established the definition that stands today. In a case titled *Miller v. California,* the chief justice laid out a three-part test for obscenity:

- The material, taken as a whole and applying contemporary community standards, appeals to the prurient interest (that is, to a "shameful or morbid interest in nudity or sex");
- The material depicts sexual conduct in a patently offensive way;
- The work lacks serious literary, artistic, political, or scientific value.

If it meets this definition, it's "Miller-obscene," in legal parlance, and can be prohibited. As you can imagine, the Miller definition hardly clarified matters for lower courts, much less for the general public. Within a year after Chief Justice Burger minted the definition, the Supreme Court justices themselves were sitting through a screening of the movie *Carnal Knowledge* to determine first-hand whether it was Miller-obscene, as the Georgia State Supreme Court had thought. (They ruled it wasn't, since the movie's sexual activity wasn't patently offensive.)

But the Miller-obscene standard that applies to books and movies does not apply to broadcasting. Radio and television are ruled by a more restrictive standard. The Federal Communications Commission has the power to ban material that is not Miller-obscene but merely "indecent." A case in point involved *Femme Forum,* one of the 1970s' midday "topless radio" call-in shows that lingered on sexual topics. The FCC was particularly rankled by the segment on keeping your sex life alive. (One listener called in to suggest non-nutritive uses of peanut butter.) The commission found *Femme Forum* to be "titillating and pandering" and fined the guilty station $2,000.

A few years later, in 1979, the Supreme Court endorsed the FCC's authority to regulate "indecent" material on the air. The Court upheld a ban on the radio broadcast of comedian George Carlin's monologue discussing (quite presciently, as it turned out) seven dirty words that "you couldn't say on the public airwaves." The words were not Miller-obscene, but they could still be banned from broadcasting for two reasons, the Court said. First: The broadcast media are "a uniquely pervasive presence in the life of all Americans." By "pervasive," the Court apparently meant that the radio is located in the "privacy of the home." (Ironically, the case was pressed by a man who heard the monologue while riding in his car with his son.) Radio is also considered pervasive because listeners frequently tune in and out of programming—those who want to avoid George Carlin's language cannot be completely protected by prior warnings.

Second: The seven dirty words could be suppressed because broadcasting is "uniquely accessible to children." There's no way to prevent children from listening in. A decade earlier, in a case involving the sale of "girlie magazines," as the justices repeatedly called them, the Court had ruled that the magazines, even if not obscene, could not be sold to children. When children are involved, a lesser offense is offense enough.

So it is with offensive sexuality in broadcasting. The FCC decides what's indecent, subject to appeal to the federal courts. When the material is politically offensive, however, the commission stands aside. Those matters are left to individual broadcasters. With the Supreme Court's backing, the FCC has upheld the broadcasters' right to decide who can buy air-time. As Justice William Brennan noted in dissenting from this decision, leaving this power with the broadcaster means that only moderate and established views are heard on the airwaves: "Indeed, in light of the strong interest of broadcasters in maximizing their audience, and therefore their profits, it seems almost naive to expect the majority of broadcasters to produce the variety and controversiality of material necessary to reflect a full spectrum of viewpoints. Simply stated, angry customers are not good customers, and in the commercial world of mass communications it is simply 'bad business' to espouse—or even to allow others to espouse—the heterodox or the controversial."

Justice Brennan's dissent notwithstanding, the line was drawn: The airwaves were to be sanitized to protect the unwilling viewer and listener. Those so inclined could acquire indecent material on their own and partake in private.

That was the simple truce that cable television has irrevocably upset. With a large number of channels to fill, cable companies had to find programming to differentiate the channels, each of which would pull in a different audience. And because the individual subscriber was not only selecting but paying for programs, cable operators felt at liberty to run those too "indecent" to appear on broadcast television. The new offerings ranged from mild R-rated movies to "adult" programming, consisting in large part of X-rated movies that had been edited into "soft-core" versions.

The second remarkable change in programming was brought on, not by commercial motives, but by a desire to serve the First Amendment. Public access channels were set aside, usually at the city's demand, to allow residents to speak freely on television without censorship, first-come, first-served. This has resulted in a host of innovative programs serving diverse segments of the population and covering issues that the mass media customarily ignored. Reflecting a community's diversity, however, some of this free speech often affronts the tastes and beliefs of the majority.

Some viewers, and the politicians representing them, were not only outraged but baffled that television could be allowed to change so radically. As the City of Miami's lawyer said in defense of the city's law against indecent cable programming: "I don't see any fundamental difference between cable and broadcasting. In both situations people are watching the same instrument—television."

But courts have found fundamental differences, and so far have struck down the anti-cableporn laws that came before them in Miami and Utah. One difference found between broadcasting and cable is that cable is not as "pervasive" as broadcasting—not because cable enters fewer homes, but because viewers can more readily avoid offensive programming on cable. They can simply elect not to take a pay service such as HBO or the Playboy Channel, while still receiving the other channels cable has to offer. People don't have this same freedom with broadcasting, according to the courts. (Of course they could elect not to have a television set at all, but there is an implicit assumption at work that broadcast TV is a necessity of life.)

The courts also noted one of the most pertinent technological differences between cable and broadcasting: Cable's viewers themselves have the ability to censor programming. In fact, federal law requires that, as of the end of this coming June, all cable television operators must provide "lock boxes" to subscribers who request them. These devices will permit parents, for example, to keep certain potentially offensive channels off their television screens. This technological fix seems to be an ideal solution to a First Amendment dilemma. Don't-want-to-sees can keep their homes free of offensive television without interfering with the rights of want-to-sees.

But, alas, no free-speech issue is ever that simple to resolve. The don't-want-to-sees demand protection not only for their families, but for their communities as well. They know a lock box on their set at home won't prevent their children from seeing morally offensive programs at a friend's house. They fear the Klan's racial hatred will be legitimized by television appearances, and violence encouraged among their neighbors. They call upon the government to use its inherent police powers to safeguard the community's quality of life.

The other side opposes any censorship, arguing that any individual's right to speak is paramount over the community's right to suppress it. It may be a knee-jerk response, but it's a necessary one where factions are claiming rights that are irreconcilable.

Assuming that First Amendment protections survive on cable television, sooner or later there will be programs to appall every taste. Former Justice

Potter Stewart has acknowledged that "the consequences of rigorously enforcing the guarantees of the First Amendment are frequently unpleasant. Much speech that seems to be of little or no value will enter the marketplace of ideas, threatening the quality of our social discourse and, more generally, the serenity of our lives. But that is the price to be paid for constitutional freedom."

The price is greatest, however, for those who are most offended. The damage they feel, and the community's interests, shouldn't be ignored or dismissed. The First Amendment's most effective defenders may be the civil libertarian who urges that cable operators voluntarily delay sexually explicit programs until after children's bedtimes, or the political activist who produces access programs to counter the other side's. The oncoming battles over cable's new obnoxiousness will be less bitter, divisive, and dangerous if the advocates of free speech recognize what a high price they are asking from some of their neighbors.

John Schwartz

AUSTIN GETS AN EYEFUL: SACRILEGE AND THE KLAN

A broken crucifix twitches across the screen. In front of the crucifix, a man in a Charles Manson mask dances and chants incoherently about sex and religion. It's 10:30 P.M., and *Hymns for Heathens*, a program produced by a construction worker who likes punk music, erupts on Channel 10 in Austin, Texas.

A few nights later on the same channel, a Ku Klux Klan leader interviews a man who was imprisoned in 1973 for fire-bombing school buses during Detroit's busing controversy. An Austin man submitted the program, *Race and Reason*, for cablecasting, but a former Klan official in southern California produced it.

What hath public access wrought?

Not everyone in town wanted these programs to appear on an Austin Cable Vision public access channel. The opposition was roused last fall when a local television reporter interviewed offended Austinites. Other local media followed suit, and soon callers to the city cable commission demanded that the shows be banned. The city manager authorized a study to "set up community standards that, if violated, would pave the way to bar access." And the cable commission extended access hours; the next time *Hymns for Heathens* appeared, it was at 1 A.M. instead of 10:30 P.M.

Two channels on the city's cable system, and half the time on a third channel, are devoted to public access. Controversial topics are featured often but don't dominate the schedule. One of the access channels is filled entirely with religious programs. The Jaycees and the bar association produce shows for the access channels, which also provide city council coverage and such programs as *Access for Youth,* a series that preteens produce; *Stretch and Shine,* a daily bout of gentle exercise for older folks, and *Colorsounds,* a music-video series with superimposed lyrics to help teach reading.

Before last fall's controversy, the biggest uproar for Austin Community Television (ACTV), which manages the access channels under contract with the city, had occurred on Halloween 1982. An access program was interrupted with reports that a "slime monster" had come out of nearby Lake Travis and was killing everyone in its path. Nearly 200 calls poured into emergency switchboards. ACTV program director Paula Manley is still surprised that the report alarmed so many people. "The slime monster was wearing tennis shoes," she says, "I mean, come *on!*" To ACTV, the response was good news; it meant people were watching.

Hymns for Heathens and *Race and Reason* caused a different reaction last October, stirring talk that Austin should abandon its liberal access policy. But Austin was bound by its cable franchise, and ACTV maintained its policy toward people who submit programs. "Our position is that all the shows they turn in will be run eventually," says Manley. The only restriction is that producers must promise that their programs aren't libelous, obscene, or commercial in nature. According to ACTV policy, it must schedule a local resident's program, even if it was produced in another city, as were *Race and Reason* and another Klan talk show.

Mark G. Yudof, dean of the University of Texas Law School, led the criticism of access. "I think many of the access people have the legal question backward," he says. "It's not whether access is constitutionally required, rather it is whether it is unconstitutional for a city *to require* access programming." That requirement violates the cable operator's First Amendment rights as an electronic publisher, Yudof says. He believes the amendment doesn't require the government to give anyone a soapbox.

Yudof also objects to the cost of access, which all cable subscribers bear indirectly. Last year Austin's cable operator paid the city $450,000 to subsidize access, and most of that went to ACTV. In addition to its $380,000 budget—unusually large for an access center—the Austin access group has a $1 million equipment fund and a new studio in the works. (Yudof does admit that the money appears to have helped improve dramatically the quality of access programming.)

When City Manager Jorge Carrasco expressed interest in setting standards barring certain producers from the access channels, the Texas Civil Liberties Union fired off a letter in defense of access. "The fact is, there are legal standards," says executive director Gara LaMarche. "Nobody in this debate is arguing that the couple of programs in question are obscene, or even really indecent . . . But offensiveness is not a legitimate ground for restricting freedom of expression." That view seems to have penetrated city hall because Carrasco's study has been all but dropped. "I'm not sure when we'll get back to it," says an attorney for the city.

Other people in Austin are trying to keep the debate alive, arguing that some of the matters at stake are far more vital than strict observance of the First Amendment. Trella Loughlin, a college teacher and frequent producer for the access channels, wants the Ku Klux Klan programs off the cable. "I would not have put Hitler on in 1937, and I would not put the Klan on today." She notes that attacks on local blacks increased after recent Klan marches in Austin, and says that seeing the Klan march or appear on television brings out violence in nonmembers who make up a "closet Klan." She suspects Klan involvement in 10 unsolved murders in Texas.

Loughlin flatly refuses to discuss free speech in connection with the Klan. That is a "red herring" issue in her mind. "Some of that thinking is what made people end up in the gas chamber."

Loughlin hasn't had to picket ACTV's offices or wave signs in her campaign to get the Klan off cable because she can address the issue on her own regular access show. Others are doing the same. On a panel show that volunteers put together, Austinites of all colors related their experiences with racism. Appropriately enough, the debate over public access has continued in the electronic forum of public access.

*S*tudy *Q*uestions: *A*lderson

[?] *Why do many communities believe it is important to have public access channels on their cable systems? Why should it matter to a community and to our society whether we have such channels? Should the holders of cable franchises in every community be required to supply at least one access channel? If you think they should, how do you believe a community can justify forcing cable operators to use part of their resources in this way?*

If access channels are as good as Alderson suggests, why do many cable companies oppose having them?

What is "narrowcasting"? How does it differ from "broadcasting"?

What does Alderson mean by an "aesthetic of reality"? In analyzing television, or other media, is this a useful concept? Do you agree with Alderson that access shows define such an aesthetic? Why?

Jeremy Weir Alderson

EVERYMAN TV

On public access, people do and say whatever they like.
Why are efforts under way to kill it off?

How can anyone defend Public Access Television? Critics point out that "Access" (as it's called) has presented some of the worst conceived, worst produced programs in television's history, punctuated by sensational features like a transsexual's striptease, cock tattooing, and even a horrifying repeating loop of a puppy being shot to death. Nonetheless, Access has not only defenders but vigorous proponents who see in it vitality, honesty, variety, relevance, and television's brightest hope. At the root of these conflicting views is one central fact: Public Access Television is the world's only form of television in which no authority decides what can or cannot be televised. For better or worse, Access is the one place where people can televise almost anything they want.

Access arose from circumstances so prosaic that no one foresaw what they would produce. Those circumstances included the exasperating tendency of TV signals to bounce off Manhattan's skyscrapers, creating so many ghosts that the multiple images on many home screens could be cleaned up by no method short of exorcism. In 1965, two exorcists arrived in the guise of cable companies convinced that New York was ripe to become the first metropolis with cable television.

Because there were no appropriate precedents, the city moved cautiously, granting, at first, only temporary operating authority, so as to have time to study alternatives. The city felt it had the right to demand something from the cable companies in return for the city services and rights of way the companies would require. In 1970, after considering recommendations from almost every conceivable community source, the city and the cable companies settled on franchise contracts that included landmark provisions for Public Access.

In 1972, the FCC imposed modified Access requirements on all cable companies with 3,500 or more subscribers. Today, dozens of cable systems (no exact count is available) offer some form of Public Access. It flourishes in such diverse locations as San Diego, East Lansing, Michigan, and Ohio's Miami Valley, but in terms of the sheer quantity and variety of programming produced, New York City remains the leader.

Under New York's rules, transmission time on either of two Public

Jeremy Weir Alderson is a free-lance writer living in upstate New York.

Access channels (there are twenty-six cable channels in all) is available on a first-come-first-served basis for up to an hour per person per week. Regular time slots can be reserved, and there is no charge for use of the channels, but programs cannot carry advertising. On a third, so-called Leased Access channel, there is a nominal transmission fee (fifty dollars per hour per cable company), and commercial programs are permitted.

Though in some locales cable companies are required to provide production assistance, in New York they are required only to transmit, without interference, whatever programs the Access producers provide, either on tape or via live feed. There is just one exception to the noninterference rule: cable companies are not required to transmit material so obscene that they themselves might be prosecuted. Some producers fear the companies will use this loophole to get control of Public Access channels.

Access was a radical departure from the policy of previous eras in which no one had dreamed of demanding free public access to the printing press, telegraph, radio, or telephone. In theory, Access was to be a sort of televised Hyde Park in the center of the "Global Village," returning to the individual the opportunity to be heard that mass society had taken away. In practice, Access was greeted with more enthusiasm than anyone anticipated, as scores of would-be producers lined up to reserve time for their shows.

By 1974, the nonprofit Experimental Television Cooperative (ETC) had opened in a cramped lower-Manhattan loft. By relying on volunteers for labor, and by using undersized industrial or homemade equipment, ETC brought the cost of television production down to as little as twenty dollars per black-and-white half hour. Though the technical inferiority of ETC-produced programming often turns off network-nurtured viewers (without capital, Access producers can only lament that if God Himself were to appear on Access most people would pass Him by as a low-budget production), ETC's opening was a tremendous spur to Access's development in Manhattan, where most producers must pay production costs out of their own pockets.

Today, Manhattan's three Access channels present more than 300 programs each week, including almost as much original prime-time programming as the three networks combined. Most of these programs can't be seen beyond Manhattan, and, of course, many of them are awful, but, as one hardly need point out, many network programs are awful too.

Through Access, countless new writers, performers, and technicians have gained their first television experience. So many women, blacks, Hispanics, and members of other minorities have their own programs as to put network tokenism to shame. But Access is more than the sum of its opportunities or the "Vanity Video" for which it is sometimes mistaken. The viewing public, too, has benefited from Access. Despite its rampant amateurism, Access has redefined television's potential by creating new kinds of programming and a new television aesthetic.

"I think broadcasting is over," declares "Coca Crystal," whose popular program "If I Can't Dance You Can Keep Your Revolution" mixes drugs (she often smokes marijuana on camera), radical politics (no nukes, no draft, etc.), and black humor (e.g. an "ad" for "Sado-Maspirin"—increases your sensitivity to the lash), to form what she calls "an eighties version of an underground paper." "Making pabulum for the masses is finished," she continues with the characteristic fervor of an Access partisan. "I believe in *narrow*casting."

"Narrowcasting"—gearing programs to a limited target audience—is possible on Access because of its small expense, and because a program doesn't have to be popular, or even potentially popular, to be on Access. As a result, weekly programs are devoted to a seemingly endless list of topics seldom treated seriously by the networks, including astrology, consumerism, feminism, haute couture, salsa music, comic books, radio serials, gospel singing, sports handicapping, hypnotherapy, parapsychology, and even a little known theology called "Absolute Relativity."

Some of the better examples of New York's Access narrowcasts would be *Impact on Hunger,* which each week deals with a different facet of world malnutrition, including starvation in New York City itself; *The Irish Freedom Show,* which regularly presents such features as an interview with an Irish socialist giving his party's platform for peace in Northern Ireland; and *Towards Aquarius,* hosted by ghetto activist "Kanya," who addresses such topics as Harlem hospital closings, which he asserts are intended to drive blacks from the inner city to make way for white real estate development. Many Access advocates believe that programs like Kanya's, which tackle tough community issues, represent one of Access's greatest strengths.

Not all Access programs are narrowcasts. Many shows are intended for a mass audience and some of these, taking advantage of cable's less restrictive regulatory framework, present material that could never be broadcast. The best known examples of this genre are the sex shows, including: *Midnight Blue,* television's first "erotic variety show," whose executive producer is Al Goldstein of *Screw* magazine; *The Ugly George Hour of Truth, Sex, and Violence,* which consists in part of interviews with women whom George has lured off the street and talked into undressing on camera; and *Maria At Midnight,* hosted by stripper Maria Darvi, who hopes her Access exposure will one day land her a lucrative movie contract.

Not surprisingly, the sex shows have aroused a lot of censorious ire. At one point, Manhattan Cable Television threw *Midnight Blue* off its system for several weeks, and an outraged New York congressman played tapes of it for the House Communications subcommittee, demanding that this immorality be stopped. (At the moment, a fragile compromise has Access producers voluntarily sticking within the limits of an "R" rating.) But morality isn't the only issue. The Access sex shows are moving into a lucrative market that broadcasters can't directly enter. *Midnight Blue* is already being syndicated around the country, and Ugly George is seeking European distribution. Certainly the networks can have no enthusiasm for one day seeing Leased Access programs compete for audiences and advertising.

Even if one is not enthralled by the Access sex shows, one may see in them the price that must be paid for the salutary freedom that Access producers enjoy—a freedom that has been put to many non-pornographic uses. At a time when the networks still sought ways to "treat" the topic of homosexuality, Leased Access was regularly transmitting *Emerald City*, a well-crafted program which "started out to show anything gay," one producer said, and included scenes of men kissing, reviews of gay bathhouses, and anti-homophobia editorials. Though *Emerald City* caught on in New York and San Francisco, it died because it couldn't expand into enough markets to command the ad rates it needed to survive. Where Leased Access rights were not legally guaranteed, *Emerald City* could not secure a regular time slot.

Waste Meat News is another now-defunct program which benefited from Access's free environment. It consisted entirely of skits satirizing a "typical" day of network television. One continuing skit was a supposed weather report entitled "Leather Weather," in which a bound, reclining woman in a kinky leather costume was used as a weather map, getting doused with water where it rained, covered with shaving cream where it snowed, etc. Some other skits featured:

- A consumer report on a "Foreign Language Cursing Detector," a must item for traveling xenophobes afraid that a foreigner might curse them out without their knowledge;
- An advertisement for a self-improvement school teaching the quality most necessary for success: meanness;
- A David Susskindian interview with the latest group to come out of the closet demanding recognition and respect: people who have murdered their spouses;
- An adventure series, "Suicide Emergency Squad," in which three Charlie's Angelish women who (according to the intro) "really know how to stop a suicide and still turn on a TV audience" try to prevent a man from killing himself by eating a Burger King Whopper;
- A late-night movie, "Frightened At Sea," in which two World War Two submarine commanders track each other until they realize they're on the same ship;
- An "Incredible Hulk" type series entitled "Sewerman," about a child abandoned for safekeeping in Manhattan's sewers during the Cuban Missile Crisis, now grown up and prowling the city;

▪ An advertisement for a new phone company service, "Dial-A-Thrill," which offers callers pre-recorded messages appealing to every possible sexual appetite.

At least *Waste Meat News* came to a better end than *Emerald City*. Its creator, Ferris Butler, voluntarily withdrew it from circulation last fall when he was hired to write for the revamped *Saturday Night Live*. Butler is quick to credit Access for his success: "The freedom to discuss things, to write on a wide variety of subject matter, enabled me to open up my creativity and use my talents better, and as a result, that helped me to move on to something else."

Taken together, the Access shows define a new television aesthetic—an aesthetic of reality, as opposed to the network aesthetic of illusion. On Access, people appear more natural, talk more freely, and address more issues of real concern than on any form of television. To this may be added the spontaneity of the live transmissions preferred by many Access producers. Access is the true progenitor of programs like *Saturday Night Live* and *Real People,* but unlike the subjects of *Real People* the real people on Access don't need glib Hollywood types to introduce them and thus distance their own real lives from the real lives of their audience.

How many people are watching? Nobody knows for sure, because no rating service includes Access programs. There are, however, some interesting indications. A survey conducted in East Lansing showed that some people there subscribe to cable just to receive the Access programs. A Manhattan Cable Television survey profiled Access viewers as younger, better educated, and more upwardly mobile than average. Evidence that Access is finding a growing audience may be found in the rapidly overloading switchboards of some Access phone-in shows and the recognition that Access stars like Coca Crystal and Ugly George receive as they walk down the street.

Leonard Cohen, the coordinator of New York City's Office of Telecommunications, has dubbed the city's experiment with Access "an absolutely great success," but, despite its many achievements, the Access concept is in deep trouble. Cable companies, many of which are owned by giant conglomerates that also own pay-TV syndicates, were not happy when the FCC promulgated its Access requirements. They saw in Access the nuisance of dealing with dozens of local producers, and a large potential for pressure group complaints about controversial Access shows. Most importantly, they were reluctant to give up channels which, they hoped, would prove more lucrative carrying pay television services (often from their own parent companies) or free services (old movies, sports, news, etc.) that might be more effective than Access in attracting new subscribers.

In 1976, Midwest Video, a small cable company chain, sued the FCC to be freed from Public Access obligations. It won in the Supreme Court, which ruled that the FCC had exceeded its statutory authority in ordering Access, but the case had an unintended boomerang effect. Mike Botein, a New York Law School professor who fought on the losing side, says the decision "turned out to be one of the best things that ever happened to Access," because, after the Court ruled, local governments which had previously relied on the FCC started following New York's lead in insisting on Access as a franchise condition. As competition for cable franchises has heated up, local governments have frequently gotten more Access channels (and even Access studios) through negotiation than they would have under the FCC rules. Still, the battle is far from over.

For one thing, what's passing for Access in many places has little or nothing to do with the experiment started in New York. According to Sue Buske, the executive director of the National Federation of Local Cable Programmers (NFLCP), a pro-Access umbrella group, "The cable companies are trying to blur the distinction between Local Origination [cable company controlled] and Access by introducing the concept of 'Community Programming,' in which the topic is community oriented but is ultimately chosen and presented by the cable operator, not by the community." Access has also been subverted by the imposition of rules that make Access time difficult to obtain or subject to the discretion of the cable operator.

In their determination not to be forced into giving up channels, even for limited Access, the cable companies have taken their fight to Congress. Last summer, with the before-the-fact advice and after-the-fact support of two cable company organizations—The National Cable Television Association and the Community Antenna Television Association—Senators Hollings, Cannon, Packwood, Stevens, Goldwater, and Schmitt introduced a bill (S.2827) that would have forbidden any level of government to "require or prohibit any program origination by a telecommunications carrier . . . or obligations affecting the content or amount of such program originations."

The NFLCP, the National Citizens Committee for Broadcasting (currently chaired by Ralph Nader), the National League of Cities, and a host of other nonprofit organizations rushed to oppose S.2827, which was scheduled to come to a vote without a hearing. The bill's sponsors insisted that its provisions had been misread and that it had never been intended as an attempt to eliminate Access, but the bill's opponents simply did not believe that claim. Although S.2827 eventually stalled, many are still worried that the 97th Congress will produce its own brand of anti-Access legislation— a possibility that appears all the more likely in the light of Reagan's election and the conservative shift in Congress.

If Access survives, technological innovations may greatly expand its horizons. The increasing availability of satellite time would permit linked

Access channels across the country to form an alternative distribution network, and the continued development of interactive (two-way) television could make Access an ideal medium for electronic town meetings. (Promising experiments in both of these directions have already been made.) Ironically, Access's dreams won't be fulfilled until the viewing public wakes up to what it has been missing. If that doesn't happen soon, television's brightest hope may be buried in the wasteland.

Study Questions: Lewis

?   *Why has MTV been so important to the recording industry?*

What does Lewis mean by "female authorship"? By "woman-identified videos"? By reading videos "against the grain"? By making "music videos into a major site for the contestation of gender inequality"?

In what sense can a vocalist have "authorship" of a song even though she did not write it? What techniques does Lewis claim are used by performers to assert a female authorial voice in the male-dominated medium of music video?

Do you think Lewis' interpretation of the videos she analyzes is justified? Why or why not? Are there different ways to "read" these videos than the way Lewis does? How? What kinds of meanings can you obtain if you read them against the grain? If you read the Lewis article against the grain?

Do you think entertainment should be an arena for gender politics? Why or why not? What other uses of music videos to express an individual viewpoint or opinion have you observed?

Why does Lewis think music videos afford a musician greater range for performance than the concert stage does? Do you agree with her?

Do you see changes in music videos since Lewis wrote this paper? Does her description fit today's videos that feature female artists, or is something different going on now? Are different views of women and women's lives being communicated today by this medium?

Lisa A. Lewis

FORM AND FEMALE AUTHORSHIP IN MUSIC VIDEO

Form and female authorship combine textually in music video to negotiate gender inequalities. The use of the song as video soundtrack, and the musician as on-screen performer, are generic conventions that textually facilitate the activation of female musicians' voices. Creative interventions in song and video content by female musicians, themselves, contribute to the creation of female authorship. Thematic motifs, centering around a male adolescent discourse, are appropriated by female musician authors in the interest of directing an address to female spectators.

"**S**exist and violent against women." That's the reputation that MTV has acquired since its inception in 1981 as America's 24-hour music video channel.[1] What with parents buying lock boxes to prevent music video viewing, and senators' wives on the trail of pornographic rock lyrics,[2] it's small wonder that women critics have been reluctant to speak up in its defense. Austin, my adopted home, has a proud and progressive musical heritage traditionally supportive of female musicians, yet when the local magazine that covers the music scene asked writer Brenda Sommer if she'd like to do a regular column on music video, she turned it down. *The Austin Chronicle* printed her explanation (Sommer, 1985:9):

> You asked me to tell you why I couldn't review music videos for you. And I told you that I realized I couldn't because I didn't have anything nice to say about them.

It's true music video does bring together two cultural forms that have notorious histories as promulgators of female objectification—rock music and television imagery. And specific examples of women in chains, in caged boxes, and strewn across sets in skimpy leather outfits can certainly be called upon to justify such claims. But focusing on the sexist representations present in many male videos overshadows an aggregate of videos produced for songs sung by female musicians and their popularity with female fans. Several news magazines and television news broadcasts have featured stories on "rock's new women," acknowledging the fact that female rock musicians have never been so popular. *Ms.* (January 1985) magazine, the mouthpiece for liberal American feminism, has helped give musician Cyndi Lauper the feminist recognition she deserves by placing her on the cover as a "Woman of the Year." Still, music video's role in popularizing female musicians and in serving as the newest terrain for the negotiation of gender politics has been largely ignored, particularly by the academic press.[3]

"Girls Just Want To Have Fun," "Love Is A Battlefield," "She Works Hard for the Money," and "What's Love Got To Do With It?" are among the music videos that explicitly work toward overturning sexist representations of women, addressing a female audience as women through forceful references to female experience and desire. They are examples of what I call "woman-identified" videos after Adrienne Rich's (1983) characterization of "woman-identification" as "a source of energy, a potential spring-head of female power" (p. 199). It isn't necessary to read the videos "against the grain"[4] to recoup specific sequences in the name of the female spectator, or to ignore a narrative closure that "claws back"[5] to patriarchal relations—familiar recourses for feminist critics interested in retrieving a female voice from dominant media. Much of the feminist content in woman-identified videos is readily accessible, although its processing by the audience is indisputably complex.

Each of the videos contains images in which women are shown appropriating space that is culturally the privilege of men. Each one includes scenes prominently displaying female subjectivity and solidarity. And each makes symbolic references to modes of patriarchial power which oppress women. The on-screen women's roles in these videos are expansive, even omnipotent. The generic form itself structurally contributes to female musicians' control over the soundtrack and visual action. It is the forceful presence of the female musicians in these videos that presents a struggle to regain (if ever it were truly lost) woman's image on the screen for women, and makes music video into a major site for the contestation of gender inequality.

Crucial to the creation of woman-identified music videos are the agency of the female musician, the formal conventions of the music video genre, and ultimately the audience's interpretation. Exposure on MTV has and is contributing to an upsurge in female rock and roll musicianship. Female musicians are actively participating in making the music video form work in their interest, to assert their authority as producers of culture and to air their views on female genderhood. The generic emphasis in music video on using the song as a soundtrack, together with the centrality of the musician's image in the video, formally support the construction of female authorship. The result is a body of video texts that refer to an explicitly female experience of life, addressing a gendered spectatorship even as they maintain a generic consistency that secures their broad appeal.

First, consider the importance of MTV in providing female rock musicians the opportunity to gain the audience recognition and industry backing that women interested in music have historically been denied.[6] In the years leading up to the start of music video programming, female rock musicians were struggling for recognition both as vocalists (the traditional female niche), and as instrumentalists and composers. The contemporary women's movement in the late 1960s and early 1970s provided momentum for change, but the early punk movement in Britain at the end of the 1970s was equally, if not more, important to female musicians. Although punk emerged essentially as a working-class male subculture, Hebdige (1983) makes the point that punk included a minority of female participants who aggressively tried to carve out a specifically female form of expression, a sharp contrast to the usual subsuming of women by subcultural phallocentrism:

> Punk propelled girls onto the stage and once there, as musicians and singers, they systematically transgressed the codes governing female performance. . . . These performers have opened up a new space for women as active participators in the production of popular music (pp. 83–85).

Punk's advocacy of "defiant amateurism" (Swartley, 1982:28) undermined the devalued status of the amateur musician, granting women unprecedented access to musical information and audiences.

Under the capitalist economic system that operates rock and roll as a commercial enterprise, commercial distribution commands the largest audiences and the financial backing to produce music. Indeed the aspirations of most rock musicians, women included, lie with commercial distribution. But in 1979, just when new female musicians were preparing to break into the music scene, the U.S. recording industry went into a tailspin as the combined effects of a sluggish economy, home-taping, and the diversification of the home entertainment market began to be felt. Any individual or group without a proven track record, and this especially applied to women musicians, was hard pressed to win a record company contract, an essential step in the quest for a large audience. That began to change, however, in the summer of 1981 with the introduction of music video programming.[7]

Six weeks after MTV went on the air in selected test markets like Tulsa, Wichita, Peoria, Syracuse, Grand Rapids, and Houston, record sales rose for certain musical artists getting heavy play on the channel. Retailers in these areas received requests for music that was not even getting airplay on the radio in their communities. A Nielsen survey, commissioned in 1983 by MTV owner Warner-Amex, showed MTV to be influencing 63 percent of its viewers to buy certain albums. For every nine albums bought by MTV viewers, four purchases could be directly attributed to the viewing of the record company-produced music videos. Lee Epand, vice-president of Polygram Records, one of the companies originally reluctant to turn over free copies of music video tapes to MTV, finally admitted that the cable channel had proved to be "the most powerful selling tool we've ever had" (Levy, 1983:78).

MTV initiated an upward spiral for many new and unknown bands and vocalists, women musicians included. As album and singles sales began to rise to all time highs, in some cases even surpassing industry sales records, financing and promotion brought new female faces to MTV. A national audience rewarded its favorites by buying more records, thereby catapulting the new and unknowns to star status virtually overnight.

In 1982, the Go-Gos became the only all-female vocal and instrumental group ever to make the top 10. Their first album, *Beauty and the Beat,* was also the first album by an all-women rock band to hit number one on the charts. That same year, *Ms.* magazine ran an article entitled "At Last . . . Enough Women Rockers to Pick and Choose" (Brandt, 1982). Although many women gained recognition as instrumentalists, the real success story was in the musical category where women had traditionally excelled, that of vocalists. But seldom has success come so big and so fast as it did on MTV.

The 1985 winner of the top Grammy award, Tina Turner, was a woman without a record deal one year, and with a top hit single the next. Cyndi Lauper's debut album, *She's So Unusual,* remained in the top 30 for more than 60 weeks, having sold close to 4 million copies in the U.S. alone. Lauper's album produced four Top 5 hit singles, a new record for a female singer. In a February 1985 *Rolling Stone* Readers' Poll, Lauper was ranked first in the category for "New Artist," second to Tina Turner in the "Female Vocalist" category, and while a distant third to Bruce Springsteen and Prince as "Artist of the Year," she outranked Michael Jackson. Madonna, the newest female vocalist success story, sold 3.5 million copies of her album *Like a Virgin* in just 14 weeks. The album was "triple platinum" before its artist had even set foot on a touring stage, the principal promotion device before the age of music video. Female musicians such as Pat Benatar, Chaka Khan, and the Pointer Sisters have all reached a million in sales with recent albums.[8] . . .

The relations of production of the song tend to assign authorship to the vocalist, particularly the responsibility for the lyric content, despite the fact that the division of labor in the production of pop songs often means the vocalist has neither written the song nor its instrumentation. Expanding on this tendency for vocalists to be handed authorship on a platter, female musicians have employed several tactics to insure that their authorship takes a woman-identified form, to counter-balance the fact that they must often work with male writers' lyrics. Neither Tina Turner nor Cyndi Lauper, for example, wrote the songs that have made them famous, yet each has won female authorship through their vocalization style, their rewriting of selected lyrical phrases, and their manipulation of their images in the promotional press.

In constructing her authorship of the song "What's Love Got To Do With It?," Tina Turner concentrated on vocalization style. She self-consciously describes in the fan magazine *Record* how she made the award winning song her own by reworking its musical rendition:

> The song was this sweet, little thing. Can you imagine me singing like Diana Ross or Barbara Streisand, trying to sound velvety and smooth? I really fought. Eventually, we roughened it out instrumentally and I added some (rock) phrasing, and we changed the song's attitude and got a hit. I have input, not just in song selection but in treatment too. I'll never be a musician, but I know what's right (Mehler, 1984:20).

Turner's self-deprecating assessment of herself as a non-musician at the end of the statement is in line with what Rieger (1985) suggests is a historically-constructed myth that positions performance outside of creative practice. The false distinction between performance and composition as it relates to creative contributions is in effect responsible for the disproportionately high number of female vocalists compared to female lyricists and composers: "Women have always only been allowed a first foothold in those areas where creativity was considered to be of secondary importance" (p. 136). In fact, the example provided by Turner reveals musical rendition to be not only a creative process but a politically empowered one.

A promotional blitz, timed to coincide with the release of Turner's album, *Private Dancer* (on which "What's Love Got To Do With It?" appears), publicized the previously hidden details of her years as a battered wife and personal slave to her ex-music partner and husband, Ike Turner. The biographical information functions to turn the lyrics of her songs into autobiographical statements. Stanzas of "What's Love Got To Do With It?" may not have been written by Turner, but her authorial voice is created as a consequence of the fan's attempt to reconcile the text with the extratextual information about the singer's personal history:

> It may seem to you,
> that I'm acting confused
> when you're close to me.
> If I tend to look dazed,
> I read it someplace,
> I've got cause to be.[9]

Quotes by Turner in the press saying things such as "I've never sung anything I couldn't relate to" (Mehler, 1984:21) lend credibility to autobiographical readings of the songs she sings. In fact, Turner's appeal to women seems largely based on the notion of experience. Her ability to survive and come out on top after many years of male harassment and lack of professional recognition makes her a fitting female hero. Her courageous image is only underscored for women by the rumble of reactionary male attraction to counter-statements by Ike Turner such as the feature article in the new music magazine, *Spin* entitled "Ike's Story": "Yeah, I hit her, but I didn't hit her more than the average guy beats his wife" (Kiersh, 1985:41).

The appearance of Cyndi Lauper's mother in the video, "Girls Just Want to Have Fun," works to turn song lyrics that specifically address a maternal figure into a reference to the singer's own life experience in much the same way that autobiographical notes in the press serve Tina Turner's association with the songs she sings. Lauper also picked the authorship strategy of selectively rewriting lyrics to make the song "Girls Just Want to Have Fun" better match the woman-identified image she was constructing. Songwriter Robert Hazard's first version of the song is fashioned as an inflated male fantasy of female desire:

> My father says, 'My son,
> what do they want from your life?'
> I say, 'Father, dear, we are the
> fortunate ones.
> Girls just want to have fun.'

But Lauper's alteration of the song's lyric text, as suggested by producer Rick Shertoff, results in a custom-made vehicle for the expression of her views on female inequality:

> My mother says, 'When you gonna
> live your life right?'
> 'Oh, Mother, dear, we're not the
> fortunate ones.
> And girls just want to have fun.'

It is the conventional usage of the song as soundtrack in music video that formally extends female musician authorship to the video text. In videos that feature a narrative scenario, the soundtrack provided by a female vocalist can operate like a narrator's omnipotent voiceover guiding the visual action. Sometimes she manages to literally put words in the mouths of other characters (sometimes male) through the use of a common music video device whereby a selected lyrical phrase is lip-synched as if it were dialogue. In "Girls Just Want To Have Fun," the burly ex-wrestler Lou Albano, as Cyndi Lauper's father, lip-synchs Cyndi's lyric, "What you gonna do with your life?" as she is shown pinning his arm behind his back in a self-reflexive wrestling manuever. The technique in this scene, by replacing the father's scolding voice with the daughter's, parodies and undermines the authority of the father, and by symbolic extension, patriarchy itself.

In terms of the videos' conventional visual representation, the generically-mandated appearance of the musician becomes another structure operative in the authorship construction process. Musicians actually appear in one of two roles in music video. Usually they are formally distinct, but sometimes they are so convergent that separation becomes difficult: (1) the role of musician, and (2) the role of actor in the video's narrative scenario, a role that is realized through the interaction of the musician in performance contexts and the musician as protagonist within the narrative line constructed by the video.

"Girls Just Want To Have Fun" and "Love Is A Battlefield," for instance, both maintain the musician in the role of protagonist in narratives that remain intact, undisrupted by the intercutting of performance footage. "She Works Hard for the Money," on the other hand, features Donna Summer primarily in performance shots that periodically interrupt a narrative which unconventionally uses an unknown actor instead of the musician in its central role. The lines between the two categories blur in "What's Love Got To Do With It?" The video presents itself essentially as a performance video in which city streets appear as backdrop for Turner as musician: yet as the video unfolds, her interactions in 'mini-dramas' with the various street characters she encounters create an impression of her as a character.

Vocalists are privileged actors in the videos because they play lead roles and lip-synch most of the lyrics. Feminist critics, in their desire for female musician parity with male musicians in the broad spectrum of divisions of labor in music, have sometimes pointed to and criticized the assignment of female musicians to the category of vocalist. In music video, however, the prerogative rests most squarely on the shoulders of the vocalist, making female musicians' traditional role into an asset.

The visual appearance of the musician in the video affords a greater range for performance than that offered on the concert stage. Eye contact and facial gestures available to only a few concert-goers are equally accessible to all video viewers. Role-playing, limited to costuming changes and the use of props on the stage, can be intricately elaborated in music video through location shooting, the use of sets, and interactions with other actors. In other words, the full gamut of devices available to television productions is opened up to musicians in music video.

Many female musicians have proved to be quite adept at manipulating elements of visual performance in their video act, thereby utilizing music video as an additional authorship tool. In "What's Love Got To Do With It?," the gestures, eye contact with the camera and with other characters, and the walking style of Tina Turner add up to a powerful and aggressive on-screen presence. Her miniskirt, show of leg, and spike heels could operate to code her as a spectacle of male desire. Instead, the image she projects struggles for a different signification. It's easier to imagine the spikes as an offensive weapon than as a sexual lure or allusion to her vulnerability. Turner's control over her own body and interactions with others in the video, particularly with men, encourages a revaluation of her revealing clothes and high heels from indices of her objectification to signs of her own pleasure in herself.[10] Similarly, in "Girls Just Want To Have Fun," Cyndi Lauper's kinetic body movement mediates against the voyeur's gaze. Almost constantly in motion, Lauper's choreographed performance fills the frame, her gyrating arms and legs stealing space away from men on city streets in location footage. . . .

Music video reproduces adolescence as a male-defined discourse through its use of characteristic themes and symbolic representations. The city street is a central symbol of freedom from parental authority which allows young viewers to participate vicariously in an independent, public existence outside the limitations that school and home life impose on middle-class youth. The endless array of images of video characters loitering on sidewalks, strolling the avenues, dancing in the street, and traveling in cars also celebrates the specifically male youth attachment to the street as a site of sociability and escape, of subcultural formation and male bonding. At the same time, the images valorize leisure activity, the socially-extended right of middle-class adolescents and the socially-induced fate of lower-class and minority teenagers. It is in leisure activity that adolescent boys carve out their own domain in the world. As McRobbie (1980) suggests, it represents a privileged "space" for the "sowing of wild oats" and for experimentation with roles and dangers before a lifetime of work.

But herein lies the problem for adolescent girls, for they are subject not only to expectations based on their age, but overwhelmingly by those assigned to their gender. The female gender experiences streets as dangerous and fearful places. What Reiter (1975) described as a "sexual geography" in her study of male and female use of public space in southern France applies to the United States as well. Women are expected to use streets as the route between two interior spaces, be they places of employment or consumption activity. The social consequence of street loitering or strolling is the label "prostitute" and the coding of one's body as available for male pursuit. Women's level of comfort on city streets is tenuous at best; rape and harassment are constant threats structuring their behavior. Girls learn early the gestures of deference: to avoid making eye contact, to cause one's body to "shrink" so as to take up as little space as possible.

Leisure time and leisure practices are also subject to a division along gender lines. Middle- and lower-class girls in the United States grow up in a culture in which women's work in the home is a constant, yet devalued, activity and where work outside the home is still underpaid and limited in form. In the many instances where women work outside the home, domestic laboring becomes an even more relentless form of double duty. As teenagers, girls encounter the expectation that they will assume the role of invisible worker at home, even when they are encouraged to seek a higher education and a career. Leisure practices engaged in by boys are, as well, often deemed inappropriate for girls. Subcultural youth groupings, often allied in part by their musical preferences, are usually off limits to girls. McRobbie (1980) confirms this point in "Settling Accounts with Subcultures," saying that subcultural use of the street as a primary site of activity tends to preclude female participation (p. 120). Girls' leisure takes different forms as a consequence, or perhaps more aptly stated as a result, of female resourcefulness and the will to resist subordination.[11]

In music video, representations of leisure make up the symbolic arena where gender battle lines are drawn. Woman-identified videos rely heavily on images that signal both the appropriation of male leisure forms and practices, and the celebration of specifically female ones. In this way, motifs based on street symbolism and leisure themes can become powerful social commentaries for female audiences. This is the context in which feminists have made the refrain of "Girls Just Want to Have Fun" into a slogan. The song gets its hard edge from the audiences' reading of the music video's image content and the quality of Cyndi Lauper's look and performance.

Shots of a mother (played by Lauper's own mother) at her morning duties in the kitchen contrast with the Lauper character's role as her adolescent daughter who comes bounding into the kitchen after a wild night out. The mother, to express her distress over the daughter's disregard of appropriate feminine behavior, breaks an egg over her heart. A montage sequence of the daughter chattering on the phone with her many girlfriends celebrates a girl leisure practice which is usually ridiculed in the public media. The bouncing Lauper then leads her band of girlfriends through New York City streets in a frenzied snake dance, a carnivalesque display that turns women's experience of the street upsidedown. Their arms reaching out for more and more space, the women push through a group of male construction workers who function as symbols of female harassment on the street. The image of men cowering in the wake of the women's dance epitomizes female fantasies of streets without danger or fear, and women's desire for an unmitigated release from socially-imposed restrictions on female bodily expression. The men, their threatening status overturned, are brought back to the daughter's home to experience female fun: dancing with wild abandon in one's bedroom. . . .

The multiplicity of authorship opportunities for female musicians and the strong woman-identified statements that MTV and the music video genre have made possible should by now be apparent. This is no small accomplishment in a mass medium largely closed to personal expressions from a female perspective and to portrayals of female fantasies of the overthrow of male domination and the forming of alliances among women, and where creative control over production by women is severely limited. Far from being the absolute bastion of male desire, as some critics argue, MTV is providing a unique space for the articulation of gender politics by female artists and audiences.

NOTES

[1]MTV is an advertiser-supported cable television channel dedicated to the programming of record company-produced music video clips for a target audience aged 12 to 34. It premiered on August 1, 1981. Its owner/operator is the Warner Amex Satellite Entertainment Company, a joint venture between Warner Communications and American Express. In 1985, MTV was sold to Viacom, a television syndication company. Examples of popular criticism that describe music video as sexist and violent include Levy (1983) and Barol (1985).

[2]The co-founders of the Parents Music Resource Center, organized in protest of "pornographic" rock music lyrics, includes Susan Baker, wife of Treasury Secretary James Baker; Tipper Gore, wife of Senator Albert Gore (D-Tenn.); and Ethelynn Stuckey, wife of Williamson Stuckey, a former representative from Florida. Hoping eventually to see the enactment of a system for rating records similar to the one used for rating movies, the Center won a lesser concession in August 1985 when 19 top record companies agreed to start printing warnings of sexually explicit lyrics on album and music video packaging. Although male musicians, such as Prince and Twisted Sister, are most under fire, Cyndi Lauper's song "She Bop" has been targeted because of its reference to female autoeroticism. For more information see *Broadcasting* (July 15, 1985).

[3]Frith and McRobbie (1978/79) provide an early exploration of gender and rock music. McRobbie's work on girl subcultures (1976, 1980) and dance (1984) is pertinent to the analysis of music video and female audiences although it has not been used as such. Steward and Garratt (1984) trace the history of female musician involvement in rock and roll and provocatively suggest ways that pop's success depends on female fan support. Brown and Campbell (1984) focus on gender in their content analysis of music video, but without attention to female musicians or woman-identified videos. Holdstein (1985) provides a textual reading of Donna Summer's "She Works Hard for the Money," arguing against a feminist interpretation. Kaplan has explored female representation in music video in several papers (1985a, 1985b, 1985c, and 1985d).

[4]Here the notion of "reading against the grain" refers to the interpretive practice of reading "through" a dominant male discourse to locate a subtextual female one. The practice is linked historically to theoretical debate within feminist film criticism. By challenging the concentration of Mulvey (1975) and others on film as the domain of voyeuristic male pleasure, the practice of "reading against the grain" raises issues related to the complexity of the interpretive process and to female pleasure in film texts. Still, as the practice involves conceptualization, it assumes that the female voice in a text exists as a secondary and embedded texture or quality. I am arguing against the appropriateness of this model for the analysis of woman-identified music videos although my concern with female

reception is consistent with this approach. See Gaines (1985) for a survey and critique of theories pertaining to female representation on the screen, and de Lauretis (1984) for a discussion of modes of analysis that foreground female pleasure.

[5]"Claw back" is a term used by Fiske and Hartley (1978) to describe the way television functions to maintain a socio-central position, thereby mediating against ideologically aberrant readings by audiences.

[6]Rieger (1985) dates the institutional exclusion of women from musical composition and performance back to the beginning of these institutions themselves. Churches in the middle ages made it an official practice to bar females from participation in liturgical rites, effectively creating a gender boundary to "high music" culture. Early educational institutions reserved musical training and opportunities primarily for their male students. Women's music-making was forced into popular culture forms, and, with respect to the formation of the bourgeoisie in the 18th century, into domestic space. Female piano playing and singing were designed as appropriate forms of musical expression for women and incorporated into the bourgeois woman's role in the family: "It was important to a man's prestige that his wife could entertain his guests with music, and of course a musical education for his daughter served as a good investment for an advantageous marriage" (p. 141). Music performed by women was conceived as a service provided for fathers, husbands, and children, not as a source of pleasure for themselves, or as a career direction, a means for making money. Prior to the influx of women, men were accustomed to performing music in the home. But as music in a domestic setting became associated with bourgeois female roles, men responded by establishing professional standards and devaluing the amateur status. The legacy of too little institutional support and the ideological attitude toward the suitability of musical expression for women form the basis for male-dominated musical forms today, including rock and roll.

[7]The following sources enabled me to trace the decline of the record industry and to feel justified in crediting the start of music video cable distribution with its subsequent turnaround: Henke (1982), Hickling (1981), Kirkeby (1980), Loder and Pond (1982), Pond (1982), Sutherland (1980), and Wallace (1980).

[8]Information about sales and rankings of female musicians were constructed from the following sources: Brandt (1982), Loder (1984), Miller, et al. (1985), *Rolling Stone* (Feb. 28, 1985), and Swartley (1982).

[9]These are selected lyrics from "What's Love Got To Do With It?" Written by Terry Britten and G. Lyle, the song was recorded under the Capitol Records label. Copyright © 1984 by Myaxe Music Ltd. & Good Single Music Ltd. Myaxe Music Ltd. published in U.S.A. by Chappell & Co., Inc. International Copyright Secured. All rights reserved. Used by permission.

[10]The term "revaluation" is borrowed from the work of anthropologist Marshall Sahlins (1981). In this regard, I have also found useful the discussions of "active" signs in Volosinov (1973) and de Lauretis (1984). Another example of Tina Turner's attempt to revalue signs that have acquired an association with male desire is her adoption of the song "Legs," popularized by a ZZ Top video, for her concert stage act.

[11]See Brake (1980) and McRobbie (1976) for reviews of literature pertaining to subcultures and feminist critiques of this literature; see Criffin (1985) for a discussion of leisure as it relates specifically to girls.

REFERENCES

Barol, Bill. "Women in a Video Cage." *Newsweek*, 4 March 1985, p. 54.

Berland, Judy. "Sound, Image and the Media: Rock Video and Social Reconstruction." *Parachute*, December 1985, forthcoming.

Brake, Mike. "The Invisible Girl: The Culture of Femininity Versus Masculinism." In *The Sociology of Youth Culture and Youth Subcultures*. London: Routledge & Kegan Paul, 1980.

Brandt, Pam. "At Last . . . Enough Women Rockers to Pick and Choose." *Ms.*, September 1982, pp. 110–116.

Broadcasting. "The Women Behind the Movement." 15 July 1985.

Brown, Jane D. and Kenneth C. Campbell. "The Same Beat but a Different Drummer: Race and Gender in Music Videos." Paper presented at the University Film and Video Association Conference, Harrisburg, VA, January 1984.

Cretcher, Jeff. "Hard Up Was Hard to Do: The Production of a Rock Video." *American Cinematographer*, September 1983, pp. 56–59, 108–113.

Cubitt, Sean. "Box Pop." *Screen* 26 (1985):84–86.

de Lauretis, Teresa. *Alice Doesn't: Feminism, Semiotics, and Cinema*. Bloomington: Indiana University Press, 1984.

Dyer, Richard. *Stars*. London: British Film Institute, 1979.

Fiske, John and John Hartley, *Reading Television*. London and New York: Methuen, 1978.

Frith, Simon. *Sound Effects; Youth, Leisure, and the Politics of Rock 'n' Roll*. New York: Pantheon Books, 1981.

Frith and Angela McRobbie. "Rock and Sexuality." *Screen Education* 29 (1978/1979):3–19.

Gaines, Jane. "Women and Representation." *Jump Cut* 29:25–26.

Griffin, Christine. "Leisure: Deffing Out and Having a Laugh." in *Typical Girls? Young Women from School to the Job Market*. London: Routledge & Kegan Paul, 1985.

Hebdige, Dick. "Posing Threats, Striking Poses: Youth, Surveillance, and Display." *Substance* 37/38:68–88.

Henke, James. "1981: Another Bad Year for the Record Industry." *Rolling Stone*, 4 March 1981, p. 51.

Henley, Nancy. *Body Politics*. Englewood Cliffs, NJ: Prentice Hall, 1977.

Hickling, Mark. "Record Sales Hold Steady with Last Year's." *Rolling Stone*, 15 October 1985, p. 52.

Huswitt, Mark. "Rocker Boy Blues." *Screen* 25(1984):89-98.

Kaplan, E. Ann. "A Postmodern Play of the Signifier? Advertising, Pastiche and Schizophrenia in Music Television." In *Proceedings of the International Television Conference*, edited by Richard Collins, et al. London: British Film Institute, 1985.

Kaplan, E. Ann. "History, the Historical Spectator and Gender Address in Music Television." Paper presented at the Yale Conference on History and Spectatorship, March 1985.

Kaplan, E. Ann. "The Representation of Women in Rock Videos." Paper presented at Lafayette College, April 1985.

Kaplan, E. Ann. "Sexual Difference, Visual Pleasure and the Construction of the Spectator in Rock Videos on MTV." Paper presented at the Conference on Sexual Difference, Southampton University, July 1985.

Katz, Cynthia. "The Video Music Mix." *Videography*, May 1982, pp. 28–35.

Kiersh, Edward. "Ike's Story." *Spin*, August 1985, pp. 39–43, 71.

Kinder, Marsha. "Music Video and the Spectator: Television, Ideology and Dream." *Film Quarterly*, no. 38 (1984), pp. 2–15.

Kirkeby, Marc. "The Pleasures of Home Taping." *Rolling Stone*, October 1980, pp. 2, 62–64.

Laing, Dave. "Music Video: Industrial Product, Cultural Form." *Screen* 26 (1985):78-83.

Levy, Steven. "Ad nauseam: How MTV Sells Out Rock and Roll." *Rolling Stone*, 8 December 1984, pp. 30–37, 74–79.

Loder, Kurt. "Sole Survivor." *Rolling Stone*, 11 October 1984, pp. 19–20, 57–60.

Loder, Kurt and Steve Pond. "Record Industry Nervous as Sales Drop Fifty Percent." *Rolling Stone*, 30 September 1982, pp. 69, 78–79.

Marchetti, Gina. "Documenting Punk: A Subcultural Investigation." *Film Reader* 5 (1982):269-84.

McRobbie, Angela. "Girls and Subculture." In *Resistance Through Rituals: Youth Subcultures in Post War Britain*, edited by Stuart Hall and Tony Jefferson, London: Hutchinson, 1976.

McRobbie, Angela. "Settling Accounts with Subcultures: A Feminist Critique." *Screen Education* 34 (1980):37-49.

McRobbie, Angela. "Dance and Social Fantasy." In *Gender and Generation*, edited by Angela McRobbie and Mica Nava. London: Macmillan Publishers, 1984.

Mehler, Mark. "Tina Turner's Still Shaking that Thing." *Record*, December 1984, pp. 17–21.

Miller, Jim et al. "Rock's New Women." *Newsweek*, 4 March 1985, pp. 48–57.

Mulvey, Laura. "Visual Pleasure and Narrative Cinema," *Screen* 16 (1975):6-18.

Pond, Steve. "Record Rental Stores Booming in U.S." *Rolling Stone*, 2 September 1982, pp. 37, 42–43.

Reiter, Rayna R. "Men and Women in the South of France: Public and Private Domains." In *Toward an Anthropology of Women*, edited by Rayna Reiter. New York: Monthly Review Press, 1975.

Rich, Adriene. "Compulsory Heterosexuality." In *Powers of Desire*, edited by Ann Snitow, et al. New York: Monthly Review Press, 1983.

Rieger, Eva. "'Dolce Semplice'? On the Changing Role of Women in Music." In *Feminist Aesthetics*, edited by Gisela Ecker. London: The Women's Press, Ltd. 1985.

Rolling Stone. "The Winners: Readers' Poll/Critics' Poll." 28 February 1985, pp. 26–27.

Sahlins, Marshall. *Historical Metaphors and Mythical Realities*. Ann Arbor: University of Michigan Press, 1981.

Sommer, Brenda. "At Home with Video." *Austin Chronicle*, 22 February 1985, p. 9.

Stern Bert. "Let the Mascara Run." *Vanity Fair*, August 1985, p. 71.

Steward, Sue and Sheryl Garratt. *Signed, Sealed, and Delivered: True Life Stories of Women in Pop.* London: Pluto Press, 1984.

Sutherland, Sam. "Record Business: The End of an Era." *Hi Fidelity,* 1980, p. 96.

Swartley, Ariel. "Girls! Live! On Stage!" *Mother Jones,* June 1982, pp. 25–31.

Volosinov, V. N. *Marxism and the Philosophy of Language.* New York: Seminar Press, 1973.

Wallace, Robert. "Crisis? What Crisis?" *Rolling Stone,* 29 May 1980, pp. 17, 28, 30–31.

Worrel, Denise. "Now: Madonna on Madonna." *Time,* 27 May 1985, pp. 78–33.

VIDEO CREDITS

Pat Benatar, "Love Is a Battlefield," (Chrysalis Records: Mary Ensign, producer; Bob Giraldi, Director, 1984).

Cyndi Lauper, "Girls Just Want to Have Fun," (Epic Records: Ken Walz, producer; Ed Griles, director, 1983).

Donna Summer, "She Works Hard for the Money," (Polygram Records: Chryssie Smith, producer; Brian Grant, director, 1983).

Tina Turner, "What's Love Got to Do with It?" (Capitol Records: John Caldwell, producer, Mark Robinson, director, 1984).

Special thanks to Jane Marcus, Horace Newcomb, and Robert Sabal for their editorial contributions and to John Fiske for encouragement.

MEDIA AS ECONOMIC AGENTS

As discussed in various articles in Sections 1–3, media form and content are determined by such forces as cultural norms, political agendas, and people's need to receive and to communicate information and ideas. However, media form and content also are shaped by economic forces, particularly by means of support such as sales of newspapers, magazines, books, movie tickets, and advertising. It is impossible to understand the mass media adequately without understanding them as economic agents. The relationship between economic forces and content is the general topic of the articles presented in this section. In a variety of ways, the authors talk about constraints that operate in the media marketplace. They take different stances toward the effects of economic constraints on the information offered to audiences, as well as on creative people and the works they produce. In effect, the authors also debate whether we are headed for the production of more and more information or simply for increased repetition of a smaller and smaller pool of ideas.

We begin with the regulatory environment for information production and distribution. Two communications attorneys (one a former Federal Communications Commission chair and the other a former FCC commissioner) argue that the public benefits from a relatively unregulated media marketplace. Richard E. Wiley and Richard M. Neustadt identify a raft of public policy issues raised by developments in communications technology. The authors, nonetheless, advocate reducing government restraints on communications industries to ensure a future brightened by the availability of more, and more diverse, information. Developments in communications and in the regulation of communications industries are occurring so rapidly that changes have taken place since Wiley and Neustadt wrote. To cite just one example, the authors mention a change in attitude on the number of AM radio, FM radio, and television licenses a single owner may control. They had barely committed those words to paper when the FCC increased the number of each from seven to twelve. Although many such changes have occurred, the basic issues about regulation that Wiley and Neustadt discuss remain as valid and important as ever.

Nicholas Johnson, also a former FCC commissioner, views media regulation very differently from Wiley and Neustadt. His essay focuses on the cable television industry. Johnson maintains that cable television is anything but a free marketplace and that cable companies have too much control over the content of what goes out to homes. He argues that satellite and cable distributors should be regulated as common carriers, that—like the telephone company—have no say about the content of messages they carry.

Ben H. Bagdikian shifts the focus to the effects of increased consolidation of media ownership in ever larger conglomerates. He urges government regulators to recognize that control of mass media amounts to control of the American public's attention. "Serious social consequences," such as the homogenization of information and popular culture, are results of the increasingly monopolistic market that Bagdikian observes.

The essays by George G. Kirstein and the National Association of Broadcasters turn our attention to the locomotive of American media, advertising. They draw two contrasting scenarios for a time when advertising is abolished. Kirstein describes a glorious day brought about by a successful campaign by women to ban advertising of all kinds. The second essay shows us a doomsday—mass layoffs of information workers, retail clerks, manufacturers, and freight workers that lead to economic collapse. In the second view, advertising is the keystone of American capitalism, without which our entire society would fall to pieces.

Frank Packard examines the business of publishing. He describes the disappearance or transformation of small, independent publishing houses into big, corporate businesses. The section concludes with Richard A. Peterson's case study of the economics of the music recording business. His essay explores the relationship between the radio and music industries, as well as economic influences on what music gets produced and on what music ultimately gets heard by the popular music audience.

The essays in this section demonstrate that media business is big business and, as such, reflects overall trends in the economic scene. One of the important questions raised by the debate over economic and regulatory issues centers on the homogenization of American mediated culture—a trend which seems inexorable. The creation of entertainment requires creative people. Glamour industries that they are, the media have enormous resources to attract the most creative talent available. Then, to maintain their positions in the marketplace, those same industries must make certain that nobody gets *too* creative. Abundant resources and talent also assure that the big media's production values are the standard by which we judge all productions and performances. We become less appreciative—less tolerant—of technically primitive independent work and the amateurism of small-market media and public access. The questions you should keep in the back of your mind as you read this section spring from Lidz of Section 2: *Are the authors of Section 4 illustrating the influence of middle-class tastes and morality on the popular culture marketplace? If so, why don't you feel more powerful?*

Study Questions: Wiley and Neustadt

? │ *Wiley and Neustadt discuss two kinds of regulatory (or deregulatory) policy: policy that is designed to increase competition and policy that is designed to eliminate government control of industry. Which of those policies do they think is preferable? Why? Which do you think is preferable? Why?*

As the authors point out, "quality programs require talent and money." Does the move toward breaking the audience for individual programs into smaller and smaller segments increase or decrease the talent and money available for individual programs? What are the implications of this trend?

What do you think of the idea of awarding licenses for new radio and television stations by lottery instead of holding hearings to try to determine which applicants would provide the best service to listeners and viewers? What are the advantages and disadvantages of each system?

What are the major issues that face Congress and the FCC, according to the authors? Among these, which one do you believe is most important?

Of all of the technological developments that Wiley and Neustadt mention, which one do you believe can bring the greatest benefits to our society? Why? Which one do you believe poses the greatest dangers to society? Why?

Richard E. Wiley and Richard M. Neustadt

U.S. COMMUNICATIONS POLICY IN THE NEW DECADE

Policy leaders for two administrations review the prospects for the 1980s.

In the fall of 1981, the Federal Communications Commission (FCC) asked Congress to repeal the keystones of government control over broadcasting content: the Equal Time Rule and the Fairness Doctrine. At the same time, the Commission reaffirmed a decision to let AT&T enter important new markets without FCC regulation. These attempts at self-denial are more than antiregulatory spasms from a conservative administration. They represent a fundamental shift in U.S. communications policy.

Richard E. Wiley and Richard M. Neustadt practice communications law in the Washington office of Kirkland & Ellis. Wiley served as chairman of the Federal Communications Commission during the Nixon and Ford administrations. Neustadt was the White House communications policy advisor during the Carter administration.

Deregulation has been the theme song in this field for a decade, but the tune has changed. During the 1970s, deregulation meant promoting competition. The goal was to eliminate the federal rules that limited entry into the communications business. This policy was controversial—the "ins" fought hard to keep the "outs" out—but it gradually prevailed. The FCC dismantled the barriers, and entrepreneurs and engineers rushed in with a myriad of new communications services.

Now the focus is shifting. Deregulation now entails an assault on all kinds of regulations—including those that have constrained the "ins." New battles over whether to continue regulation of broadcasting content, AT&T's rates, cable TV services, and other such issues will dominate communications headlines for the next few years.

After years of unchallenged domination, the three broadcasting networks and AT&T encountered an army of competitors over the past 10 years. Technological advances and private initiative deserve a lion's share of the credit for this development. But dramatic changes in public policy, reshaping the FCC's basic approach to the mass media and common carrier industries, also played an important role.

When the dust settles, deregulation will have taken a deep bite out of traditional communications law. Communications policymakers will still have busy days, however. Ironically, the FCC probably will be immersed in the very work that motivated its creation nearly 50 years ago: managing a seemingly unquenchable demand for radio frequencies. In addition, a new policy agenda is emerging which will pose novel challenges for the decades ahead.

The 1970s Were a Decade of Diversity in the Media Field, as Competition Surged in Five Areas: UHF Television, Radio, Cable Television, Pay Television, and Videocassettes and Discs.

UHF   Once the hard-to-receive stepchild of television, this service finally is coming into its own. Congress forced manufacturers to build TV sets that receive UHF, and the FCC mandated "click" tuning and improved reception. Specialized programming—pay, religious, public, and other—helped build audiences. Currently, about 400 UHF stations are on the air, with more to come. The growth of UHF helped boost the total of TV stations to over 1,000—more than double the number in 1960.

Radio   Some analysts once thought television would kill radio, but the U.S. now has over 9,000 stations, also double the 1960 number. Most of the increase is in FM; improved radios, better programming, and the creation of FM stereo have made FM fully competitive with AM.

Cable Television   In the past seven years, the courts and the FCC have removed most of the regulations that had stifled cable growth. Other Commission actions opened the skies to the satellites that have made cable networks possible. Cable now reaches almost 30 percent of households, and is growing rapidly. Most new cable systems have over 30 channels, and the competition for franchises is so fierce that a number of applicants have proposed systems with as many as 200 channels.

Pay Television   The FCC is completing a decade-long process of lifting its restrictions on pay TV. Half a dozen pay networks distribute movies or sports events without advertisements, and more will be operating soon. A large proportion of cable subscribers now receive at least one pay channel, and another 1.5 million subscribe to pay services delivered over the air by UHF stations (STV) or the microwave Multipoint Distribution Service (MDS).

Videocassettes and Discs   Over one million videocassette and videodisc players are now in use, and sales of the devices are accelerating. The technology involved—which developed without government intervention—gives the viewer freedom from the constraints of fixed programming schedules.

This proliferation of outlets is yielding an explosion of programming choices for U.S. audiences. In addition to the three major networks, broadcasters across the country transmit public radio and television, an Hispanic network, and several religious networks. Cable subscribers can receive a host of additional services, including a children's service; several news, sports, and cultural networks; a health channel; a weather channel; and live coverage of the House of Representatives. All these channels are providing the economic base for "narrowcasting"—i.e., programming aimed at particular groups of viewers instead of the lowest common denominator.

This abundance has not lead to a utopia. Quality programs require talent and money no matter how many channels are available. However, the new diversity is giving people the services they want, as demonstrated by cable's explosive growth. And just as radio survived television, the new competition seems to be supplementing, rather than jeopardizing, basic local and network broadcasting service; most stations continue to show healthy profits.

Meanwhile, Technological Advances and Deregulation are Creating Even More Media Options for U.S. Audiences.

Direct Satellite-to-home Broadcasting (DBS)   The FCC has launched a proceeding to authorize television broadcasting from satellites to small earth stations on roofs and in backyards. DBS may provide more than 20 channels of advertiser-supported and pay TV.

Radio Expansion   The 1979 World Administration Radio Conference accepted a U.S. proposal to expand the AM radio band by 10 percent during the 1980s. The FCC has acted to reduce the coverage of the "clear channel" AM stations, creating vacant frequencies for new, local stations and allowing some "daytime" stations to broadcast at night. These two steps together may produce space for as many as 500 new stations.

Low-power Television   The FCC has proposed to create a new class of community-oriented stations, slotted into gaps in existing stations' coverage. These stations will cover areas of 700–1,200 square miles each and will cost much less to start and run than regular stations. The FCC has received thousands of applications to start such stations—so many that the Commission has been forced to delay starting the service while it decides among competing applicants.

The Recent Antitrust Settlement Splitting up AT&T Continues a Pattern of Equally Dramatic Changes that Have Taken Place in the Telephone and Data Transmission Business.

Equipment   The FCC cracked open the telephone equipment monopoly just 14 years ago. Today, consumers are free to buy or lease their phones— in models ranging from plain black to Mickey Mouse designs—from anyone and plug them into Bell's outlets. The spur of competition is driving AT&T and its competitors to produce ever more sophisticated communications equipment for homes and offices.

Long-distance Transmission   The decision to allow competition in long-distance transmission is even more recent, but already MCI, Southern Pacific, and other companies are offering competitive voice services in most large cities. Satellite Business Systems and others are launching satellites to provide sophisticated voice and data links for businesses.

Local Transmission   The local telephone exchange is the last remaining monopoly territory, and even there competition is beginning. The FCC's new Digital Termination Service will provide local data links by microwave. The Commission is establishing another local service—cellular radio— which will allow large numbers of mobile telephones to connect with each other or with the local exchange. Some cable companies are providing local transmission service, just like telephone companies.

In sum, while the rest of the world has maintained monopoly structures for telecommunications, the U.S. is committed to competition. AT&T—whether in one part or two—still dominates and, in some fields, competition is still fragile. However, the regulators have opened a door which will never again be closed. Now, the focus in Washington is shifting; the argument is about whether government should leave the room.

The Current Debate Over U.S. Communications Policy Centers Around the Idea of "Unregulation."

The foundation of much of U.S. communications policy is scarcity. Because channels are limited, regulation is needed to decide who gets them and is applied to ensure that their use serves the public. The advent of competition is undercutting this rationale. Critics of FCC regulation agree that it interferes with broadcasters' First Amendment rights, imposes needless costs, and delays introduction of new services. This view is in line with the widely accepted philosophy in Washington that regulation in general has been excessive and must be cut back. FCC Chairman Mark Fowler has announced an "unregulation" policy which will involve a review of almost every rule on the books and the removal of many of them.

The FCC has been cutting back its restrictive regulations since the early 1970s, but the pace has accelerated since the 1980 election. The new approach suggested by the "unregulation" policy will affect a number of areas.

Broadcasting   In addition to the Fairness Doctrine and the Equal Time Rule, the FCC has long administered an elaborate set of broadcasting regulations including controls on formats, frequency of advertisements, time dedicated to public affairs programs, multiple ownership, etc. In 1980, the Commission dropped many of these rules for radio. Congress has already given radio and TV stations longer license terms, and it is now considering broad deregulation legislation for the entire industry.

One example of the shift in focus from competition to unregulation involves the Carter administration's proposal to narrow the spacing between AM stations in order to create several hundred new stations. The current commissioners agreed with industry complaints that this change would be too costly and decided against the proposal.

Media Ownership   Another example of the change in attitude involves the FCC rules that limit the number of radio and TV licenses a single owner may control and restrict common ownership of communication outlets (broadcast, cable, newspaper, and telephone) in any individual market. In 1980, the FCC was studying whether to break up existing AM-FM radio combinations. Now that proposal is dead, and Chairman Fowler has expressed the view that competition is so strong that many of the ownership rules may not be needed.

Cable Television   The FCC and the courts eliminated most of the federal cable rules several years ago, but regulation remains vigorous at the local level. In many jurisdictions, local authorities are overseeing subscriber rates and are requiring access channels for the public. In 1981, the Senate considered legislation to preempt most local authority over cable on the theory that cable complies with other media and that regulation is harmful. This bill died, but similar proposals are expected in 1982.

Carrier Deregulation   Based on the theory that competition will control prices, the FCC has proposed to eliminate rate regulation for some long-distance services, and the Senate has passed a bill that would go further and sweep away much of the FCC's rate authority. The new antitrust settlement also confirms a 1980 FCC action, *Computer II,* effectively lifting limitations on AT&T's activities which stemmed from an earlier Consent Decree. Assuming the court approves the new settlement, AT&T will be permitted to enter dynamic markets (such as data processing) on an unregulated basis. The *Computer II* decision ordered AT&T to form an arms-length subsidiary which supposedly will prevent the carrier from using its near-monopoly in long-distance transmission to compete unfairly in unregulated markets. A tougher restriction applies to the local operating companies which are to be divested—they are limited to regulated transmission services.

Predictably, these and other "unregulation" policies are controversial. In the media area, opponents argue that the promised abundance of television channels has not yet reached most people, so government protections are still needed. In the common carriage field, critics argue that Bell still controls 96 percent of the long-distance telephone market, so continued rate regulation and very strict separation of the subsidiary are needed.

Proponents of regulation also argue that marketplace forces are inadequate. For example, some say that the airwaves belong to the public, so it is appropriate to impose requirements for their use or to make broadcasters pay for them. Others contend that the AT&T divestiture, competition, and deregulation will drive local telephone rates through the roof in costly-to-serve rural areas and that the government should mandate subsidies to prevent such results. Still others argue that the government should mandate access to cable, satellite-to-home broadcasting, and other services, to increase diversity and offset the advantage that well-funded groups have in using the media.

Although positions differ from issue to issue, the "unregulation" view generally is dominant at the FCC and in the Senate, while supporters of regulation are strong in the House. Thus, some proposals—such as repeal of Equal Time and Fairness rules—may end in deadlock. In many cases, however, the unregulation cause has the arguments and the votes to shrink substantially the communications rulebook during the next few years.

A New Communications Policy Agenda for the 1980s Is Emerging Even as the Fight Over Old Rules Swirls Through the FCC and the Congress.

These new issues are driven by the rapidly expanding uses of communications and the increasing importance of communications technology in the world economy. Some of these items will be resolved at the FCC, but many will be debated in a broader setting.

Spectrum Management   The drive to replace regulation with marketplace forces is running into a limitation that the government cannot remove: the physical properties of the radio spectrum. As indicated, the need to manage the spectrum in order to prevent interference was the reason the FCC was created in the first place, and that job is becoming more difficult. Radio frequencies are used for broadcasting, telephone circuits, taxi fleets, police cars, airplanes, radar, satellites, and even astronomy. Clear channels are essential to the Buck Rogers marvels we can expect in this century—from wristwatch telephones to high-resolution television to factories in space. These often-competing uses are creating a serious problem in frequency overcrowding.

Spectrum management is becoming a hot international issue as well. At the 1979 World Administrative Radio Conference, over 100 nations spent three months debating and deciding on spectrum issues. That process worked out fairly well, but the Conference deferred the toughest problems to seven specialized conferences to be held throughout the decade. These sessions will deal with such thorny issues as how to regulate DBS and whether to carve the band of space available for satellites into segments owned by individual countries. The process will be particularly challenging because many Third World countries want to stake out their claims on frequencies even though they may be years away from actually needing them.

Another focus of attention is the executive branch of the government, which uses a large portion of the spectrum for defense, air traffic control, and other purposes. In the past decade the executive branch transferred almost a quarter of its spectrum to the FCC for private use. (The usable spectrum now breaks down as follows: 35 percent private, 25 percent government, and 40 percent shared.) However, the current surge of high-technology defense programs may reverse that trend.

On the private sector side, the FCC has to umpire more and more struggles over the best uses for valuable frequencies. The flood of applications for low-power TV licenses is one of many examples.

Unfortunately, the rules of this game are obsolete. The Commission usually decides among competing applicants by holding a "comparative hearing" to determine which one would do the best job. This process can take years, and it places an impossible burden on an FCC staff already being thinned by budget cuts. Frequently, most of the applicants are qualified to provide the service, and the resulting litigation over corporate virtue is often wildly expensive. Moreover, these contests threaten to push the FCC right back into the regulatory control that it is trying to shed.

Some uncharitable souls say that the main effect of the comparative hearing process is to delay service while part of the scarcity value of a frequency is being transferred from users to lawyers. In any case, the process means long delays in the introduction of valuable new services.

New assignment techniques also are needed as incentives to conserve spectrum. Users should have an economic spur to improve equipment, drop or transfer frequencies they do not employ, and utilize bands that are least in demand.

Congress and the FCC are beginning to respond. During the summer of 1981, Congress passed a law authorizing the Commission to use lotteries instead of hearings to award frequencies, although this legislation has restrictions that the FCC feels make it unworkable. The Commission broke precedent by allowing FM radio stations to use portions of their signals for industrial purposes instead of broadcasting. Both bodies must take more such creative steps if the FCC is to avoid becoming a bottleneck in the progress of communications technology.

In Addition To Spectrum Management, a Number of Other Issues Will Be Featured on the Communications Agenda of the Eighties.

Government Systems   The government spends over $15 billion per year on telecommunications and data processing. Strong oversight of this spending is needed to avoid waste and duplication while taking advantage of new technologies. For example, the government should consider use of teleconferencing to reduce travel and use of electronic mail and storage to streamline information flow. Congress passed legislation in 1980 to create a new Office of Management and Budget to oversee this area and plan how to bring the "electronic office" to Washington.

While the government should take advantage of the new technologies, it also must be cautious. While many of the new systems are clearly useful, enthusiasts have more to do with trying out new equipment than with delivering government services. The fact is that Congress appropriates money to pay for specific programs, and communications usually is a means, not an end. In general, an agency should invest in new communications systems only if they offer cost-effective ways to do the agency's job.

Property Rights   Information is an unusual commodity in that one can transfer it and still have it. As communications channels multiply, the demand to share information—at a minimum price—increases. At the same time, demand for *new* information is increasing, and that means more incentives to produce the information—i.e., a high price. This permanent conflict has surfaced in three current debates in Congress—over use of videotape recorders to record TV programs off the air, cable TV operators' payments for broadcast programs, and technology transfer abroad. In the next few years, Congress will find itself constantly reexamining the balance struck in the patent, copyright, and trade laws.

Home Information Systems   Broadcasters, newspaper publishers, and others are launching systems that transmit data from computers to people's homes—usually displayed on TV sets. The information can include news, theater listings, airplane schedules, advertisements, etc. Two transmissions systems exist: teletext, which is one-way and uses broadcasting or cable TV; and videotex, which is two-way and uses telephone lines or cable TV. These systems eventually may become an important new mass medium. Because videotex operates two-way, it also can provide transaction services. In a few years, we may be using telephone lines or cable to shop and bank from home, and send mail, turn on appliances, play computerized games, and so on.

   This technology poses tricky policy questions. It combines publishing and broadcasting, and no one knows yet whether the FCC content regulations and other broadcasting rules will apply. Cable operators are interested in the data business but fear that it might expose them to regulation as common carriers. AT&T wants to put its Yellow Pages on videotex, but congressional leaders are opposed because the carrier could compete unfairly against other information providers who depend on telephone lines. Many existing consumer protection rules were written for transactions on paper, and electronic funds transfer rules were designed for automatic teller machines. Banking and shopping from home will demand new policies in both areas.

International Issues   In addition to spectrum negotiations, the progress in communications is producing other difficult international issues. First, our economic growth demands increasing exports of equipment and software, and this requires that hitherto closed markets be opened to U.S. products. The task is particularly difficult because telecommunications is a government-controlled monopoly almost everywhere in the world except the U.S. In addition, trade negotiators must deal with the new threat of foreign controls on transborder data flows, which may create additional trade barriers and perhaps even disrupt international communications. Second, rapidly increasing demand for international circuits is straining international planning procedures for new satellites and undersea cables. Finally, some Communist and Third World countries are supporting a world information code that could legitimize censorship of the press. Appropriately, the U.S. is leading the fight against such proposals.

Information Institutions   The rising cost of print and physical delivery and the falling or stable costs of electronics make it likely that much information now disseminated on paper will be provided through computerized data bases. This is presenting challenges to many of the institutions that have relied on paper to process information. The library tradition of free access for all is baffled by information stored in data bases that charge by the hour. Schools may be unable to afford needed, large investments in computers and other new teaching devices. The Postal Service faces inexorable increases in its expenses, while the declining cost of electronic messages pulls customers away from the mails. Some magazines may be unable to survive the rising costs of printing and postage and the shift to electronic information services.

These trends will produce friction between paper-based and electronic-based institutions. Already, for example, the Postal Service is locked in a fight with telecommunications carriers over its role in electronic delivery of mail. In addition, those who will be hurt by the changes may seek help, directly through grants or indirectly through special postal rates or tax expenditures. While the government has a responsibility to maintain some of these services, it should look skeptically on proposals to preserve old delivery technologies.

Privacy   Computer records of people's habits in shopping, banking, and movie-viewing also raise privacy concerns; laws or guidelines are needed to ensure that such sensitive data are handled responsibly. However, public policy has not kept pace with advancing technology in this area. A loophole exists in the wiretapping laws for nonoral messages such as electronic mail. Two-way systems will computerize records of the things we read and buy. That information belongs to the system operators, and no laws (except one state law and a few cities' cable franchises) restrict their disclosure. Legislation or industry guidelines are needed that will prevent misuse of these data without hampering the services involved.

Equity and Employment Issues   The new communications technologies offer increased business productivity but they pose serious social problems. As these systems spread, they will make the job market more specialized, with less need for low-skilled labor. For example, electronic mail, banking, shopping, newspapers, and offices will reduce the need for postal workers, tellers, retail clerks, newspaper carriers, and secretaries. In addition, information available only on data bases that charge for access may be out of reach for the poor. Television programs that now can be watched for free may become available only for charge. We must anticipate those changes, and put in place programs such as job retraining to soften the blows.

Political Process   The new technologies may alter political campaigns and the process of government may tailor advertising to the special interest audiences of "narrowcasting" channels. Lobbying might be conducted through teleconferences, giving interest groups another tool to pressure members of Congress. We already are seeing instant electronic polls—on the QUBE two-way cable system in Columbus, Ohio—and the new technology will revive the old debate between representative government and direct democracy.

The coming advances in communications will reverberate throughout our society during the 1980s, as new technologies alter our daily activities. These changes should help with some of our most pressing problems, from stagnant productivity to dependence on imported energy. They also will pose new questions and challenges.

The first stage of the deregulation policy helped unleash these innovative forces and the second is removing some of the regulations that competition has rendered obsolete. As traditional regulation shrinks, communications policy will move to novel issues, often in unfamiliar forums. However, the field as a whole will be even more challenging and important in the next decade than it was in the past.

Study Questions: Johnson

⟨?⟩ *Johnson reminds us that the public has no legally enforceable right to use a local radio or television station (except for some kinds of advertising or political campaigning). Should we have that right? Why or why not?*

Should we who do not own cable systems have a legally enforceable right to use them? What are the arguments for such a right? What are the arguments against it? Should the policy on this matter be the same for a member of the community who wants to promote a particular charity, for a political candidate, for an advertiser of toothpaste, and for a seller of programming such as Ted Turner?

Cable technology allows viewers to receive more than 100 channels in their homes. Has this development resulted in adequate access for people and ideas? Why or why not?

What is Johnson's solution to the access problem? Do you agree with his analysis and proposal?

Nicholas Johnson

THE MYTH OF THE MARKETPLACE

Consider this imaginary conversation:

"Is this the phone company?"

"Yes."

"I'm new in town. Do you have phone lines available?"

"Perhaps. But if we were to put one in, what kinds of things would you be talking about on the phone?"

The conversation is absurd because the phone company doesn't control content. At least, not yet. Anyone can get access to the system. Freedom of speech by phone is so fundamental that people can organize protests over telephone rates—and use the phone to do it. Any alternative would be so outrageous we don't even think about it. But the ground rules we take for granted with the telephone are unique among communications networks—and fast eroding.

First Amendment rights have to be rewon with every new communications technology. And right now it looks as though Thomas Jefferson is getting the worst of it.

Consider broadcasting. You have no legally enforceable right to use a local radio or TV station. The station's management *does* ask you, in so many words, "Suppose we were to let you use our radio or television station—what kinds of things would you be talking about over the air?" Individuals have no right to appear if station management would rather censor them; the only exception is candidates for federal office.

Cable television was supposed to change all that. Broadcasting's "economy of scarcity" (with one to five stations per community) would become an "economy of abundance," with cable's 12, 20, 35—and now over 100—channels.

What about regulation? According to the cable industry, there was no need: with dozens of empty channels, the "marketplace" would see to it that all people and ideas got access. It would be safe to abandon the FCC's "fairness doctrine" (that controversial issues be covered, and some time provided for a range of views) and other legal guarantees of diversity. And it would not be necessary to limit the number of cable systems one company could own.

These ideas sounded plausible, and many Washington policymakers were persuaded. The volume went up on the rhetoric of cable "deregu-

Nicholas Johnson was Federal Communications Commissioner from 1966 to 1973. He is now a lecturer and writer, teaching cable policy at the University of Iowa, and a member of the Iowa City cable commission.

lation." The only problem was one enormous oversight, one leap of logic. The arguments simply assumed that access to cable was open to all, like access to the telephone network.

But whatever the virtues and vices of "marketplace regulation," one thing is certain: without a marketplace, the rhetoric becomes hollow. At a minimum, a marketplace enables a willing buyer and seller to exchange goods and services for money. That is not possible with today's cable systems. Here's an example:

Ted Turner offers cable subscribers a 24-hour news service called Cable News Network (CNN). He charges them 15 cents a month. CNN is distributed nationally by communications satellite. Every cable system receives it, but not all use it.

In Iowa City, Hawkeye CableVision has been asked to supply subscribers with CNN, but Hawkeye has stalled for two years. Hawkeye is owned by ATC, headquartered in Denver. And ATC is owned by Time, Inc. in New York. Time, Inc. also owns a pay-cable service called Home Box Office (HBO). HBO is on its Iowa City cable system; CNN is not. Time, Inc. does not own CNN.

Ted Turner wants to sell CNN in Iowa City. Subscribers want to buy. Why is there no sale? Where is the "marketplace"?

Simple—there is no "marketplace." Cable is just not available to entrepreneurs, Hollywood producers, or ordinary citizens if the company doesn't feel like it. (Hawkeye also denied access to a local candidate for county commissioner.) And when a company controls all cable channels in a community (TV plus data, banking, and security systems), the potential for abuse becomes alarming.

Cable is only the most immediate and dramatic of the censored communications technologies. Similar censorship threats occur with videodiscs, direct-broadcast satellites, videotex and teletext (electronic database services via telephone and television, respectively), and computer conferences.

The issue cannot be ignored, and the answer is seemingly simple: to legally guarantee access and separate distribution and content. Don't let Time, Inc. own both Hawkeye (distribution) and HBO (content). Don't let Comsat own both satellites and network programming. Keep the phone company out of "the knowledge business."

Guarantee the right to buy access to any communications distribution system the way we now guarantee access to the telephone network—for you and me as well as for Ted Turner, Norman Lear, and Mobil Oil. Ensure that the quest for profit drives distribution systems to move as much information as possible rather than choke it off.

If we're actually going to apply the conservative doctrine of regulation by the marketplace, not just use it as a fraudulent cover for unrestrained greed, "access" is an idea whose time has come.

S*tudy* Q*uestions:* B*agdikian*

[?] *What does Bagdikian mean by "The power to shape the nation's new and popular culture is up for sale"? Do you agree or disagree with his assessment of the seriousness of the problem? Would your opinion be different if you were nearing retirement and your pension fund owned stock in media conglomerates, making the size of your pension dependent on the profitability of these firms?*

Two of the major reasons cited by Bagdikian that corporations influence the news produced by the media they own are the following: (1) to influence public or government views about things of particular concern to the corporation or its executives and (2) to squeeze as much short-term profits from their news media as possible. For which of these two does Bagdikian make a better case? Which of the two do you believe poses greater threats to the quality of information available to American citizens?

Is Bagdikian's analysis more in agreement with Johnson's or with Wiley and Neustadt's? Do the information and arguments presented by Bagdikian shed any new light on the issues presented in those articles?

Considering the arguments made in all of the articles you have read to date, do you believe the government should stop the increasing concentration of media ownership or not?

Ben H. Bagdikian

THE MEDIA GRAB

The country's news columnists have had an instant revelation: After 20 years of reporting on take-overs and attempted take-overs of media companies, they are finally conceding in front-page stories that the power to shape the nation's news and popular culture is up for sale to the highest

Ben H. Bagdikian, author of *The Media Monopoly,* teaches at the Graduate School of Journalism, University of California, Berkeley.

bidder. Editors who have long been reporting about mergers and acquisitions among the country's newspapers, magazines, broadcast properties, and book publishers are now surprised to find that all this consolidation may have consequences for the national character as well as the earnings statements.

When Capital Cities acquired ABC it was obvious that Peter Jennings had a new boss on the nightly news. But there were public assurances, as there had been for other mergers over the years, that the public had nothing to worry about, since Capital Cities was already in the media business. The recent purchases of Teleprompter Inc. by Westinghouse; the Southern Progress magazines by Time Inc.; Ziff–Davis by Rupert Murdoch and CBS; *U.S. News & World Report* by Mortimer Zuckerman, and *The New Yorker* by S. I. Newhouse Jr. were accompanied by the same reminders that the new owners were already in the business. Behind this assurance stands the apparent assumption that an inflexible morality among media owners restrains them from unduly influencing news and entertainment.

It is an illusion without support in history or human nature. Gross propagandizing, it is true, can reduce profits. But where monopoly reigns, as in 98 percent of the cities with local papers, consumers have no alternative and owners have great latitude. Even owners in competitive situations will generally use their power for personal reasons if they feel that the stakes are high enough, or if their most passionate interests are involved. Some will even publicize their politics at the expense of profits, as William Randolph Hearst Jr. once did and as Rupert Murdoch does today. Yet the usual news reports on take-overs dwell almost entirely on which investment house won out, and how corporate dividends will be affected.

It is true that when Murdoch took over the *Chicago Sun-Times* the top editors and reporters reacted the way the Romans did to Alaric the Visigoth. Murdoch does have some peculiar ideas about what to feed the American public as "news." But he was considered a flaming exception, though in fact he is only less patient and subtle than most media owners in making his inroads on the editorial process. And now, of course, he's branching into television with his probable acquisition of the Metromedia stations.

The long silence on problems of concentrated media ownership ended dramatically when outsiders tried to break into a game previously reserved for original players. When the ultra-conservative Jesse Helms and the Fairness in Media group said they would try to buy CBS in order to reshape the network's news along right-wing lines, the arcane truth that control of the mass media has serious social consequences suddenly became obvious to those who had neglected it before.

Building and using media empires is not a new phenomenon. Hearst and Pulitzer did it in the nineteenth century; Luce, Sarnoff, and dozens of others in the twentieth. But something new began in the 1960s. Large newspaper chains, and then giant ones, began to buy one another, electronic firms bought book publishing houses, and big fish generally indulged their appetites for smaller ones. Soon media companies became large enough to diversify into other kinds of media with which they once competed. ABC boasted this year that its TV and radio networks each earn greater advertising revenues, and its magazine group carries more ad pages, than any competitors in their respective media, while its cable ventures make it the nation's largest supplier of cable programming. Cable and the other new media came under the control of companies with deeply vested interests in the old media, who found it in their interest to thwart innovations. This was why a regulation was adopted in 1971 prohibiting network ownership of cable systems. More recently, the development of teletext was effectively halted when most local stations refused to accept the teletext transmissions of CBS and NBC, fearing the viewers would tune out to use them during the commercial breaks.

The giants pursued these acquisitions for the same reason giants do it in soap and oil—a relatively small number of corporations, they know, can effectively control their market. But soap is only a commodity; those who control the media control information, knowledge, social values. It should come as no surprise that the social implications of media concentration receive such scanty news coverage.

Media corporations represent money: Daily papers and broadcasting have consistently been among the leading profit makers in American industry. And they represent power: The major media have enormous political and social influence. Those who control the media can make the most empty-headed political hack sound like a Founding Father and the most self-serving piece of legislation resemble the Golden Rule. What they dislike, they can ignore or condemn. To control the media is to control the attention of the American public.

Yet this issue rarely finds its way onto the front page or the evening news. In 1979, when American Express tried to take over McGraw–Hill, a major publisher of business magazines, Harold McGraw, chairman of the latter, publicly stated that it would be unwise for a major banker to exercise control over news about banking. The tactic worked, but rarely since then has the forbidden issue of conflict of interest been raised in the mainstream media.

Journalists, who tend to be naive about owner influence, commonly deny the problem by saying, "No one tells me what to write." They seem to ignore editors, who are responsible to owners, who every day tell them what to cover and therefore what *not* to write. Journalists take exaggerated comfort from the few chains with moderately good records, such as Otis Chandler's Times Mirror and the Knight–Ridder newspapers, with 40 papers between them. They ignore the majority, who cut back real news and emphasize inexpensive fluff in order to maximize profits. The Thomson and Donrey chains, with 130 papers between them, are two of many examples.

Concentration of ownership continues. When I completed research on a book in 1981 there were 50 national and multinational corporations that controlled most of the 25,000 media outlets in the country (daily papers, magazines, radio and television stations and networks, book publishers, and movie studios). In the intervening four years the 50, by my informal calculation, have been reduced to 43, with the number getting smaller each year.

There are several dangers inherent in this trend. Democracies depend on the sort of rich mixture of information that can only come from a large number of owners with diverse views. Individuals are thus free to choose the ideas, the kinds of information, that suit their own needs and interests. Yet we now have a small group of powerful owners with remarkably similar political and social views. As a result, our major media probably offer the narrowest range of ideas available in any developed democracy.

Most media-owning giants have also invested heavily in other industries, or have on their boards executives from other industries. Among them are RCA and Gulf & Western, which own subsidiaries that produce defense products and have board members from the weapons industry: *The New York Times* and Time Inc., which have interlocking directorates with the oil and gas industry; and Gannett and Times Mirror, which interlock with space research. These are all industries whose profits are extremely sensitive to public opinion and government policy. What a company's media subsidiary reports as news could seriously affect the parent's profitability. As the major media have become integrated into the top levels of the country's industrial and financial structures the problem has become more profound. And as more foreign interests buy into the American media—their participation is already significant in newspapers, magazines, and book publishing—the problem becomes global and influences the reporting of foreign affairs.

Since most of these firms are publicly traded on the stock market their stock can be bought by anyone with enough money or credit. The firms, in turn, must conform to the demands of Wall Street investors. Few big investors will tolerate low dividends while basic institutions are being built, so most companies are under pressure to show maximum short-term profits. That is not the way for a company to develop good television programs—or many other kinds of products, for that matter.

Media giants are more and more likely to own interests in several media. CBS, for example, is as ramified as ABC. Until recently each medium jealously watched other media, objecting publicly or through their lobbyists in Washington to every sign of unfair advantage gained by the competition. The broadcast networks, for example, used to ridicule the promise of cable at every turn. Now, when the government is virtually encouraging gigantism (through the FCC's rule allowing a single firm to own 12 television stations, for instance), all the watchdogs live incestuously in the same kennel.

The ultimate interest of any of these new media giants is to maintain the status quo, an interest that news coverage is sure to reflect. I don't mean to suggest that the chief executive officer of each media-owning corporation personally makes news assignments or edits stories and broadcasts reports. That would be impractical and unnecessary. He merely hires and fires the people who do. And surely many owners are inhibited by professional standards, though the standards vary widely from one organization to another. Owners will not quash every piece of news that displeases them, if only because crude censorship can damage their reputations. Nevertheless, when it comes to the central interests of the owners, management does not hesitate to override the policies or convictions of professional employees. In 1974, for example, Funk & Wagnalls, a book publishing subsidiary of Readers' Digest Inc., cancelled a book one month before publication because its anti-advertising message might have offended *Readers' Digest* advertisers. In 1978 staff members of the Horvitz newspaper chain were ordered not to cover or report on a public lawsuit embarrassing to owners of the newspaper chain. Television news rarely reports on issues concerning broadcasting—deregulation, for a recent example. There's good reason for this: The industry is better off when the public is not too well informed.

The encouragement that the Federal Communications Commission and the Reagan Administration are giving to the dominating few in the mass media represents an alarming return to the early days of monopoly in broadcasting. Radio began in the United States as a monopoly of the Navy, and was replaced in 1919 by a commercial cartel consisting primarily of AT&T, Westinghouse, and General Electric, which in turn created the Radio Corporation of America (RCA). It took governmental action to compel a more competitive, democratic broadcast system. With the new communications act in 1927, newcomers felt welcome. A young cigar firm executive, William Paley, formed CBS to compete with RCA's broadcast arm, NBC. And an FCC order had to come down before NBC would divest itself of one of its two radio networks. The divestiture led to the creation, in 1943, of the American Broadcasting Company. It will take similar action to prevent broadcasting and other major media from returning to the unhealthy, primitive state of diminished competition in news, ideas, and popular culture.

Study Questions: Kirstein / National Association of Broadcasters

[?] *Is there any way in which the issues or arguments raised by these articles have changed in the decade or two since they were written?*

Which of these forecasts of an advertisement-free society do you believe is most valid? Why?

What elements of each essay reveal the different audiences for which these authors wrote?

Why do you think the National Association of Broadcasters' essay insists that Americans need to be sold on the virtues of advertising? Is that still true today?

Debates on the elimination of advertising were prevalent two decades ago, but we seldom encounter them today. Why?

George G. Kirstein

THE DAY THE ADS STOPPED . . .

The day the advertising stopped began just like any other day—the sun came up, the milk was delivered and people started for work. I noticed the first difference when I went out on the porch to pick up *The New York Times*. The newsdealer had advised me that the paper would now cost 50¢ a day so I was prepared for the new price beneath the weather forecast, but the paper was thinner than a Saturday edition in summer. I hefted it thoughtfully, and reflected that there really was no alternative to taking the *Times*. The *News* had suspended publication the day before the advertising stopped with a final gallant editorial blast at the Supreme Court which had declared the advertising prohibition constitutional. The *Herald Tribune* was continuing to publish, also at 50¢, but almost no one was taking both papers and I preferred the *Times*.

As I glanced past the big headlines chronicling the foreign news, my eye was caught by a smaller bank:

1 KILLED, 1 INJURED IN ELEVATOR ACCIDENT AT MACY'S.

The story was rather routine; a child had somehow gotten into the elevator pit and his mother had tried to rescue him. The elevator had descended, killing the woman, but fortunately had stopped before crushing the child. It was not so much the story as its locale that drew my attention. I realized that this was the first time in a full, rich life that I had ever read a newspaper account of an accident in a department store. I had suspected that these misfortunes befell stores, as they do all business institutions, but this was my first confirmation.

There were other noticeable changes in the *Times*. Accounts of traffic accidents now actually gave the manufacturers' names of the vehicles involved as, "A Cadillac driven by Harvey Gilmore demolished a Volkswagen operated by . . .." The feature column on "Advertising" which used to tell what agencies had lost what accounts and what assistant vice-president had been elevated was missing. As a matter of fact, the whole newspaper, but particularly the Financial Section, exhibited a dearth of "news" stories which could not possibly interest anyone but the persons mentioned. Apparently, without major expenditures for advertising, the promotion of Gimbels' stocking buyer to assistant merchandise manager was not quite as "newsworthy" as it had been only yesterday. Movies and plays were listed in their familiar spot, as were descriptions of available apartments in what used to be the classified section. The women's page was largely a catalogue of special offerings in department and food stores, but no comparative prices were given and all adjectives were omitted. One could no longer discover from reading the *Times*, or any other paper, who had been named Miss National Car Care Queen or who had won the Miss Rheingold contest.

Driving to work, I observed workmen removing the billboards. The grass and trees behind the wall of signs were beginning to reappear. The ragged posters were being ripped from their familiar locations on the walls of warehouses and stores, and the natural ugliness of these structures was once more apparent without the augmenting tawdriness of last year's political posters or last week's neighborhood movie schedules.

I turned on the car radio to the subscription FM station to which I had sent my $10 dues. The music came over the air without interruption, and after awhile a news announcer gave an uninterrupted version of current events and the weather outlook. No one yet knew which radio stations would be able to continue broadcasting. It depended on the loyalty with which their listeners continued to send in their subscription dues. However, their prospects were better than fair, for everyone realized that, since all merchandise which had previously been advertised would cost considerably less on the store counter, people would have funds available to pay for the news they read or the music or other programs they listened to. The absence of the familiar commercials, the jingles, the songs and the endless repetition of the nonsense which had routinely offended our ears led me to consider some of these savings. My wife's lipsticks would now cost half as much as previously; the famous brand soaps were selling at 25 percent below yesterday's prices; razor blades were 10 percent cheaper; and other appliances and merchandise which had previously been nationally advertised were reduced by an average of 5 percent. The hallowed myth that retail prices did not reflect the additional cost of huge advertising campaigns was exploded once and for all. Certainly these savings should add up to enough for me to pay for what I listened to on my favorite radio station or read in the newspaper of my choice.

After parking my car, I passed the familiar newsstand between the garage and the office. "*Life* $1," the printed sign said "*Time* and *Newsweek*, 75¢." Next to these announcements was a crayon-scrawled message! "*Consumer Reports* sold out. Bigger shipment next week." I stopped to chat with the newsie. "The mags like *Consumer Reports* that tell the truth about products are selling like crazy," he told me. "*Reader's Digest* is running a merchandise analysis section next month." I asked about the weekly journals of opinion. He said, "Well now they are half the price of the news magazines—*The Nation* and *The New Republic* prices have not gone up, you know, but I don't think that will help them much. After all, a lot of magazines are going to begin printing that exposé-type stuff. Besides, people are buying books now. Look!" He pointed across the street to the paperback bookstore where a crowd was milling around as though a fire sale were in progress.

I walked over to the bookstore and found no special event going on. But books represented much better value than magazines or newspapers, now that the latter were no longer subsidized by advertisements, and the public was snapping up the volumes.

Sitting in my office, I reviewed the events and the extraordinary political coalition that had been responsible for passing the advertising prohibition law through Congress by a close margin. The women, of course, had been the spearhead of the drive. Not since the Anti-Saloon-League days and the militant woman-suffrage movement at the beginning of the century had women organized so militantly or expended energy more tirelessly in pursuit of their objective. Their slogans were geared to two main themes which reflected their major grievances. The first slogan, "Stop making our kids killers," was geared mainly to the anti-television campaign. The sadism, killing and assorted violence which filled the TV screens over all channels from early morning to late at night had finally so outraged mothers' groups, PTAs and other organizations concerned with the country's youth that a massive parents' movement was mobilized.

The thrust of the women's drive was embodied in their effective two-word motto, "Stop lying." Women's organizations all over the country established committees to study all advertisements. For the first time in history, these common messages were analyzed in detail. The results were published in anti-advertising advertisements, by chain letter and by mouth. The results were devastating. No dog-food manufacturer could claim that pets loved his product without having the women demand, "How in the name of truth do you know? Did you interview the dogs?" . . .

Women led the attack, but the intellectuals soon joined them, and the clergy followed a little later. The intellectuals based their campaign largely on the argument that the English language was losing its usefulness, that word meanings were being so corrupted that it was almost impossible to teach youth to read to any purpose. One example commonly cited was the debasement of the superlative "greatest." The word had come to mean anything that didn't break down; viz., "the greatest lawn mower ever," interpreted realistically, was an instrument that, with luck, would cut grass for one summer. The clergy's campaign was geared simply to the proposition that it was impossible to teach people the virtues of truth when half-truths and lies were the commonly accepted fare of readers and viewers alike.

Opposition to the anti-advertising law was impressive, and at the beginning it looked as if all the big guns were arrayed against the women. Spokesmen for big business contended throughout the campaign that elimination of advertising meant elimination of jobs. The fallacy of this argument was soon exposed when all realized that it was not men's jobs but simply machine running time that was involved. By this decade of the century, the cybernetic revolution had developed to a point where very few men were involved in any of the production or distribution process. No one could feel much sympathy for the poor machines and their companion computers because they would be running only four hours daily instead of six.

Some merchants tried to blunt the "stop lying" slogan by telling the absolute truth. One San Francisco store advertised:

> 2,000 overcoats—only $12. Let's face it—our buyer goofed! These coats are dogs or you couldn't possibly buy them at this price. We're losing our shirt on this sale and the buyer has been fired. But, at least, many of these coats will keep you warm.

The trouble with this technique was that it backfired in favor of the women. The few true ads, by contrast, drew attention to the vast volume of exaggeration, misrepresentation and outright lies that were printed as usual. The advertising industry published thirteen different editions of its "Advertisers Code" in the years preceding the law's passage, but few could detect any difference from the days when no code at all existed.

The press, of course, was the strongest opponent and loudest voice against the advertising prohibition. Its argument was largely legalistic, based on the First Amendment to the Constitution, for the publishers had decided at the outset of their defense not to emphasize the fact that if advertising stopped, readers would actually have to pay for what they read, rather than have America's largest corporations pay for the education and edification of the public. However, the words "Free Press" came to have a double meaning—both an unhampered press and a press that charged only a nominal fee for the publications.

The constitutional argument was really resolved in that final speech on the floor of the Senate before a gallery-packed audience, by Senator Thorndike of Idaho. His memorable ovation, certainly among the greatest in the Senate's distinguished history, concluded:

> And so, Mr. President, the opponents of this measure [the advertising prohibition] claim that the founders of this republic, our glorious forefathers, in their august wisdom, forbade the Congress to interfere with the freedom of the press to conduct itself in any way it found profitable. But I say to you, that the framers of the Constitution intended to protect the public by permitting the press, without fear or favor, to examine all of the institutions of our democracy. Our forefathers planned a press free to criticize, free to analyze, free to dissent. They did not plan a subsidized press, a conformist press, a prostitute press.

The applause was thunderous and the bill squeaked through the Senate by four votes. Three years later, the Supreme Court upheld Senator Thorndike's interpretation. That was two days ago, and today the advertising stopped.

All morning I worked in the office, and just before noon I went uptown for lunch. The subway cars were as drab as ever and seemed a little less bright because of the absence of the familiar posters. However, in one car the Camera Club of the Technical Trades High School had "hung" a show of New York City photographs chosen from student submissions. In another car, the posters on one side carried Session I of a course in Spanish for English-speaking riders, while the opposite side featured the same course in English for those speaking Spanish. This program was sponsored by the Board of Education which had subcontracted the administration of it to the Berlitz School. A poster in both languages in the middle of the car explained that the lessons would proceed on a weekly basis and that by sending $1 to the Board of Education, review sheets and periodic tests would be available upon request.

On Madison Avenue, the shopping crowds were milling around as usual, but there was a noticeable absence of preoccupied and hatless young men hurrying along the street. The retirement plan that the advertising industry had worked out through the insurance companies was fairly generous, and the majority of key personnel that had been laid off when the agencies closed were relieved not to have to make the long trek from Westport or the nearer suburbs each day. Some of the copywriters who had been talking about it since their youth were now really going to write that novel.

Others had set up shop as public relations counselors, but the outlook for their craft was not bright. Without the club of advertising, city editors looked over mimeographed press releases with a new distaste, and it is even rumored that on some newspapers the orders had come down to throw out all such "handouts" without exception. On the magazines, the old struggle between the editorial staff and the advertising sales staff for dominance had finally been resolved by the elimination of the latter. There were even some skeptics who believed that public relations counseling would become a lost art, like hand basket weaving. So most former advertising copywriters planned to potter about in their gardens, cure their ulcers and give up drinking. They were not so many. It was a surprise to most people to learn that the advertising industry, which had had such a profound effect on the country's habits and moral attitudes, directly employed fewer than 100,000 people.

Outside 383 Madison Avenue, moving vans were unloading scientific equipment and laboratory accessories into the space vacated by Batten, Barton, Durstine & Osborn. The ethical drug industry had evolved a plan, in the three-year interim between the passage of the advertising prohibition and the Supreme Court's validation of it, to test all new drugs at a central impartial laboratory. Computers and other of the latest information-gathering machinery were massed in the space vacated by this large advertising agency to correlate the results of drug tests which were being conducted in hospitals, clinics, laboratories and doctors' offices throughout the world.

The Ford Foundation had given one of its richest grants, nearly three-quarters of a billion dollars, to the establishment of this Central Testing Bureau. The American Medical Association had finally agreed, under considerable public pressure, to take primary responsibility for its administration. It was pointed out to the doctors that when the drug companies could no longer make their individual claims through advertisements in the AMA bulletin or the medical society publications, a new and more reliable method of disseminating information would be required. At the outset, the AMA had joined the drug companies in fighting bitterly against the prohibition, but the doctors now took considerable pride in their centralized research and correlation facilities. The AMA bulletin, once swollen to the bulk of a small city's telephone directory, was now only as thick as a summer issue of *Newsweek*. Doctors no longer would find their mail boxes stuffed with throw-away material and sample pills; but they would receive the weekly scientific report from Central Testing Bureau as to the efficacy of and experience with all new preparations.

Late in the afternoon, I began to hear the first complaints about the way the new law worked. One of the men came in and picked up a folder of paper matches lying on my desk. "I'm swiping these; they're not giving them out any more, you know." Someone else who had been watching TV said that the two channels assigned to the government under a setup like that of the BBC, were boring. One channel showed the ball game, but the other had been limited to a short session of the Senate debating the farm bill, and a one-hour view of the UN Security Council taking up the latest African crisis. My informant told me the Yanks had won 8 to 0, and the Senate and the UN weren't worth watching. I reminded him that when the channel that was to be supervised by the American Academy of Arts and Sciences got on the air, as well as the one to be managed by a committee of the local universities, things might improve. "Cheer up," I told him, "At least it's better than the Westerns and the hair rinses."

Oh, there were some complaints, all right, and I suppose there were some unhappy people. But personally I thought the day the advertising stopped was the best day America had had since the last war ended.

*N*ational *A*ssociation of *B*roadcasters

ADVERTISING STOPPED AT 10 O'CLOCK

All advertising in the United States was stopped at 10 o'clock this morning.

The nation's more than 6,600 commercial radio stations, stunned by the loss of their only revenue, announced plans immediately to suspend operations indefinitely.

All of the nearly 700 commerical television stations, also financed solely by advertising, are expected to go dark in a matter of days.

The major radio-TV networks have announced an imminent halt in all services.

The nation's newspapers and magazines, primarily dependent on advertising revenue, are trying desperately to adjust.

Many newspapers hope they can hang on—by trimming the size of editions and doubling or tripling prices to subscribers. Most magazines were pinned to the wall and ceased publication, but a few talked of joining the cost-cutting, price-boosting move.

Hundreds of thousands of people in advertising, broadcasting and the print media are looking for jobs—or soon will be. They will be joined shortly by thousands more employed in program production, equipment manufacturing and similar allied industries.

Economists predict that thousands of retail clerks in stores across the nation will be out of work within a week. They figure that, without advertising, stores won't have enough buying traffic to justify big payrolls.

Store owners and managers already are cancelling orders placed in anticipation of normal business. Manufacturers and wholesalers are slashing production and inventories and some are shutting down their plants.

Freight carriers recognize that there soon will be nothing to carry for profit and are cutting back on operations and laying off employees.

Prices are plummeting on the stock exchanges and grain and cattle markets. Many investors seem convinced that the nation is heading into a general business bankruptcy. Trading is at a standstill. There are plenty of sellers, but no one is buying.

Breadlines already are forming in areas hit hardest by widespread unemployment and demands are being heard for large doses of government aid.

To forestall panic and to deal with the fast-developing crisis, emergency meetings of the Cabinet and the Congress are underway in Washington and Governors have called special sessions of their state legislatures.

On orders of the President, all government departments and agencies are reviewing their programs and policies in a belt-tightening move designed to divert for emergency use as many spare dollars as possible.

But experts at the Internal Revenue Service are gloomy over prospects of collecting even a fraction of the taxes needed to meet even the normal requirements of government.

A leading constitutional authority warns that the nation is well down the road to dictatorship, with little chance of turning back.

Prof. I. M. Doingood of Snodgrass University, a leading critic of advertising who led citizen groups in a nationwide assault on advertising in all its forms, commented: "This is awful!"

(The professor had just been told by the university that his faculty post is being abolished because so few students have the necessary funds to return to campus next term.)

Officeholders, including those who gave the anti-advertisers lip service in their own protests on news coverage, are beginning to wonder how they'll campaign now that radio and television are blinking out and so many newspapers are folding.

A man in the Kremlin greeted the news with an enigmatic smile. What happened in America today reduced a great world power to shambles as quickly and completely as if it had been hit by a rain of nuclear bombs.

All this *could have happened* in America today if advertising had been stopped at 10 o'clock this morning.

All this *could have happened* if advertising had been so restricted by government regulation that it no longer could function.

It *could have happened* because . . .

- There no longer would have been any means to sustain the only voice that tells the American people about the product of their labor.
- There no longer would have been any means to provide people with the day-to-day, hour-by-hour information that is so essential in keeping America's free-wheeling free enterprise system rolling.
- The only alternative—dictation by government of what people should buy, and why, and when—would be a long step toward complete government control and the loss of all freedom.

Despite its recognized contributions to the nation's economic and social growth, advertising throughout its history has been disparaged by super idealists as frivolous or fallacious—and just about everything between.

Some critics claim advertising is a needless luxury that merely adds to the cost of goods and services. Others argue that it spawns monopolies by stifling competition. A few denounce all advertising messages as wicked siren songs designed to seduce a nation of gullible consumers.

No professional in advertising or the mass media it supports quarrels with those—in or out of government—who object to advertising that is fraudulent or misleading. They firmly agree that the schlock operator who blatantly lies or tries to sell shoddy or worthless merchandise should be run out of business.

Neither do they—except in rare and obvious instances—distrust the motives of those who would change advertising. They only distrust their *conclusions* that advertising is bad and should be reformed drastically or abolished completely.

What these critics overlook—and in many instances deliberately ignore—is that advertising is the vital sap of the free enterprise system, a necessary and irreplaceable ingredient in the nation's growth and progress.

The American free enterprise system, the greatest prosperity economy ever devised by man, is a delicate balance of three essential ingredients: *mass production, mass distribution,* and *mass consumption.*

The keystone in the triumvirate is advertising—the irresistible force in selling that gives birth to the common benefits of mass production, mass distribution and mass consumption.

Remove the keystone and the entire economy could come crashing down as suddenly as the Roman Empire tumbled in another era.

In the light of world history, it seems like it was only yesterday that all communication was by word of mouth, tom-toms, smoke signals or simple symbols scratched on a strip of birch bark. Here in America, there was little culture, very little comfort and hardly any progress.

Suddenly, especially in America, there was a spurt in growth and progress that has, in the span of two centuries, enabled the United States to reach a point in enlightenment and living standards beyond the dreams of its Founding Fathers.

Woven deeply into that fabric of growth are the many means of mass communication, supported by advertising, which—like our nation—has had a phenomenal growth.

- From smoke signals and birch bark messages through Gutenberg and moveable type to the great periodicals of our day . . .
- From tom-toms and whispers on the wind to electronic voices heard round the world and seen in living pictures in our homes.

Inventors and scientists gave us these basic treasures one by one. But it was advertising that introduced them to millions and made them available and useful at prices even the less affluent could afford.

Advertising rightly can claim much of the credit for providing us with news of current events as they happen here at home, around the world, and out in space.

Advertising dollars paid the bills to bring into our living room radio reports and live television pictures when Neil Armstrong stepped on the moon in that "one giant leap for mankind."

Advertising dollars paid the bills for the nonstop coverage of the changeover in administrations when President Nixon resigned and was replaced by President Ford.

Advertising dollars also pay for news coverage and interpretation of day-to-day events as well as the political conventions, presidential elections and inaugurations and other special events.

Advertising also picks up the tab for the music, drama and other entertainment Americans enjoy in their pursuit of happiness.

Advertising can claim much of the credit, too, for the abundance and choice of all the other good things in life—the new or the old in fashions displayed at department and specialty stores; the wide variety of foods at the supermarket, the latest in appliances to ease the homemaker's burden; the millions of new automobiles of domestic or foreign make; tires for the wheels and gasoline for the tank; and the jet line to fly when you leave the car at home.

Examples are endless. Chances are that whatever one names is advertised.

Vincent T. Wasilewski, president of the National Association of Broadcasters, feels firmly that advertising's net effect is good.

"It helps promote the greatest good for the greatest number," he says. "It helps to satisfy the needs and desires of human beings. It makes possible many more good things of life, not only for the affluent but also for those who can least afford them."

Senator Sam Ervin of North Carolina, a keen observer of things American has observed from his strategic post in Congress:

> Advertising in America has been one of the most significant of all factors in altering our living habits, our social attitudes, and our personal expectations . . .
>
> Advertising has brought to millions of Americans new ideas about various possibilities of life styles available in our great country . . . not only about which soap to buy, but where to live, for which goals in life to aspire, what jobs to seek, and what to do with our increasing amount of leisure time . . .
>
> To dismiss advertising as we know it today as nothing more than an offer to sell or an offer to buy is not only to ignore its total impact but it is to forget about our traditional belief in the importance of communication of ideas—all kinds of ideas—to the advancement of civilization.

The proponents of advertising warn that all these benefits would vanish if counter-advertising and many of the other proposed restrictive measures were adopted.

Gilbert H. Weil, legal counsel to the Association of National Advertisers, has served notice that the threat to advertising has reached "a point critical to its continued existence."

"Even those who do not deliberately seek the abolition of advertising as such," he said, "are vigorous and effective proponents for changes in its nature and function which are quite likely to result in its extinction."

The *Starbuck Times*, a weekly newspaper published in Starbuck, Minn., once offered some "Words of Wisdom" to nonadvertisers that carries an equally strong message for antiadvertisers. Under a "Why Advertise?" headline, the article said:

> A man wakes up in the morning after sleeping under an advertised blanket in advertised pajamas. He will bathe in an advertised tub, wash with an ad-

vertised soap, shave with an advertised razor, drink advertised coffee after his advertised juice, cereal and toast (prepared in an advertised toaster), put on advertised clothes and an advertised hat.

He will then ride to work in an advertised car, sit at an advertised desk, smoke advertised cigarettes and write with an advertised pen.

Yet this man hesitates to advertise, saying it does not pay.

Finally, when his unadvertised business goes under, he will then advertise it for sale.

It is no accident that the United States has both the highest standard of living in the world and the world's most and best system of advertising. They are linked inseparably and one complements the other.

The Census Bureau publishes regularly statistics that show how the good life in advertised America keeps getting better.

Ownership of TV sets is a good example. The Bureau found in 1960 that 86.5 percent of all American homes owned at least one TV set. By 1973 the figure had climbed to 96 percent and half the sets in use were in color. Even in households with incomes under $5,000, 94 percent had at least one set.

Latest available figures show there now are 401 million radio sets in use—one and a half sets per person, or roughly five in each family.

Four families in five owned at least one automobile in 1975 and three in 10 had two cars or more. Nine of every 10 cars sold was equipped with a radio.

By 1971, three families in five owned their own homes and families in increasing numbers were buying second homes in the country or at the seashore.

Census figures on appliances are also indicative of the increasing affluence of American families.

Three families in four owned washing machines in 1975 and nearly half of all families had clothes dryers. A third of all families owned freezers and one in four had dishwashers. Almost every family (98.6 percent) owned a refrigerator. Three families in 10 had at least one room air conditioner and 16 percent of all families enjoyed central cooling systems.

Advertising not only is a bulwark of our economy, but also is closely tied to the very survival of our freedom.

William Green, late president of the American Federation of Labor, said it well when he observed:

In a very real sense, advertising is a bright symbol of freedom. It is a method of urging which immediately indicates the existence of freedom of choice. If there were no liberty, there would be no advertising. Someone would *tell* us, not *coax* us.

Obversely, it also is true that if there were no advertising there could be no freedom.

Frank Stanton of CBS, Inc., a staunch defender of broadcast freedoms, has said, "Advertising is the foundation of a free press. Remove this source of support and the whole structure falls. It's as simple as that . . ."

Former U.S. Senator Sam Ervin, a foremost constitutional authority and an indefatigable defender of First Amendment freedoms, has said that advertising is "commercial speech" and is entitled to the same protection as the printed word.

In a speech entitled *Advertising—the Stepchild of the First Amendment,* the former Senator said any effort to make the government "an arbiter of the truth of ideas" would constitute "the very evil the First Amendment was written to avoid."

While conceding that some restrictions may be necessary, he observed:

> The expression of ideas in advertising is a vital part of the total system of free expression of thought which the First Amendment was designed to protect.
>
> If government at any level ever assumes the authority to prohibit absolutely the advertisement of perfectly legal products, if it even assumes the role of final arbiter as to what is truth in advertising, if it develops the power to dictate to the people what they should buy and for what reason, then not only will the dissemination and exchange of economic ideas be dead, but freedom in all its many facets will soon disappear from our land.

Yes, it *could* happen in America . . . if advertising was stopped at 10 o'clock.

Yes, it *could* happen in America . . . if advertising was so seriously restricted that it no longer could function.

Study Questions: Packard

? *Do you believe books once "constituted the core of our verbal thought and culture," as Doctorow argues in the quotation heading this article? Why?*

Why does Packard believe publishers' traditional balancing of the pursuit of profit and the advancement of literature and talented writers has changed?

How do you explain the disappearance of the independent publishing houses, their takeover by conglomerates? What arguments for the positive effects of this consolidation are presented in this article? What arguments for the negative effects? Overall, do you see the effects as more positive or more negative?

What is the "blockbuster phenomenon"? What are its consequences for the publishing industry and for the publishing of high-quality books?

What relationship, if any, do you see between Packard's concerns in "Literature as Big Business" and Bagdikian's concerns in "The Media Grab"? Do you suppose they would propose the same solutions?

Frank Packard

LITERATURE AS BIG BUSINESS

> Books have constituted the core of our verbal thought and culture. They have been the medium by which our country has maintained its historical argument with itself, in all of its voices, in all the aspects of its soul. Because of that they have stood traditionally as the source of ideas and thought drawn upon and used and disseminated by the other media. A professor's painfully worked-out ideas, his scholarship, over the years of study, is reported in newspapers, excerpted in magazines; a novelist's work forged from the privacy of his imagination is reviewed in the papers and journals and possibly adapted for film. Traditionally all the other media have stood toward our books as extenders, popularizers, commentators—but the impulse from the book precedes all.
> —E.L. Doctorow

Book publishing has always suffered an uneasy tension between aesthetic and economic priorities. On the one hand publishing is one of society's most essential institutions, providing a marketplace for ideas, enhancing our freedom and the nation's intellectual and artistic life. On the other hand it is a business, with balance sheets and financial accountability.

The problem is simple in conception but complicated in practice: book publishers must sell to survive. Unfortunately, writing of artistic merit—literature—often is less marketable than books that fulfill the popular demand for unsophisticated entertainment or information. The public,

Frank Packard, a senior, majors in history at Princeton University. Stephen Schaible assisted in researching this article.

observed Alexis de Tocqueville in the mid-nineteenth century, prefers "books which may be easily procured, quickly read, and require no learned researches to be understood. The ever-increasing crowd of readers, and their continued craving for something new, ensure the sale of books that nobody much esteems."

Despite the scattered resentment of writers throughout history, the publishing industry has had a proud tradition of balancing the pursuit of profit with investment in authors whose work, though not necessarily best-selling, shows promise of cultural value. Publishers, always in the business for the love of books as much, or more, than the rate of return, have been content with smaller profit margins than conventional businessmen.

PRIORITY ON PROFITS

The balance between profit and art in the publishing industry, satisfactory for many years as a means of both advancing literature and keeping pub-lishing houses in business, seems to have been upset in recent years. A 20-year trend of mergers between once-independent publishing houses and large, diversified, publicly owned conglomerates has roused the anxieties of authors who see an ever-increasing priority afforded to profits at the expense of literary value. Says E.L. Doctorow, author of *Ragtime* and *Loon Lake*, and a spokesman for the writers' organization, PEN:

> The best publishers of the past always knew how to float their good books on the proceeds of their commercial books, pay for one with the other, make money, and be proud of their contribution to literature and ideas at the same time . . . This delicate balance of pressures within a publishing firm is upset by the conglomerate values—the need for greater and greater profits and the expectation of them overloads the scale in favor of commerce.
>
> The individuals who dominate publishing today are not publishers, laments author Kurt Vonnegut, they are "either from Harvard Business School or Accountants. There are no romantics in the business anymore."
>
> Through the 1950s American publishing was a cottage-industry. Character-ized by a decision making process dispersed among thousands of independent parties, the publishing industry was able to cultivate expression of every kind, from the poetic to the analytic. All this began to change when the booming economic climate of the 1960s brought the sights of expansion-minded con-glomerates upon the education industry.

THE EDUCATION BONANZA

If the liberal consensus wrought by the Great Society of Kennedy and Johnson had any positive nexus with conservative interests in the sixties, it was in the establishment of education as a lucrative investment. Government spending in scientific research received a further boost from the shock of the Sputnik launch. The education explosion became an investor's bonanza. With high expectations for the synergism of technology and education industries, other electronics corporations followed RCA's lead. General Electric and Time Inc. founded the General Learning Corporation, adopting the Silver Burdette textbook house as a publishing base. Similarly motivated, CBS, IBM, IT&T, Litton Industries, Raytheon, and Xerox established their own "information companies." The educational side of a publishing house—the tail that wags the dog, comprising, for example, 80 percent of Random House—ripened in the eyes of investors.

"No harm was done to the industry, but (neither) was any value added," says William Knowlton, president of Harper & Row, Inc. The marriage of education and electronics failed to produce the ideal return on investment—in part because traditional teaching methods proved to be cheaper—and many of the conglomerates abandoned the integration experiment. The General Learning Corporation was dissolved in 1974. RCA sold Random House at the end of last year.

GOING PUBLIC

How had the independent publishers become so accessible to their enterprising buyers? Upon the lifting of World War II price freezes, book production costs soared by more than 80 percent in two years. Afraid of losing customers, the industry reacted by holding prices for their books artificially low. Inflation added to the rising cost of production, creating a capital crisis. Most houses saw no solution but to go public and issue stock as a means of raising capital.

Though the convergence of electronics and education during the 1960s had proven premature, the concentration fever started anew after the economic recession of the early 1970s. Conglomerates both within and without the communications field began acquiring publishing houses. Time Inc. purchased Little, Brown in 1968; Times Mirror took over the New American Library in 1963; Gulf + Western acquired Simon & Schuster merely for the sake of diversification. American Express attempted to take over McGraw-Hill unsuccessfully and Houghton-Mifflin stopped an acquisition effort by Western Pacific Industries, a railroad conglomerate, only when a number of its authors threatened to take their business elsewhere. Houghton-Mifflin had to spend $10 million to preserve its independence.

Even today, facets of the communications industry continue to combine with others to such an extent—Newhouse Newspapers now owns Random House, for instance—that in ten years it may no longer be possible to distinguish by function companies that were once regarded as distinct, such as a large newspaper, magazine, book, broadcasting, and motion picture interests. The trend toward concentration among publishers themselves has lead to the combination of hardcover and softcover houses: Doubleday and Dell; Viking and Penguin; Holt, Rinehart and Winston (owned by CBS) and Fawcett Paperbacks.

A look at today's ten largest trade book publishers provides an accurate portrait of industry convergence in the last twenty years. The top eight are either part of large corporations—Random House (Newhouse Newspapers); Grosset & Dunlop (Filmways, Inc.); Little, Brown (Time, Inc.)—or, like Harper & Row, Macmillan, and Doubleday (which also owns the New York Mets) are conglomerates in and of themselves. Both of the next largest trade publishers, Crown and Houghton-Mifflin, are independent yet own several smaller publishing firms.

RETAILING THE BEST SELLER

In addition to the concentration of the publishing industry, the retail side of the book business has experienced a similar refinement of power. Large retail book chains such as B. Dalton and Waldenbooks emphasize best-sellers to the detriment of small and large publishers alike. The smaller houses, which may not offer books appealing to the lowest common denominator of taste, must compete furiously for shelf space. "The bookstore chains," says Roger Straus, president of the independent house Farrar, Straus and Giroux, "emphasize the best-seller because they are interested in the highest possible turnover . . . If the second-rate books don't take off very quickly they are returned." Furthermore, the chain retailers complicate the business of a maverick or risk-taking publisher in search of young writers by tying up capital. Complains Straus, "Another problem nobody talks about is the 90 to 160 days it takes for these stores to pay for books. They're supposed to pay in 30 days. They come up with every imaginable excuse for taking so long. What can you do? Shut them off? That's slitting your wrists."

The blockbuster phenomenon, however, does not have its roots in today's changing retail system alone. Paperback publishers and movie producers have created a market in the sale of subsidiary rights for books. Armed with enormous promotional budgets, paperback publishers have set out to make their fortune on a handful of "big books." The stakes are high in today's blockbuster business; subsidiary rights to E.L. Doctorow's *Ragtime* earned $1.85 million; Colleen McCollough's *The Thorn Birds* fetched $1.9 million; Mario Puzo's *Fools Die* $2.2 million; and Judith Krantz's *Princess Daisy* a tremendous $3.2 million. That paperback publishers have come to invest so heavily in the best-seller is an indication of their subservience to the mass common culture.

Given economic realities, this should come as no surprise. Yet the implications of the blockbuster phenomenon are serious for beginning novelists whose work is not destined for the wire racks of drugstores. Paperback publishers have a stronghold on the access of writers to average American readers. Mass-market paperbacks have a final distribution estimated to be between 100,000 and 150,000 outlets—versus 7,000 bookstores for hardcover and trade paperbacks—because the mass-market "pipeline" for paperbacks rides on top of the national magazine distribution system.

Hollywood has given the big book boom another source of support. The auction prices for movie rights on successful novels such as Peter Benchley's *The Island* ($2.4 million) and Gay Talese's *Thy Neighbor's Wife* ($2.5 million) have made it more advantageous for a motion picture company to commission books themselves. In 1979, Metro-Goldwyn-Mayer paid Sharon and Paul Boorstin $50,000 to write *The Glory Hand*, a semioccult novel. If the book makes *The New York Times* best-seller list, the authors will receive another $50,000.

"QUESTION OF ECONOMICS"

How to interpret the effects of the concentration trend upon literature has caused a rancorous debate among writers and publishers, particularly in the past few years. "The question of what is publishable becomes a question of pure economics," claimed author Herman Wouk in 1977. "Publishers are now going for the big book. It is more and more a choice of whether a book will sell, not whether it will contribute to culture." E.L. Doctorow portrays his fears of concentration this way: "Regardless of the good intentions of the people working in publishing today, regardless of the enlightenment at the top levels of editorial management, the narrowing of divergent decision making power into fewer corporate organization, . . . both at the publishing and retailing ends of the business, provides the structure for a time when enlightenment no longer prevails, when the people who we have now have died or retired . . . (taking) their standards of excellence . . . with them. And the people who take their place, a career generation or two from now, no longer come into publishing or bookselling because they love books but because it is corporate life."

Some publishers are far less disturbed by the concentration trend than writers, however. William Knowlton of Harper & Row finds that two aspects of concentration bother him: the power within the hands of a few retailers, and the buying power of the integrated book clubs and paperback houses. "The first is somewhat overdramatized. The turn-over ratios (shelf life in a bookstore) do change the emphasis given to books. Unquestionably some books—poetry and first novels—get lost. And that should be of concern to young writers today." The second is a hypothetical concern, he believes, causing more agitation among writers than any real effect.

Knowlton sees the development of chain bookstores as very beneficial to the book business in general. "They have put bookstores where they never were before. More books are being sold." However, he adds, the bookstore chains have "diminished the prospects for a segment of the spectrum (of available books)." Curtis Benjamin, the retired chairman of McGraw-Hill Books, also approves of the chain bookstore trend: the chain stores backlist books, pay bills, have shelf space, and—most importantly—know how to sell books, he says. The smaller stores, Benjamin feels, do not meet these challenges as well, despite their love of books.

As for the effect of concentration of publishing houses upon contemporary literature, Knowlton observes no drop in quantity or quality: "The amount of fiction published by the larger houses—the Random Houses, Doubledays, and Simon & Schusters—is greater than that published by the smaller houses despite the assertions of the latter that they are innately more tasteful, more virtuous and more courageous because of their commitment to this kind of work. . . . There is a terrific choice for consumers— over 800 different cookbooks. Ten or fifteen years ago there was one guidebook to Mexico, now look at the travel books. With lots of competition the consumer is getting more than enough." The larger publishers, according to this point of view, can actually afford more advances and commissions and take greater chances with unestablished writers due to the strength of their financial resources. "We pay what we think we can get back on it," says Knowlton. "Often we're wrong and it doesn't come true. With competitive bidding, which is often the case with (literary) agents, . . . we pay more than we will get back on it." As evidence of Harper & Row's support for writers with no regard for profit he cites some slow-selling authors in the publishing house. Ruth Jhabvala and Anita Desai are two Indian novelists on the Harper & Row list whom Knowlton admires. Harper & Row has published *Blackbird Days* by Kenneth Chowder and Thomas McHahon's *McKay's Bees* with little concern for their sales potential. Knowlton is also proud that his company published Jean Rhys' autobiographical excerpt, *Smile Please*, as well.

LOSING ONLY "DEADWEIGHT"

Some publishers and editors feel that literature's only loss has been the deadweight. One editor who has worked with several prominent writers at Random House believes that the number of writers has not diminished, only the number of good writers, because inflation and soaring costs have tightened bidding between publishers. This editor feels that today's increased competition has paid deserving writers quite well. Moreover, he says, "quality will always have a market."

That the quality of contemporary prose has declined may not have anything to do with recent convergence of power at the top of the publishing industry. "There's lots of slovenly editing today," says William Knowlton. "It is probably a little worse than in the past. Young editors are in a hurry. This business is editorially misperceived: the fact of the matter is that you've got to read lots of crap, thousands of details. (Since) it is such a tough, meticulous, disappointing business, it is damn hard to find good people who have stuck with it ten to fifteen years. Their standards are unrealistic; they want quicker rates of return." Says Genevieve Young of Little, Brown, "something really happened in the 1960s. People forgot how to spell, didn't recognize run-on sentences. I gather it was considered elitist to teach proper English in some places."

Yet even seasoned authors are suffering grammatical lapses. Judith Krantz's *Princess Daisy* contained this nugget: "Thank heavens they'd all be in the staterooms, intently adjusting their resort dinner clothes, caparisoned for the delectation of each other." Gay Talese wrote these prosaic perfections in *Thy Neighbors Wife:* "What would prove to be decisive in her decision . . ." and "Men who noticed that their wives aroused other men became in many cases aroused by her themselves." If current editors had stronger backbones, William Knowlton believes, these problems would not occur. "Lots of manuscripts come in that are rankly sentimental, late, or long, or not what the (authors) said they would be. Editors can't confront the (writers), and so they get published." Writer John McPhee blames the current spate of imprecise verbosity upon authors who have exchanged the pen for the microphone: "There are a lot of books around that smell of tape-recorder. Writing is so difficult that if a writer is looking at words on paper, say the transcript of a tape recording, it's damn difficult to resist them. So a lot of books go on too long because he recorded too much."

Since publishers can charge more for fat books, the editors feel no pressure to curb the muddled prolixity that abounds. An editor may indeed refrain from trimming and tightening an author's prose if he is confronting a large ego. These egos in turn are the product of the blockbuster phenomenon. If publishers are paying several million dollars for one's books, it is natural that a writer's self-regard and intolerance of criticism should also soar.

BREADTH OF VISION

Since quality in literature is such a delicate matter of taste, it may suffice to say that a difference of opinion exists as to the consequences of concentration within the publishing industry. The age-old tension between profits and aesthetics may be no stronger now than in the days of de Tocqueville. There seems to be no doubt, however, that the attention today's publishers are giving to the bottom line has bared the nerves of the writing community.

People have always entered the publishing business for a variety of reasons: the love of literature, the prestige of hobnobbing with famous writers, or for the pleasure of being a patron of the arts. Rarely, though, has a publisher motivated by profit alone succeeded in producing quality books at the same time.

As economic necessity drives profit further and further ahead of aesthetics among publishers' priorities, it will remain to be seen if the industry has not indeed lost its breadth of vision.

Study Questions: Peterson

[?]   *Peterson presents two ideas about the sources of change. Which of them do you believe is more valid? Do you agree with Peterson that the "apparatus" interposed between creator and consumer is the most important of all?*

In what sense is there a "symbiotic relationship" between the radio and recording industries?

What were the factors that led many radio stations to switch to a country music format?

What effect did radio and economics have on the sound or style of country music? How has radio brought some forms of country music and some performers to the fore while, in effect, burying others? Explain the reasons for these changes as fully as possible.

How are shifts in music related to shifts in the music industry?

What does Peterson mean by a "crossover strategy"? Have you detected the effects of that strategy on other kinds of music in recent years?

How much influence has the general listening public had on these various developments?

Richard A. Peterson

THE PRODUCTION OF CULTURAL CHANGE: THE CASE OF CONTEMPORARY COUNTRY MUSIC

On Tuesday, November 5, 1974, a group of about fifty established country-music entertainers met in the suburban Nashville home of Tammy Wynette and her husband George Jones. It was a stormy session; the future of country music seemed to be at stake. Four of the top awards given at the annual Country Music Association (CMA) show two weeks earlier had gone to persons whom many at the meeting did not consider "country music" artists.

From this initial meeting came the Academy of Country Entertainers (ACE). The original purpose of the new organization was to establish a definition of country music that would exclude the cultural carpetbaggers coming from the field of popular music, but it was not universally welcomed. Many people in the music industry dismissed the new organization as an attempt of fading stars to stand in the way of changes taking place in the music in a vain effort to prolong their own careers. The critics of ACE saw these changes as inevitable either because of the efforts of new creative artists entering the field or because of changing audience tastes.

While the formation of ACE was triggered by one event, over the next several years the organization developed an explanation for the changes taking place in the music. The leaders of ACE argued that change was due neither to the creative evolution of the genre of country music nor to changing audience tastes, but instead was due to certain structural changes taking place in the complexly interrelated institutions that make up the contemporary commercial-music industry, changes which altered the way country music was produced, marketed, and merchandised, changes which threatened to destroy country music.

SOURCES OF CULTURAL CHANGE

The assertions made by defenders of the music industry against the ACE critics fit most conventional theories of how cultural elements change. In varying degree these theories blend two distinct ideas. On one hand there is the idea that change can be explained as a product of the innovative interaction of creators, whether scientists, theologians, painters, or musicians. On the other hand, there is the idea that change is the result of evolving consumer demand, caused either by a natural ebb and flow of fads and fashions or by changing social-structural imperatives. In either case, elements of culture reflect the particular society in which they are consumed.

All of these explanations of cultural change tend to ignore the influence of the increasingly complex apparatus which is interposed between culture creators and consumers. The influence of this intervening apparatus, however, *is* focal in the rapidly crystalizing "production of culture" perspective which is widely represented in this issue of *Social Research*. An examination of the ACE case thus provides a convenient opportunity for exploring in detail the sorts of mechanisms of change unintentionally built into the complex commercial systems which produce and disseminate cultural goods.

By any conventional yardsticks, country music changed rapidly from 1972 to 1977. Lyrical themes focused more exclusively on love problems and were more explicit in discussing various sorts of deviant behavior. Chord structures and rhythms became more complex, orchestrations became fuller, and the singing styles became smoother. In all these ways, the most widely heard country music sounded more like the other genres of popular music in 1977 than it had in 1972. These changes are illustrated in the difference between the singing style of Loretta Lynn, three-time Female Vocalist of the Year between 1967 and 1973, and the 1977 winner, Loretta's kid sister, Crystal Gale. While Lynn sang "Coal Miner's Daughter," "Don't Come Home A'Drinkin' with Lovin' on Your Mind," and "You're Looking at Country," Gale sang "I'll Do It All Over Again" and "Don't It Make Your Brown Eyes Blue?"

Although the hard nasal country sound of Loretta Lynn is self-evidently different from the countrypolitan stylings of Crystal Gale, the structural shifts in the music industry underlying the changes are not so easily unraveled. In the discussion which follows, we will first show the interdependence between the commercial-music industry and its Siamese twin, the radio-broadcasting industry; second, illustrate the changes which have taken place in country-music radio; and third, show how these changes had an impact on record-making artists' careers, and eventually on the genre of country music itself. Throughout, the analysis is fueled by the irony that the wider acceptance of country music has been achieved in ways that threaten to destroy the unique elements of the genre and the social institutions necessary for its long-term survival.

RECORDS AND RADIO

Commercial-music firms are geared almost entirely to the creation, production, distribution, and selling of large numbers of *new* records. Except for the few long-playing records that attain very large sales, country-music phonograph records are withdrawn from distribution within a few months after they are first put on sale. The record industry has developed no mechanism for advertising this profusion of new releases, relying instead on radio stations to, in effect, advertise its product by repeated air play. These records, in turn, provide free programming material for radio stations.

This peculiar symbiotic relationship between the record and radio industries has existed since the commercial success of TV in the 1950s led radio stations to program to specific demographic segments of the population. The dependence on radio air play for merchandising new records has a number of consequences which shape contemporary country music. First, only those records which are played on the air have a chance to become commercially successful. Second, record makers consciously tailor their productions so that they are likely to be aired, that is, be acceptable to radio-station programmers. Third, the careers of artists and eventually whole genres of music are facilitated or frozen out in the process.

If radio programmers selected a record on the basis of its popularity with the public at large, the mechanisms just described would ensure that commercial music reflected public tastes. But the public is not the *prime* concern of radio programmers. Commercial radio depends on attracting advertisers, who pay for as much as 18 minutes of the broadcast hour to sell their wares. In this sense, commercial radio and television are like political rallies or the old medicine shows in that the entertainment is provided free to attract potential customers. Understandably, then, advertisers support those stations that can show they deliver an audience of the sort to which the advertiser wants to pitch his wares.

Advertisers and radio-industry programmers in turn rely heavily on market research to know who their audience is, so the particular research tools and means of classifying people that are employed in the research methodology significantly color the industry's understanding of public tastes. In the final analysis, an individual's aesthetic taste has an influence in shaping commercial music only insofar as he/she is considered a likely customer and, what is more, a customer who is identifiable as likely to listen to the radio.

This latter proviso introduces another important chain of consequences. If people do not hear what they like on the radio, they are likely to turn the radio off and thus, given current polling techniques, not count in shaping popular culture. This alienation factor is not systematically recognized by the radio industry. Thus, ironically, even though the commercial industry is set up to sell people whatever music they want, there has been a very large unsated demand for certain types of popular music because the industry only poorly understands its audience.

Anticipating our later discussion a bit, here is one telling example of disjunction between demand and supply. Recent surveys show that more men than women prefer country music and that country-music radio listenership is predominantly male, more so than for any other musical format.[1] But the advertisers who purchase time on country music stations today target their appeals to females in the 18-to-49 age range who they feel make most consumption decisions. As a result, country-music stations program to this segment of the population. As country-music radio programmer Mike Hoyer of radio station KBUL–Wichita said recently: "It's the 18–49 age audience we're after, and we love women in that age group. We look for female appeal."[2]

THE EXPLOSION OF COUNTRY RADIO: 1961–1974

Having introduced the prime classes of actors, we are now prepared to see their interplay in one particular drama, the reshaping of country music. The action is bewilderingly complex but, by focusing first on country-music radio, we can unravel the main sequences.

In 1959, the Country Music Association (CMA) was formed in Nashville by a group of country-music-industry executives who were concerned that the audience was being drawn away by the success of rock music. Touting country music as wholesome family entertainment, the CMA aimed its efforts at entertainment-industry bookers in an effort to show them the continuing profit potential in country music. An early brochure, for example, was entitled "What You Don't Know about Country Music Is Costing You Money."

A great deal of effort was directed toward convincing radio station managers to adopt a full-time country-music format. In 1961 there were only 81 full-time country-music stations in the entire country.[3] By 1965 this number had increased threefold. In the main this increase was in stations serving small towns and in stations switching from part- to full-time country format.

Most of the music programmers[4] drawn into country radio by this expansion had long experience with the genre as fans and sometimes also as performers. They knew the music, the audience, and the products they sold. They used a conversational style on the air as if they were talking casually with friends about items of mutual interest: the music, its performers, where they might be heard locally, and items for sale ranging from flour to work clothes.[5] This folksy style of presentation, so unlike that of the fast-talking pop-jockey, undoubtedly helped to foster a country-music constituency, but stations switched to the country format not so much to propagate the music as to bring advertising revenue to the station. As Ted Cramer, who in 1970 was the program director of KCKN–Kansas City, noted, the station had featured a rock format until 1961, and "It was fairly successful in (listener) ratings, but not in (advertising revenue) billings, so the whole chain of stations changed to country music."[6]

Between 1965 and 1968, the number of full-time country-music stations doubled again, reaching something over 500 in number, and by 1968 country music had caught on in all the media and in the public imagination. Glen Campbell and Johnny Cash both had network TV shows, and the country-humor program *Hee Haw* was a surprising hit. What is more, the romantic wing of the rock movement turned increasingly to rural imagery and life-ways. Influenced by Bob Dylan, the Grateful Dead, Poco, and Gram Parsons, who experimented with country sounds, songs, and instruments, country music became respectable to the youthful counterculture of the time. One related consequence was a whole new youthful audience for bluegrass music. Soon after, a partial fusion of rock and honky-tonk country, which was later called variously in the media "red-neck rock" or "outlaw country," began to emerge employing cowboy and badman imagery. Johnny Cash's Folsom Prison live album, for example, enjoyed substantial sales in the country-music market but became a genuine hit, staying on the *Billboard* list of the 200 top-selling albums for 122 weeks, because it attracted the attention of the counterculture. Even astronauts beamed "good American country music" back to Earth. "Country" was clearly commercial.

Between 1968 and 1974 the number of full-time country-music stations about doubled again so that in the latter year there were, depending on the criterion used, 856 or 1,016 country-music radio stations broadcasting in the United States. Most widely noted was the conversion, early in 1973, of the 50,000-watt New York City AM station WHN. By 1974 the prime CMA objective, to propagate country music through radio air play, had succeeded spectacularly. Every market, major as well as minor, had at least one powerful station playing country music around the clock.

But there was an unanticipated irony built into this success. With the rapid expansion from 1964 to 1974, there was an unprecedented demand for country-music programmers, and not enough could come from the ranks of committed and knowledgeable country-music people. At the same time, there were a large number of unemployed programmers who had been displaced by the switch to country. In practice many station managers solved their personnel problems by simply keeping their programmers. In consequence, several thousand programmers found themselves converted overnight, and often against their will, from popular, rock, and middle-of-the-road air personalities into country jocks, a genre few liked and fewer understood. With much coaching from record-company personnel, the Country Music Association, and trade magazines, however, they set out to become familiar with country music. In the process they developed a new concept for country radio.

By 1968, the *modern* country-radio idea had been explicitly formulated. The following introduction to country music, written by the Alan Torbet radio consultants and aimed at potential advertisers, is representative of the image of *modern* country radio, if put in more condescending terms than most advocates used:

> The name, "Country-Music," is confusing to some, since it can connote that this music is for persons living in rural areas. Modern country music has become a multi-million dollar business, and it could only do so by appealing to urban population centers—not by limiting it to the farm.
>
> Today the term "country" is synonymous with "nation." Other than jazz, this form is the only truly "national" music of the United States—telling in lyrics the stories of people, places, experience, and feelings.
>
> It is called by many names to connote this "national" feeling—Americana, countrypolitan, town and country, etc., etc. In any event, *modern* country music has no relationship to rural or mountain life. It is the music of this *Nation,* of this country, the music of the people. You find no screech fiddles, no twangy guitars, no mournful nasal twangs in *modern* Nashville sound of country music. Today you find the sweeping sound of full orchestrations, multi-voiced choruses, amplified instruments and sophisticated arrangements, and an adult lyric approach.
>
> Consequently, the *modern* country-music station is as bright, urbane, sophisticated and lively as the best contemporary middle-of-the-road or better-music station with wide adult appeal. The winning-country music stations are, first, good radio stations, regardless of the music they play.[7] . . .

THE RECORD INDUSTRY REACTS

For decades the country-music segment was considered the most stable profit center in the record industry. In fact, the steady profitability of the country-music division saved several major firms in those years when they had lost substantial sums on heavily promoted rock-music failures.[8] While country-music sales before 1970 were not often large, production costs were low, promotion costs were little more than favors to influential disc jockeys, performers were not demanding, and fans were loyal and bought records in predictable numbers. The four major record firms, RCA, Capital, Columbia, and Decca (now MCA), regularly divided a 66–89 percent market share while the rest of the country-music sales were divided among a number of small independent companies.

But the rapid expansion and redefinition of country radio changed all this. The million-selling record and the LP grossing a million dollars in sales were rare before 1965, but by 1977 they were regularly expected by company executives if still not often obtained. Beginning in the 1960s record-makers (a generic term used here to include all those behind-the-scenes people from songwriters, publishers, and producers to sales and promotion personnel) regularly increased their expectations of the number of copies a record needed to sell to be deemed successful. Production and promotion became more elaborate and expensive. At the same time the overhead on increasingly elegant corporate facilities raised costs so that the unit sales necessary to break even grew rapidly. Thus increasingly big sales were demanded of *all* performers under contract. As independent record producer Jimmy Bowen, who moved from Los Angeles to Nashville in 1977, noted: "Nashville country producers kept costs low because they worked under an (expected sales) selling of 50,000 records. I spend all I need to get a good sound; we don't go into the studio with a project unless we can project sales of 150,000."[9]

The first wave of star celebrities created by repeated air play were, of course, the darlings of the record-makers, but only so long as they enjoyed large record sales. The experience of Porter Wagoner, one of the first celebrities, who, paired with Dolly Parton, won the CMA Vocal Duo of the Year award in 1970 and 1971, illustrates the hazards of the new high-pressure industry. Many of the new country-radio programmers did not like his nasal sound. As Roy Stingley of WJJD—Chicago said in 1972, "These days I sometimes have to bear in mind just how country I can be. I have a new Porter Wagoner record maybe, and I can't play it 'cause it's *too* country."[10] Within a year Dolly Parton along with Buck Trent, Wagoner's most proficient backup musician, left Wagoner to seek more new-wave-oriented careers. In the years following, his air play and record sales dropped relative to other performers even though he remained one of the most popular performers in live shows around the country.

The new economics of the record industry had more dire consequences for many of those working below the star level. In the early and middle 1970s, record-makers cut scores of the troupers from their company rosters. This happened even if the artist was selling as many records as ever, because that level of sales could not pay for the new high level of costs. Companies wanted to concentrate on their hit-makers and publicly justified the roster cuts by noting that the troupers did not have hit records as indexed by air play. Thus in a short period of time the greater part of a generation of entertainers who played conventional country music found themselves cut off from making records, the most important tool of their artistic production.

Many music-makers in the industry tried to accommodate to the changing definition of country music implicit in the new country radio since record sales depended on radio air play. Songwriters, publishers, producers, arrangers, and all those record-industry people involved in the flow of music to the market melded their efforts to fit with the new country-radio sound. They did this even though some recognized that it was not necessarily what the country-music audience wanted. Paul Soelberg, in a prophetic 1970 article entitled "Modern Country Radio: Friend or Foe?," put the point succinctly: "The economics of country music are vitally dependent on getting air exposure for the product. As a result, product creators now must devote substantial attention to producing products calculated to appeal not necessarily to the fan, but to the new programmers now holding the power of life or death over new records." By way of illustration, Soelberg quotes a record-maker "We sometimes have to make records that go against our instincts. Theoretically we are supposed to make records meant for the fans to judge; instead we find ourselves thinking about what the (radio programmer) will or will not reject."[11] Thus, in effect, the radio programmer rather than the ultimate record-buyer becomes the "audience" for record-makers.

The processes of adapting country music to the new country-radio sound accelerated after 1973 when several corporations which were already powerful in the popular-music market, most notably Warner Brothers, United Artists, Playboy, and Motown Records, successfully entered the country-music field. These companies entered the competition geared to satisfying the new country-created market, and many established record-makers, most notably Billy Sherrill and Al Gallico, emulated their success. Finally, successful country-music artists began to drop their country-music-oriented producers for established Los Angeles easy-listening-oriented producers. For example, in 1977 Jimmy Bowen, producer of Dean Martin, Sammy Davis, Jr., and Frank Sinatra, began producing the records of several leading country artists, including Mel Tillis. In the same year, Barbara Streisand's producer, Garry Klein, began producing Dolly Parton, and Al Martino's producer, Joel Diamond, began producing Eddy Arnold.

The general strategy was to create records that would be played on country stations and would also cross over to be played on radio stations with a format other than country music. To achieve this, the hard distinctive edges of the country sound were eliminated, and elements drawn from mood music, pop, soul, or rock were added. This "search for crossovers" strategy was also adopted in much of the commercial-music industry beyond country music as well, so that in the mid-1970s the various distinct industry-defined genres of music came to sound more and more alike.

THE NEW COUNTRY PERFORMERS

All of the changes in country radio and recording described above make it possible for a number of pop-oriented artists to achieve wider acclaim through country music. The most obvious cases of this sort of crossovers to country music are Olivia Newton-John in 1974, John Denver in 1975, and Kenny Rodgers in 1977. Because of their following in popular music, these artists had a great advantage in obtaining sales and industry notoriety. As country-music trouper Johnny Paycheck noted in a 1976 interview, "If some artist in the pop field gets a crossover hit into the country field, it's a lead pipe cinch he will win the awards. Pure country artists do not have a chance. We do not care about crossover hits. We want straight good country hits, but we want to be acknowledged for them."[12] A number of established artists like Loretta Lynn, Mel Tillis, and Dolly Parton were able to modernize their sound and began to produce records *intended* to cross over from country into the other commercial radio formats.

After 1973, a potentially much more important process began to be evident as well. A whole group of performers tailored their music and images to the new country-radio sound and hoped their records would be played on other types of stations as well. The first highly successful example was the classical and jazz-trained piano-player Ronny Milsap, who was named Country Music Association Male Vocalist of the Year in 1974 and Country Music Entertainer of the Year in 1977. Both the similarities and the diversity in the new country sound, however, are best illustrated by the successful new females—Tanya Tucker, Barbara Mandrell, Linda Ronstadt, Emmie Lou Harris, and Crystal Gale—and their male counterparts—Don Williams, Larry Gatlin, Gene Watson, Eddy Rabbit, and Gary Stewart. The rapid and profound shift in the country music played on commercial radio stations is indexed by the list of the twenty most-played records of 1977. Only three of these twenty were by artists like Loretta Lynn and Merle Haggard who represented the pre-1974 sound, while five were by popular-music artists, including Tom Jones, whose records had crossed over to country, and eight were by the new pop-country artists such as Ronny Milsap, Crystal Gale, and Linda Ronstadt.[13] Obviously, the new style country radio had a profound impact.

CONCLUSIONS

The several interrelated sequences of events in the radio and phonograph-record industries just described have had important consequences for the scope and nature of what is called country music. But it is not our purpose here to detail them fully. Suffice it to say that the events described represent one case of the revolutionary phase of a cycle in country music which recurs every several decades. In each cycle, a kind of country music is spread and then pushed from the limelight by new media and marketing techniques. These, in turn, facilitate the emergence of a new-sounding generation of country-music artists. Typically, the displaced forms of music do not die; instead they become distinct genres with loyal creators and fans. The bluegrass style is an excellent case in point. A derivative of the string-band music of the 1930s, it was kept alive and revived in the 1960s as a folk-music form.

In tracing the ACE case in terms of the production-of-culture perspective, we have placed the greatest emphasis on changes taking place in the radio and record industries. A complete analysis in this perspective would pay more attention to creators and consumers as well, because creative innovations are being made all the time for an audience whose tastes do change. But in country music, as in all the arts which depend on commercial media, the questions of *which* creative efforts will be fostered and *whose* tastes will be catered to depend increasingly on the intervening technological and organizational elements in the production of culture.

NOTES

[1] Richard A. Peterson and Russell Davis, Jr., "The Contemporary American Radio Audience," *Journal of Popular Music and Society* 6 (Spring 1977): 12–18; and Michael D. Hughes, Richard A. Peterson, and Michael S. Swafford, "Patterns of Cultural Consumption in Contemporary America," paper presented at the 1978 Southern Sociological Society meetings, New Orleans.

[2] Quoted in the Country Music Association's 1977 Broadcasters Kit.

[3] All data on the number of country-music stations are drawn from the Country Music Association's listings. The Association's kind cooperation in providing these and other data is gratefully acknowledged. No other musical genre, including classical music and opera, enjoys such a diligent advocate.

[4] The generic term "programmer" is used to refer to all those involved in selecting the station format. This includes announcers (usually called disc-jockeys or dee-jays), music directors, and, at the general-policy level, station managers.

[5] This style of presentation is increasingly hard to find on the air, but was still an element of WSM's Grand Ole Opry presentation in the late 1970s.

[6] *Billboard,* 26 December 1978, p. 28.

[7] The spelling and punctuation are taken directly from the news release.

[8] This has been recounted to me by executives of three different record firms. None wished to be quoted on the point. All of the uncited assertations of this selection have been drawn either from my own observation, unpublished industry records, or informants wishing anonymity.

[9] In an 8 January 1978, personal interview.

[10] *Country Music,* November 1972, p. 17.

[11] See Paul W. Soelberg, "Modern Country Radio: Friend or Foe? *Billboard,* 17 October 1978.

[12] The distinctively personal and candid nature of country lyrics is illustrated in the titles of Paycheck's best-selling records: "I'm The Only Hell My Mama Ever Raised," "Slide Off Your Satin Sheets" (sung to a dissatisfied upwardly mobile woman), "Eleven Months and 29 Days" (about jail), and "Take This Job and Shove It!"

[13] The other four were by persons identified as ex-rockers, Waylon Jennings and Charlie Rich, or by Elvis Presley, whose death in 1977 signaled a jump in the sales of his records in all markets. See *Radio and Records,* 23 December 1977.

MEDIA AS SHAPERS OF PERCEPTION

Each of the essays in this section is about stereotypes—stereotyped images of people, events, and ideas or stereotyped ways of thinking and working. In most cases, the authors are not talking about deliberate attempts by media creators to offend anyone or to mislead the public. Rather, these articles describe and analyze the powerful workings of the mostly subtle assumptions humans make about other people. In everything we do, whether writing news reports, composing novels, or speaking with friends, we use stereotypes to process and organize information. Stereotypes are relatively easier to discern in mass media because they are often blatant and because we are more likely to question media portrayals than we are the portrayals we or our friends and family members construct. Critics, too, are often quick to attack glib or stereotyped portrayals in the media. This section does not catalog obvious media stereotypes. Rather, it frames the subject of stereotypes more broadly to include all kinds of perceptual errors born of oversimplification and unquestioned assumptions. Although media still are the focus of discussion, the implication of the authors' observations reach well beyond the media.

The section begins with Walter Lippmann's classic articulation of the idea that we humans create—not merely observe—the "realities" that form the basis of our actions. To Lippmann, stereotyping realities is normal and inevitable. His analysis, which we have excerpted briefly, predates the terminology of information theory and perceptual psychology that we now use to describe the behavior he discusses. His work also anticipates such concepts as the "pseudo event," which Daniel Boorstin later developed, and the growth in newsmakers' manipulation of their mediated images. Lippmann is responsible for our current use of the word *stereotype* to mean an oversimplified conception of something or someone. His distinction between "the world outside and the pictures in our heads" remains valid, powerful, and relevant to an understanding of mass communication processes, even though Lippmann wrote before the existence of many contemporary mass media.

Bernard Rubin acknowledges Lippmann's contribution and then offers a critique of his work, not to discredit Lippmann so much as to underscore his main points: that stereotypes are very powerful and that the most difficult place to discern them is in our own thinking. For example, Rubin points to Lippmann's blind spots where gender and the persecution of European Jews were concerned.

Mel Watkins' article is about images of black people in the media, especially television. He offers a historical review of famous black television characters and describes what it was like to grow up with television's limited portrayal of his race. Watkins points out that most current portrayals remain inaccurate and suggests that the most authentic pictures of black people are created by black people.

The next four essays in this section address the tension between the journalistic ideal of objectivity and the bias brought on by unacknowledged assumptions. Herbert J. Gans offers a compendium of enduring values in American journalism. Permeating the world view that the news media convey, these values present society as journalists think it ought to be rather than as it is. Gans asserts that these underlying messages are the real messages of the news and that they may reveal more about journalists than they do about the world.

Denise Kervin provides us with a case study for Gans's thesis. She analyzes how television network news defined the "reality" of the civil war in El Salvador from 1977 to 1982. Her detailed content analysis shows that values are present not only in journalists' words, but in their television pictures, too. Kervin connects the values she has discerned in the news coverage of El Salvador with American culture, concluding that our news pictures may say more about us than they do about El Salvador.

Herbert Schmertz agrees with Gans and Kervin that news is distorted, but he is more openly critical of newsworkers. Schmertz says the problem is that newsworkers are, from a demographic standpoint, unrepresentative of the American people. He is concerned about the press's power to manipulate images. Calling the press "unethical" and "irresponsible," Schmertz speaks as someone who often has been the subject of news stories with which he has been dissatisfied. He calls for the press to take more responsibility for covering people and events accurately.

Like Schmertz, Cal Thomas expresses strong feelings about bias in the press. His approach differs in that he calls upon those who are the subjects of the news, rather than journalists, to take action. Thomas' essay is addressed to conservatives, whose views he believes have not been accurately represented in the media. He offers practical advice on ways to handle the press, to respond to criticism, and to assure that conservatives' (or anyone else's) best image finds expression in the news. Thomas' essay provides a peek into the world of public relations, a world that, ironically, is seldom seen by the public.

It is easy to come away from these readings with the impression that we almost always play the game of perception without a full deck. One thing is certain: we can never be sure we see any picture whole. Stereotyping—the creation or use of a conventional, oversimplified image—is useful. It allows us to cope with large amounts of information quickly. Moreover, stereotyping is natural, even necessary to some extent. Studies of human perception have shown that, to process information, the sense organs and central nervous system must simplify—and systematically destroy—some of that information.

If stereotypes are useful, natural, and inevitable, how are we to contend with the negative effects they can have? Why should we bother to try? First of all, not to try is to surrender to the power of stereotypes to govern our behavior and our thinking. Second, even though stereotypes are inescapable, their power is not absolute. It is possible to minimize being misled by stereotypes if we regularly examine our assumptions and question the assumptions of others, including the media's. Such questioning sometimes will be seen as impertinent, even to ourselves. It usually is more comfortable not to do it; however, interrogating stereotypes and questioning assumptions must be lifelong endeavors because there is another certainty in all of this: the unposed question *will* go unanswered.

Study Questions: Lippmann

?

What is the moral of Lippmann's tale of the English, French, and Germans? What relevance, if any, does it have for the contemporary world? Might it have any relevance for our country's foreign policy toward Iran, Cuba, China, or the Soviet Union?

Lippmann's story is about faraway events the people on that island could not observe directly. Are there analogous situations in your home town, in your college, or perhaps even in your home that you can know only "indirectly"? Is there a moral in his story that is relevant when we are concerned about close-to-home situations?

Lippmann argues that we adjust to our environment through "the medium of fictions." What does he mean by that? Does he mean that all news stories or things people tell us are fictions? What are the implications of such a claim?

Why is it easier to find errors in our perceptions through hindsight than to perceive things accurately as they are happening?

Why do we persist in constructing erroneous pictures of others even when we know from experience that such perceptions can lead to costly mistakes?

What recent examples of costly errors induced by faulty perceptions can you think of? What role, if any, did the media play in abetting or exposing those false perceptions in your example?

Does this excerpt from Lippmann's book contain any evidence that the author had blind spots in his own vision—that some of his perceptions were faulty?

Walter Lippmann

PUBLIC OPINION

The world outside and the pictures in our heads

There is an island in the ocean where in 1914 a few Englishmen, French-men, and Germans lived. No cable reaches that island, and the British mail steamer comes but once in sixty days. In September it had not yet come, and the islanders were still talking about the latest newspaper which told about the approaching trial of Madame Caillaux for the shooting of Gaston Calmette. It was, therefore, with more than usual eagerness that the whole colony assembled at the quay on a day in mid-September to hear from the captain what the verdict had been. They learned that for over six weeks now those of them who were English and those of them who were French had been fighting in behalf of the sanctity of treaties against those of them who were Germans. For six strange weeks they had acted as if they were friends, when in fact they were enemies.

But their plight was not so different from that of most of the population of Europe. They had been mistaken for six weeks, on the continent the interval may have been only six days or six hours. There was an interval. There was a moment when the picture of Europe on which men were conducting their business as usual, did not in any way correspond to the Europe which was about to make a jumble of their lives. There was a time for each man when he was still adjusted to an environment that no longer existed. All over the world as late as July 25th men were making goods that they would not be able to ship, buying goods they would not be able to import, careers were being planned, enterprises contemplated, hopes and expectations entertained, all in the belief that the world as known was the world as it was. Men were writing books describing the world. They trusted the picture in their heads. And then over four years later, on a Thursday morning, came the news of an armistice, and people gave vent to their unutterable relief that the slaughter was over. Yet in the five days before the real armistice came, though the end of the war had been cele-brated, several thousand young men died on the battlefields.

Looking back we can see how indirectly we know the environment in which nevertheless we live. We can see that the news of it comes to us now fast, now slowly; but that whatever we believe to be a true picture, we treat as if it were the environment itself. It is harder to remember that about the beliefs upon which we are now acting, but in respect to other peoples and other ages we flatter ourselves that it is easy to see when they were in deadly earnest about ludicrous pictures of the world. We insist, because of our superior hindsight, that the world as they needed to know it, and the world as they did know it, were often two quite contradictory things. We can see, too, that while they governed and fought, traded and reformed in the world as they imagined it to be, they produced results, or failed to produce any, in the world as it was. They started for the Indies and found America. They diagnosed evil and hanged old women. They thought they could grow rich by always selling and never buying. A caliph, obeying what he conceived to be the Will of Allah, burned the library at Alexandria. . . .

We can best understand the furies of war and politics by remembering that almost the whole of each party believes absolutely in its picture of the opposition, that it takes as fact, not what is, but what it supposes to be the fact. And that therefore, like Hamlet, it will stab Polonius behind the rustling curtain, thinking him the King, and perhaps like Hamlet add:

> Thou wretched, rash, intruding fool, farewell!
> I took thee for thy better; take thy fortune.

Great men, even during their lifetime, are usually known to the public only through a fictitious personality. Hence the modicum of truth in the old saying that no man is a hero to his valet. There is only a modicum of truth, for the valet, and the private secretary, are often immersed in the fiction themselves. Royal personages are, of course, constructed personalities. Whether they themselves believe in their public character, or whether they merely permit the chamberlain to stage manage it, there are at least two distinct selves, the public and regal self, the private and human. . . .

The only feeling that anyone can have about an event he does not experience is the feeling aroused by his mental image of that event. That is why until we know what others think they know, we cannot truly understand their acts. I have seen a young girl, brought up in a Pennsylvania mining town, plunged suddenly from entire cheerfulness into a paroxysm of grief when a gust of wind cracked the kitchen windowpane. For hours she was inconsolable, and to me incomprehensible. But when she was able to talk, it transpired that if a windowpane broke it meant that a close relative had died. She was, therefore, mourning for her father, who had frightened her into running away from home. The father was, of course, quite thoroughly alive as a telegraphic inquiry soon proved. But until the telegram came, the cracked glass was an authentic message to that girl. Why it was authentic only a prolonged investigation by a skilled psychiatrist could show. But even the most casual observer could see that the girl, enormously upset by her family troubles, had hallucinated a complete fiction out of one external fact, a remembered superstition, and a turmoil of remorse, and fear and love for her father.

Abnormality in these instances is only a matter of degree. When an attorney general, who has been frightened by a bomb exploded on his doorstep, convinces himself by the reading of revolutionary literature that a revolution is to happen on the first of May 1920, we recognize that much the same mechanism is at work. The war, of course, furnished many examples of this pattern: the casual fact, the creative imagination, the will to believe, and out of these three elements, a counterfeit of reality to which there was a violent instinctive response. For it is clear enough that under certain conditions men respond as powerfully to fictions as they do to realities, and that in many cases they help to create the very fictions to which they respond. Let him cast the first stone who did not believe in the Russian army that passed through England in August, 1914, did not accept any tale of atrocities without direct proof, and never saw a plot, a traitor, or a spy where there was none. Let him cast a stone who never passed on as the real inside truth what he had heard someone say who knew no more than he did.

In all these instances we must note particularly one common factor. It is the insertion between man and his environment of a pseudo-environment. To that pseudo-environment his behavior is a response. But because it *is* behavior, the consequences, if they are acts, operate not in the pseudo-environment where the behavior is stimulated, but in the real environment where action eventuates. If the behavior is not a practical act, but what we call roughly thought and emotion, it may be a long time before there is any noticeable break in the texture of the fictitious world. But when the stimulus of the pseudo-fact results in action on things or other people, contradiction soon develops. Then comes the sensation of butting one's head against a stone wall, of learning by experience, and witnessing Herbert Spencer's tragedy of the murder of a Beautiful Theory by a Gang of Brutal Facts, the discomfort in short of a maladjustment. For certainly, at the level of social life, what is called the adjustment of man to his environment takes place through the medium of fictions.

By fictions I do not mean lies. I mean a representation of the environment which is in lesser or greater degree made by man himself. The range of fiction extends all the way from complete hallucination to the scientists' perfectly self-conscious use of a schematic model, or his decision that for his particular problem accuracy beyond a certain number of decimal places is not important. A work of fiction may have almost any degree of fidelity, and so long as the degree of fidelity can be taken into account, fiction is not misleading. In fact, human culture is very largely the selection, the rearrangement, the tracing of patterns upon, and the stylizing of, what William James called "the random irradiations and resettlements of our ideas."[1] The alternative to the use of fictions is direct exposure to the ebb and flow of sensation. That is not a real alternative, for however refreshing it is to see at times with a perfectly innocent eye, innocence itself is not wisdom, though a source and corrective of wisdom.

For the real environment is altogether too big, too complex, and too fleeting for direct acquaintance. We are not equipped to deal with so much subtlety, so much variety, so many permutations and combinations. And although we have to act in that environment, we have to reconstruct it on a simpler model before we can manage with it. To traverse the world men must have maps of the world. Their persistent difficulty is to secure maps on which their own need, or someone else's need, has not sketched in the coast of Bohemia. . . .

And so before we involve ourselves in the jungle of obscurities about the innate differences of men, we shall do well to fix our attention upon the extraordinary differences in what men know of the world. I do not doubt that there are important biological differences. Since man is an animal it would be strange if there were not. But as rational beings it is worse than shallow to generalize at all about comparative behavior until there is a measurable similarity between the environments to which behavior is a response.

The pragmatic value of this idea is that it introduces a much needed refinement into the ancient controversy about nature and nurture, innate quality and environment. For the pseudo-environment is a hybrid compounded of "human nature" and "conditions." To my mind it shows the uselessness of pontificating about what man is and always will be from what we observe man to be doing, or about what are the necessary conditions of society. For we do not know how men would behave in response to the facts of the Great Society. All that we really know is how they behave in response to what can fairly be called a most inadequate picture of the Great Society. No conclusion about man or the Great Society can honestly be made on evidence like that.

This, then, will be the clue to our inquiry. We shall assume that what each man does is based not on direct and certain knowledge, but on pictures made by himself or given to him. If his atlas tells him that the world is flat he will not sail near what he believes to be the edge of our planet for fear of falling off. If his maps include a fountain of eternal youth, a Ponce de Leon will go in quest of it. If someone digs up yellow dirt that looks like gold, he will for a time act exactly as if he had found gold. The way in

[1]James, *Principles of Psychology* 2:638.

which the world is imagined determines at any particular moment what men will do. It does not determine what they will achieve. It determines their effort, their feelings, their hopes, not their accomplishments and results. . . .

Study Questions: Rubin

[?] *From your observations of the media, are Rubin's generalizations about stereotyping valid? Are there some kinds of stereotyping in the media that he has overlooked? Can you find in a recent issue of a newspaper an example of one of the kinds of stereotyping Rubin describes? How would you revise that story to overcome the problem?*

In what ways can stereotyping result from information one does not report, rather than from information one does report?

What major issues that have nothing to do with media stereotyping does Rubin discuss? What can media workers do about these issues?

What are the main points of Rubin's critique of Lippmann?

Rubin criticizes the following sentence from The Boston Globe *story about a new author:*

> Monsky tells the story in a soft-spoken Southern accent which doesn't quite seem to go with her Semitic features and intellectual-looking wire-rimmed glasses.

What is Rubin's criticism of that description? Is his criticism justified?

Assuming all of Rubin's arguments in this essay are valid, what would you do about stereotypes if you were a newspaper editor or producer of movies or television series? Can stereotypes be eliminated from the media? Is it possible to create a drama or story about the military or about religion that will be meaningful to an audience without some reliance on familiar stereotypes? What would a reasonable policy on stereotyping be for a news medium?

How should a mass communicator deal with the fact that stereotypes exist not simply in media content, but also in the minds of audience members?

Do you agree with Rubin's assertion that television has numbed our perceptual defenses against stereotyping?

Bernard Rubin

MASS MEDIA STEREOTYPING AND ETHNIC AND RELIGIOUS GROUPS

The shorthand language of stereotyping is quick, easy, and pervasive—but usually wrong.

Stereotyping can be useful whenever one needs to convey in shorthand a body of descriptive messages about a person or a group. These distillations are not inherently good or bad, beneficial or harmful, elevating or degrading, or true or false. Every such intellectual exchange, which paints a picture with a few broad brush strokes, must be examined carefully before categorization.

For example, one can applaud a clarion call from Pope John Paul to "good Christians" in the context of one of his pilgrimages around the world, without requiring proof that the masses of people observed in the television scenes live up to his high standards. "Born Again" Christians are, it seems, forever explaining to the rest of us how one arrives at such a state of grace. Stereotypes are not substitutes for identifications or definitive characterizations.

It is easier to package the "You've come a long way, baby" new woman in a cigarette advertisement than it is to depict the so-called liberated woman in a documentary film. Stereotyping works best when moral, social, economic, political, and philosophic issues are not central to the communication process. That is not to say that profound issues and values are not easily conveyed by stereotypes, but to conclude that only fools or very wise individuals would rely on stereotyping as a prime means of conveying important ideas. More accidents are possible than is appreciated when one uses stereotypes as substitutes for deeper explanatory methods of communication. Try, for instance, to typify all middle-class blacks in one short-burst word or pictorial (painting, photograph, etc.) effort. Or, try to stereotype all Native Americans, all Moonies, all of the steel industry's unemployed, or all of the students of theology at the Harvard Divinity School. It's not likely that you'll succeed.

Nevertheless, stereotyping influences more people daily for short- and long-run effects than any of us would like to admit. The highest appeals

Bernard Rubin is Professor of Government Affairs and Communication, Boston University. He presented the above paper at the Seventh National Workshop on Christian-Jewish Relations last April in Boston. The text has been lightly edited for publication.

for inspired activity as well as the crudest calls for mean work are framed in stereotypical language that describes "them" or "us." Racists find stereotyping most useful for packaging lies, slanders, deceits, and innuendoes as they go about the business of tearing at groups they would destroy. At the other end of the social scale are honest do-gooders who disseminate stereotypical messages with patient anticipation of a commonwealth devoted to personal and intergroup harmony. They paint the pictures they would like to see.

Walter Lippmann, in his book *Public Opinion* (1922), discussed stereotypes at length. He transferred the label from its usage in the printing industry (molded type plates used to produce exact copies from the originals) and signalled its utility whenever people want to catalog, categorize, or capsulate ideas or situations so that others may make easy references for easy recognitions. He made us realize that, "What matters is the character of the stereotypes and the gullibility with which we employ them." Among his illustrations we find: "He is an intellectual. He is a plutocrat. He is a foreigner. He is a 'South European.' He is from Back Bay. He is a Harvard Man." Lippmann goes on, "How different from the statement: He is a Yale Man. He is a regular fellow. He is a West Pointer. He is a Greenwich Villager. He is an intellectual banker. He is from Main Street."

Mr. Lippman, in 1922, did not realize how unsavory all of the he-this and he-that would appear to present-day humanists anxious to live in a world of opportunity and respect, regardless of gender. He was savant enough, though, to warn us that there was a direct connection between blind spots and stereotypes. "Uncritically held, the stereotype not only censors out much that needs to be taken into account, but when the day of reckoning comes, and the stereotype is shattered, likely as not that which it did take wisely into account is shipwrecked with it."

Mr. Lippmann's intellectual accomplishments in this century in the areas of punditry about public affairs—both national and international—rank him high against any contenders, but he had his own blind spots. One story that he did not deal with sufficiently was the Nazi design for destruction which decimated European Jewry. Mr. Lippmann was not without flaw.

Indeed, a conspicuous lesson about stereotyping can be learned from the famed Walter Lippmann, world affairs expert extraordinaire of the American press, a man whose influence with editorial writers and columnists exceeded that of his contemporaries in journalism. The lesson is how devastating bias can be. For reasons having to do more with his own psychological needs and fears, from the time he was a young man, Lippmann wanted to be with what he perceived as the American majority. He molded himself into a lead type slug and wrote WASP. With his German Jewish background, he cast a suspicious eye on the hordes of Jewish immigrants emigrating to the United States from eastern and southern Europe. Their looks, ways, and religious customs offended him to a large degree. Not only was he perplexed to find that they were out of step with the prevailing Anglo-Saxon heritage and drives (how could it have been otherwise?), but also he was determined to be the advice giver, showing them the way to an enlightened status.

The fascinating aspect of this Lippmann fixation was how dogged he was in its defense and how he elaborated on the theme through the years. He even refused to deal personally with the Holocaust. We are indebted to Ronald Steel, his biographer, for the incisive book, *Walter Lippmann and the American Century,* which reveals a brilliant person with some mental warts.

It is well to bear in mind that Lippmann became more and more pessimistic, as the years went by, about the virtues of public opinion as determined by the masses of citizens.

In 1922, the same year that Lippmann's book, *Public Opinion,* appeared, he wrote (I choose one of his less blatant comments to reveal his mental approach to stereotyping):

> I worry about Broadway on a Sunday afternoon, where everything that is feverish and unventilated in the congestion of a city rises up as a warning that you cannot build up a decent civilization among people who, when they are at last, after centuries of denial, free to go to the land and cleanse their bodies, now huddle together in a steam-heated slum.[1]

Eleven years later, he explained, with the disinterest of the truly dispassionate, that repression of the Jews, "by satisfying the lust of the Nazis who feel they must conquer somebody and the cupidity of those Nazis who want jobs, is a kind of lightning rod which protects Europe." To be fair, Lippmann admitted that there was "ruthless injustice . . . meted out to the German Jews," but one had to look at the whole picture and, downplaying the "annual passions of a great revolution," hear "the authentic voice of a genuinely civilized people."[2] After World War II, Lippmann never wrote about the death camps, though the full story of the Holocaust was revealed by legions of his fellow journalists.

There is an important lesson in the fact that Lippmann made stereotyping so clear to all the students of public opinion from 1922 to today, and yet he failed to appreciate how deeply intellectual prejudice could also serve as naked emotionalism to mold distorted pictures of persons and groups. One is forced to ask to what extent bad stereotyping can be traced to sheer snobbery or to stupidity in bypassing the real issues of how the press covers the poor, the distressed, and the downtrodden by the superficially educated who have trained themselves to avoid reality.

So far, the emphasis has been on the descriptive powers of stereotypes, and psychological backgrounds to what is communicated. There is another aspect which receives less attention but which is equally important. Much stereotyping evolves from what is not conveyed. Much stereotyping results from what is omitted in the mass media.

Recently, I had need to pore through the past three years of *Newsweek* magazine, looking for topics to assign for student research. I wanted to make sure that the list I drew up for term paper work for a class in public affairs and communications did not depend upon my memory alone, so I did some content analysis. It became clear as I examined the *Newsweek* stories, issue by issue, that there was extremely limited coverage of Asians, blacks, Native Americans, Hispanics, and students included in a number of examples I wanted to track.

To be sure, there were feature stories whenever some news event was linked to a group member, but there was little else. *Newsweek,* I knew, has had its troubles with coverage of women's affairs. Several years ago, in a law suit brought by its women employees, the magazine was revealed as somewhat insensitive to even such matters as the equality of its editorial personnel. Spurred by the judiciary, owners took corrective action. I also knew that for liberal critics coverage of minorities by the bulk of the American electronic and print press was not satisfactory. From turning the pages of *Newsweek,* I learned more—that actions do not necessarily lead to reactions and thereby complete the processes of relationships. Given what I didn't see in the pages of that magazine about the day-to-day, week-to-week, year-to-year lives of minorities in this country, I concluded that there must be a profound public reaction to the absence of reporting. I surmised that stereotypical images must be created when clients of the mass media have to fill in their own shorthand pictures of peoples who remain shadows or blurs in the press. Using that common illustration about the perception of content—"Is the glass half full or half empty?"—it is evident that when we deal with news, the context any of the media provide us with determines how we view the world. The empty portion of the news "glass" is actually fillable, if there were proper interest in subjects usually ignored or bypassed.

Nationally glorified politicians, those who manipulate giant businesses and industries, international terrorists, and theatrical personalities are usually found in the filled part of *Newsweek* or *The Boston Globe* or the ABC, CBS, and NBC networks' evening news programs. They typify what is considered newsworthy. In a sense, the mass media are organizational stereotypes because they so seldom stray from what was made clearer before. On the other hand, the masses of ordinary citizens are usually out of view or, if analyzed, made more shadowy by media reliance upon stereotypical coverage.

When presented fairly, the stereotypical imageries of groups depicted in the mass media have certain virtues. However, there is widespread concern among these groups at the casual manner in which they are designated or categorized. The Irish Americans must have had enough of rote comments about the "fighting Irish." "Stolid Swedes," "clannish Italians," "stupid Poles," "business-oriented Jews," "musically gifted blacks," "cruel Indians," "greasy Hispanics," "Puritanical Yankees," and "cunning Asians" should all be consigned to the archives of historical treatment about prejudice. If there be truth to such stereotype-casting as is alleged by some scholars even today, they should be forced to cite the evidence in the context of each of their reports.[3]

The persistence of stereotyping can have a discouraging effect upon young people, and may account for lack of progress in certain areas. A Mr. Romatowski, who had served on the Yonkers, New York, Municipal Housing Authority for 15 years as of early 1979, spoke to the issue in trying to account for the reason why leadership skills which he saw abundant in Polish-American organizations hadn't led to much leadership in the wider political scene: "We just don't get anywhere in politics. I could understand it with the first generation. They weren't educated. But I can't understand it with the second generation. Some of it probably stems from the old stereotypes which are just now breaking down."[4]

Television is a prime mover of stereotypes. Remember please, the contents of the glass—half full or half empty! My colleague, Dr. Earle Barcus, conducted a content analysis for Action for Children's Television. He studied 38 hours of children's programs shown in Boston during January 1981.

> Of the 1145 television characters that appeared . . . only 42 were black and 47 belonged to other minority groups . . . 3.7 percent of the characters were black; 3.1 percent were Hispanic, and 0.8 percent were Asian . . .
> As for females, Barcus said "Only 16 percent of all major characters in the program sample were female."[5]

I did a small computer run on minorities and stereotyping to get samples of how the wind was blowing during the last two years. Here are some examples, beginning with a hopeful current.

- *The Los Angeles Times,* March 31, 1982. "U.S. textbook publishers have made major changes in elementary school presentations because of highly vocal pressures brought by women's groups and minorities in past two decades. Illustrations now tend to show boys and girls in equal numbers and integration between white and black children. Racial stereotypes have been largely eliminated, along with sex-biased language and passive feminine symbols."
- *The New York Times,* October 12, 1981. "Officials of Venereal Disease National Hotline challenge stereotype of venereal disease victims as young, poor, and non-white. Reports only 18 percent of callers are under 20 years old, while about 83 percent are white and over 50 percent earn more than $15,000 annually."
- *The New York Times,* January 27, 1981. Report by University of Pennsyl-

vania's Annenberg School of Communications found that commercial television may be blocking public understanding and support of science. Survey of large samples of U.S. viewers finds that scientists are portrayed as older, less romantically involved, more dangerous, more doomed to failure, less sociable, less attractive, and shorter than other television characters. Finds science to be held in lower esteem by women, low income groups, non-whites, and less educated viewers.

- *The Washington Post,* October 28, 1979. Magda Abu Fadil asserts only U.S. minority that remains butt of ethnic jokes, slurs and outright prejudice is Arab community in U.S. Asserts most other minorities have organizations for objecting to offensive material.
- *The New York Times,* December 16, 1982. Residents of Portstewart (Northern Ireland) explain how country's political and religious troubles have impacted on their lives. Say there are few adult men or women in the country who are not conditioned, upon meeting a stranger, to mark that person automatically as either Protestant or Catholic, through clues of name, occupation or accent.

Stereotyping leads are sometimes slyly hidden in the context of an otherwise innocuous story—just enough provided to make a point whether that point is justified or not. Editors should hesitate to censor bias out of such stories, but they could justifiably ask for more data so that authors could decide if they meant what they said. *The Boston Globe* ran a story[6] by one of its staff members about a fine new author who sold her first novel on her first submission to a publisher. Susan Monsky so impressed the firm of Houghton Mifflin with sixty completed pages that they accepted the book *Midnight Suppers.* Carol Stocker's "Living Pages" feature, almost one-half page in length, was something of a tribute to the new author. At the risk of being picky with a few lines out of context, I take those gratuitous lines out for your review. "Monsky tells the story in a soft-spoken Southern accent which doesn't quite seem to go with her Semitic features and intellectual-looking wire-rimmed glasses." She grew up in Montgomery, Alabama. As for the Semitic features, one has the feeling in reading the piece in the *Globe* that Lippmann's advice for Jews to lay low in this society until they were indistinguishable from the folks he admired still festers. I call attention to what seems to be a small business of stereotyping *because it is so small.* Hidden away in an otherwise laudable account is the hint that Jews really are different.

Today, imagery through stereotypes of groups tends to harm more than help those groups. Too many issues of the most vexing and pressing sort have to be determined on an individualistic basis. Simplistic assignments of outlook on the extremely sensitive subject of abortion, for example, may be made by reference to a religious group's declared stand. As a consequence, Roman Catholics should be easy targets for identification about their outlooks and decisions. One could stereotypify any individual who was a devout Roman Catholic and who responded piously and automatically to the teachings of that Church. Most Orthodox Jews would, presumably, be susceptible to such identification, as would a great number of Protestants. The problem comes because we are such a concentric and democratic society. Individuals differ, on even so basic a subject as the rights and duties of human beings, even when they attend the same church on holy days and share the same religious traditions. One must be careful to delve deeply into the subject before mixing people into the same public opinion batter. One believer may be totally against abortion; another may see it is a morally acceptable escape route under certain conditions; still another may be at odds with the basic clerical stand for personal or humanistic or social or economic reasons.

With the subject of abortion the given, it soon becomes clear to the researcher that public opinions that can be allied sweep across faiths and vary according to time, place, condition, who, what, when, how, and where.

The Moral Majority has certainly taken its bruises from the mass media, which persist in depicting its leaders and members as all cut from the same tree. It is easy to use stereotyping when reporters can in words and pictures portray the Fundamentalists whose origins and outlooks owe so much to the so-called "Bible Belt." Any reflective review reveals far more complexity. Reporters find themselves dealing with, among other things: a basic branch of the generally conservative social movement in the country; a series of responses (under one banner) to the increased permissiveness in the presentations of the mass media—both print and electronic; comparatively recent developments affecting the nature of public and private education in the nation; an alliance of religious and civil associations calling for enhancement of what they consider to be traditional values; one series of responses to the over-urbanization of our society; an important alliance trying to shape foreign policy.

It is too darned easy to present the Moral Majority movement in stereotypical terms, although it is made up of similar but diverse groups. And the media take the easy way too often. Let them show the "old boys" and the demagogery as it exists, but also report the Moral Majority as a complex mosaic of persons, groups, interests, and views. A stereotypical picture into which the Moral Majority may fit as a whole may prevail, but that picture should be the sum of its parts and not just a corner of a bigger scene which is out of focus.

Now that I have made it clear that the Moral Majority is too complex to be digested in mere outline, may I remind you that I have not attempted organization evaluation for your review. Should you ask me to begin such a project, I warn you that if I came up with stereotypes from my research, they would be numerous and clear pictures. My stereotypes would, in the words of television, be a story board etched fine with much detail.

Can a stereotype be detailed? How else are we to conclude other than to plumb for detail, when looking into: human rights, the nuclear freeze, the middle class, the labor movement, Japanese employment, managerial and technological prowess, the contestants in the Middle East crises, child abuse, clerics in politics, obscurity in the media, oligarchies and peasants in Latin America, or "feminism" as a movement and as a cultural phenomenon.

The mass media are hungry to find ways around research—in short, to get as much out of as little research as possible. Marva Collins, a black woman teacher who lives in Chicago, initiated her own teaching experiment about six years ago, founding a private school in her home. The students were primarily black youngsters. At the Westside Preparatory School she and her staff attempted to improve academic skills, building lesson plans on methods to increase the motivation and inspiration of students, many of whom had been considered uneducable. The CBS series *60 Minutes* showed her and her students poring over Shakespeare, Tolstoy, and Plato. As is not unusual whenever fame dissolves into notoriety, controversy resulted from the publicity. In "dozens of articles in national publications," Ms. Collins had been labeled a "superteacher" and a "miracle worker."

Whatever the final judgments on her Westfield Preparatory School, she has complained, "I've never said I'm a superteacher, a miracle worker, all the names they gave me. It's unfair to expect me to live up to it. I'm just a teacher."[7]

Another complaint about stereotyping through word pictures was published in a 1982 "My Turn" essay in *Newsweek*[8] by a former professor at Hofstra Law School, who moved to the Amanda Cooperative Village in 1980. Sheila Rush describes the Village as a spiritual community located in Southern California where she went for inspiration and growth. It is a work-study community which Rush notes, "is organized as a village, with an elected government, open decision-making forums . . . There are both private and community-owned housing and businesses, a farm, a dairy, a market, schools, a meditation retreat and a temple used for spiritual observances . . . People come and go as they please . . . three rules: no drugs, no liquor, no dogs. We have a spiritual director whose influence is undeniable, yet no greater than that of the founder of any organization whose wisdom and compassion have been confirmed by experience."

What bothers Rush is that reporters who can visit and see whatever they want "with few if any restrictions on whom they can talk to, what they can quote" can then write about a community she doesn't recognize. "They call it a 'cult'—at best we are a 'commune'—our spiritual director is said to be a virtual dictator." Former Professor Rush concludes, "History reveals that public acceptance of new religious groups takes time. In the meantime, I hope and, yes, pray that offending members of the press become more aware of their biases and of all their possible consequences."

Rush has a point. When we think back to the Jonestown tragedy—one that was not grasped in its essentials by the press, the State of California, and the U.S. Government in time to save the lives of hundreds of people— we ought to expect that charges be verified, that press designations be confirmed, that sloppy stereotypes be avoided.

In 1971 Pope Paul VI approved *"Communio et Progressio,"* a document dealing with modern mass communications media. Basically, the pastoral instruction, according to the editors of *America,* "demonstrated an awareness that the rapid development of communications technology had resulted in a real shift in consciousness, from a Gutenberg era dominated by print to a video age where image, symbol, and more immediate impressions formed a new human language." The educational and social opportunities before the media gave rise to a certain optimistic tone in the instruction. A decade later, the editors of *America* cite evidence of the "cultural erosion" that the media can promote. One illustration points up how Western life has been often stereotyped: "Observers working in economically developing nations point out that mass media invariably present images of modern urban life and an affluent, Western style of living that young people in rural areas find unsettling."[9]

In my own numerous trips to the Third World in Asia and Africa, I find indisputable evidence to support the above contentions.

The *Minneapolis Star* announced a policy in late 1980 to keep injurious stereotypes and labels from its news pages. Commendations for the new policy came swiftly from the Jewish Community Relations Council, and the Anti-Defamation League of Minnesota and the Dakotas. The director of the Council wrote Stephen Isaacs, then editor of the *Minneapolis Star,* supporting the "laudatory aim, not easily accomplished considering the cultural stereotypes which have become part of our folklore and thus embedded in the mental images so many people hold of other groups."

Isaacs wrote that the newspaper strives to maintain news columns that are free of inadvertent slurs—whether based on race, color, nationality, locale, religion, marital or parental status, physical and/or mental status, sex, sexual preference or age.

. . . The policy statement calls for alertness to "unwitting complicity" in what amounts to reinforcing roles or labels tending to sustain stereotypes that may be offensive, whether blatantly or subtly.

Writers and editors are reminded that they should be sensitive to unintended but invidious dual standards sometimes applied to men and women in newspaper descriptions. Isaacs gave readers an example of citing family status when women make news, but using professional status when men do.

The *Star,* the report says, should avoid mentions of race unless that mention is specifically germane to the point of an article and should not routinely use shorthand descriptions of juries by race or sex unless race or sex is used to make a point in the article.[10]

We all have a great stake in media stereotyping, and we are reminded frequently of the moral, philosophic, political, and social consequences. I was very much disturbed, and continue to be so, by the plights of Haitian refugees who somehow made it to our shores—usually to the closest points they could reach in Florida. Within sight of some of Miami's luxury hotels, women, men, and children drowned when vastly overcrowded boats, held together by bits and pieces of wire or wood or cord, disintegrated. Others came to this haven after drifting for many days without food or water. Fleeing from political tyranny, from the poverty of the poorest country in the hemisphere, and towards the hope that the United States still represents around the world, they sought sanctuary.

They were met by a hostile federal administration, which declared that they were not necessarily political refugees but were economic refugees. As such, they were likely to be sent home. Some who made it to small Caribbean islands of other sovereign governments were sent back against their will.

Why were the Haitians not treated like the vast majority of the Cuban refugees? Was it because they were categorized as undesirable blacks who spoke *patois* French and who fled with little other than their lives? Was it because they were stereotyped as peasants—black, untutored, unskilled— who could not contribute to any grand political debates framed by East-West politics? Was it because we Americans have made a stereotype out of the word "refugee"? What was good enough for one type of refugees should be equally good for other types of refugees. We will have to come to grips with such issues.

Our middle-class aspirations—which I am devoted to—do not blind my eyes or close my heart to what is going on in the world. Those who fled from "Baby Doc" Duvalier and his henchmen, who take whatever water there is from the rock of economic despair that is Haiti, deserved better than they got. It took too long for the American public to sense the issues, even though we have at our command the best and most democratic communications system in the world.

What is at the root of such confusion and misapplications of traditional policies toward refugees? I believe that we are trained by television news to watch the pictures so closely that we are almost unmindful of the captions, as it were. We have been trained to observe interesting scenes without having the blood run hot or cold. Those scenes have sometimes been horrible, but we sense them as part of the horror of the theater or of the theatrical films of which we are such devoted fans. The smell of disaster, the sense of danger, the genuine anger at what is being done to our brothers and sisters steams out of our minds like vapors from the tea kettle just removed from the fire. A few moments and all is cold, the emotional taste of whatever contents remain is flat. We observe the scenes of the tragedies in the news like robot televiewers responding by command to electronic signals.

It is not too harsh to say that so much of what we see is falsely classified as entertainment. We have gone too far in merging fictional adventure with realism. El Salvador, Guatemala, Nicaragua, Haiti are all observable through the filter that too many of us intellectual, middle-class types find a useful mechanism to keep pain and anguish out of our consciousness. There are no left-right politics in what I am saying. Let arch ideologues deal with such. The Soviets screen Afghanistan from their people with controls over the media and idiotic word games. These enemies, according to the leftist totalitarians trading in disinformation, are "bandits," and those are "running dogs," and those are "lackeys of imperialism." When it comes to stereotyping, the anti-democratic forces in the world, from Nazis to Communists, make us look like babes.

It is equally hard for us to see the real problems of the unemployed, because there is so much juggling of pet stereotypical phrases such as "the media society," "the service society," the "automated economy." For two years we have dealt better with the price of gold than with the travesty inherent in offering butter and cheese to our poor when our granaries and storehouses overflow. Too much of what we see are partial stereotyped pictures with vital segments obliterated because of our own blind spots.

I refuse to believe that, as citizens of a community cherishing the ideal of equity, we cannot make stereotypes work more for us than against us.

One key to progress would be to recognize that we are often servants to the masters of advertising. Those masters have trained us to respond like Pavlov's dog to stimuli. "Buy this" or "want that" is what it is all about. Let us mix in the advertising more of the "know this," or "understand that," or "feel this" and "see that" with the eyes, the brain, and the heart working in conjunction with one another. At the very least, it is high time to take the first steps towards a re-evaluation of stereotypes. Above all, it is crucial that those connected with the mass media commence to study the uses of stereotypes for social purposes.

NOTES

[1] Ronald Steel, *Walter Lippmann and the American Century*, (Boston: Little, Brown and Company, 1980), p. 192.

[2] Steel, op. cit., pp. 330–31.

[3] William B. Helmreich, "Stereotype Truth," *The New York Times*, 15 October 1981. (I found Helmreich's conclusions to be less than profound.)

[4] Gary Kriss, "Proud Polish Overcoming Stereotypes," *The New York Times*, 18 March 1979.

[5]Norman Black, "Study Says Kids' Shows Hurt Minorities," *The Boston Globe*, 14 July 1982.

[6]Carol Stocker, "Published on the First Try," *The Boston Globe*, 11 February 1982.

[7]"'Superteacher' in Chicago Under Fire from Parents and Press," *The New York Times*, 7 March 1982.

[8]Sheila Rush, "Do We Have Freedom of Religion?" *Newsweek*, 19 July 1982.

[9]"Editorials, A Decade of 'Communication and Progress,'" *America*, 25 April 1981.

[10]"Anti-Stereotyping Policy Wins Praise," *Editor and Publisher*, 27 December 1980.

Study Questions: Watkins

[?] *Why do you think there were not more blacks and more realistic portrayals of blacks on television in the 1950s?*

What reasons can you think of that might explain why Watkins was attracted to negative stereotypes of black people in the media when he was young, even though he was black?

What effects of televised coverage of the civil rights movement does Watkins identify?

What is the significance of Watkins' observation that the blacks who appear on television tend to be teenagers and to appear in situation comedies rather than to be adults in other kinds of programs?

Has the picture changed since Watkins wrote this essay? If so, how? Does the current Bill Cosby Show *(not the one described in this article) overcome Watkins' criticism of other shows featuring black performers? How would you evaluate* Hill Street Blues *on the issues Watkins raises?*

Is contemporary treatment of blacks in news stories better, worse, or about the same as that of the sixties?

Are the criticisms of media treatment of blacks equally applicable to the treatment of other minority groups on television?

What changes in mediated images of black people would you expect to see if they had control over those images? Can you cite examples of changes that might occur in images of other population groups if those groups had control of their portrayal in the media?

What connections can you make between the situation Watkins describes and Rubin's discussion of stereotyping?

Mel Watkins

BEYOND THE PALE

In the fifties, you didn't see no part of no blacks on TV. You had to be creative if you wanted to see some brothers—had to sit there in your living room and imagine some black folks. And with the people you saw on the tube, it were not easy. I mean, yeah, there was Amos 'n' Andy and sometimes old pop-eyed Mantan Moreland in a movie running like hell from somethin' he thought he seen. But for the most part you didn't see nothin' resemblin' a spade. Me, I used to get up and turn on the radio, listen to 'The Shadow,' that's 'bout the closest thing to a spade they had on the air at the time.

This comment was overheard at a Harlem bar during a commercial break in a Saturday afternoon football broadcast, as a group of patrons bantered about how often they see blacks on television. The old-timer who made the remark—the bar's resident philosopher-comic—was, as usual, injecting a bit of irony and contention into an otherwise predictable conversation. And, as odd as they may have seemed to the younger patrons at the bar, his observations were basically correct.

Certainly, blacks' changing roles have made television-watching today a radically different experience from what it was in the early fifties, when I was a child in a small Midwestern mill town and my family purchased its first television set.

Then, any child old enough to spend Saturday afternoons at the movies, to scan the newspapers occasionally, or to be aware of current radio programs, knew that for some reason—illogical as it may have been—blacks were rarely seen, heard, or mentioned anywhere in the media. When they were, they appeared in the guise of some grossly distorted burlesque figure, never more than a borderline literate—or they were perpetrators of some ghastly crime. In other words, they were *not* really blacks as I knew them. (There were very few rapists among my early acquaintances, and I just didn't know anyone for whom grinning was a constant preoccupation; media images notwithstanding, growing up in the ghetto was a very *serious* and dangerous affair.) But since no one else seemed to question the situation, I simply accepted it as just another of the strange perversions of the adult world.

Even so, my initial encounters with blacks on television during the fifties

Mel Watkins is an editor at *The New York Times Book Review*. He is currently writing a book on black-American humor.

were tinged with a persistent uneasiness. I mean, to be presented with Farina, Stymie, or Buckwheat of Hal Roach's *Our Gang* comedies, with Mantan Moreland in the Charlie Chan mysteries, with Stepin Fetchit and Willie Best—and to realize that they were the *only* blacks on television—was to sense an attitude both insulting and frightening in the nonblack world beyond one's living room. *Is that the way they see me?* That question always hung there, somewhat dampening the humor of those old movies.

And if the black image in those movies (which constituted a large part of early television programming) was embarrassing, it was no better in the weekly series. One would have thought that blacks had only three occupational options: singing and dancing, working as a servant, or—again—just grinning. There was Eddie "Rochester" Anderson as a valet on Jack Benny's show, and there was Lillian Randolph as a maid on *The Great Gildersleeve*. Later on, the title role in *Beulah*, yet another maid's part, was played at various times by Ethel Waters, Hattie McDaniel, and Louise Waters. And of course, there was *Amos 'n' Andy*. Except for entertainers such as Lena Horne, Leontyne Price, the late Nat "King" Cole, Harry Belafonte, and a few smiling faces in crowd scenes, these shows offered the only representation of blacks on early television.

Still, as sparse and distorted as that representation was, I can recall waiting anxiously in front of the television set any time a black performer was scheduled to appear. (Few blacks I knew ever missed *Amos 'n' Andy*.) Despite the rapt attention, though, we rarely identified with those blacks on the home screen.

The strongest impression I derived from television in the fifties, then, was a sense of the vast distance between the black and the white worlds. Programs like *Beulah* or *The Jack Benny Show*, and movies with comedians like Mantan Moreland or Stepin Fetchit, presented blacks in white environments, portraying them in such a bizarre manner that I couldn't for a second imagine they had anything to do with reality. They were about as authentic to me as Superman or Br'er Rabbit. *Amos 'n' Andy* was the only show at the time with a nearly all-black cast, and that made it a little more familiar to me. Moreover, in private—that is, not in the presence of whites—I found Kingfish's larcenous activities hilarious, and not that far-removed from those of certain people I knew who could have been his prototype. (At the time, I don't recall that any of us were aware of the more serious consequences of the burlesque images of black professionals—doctors and lawyers—perpetuated by this show.) Still, *Amos 'n' Andy* only worked to confirm my sense of the black world as an insulated, separate place from which I could only escape at considerable risk to self-esteem and safety. I have little doubt that it did the same for the fair-skinned children I saw every day in school (but never saw afterwards).

If certain social critics are right about the medium being the message, then the message of the fifties was all too clear, *"If you white, you right. If you black, get back."* Considering the grassroots idealism and optimism still alive among blacks at that time, and the visual medium's power to mold behavior patterns, the timing for those black video images was atrocious. Not only was television not suggesting even the possibility of a racially harmonious America, it was affirming just the opposite—a separatist world, where blacks were only tolerated in white society as servants, buffoons, or entertainers. It doesn't require much hindsight to recognize that the television images of the fifties and the early sixties were ruinous to black-white rapprochement. We are probably still paying for the medium's blunder with added social unrest and racial violence.

Ordinary blacks finally made their first significant television appearances during the sixties civil rights movement—not in sit coms, but during sit-ins and on national news broadcasts. The impact was overwhelming. Suddenly, here were throngs of real, live people—until now confined by American television to the realm of the nonexistent.

For me—one of a handful of black students at a Northern college during the sixties—watching those newscasts was a shattering experience. The blatant inhumanity and brutality emerging from the confrontation between black protesters and unyielding whites brought home a hard truth: From the moment the first dog or fire-hose was turned loose on a crowd of blacks, the first black child spat upon by an enraged Southern housewife, the first skull cracked by a well-aimed nightstick, one knew that the dream of black assimilation into the fabric of American society had been set back for decades—possibly forever. For an entire generation of black children just now moving into adulthood, those were the first real images of blacks interacting with whites ever witnessed on television. They are images unlikely to be forgotten, much less forgiven.

For whites, also, this abrupt intrusion of blacks onto the television screen, and therefore into their homes, must have been appalling—whether because they empathized with the protesters and abhorred violence, or because they were hostile to those upstarts who dared step "out of their place" and threaten a monochromatic world.

The civil rights movement fizzled with minimal gains and ultimately halted under the weight of benign neglect. But it accomplished much in directing media attention to the plight of black Americans. National awareness expanded throughout the sixties with coverage of the more militant protests and race riots.

It does not seem altogether coincidental that *I Spy*, the first prime-time adventure series to feature a black in a starring role, first aired in 1965, the year after race riots erupted in Philadelphia, Rochester, New York City, and Elizabeth, New Jersey, and a month after the destruction of Watts in Los Angeles. Nor is it surprising that NBC suddenly discovered an easing of resistance among advertisers and affiliated stations to the idea of a black lead in a weekly series.

And so Bill Cosby became the Jackie Robinson of network television, co-starring with Robert Culp as a CIA agent in *I Spy*. Cosby, a twenty-seven-year-old nightclub comedian at the time, made his dramatic debut in the show and went on to win three successive Emmy Awards for "outstanding continued performance by an actor in a leading role in a dramatic series." Yet, despite the quality of his performances and the undeniable entertainment value of the show, I could never see the casting of Cosby as much more than a thinly disguised attempt to cool off the anger and bitterness that had ignited the Watts riot.

After all, he portrayed a character accepted by the system who continually risked his life to protect it. Moreover, at a time when the fight for equal rights had made racial violence endemic, the subject of race was seldom even touched on by Cosby or Culp. The show had absolutely nothing to do with the reality of America in 1965, and consequently had little or no effect on the growing racial tension. It did represent a breakthrough in casting, and apparently television executives thought this was enough.

But, just as early riots had spurred television networks to hire blacks both behind the scenes and on camera, continued violence in American cities—and the assassination of Martin Luther King, Jr.—intensified the drive for more adequate black representation in the television industry. Protests by black organizations about bias in the industry had also increased dramatically. In certain instances, lawsuits had been filed against television station owners and, as with WLBT in Jackson, Mississippi, some owners were threatened with loss of their federal licenses. The Federal Communications Commission had by this time adopted an anti-discrimination policy based on the 1964 Civil Rights Act.

So, with pressure from all sides, by 1968 the television industry had to give in to the push for racial balance. In typically premature fashion, network executives began to contend that "the day of equal opportunity" was near and, conceivably to prove this claim, they scheduled two new shows featuring blacks, ABC's *The Outcasts*, a western starring Don Murray and Otis Young (portraying a former slave) as bounty hunters in antebellum America, and NBC's *Julia*, starring Diahann Carroll.

The Outcasts was produced ostensibly to correct some of the flagrant distortions in *I Spy*. Many of the episodes depicted conflict, even animosity, between Young and Murray, and Young's color was presented as a continuing problem for him. In other words, *The Outcasts* generally paid stricter attention than the other show to real problems faced by blacks, but it foundered in the ratings and had a short life.

In *Julia*, Diahann Carroll played the widowed mother of a six-year-old child. The first television series to focus on a black family, *Julia* conspicuously lacked a father figure. But the harsh criticism the show received still seemed undeserved. While Julia and her son Corry were not typical blacks, they weren't inconceivable. They did not reflect the attitudes or mores of the black masses, but they were representative of black middle-class attitudes, which (like Julia herself) were extremely light if not quite white. But then, that was the rub.

Black, for many critics in the late sixties, meant *distinctively* black. That was associated only with the black lower classes, who were, and still are, the prime victims of American racism. *Julia* had little to do with them. Diahann Carroll herself described the show as "lightweight entertainment that was about as true to life as any other series." Still, no judgment of the show seemed more apt at the time than a friend of mine's remark. "Julia fiddles while Chicago burns."

Not until the late sixties, when militancy had become the dominant mood among blacks and the battle had literally been taken to the streets, did the television industry fully respond. And even then, its only offerings generally ignored the crisis of black-white conflict. There were exceptions, of course, such as the CBS *Black America* documentary series, which began with the Bill Cosby-narrated "Black History: Lost, Stolen, or Strayed." Ironically, that segment spent considerable time pointing out the distorted images of blacks that Hollywood had introduced and television had perpetuated—lazy, shiftless darkies, cowardly buffoons, lecherous ne'er-do-wells. The 1968 television season may have eliminated insulting portraits of blacks, but it left me with as much uneasiness as had the past distortions.

That season did at least mark the beginning of an era, however. Blacks no longer had to fight merely to appear. For nearly a decade, practically every show had a black actor or actress in a continuing role, or frequently included a black performer in one of its episodes. Variety shows usually had one or more black guests, although few blacks hosted such programs. The public pressure of the late sixties and the lagging economy of the seventies drove sponsors to seek out "special markets," so blacks began appearing regularly in commercials as well.

The number of blacks on the air reached a peak during the seventies, when several shows with nearly all-black casts (*Good Times; The Jeffersons; the original Sanford and Son; What's Happening!!*) were aired. Only *The Jeffersons* has lasted. The others have been replaced by programs featuring black performers in integrated casts. And these recent shows run the gamut: from *Diff'rent Strokes,* starring Gary Coleman as a precocious child living with his adoptive white family, to *Sanford,* with Redd Foxx as the grizzled, acerbic junk dealer playing opposite a nonblack employee. Although blacks remain plainly visible during television's peak hours, the number of blacks in regular roles on weekly, prime-time network shows has noticeably diminished in the past few years.

Moreover, as a recent Civil Rights Commission report stated, blacks appearing on television are disproportionately cast as teenagers and in situation comedies. Since 1968, almost all new weekly series starring blacks fit into one of these categories. Only the short-lived *Bill Cosby Show*, in which Cosby portrayed a schoolteacher and coach, even attempted any serious depiction of black life.

There have so far been no long-lasting dramatic series (to compare with *The Waltons, Lou Grant*, or even *Little House on the Prairie*) focusing on black life in America. Except for *Harris and Company*, which aired only briefly in 1979, and *Palmerstown, USA*, the Norman Lear-Alex Haley production temporarily shelved after an inauspicious beginning, none have even been tried. And the few dramatic specials seen on network television, with the exception of *Roots* and *Roots II*, have drawn severe criticism from blacks. Just last year an organization was formed specifically to prevent the airing of the NBC television drama *Beulah Land*. In this instance the film's title was indicative of its content, and the black organization protested the "offensive and degrading stereotypes that perpetuate the image of the slave as ignorant, oversexed, slovenly, dependent on the whim of his master and filled with love for that master and the master's land." Some minor changes were made in the script of *Beulah Land*, although the producer contends they were not in response to the protests. The film ran last October, and critics justifiably pointed out that the grossness of its stereotypes was matched only by the inanity of its plot.

Commercial television's staple program form—especially for its black performers—is not the serious drama. It is the situation comedy, which requires extreme oversimplification in its quest for humor, and practically prohibits any exploration of contemporary life. These limitations notwithstanding, two black sitcom characters—George Jefferson and Fred Sanford—have occasionally provided accurate glimpses of black attitudes.

As Jefferson, Sherman Hemsley portrays a black man who, after building a thriving laundry business, has moved his family into a luxurious Upper East Side apartment in New York City. Jefferson is an odd combination of the aggressive, materialistic, successful businessman and the pompously proud black man. He is as anti-white as Archie Bunker is antiblack, and just as Bunker's gibes about minorities are defused by his prevailing ineptitude and stubborn self-righteousness, Jefferson's insistently caustic racial remarks are made acceptable by his ultimate buffoonery. Still, humor is often double-edged; just as there is a considerable segment of the nonblack television audience sharing Bunker's attitudes toward minorities, Jefferson's cynicism about whites and most American ideals (excluding the pursuit of money) reflects the sentiments of many blacks.

Similarly, Redd Foxx's portrayal of Sanford, despite the comic guise, often provides insight into a skepticism of middle-class values common among blacks. Sanford's stubborn insistence on maintaining his own identity reflects a genuine black attitude. And he also mirrors the shift in black perspective over the recent decades—from a self-conscious denial of so-called black behavior to an assertive flaunting of it.

In both *The Jeffersons* and *Sanford,* however, the performers themselves are responsible for conveying this real-life quality. They must go beyond the script to do so. Neither show clearly expresses the style of humor traditional to black communities.

It is distressing for one who grew up with that distinctive black style of humor on street corners, and later in theaters like the Apollo, to miss it in most television sitcoms—even those with black comedians. This conspicuous lack speaks of the networks' blinkered devotion to the wants of the majority. According to some blacks inside the industry, the absence of the black style of humor may be a prime reason for the gradual disappearance of black shows on television.

According to Matt Robinson, a black writer and producer whose credits include the films *Save the Children* and *Amazing Grace,* "all comedy on television is based on the Jewish comedy style—the style of the borscht-belt standup comedians who do gags with a rapid-fire approach: set up-set up-punch line. The style was adopted because it solved the technical problem of television's having to get everything in quickly. Because it is a fast medium, you have to grab the audience, quickly, within the first thirty seconds or so, or else they change the channel.

"In a show like *Sanford,* for instance, the tone of the humor is often black, the material is black-oriented, but the structure follows the same formula as any other television show. It's based on the unlikely proposition, as we all know, that there is always someone standing around with witty, flippant responses for anything that's said. That's not a black development.

"I think black humor stopped being a dominant force with the advent of television. Black humor, to me, is that stage-show type of humor that flowed from specific characters and situations that were familiar to other blacks—almost exclusively so."

Many white writers agree with Robinson's assessment of television humor. According to Dick Baer, who has written scripts for black sitcoms like *What's Happening!!* and who now writes for *Archie Bunker's Place,* "Comedy dealing with racial matters has to do with what people expect blacks to do. To a certain extent, it's what blacks expect blacks to do. But since whites are in the majority, they make the decisions about how blacks are going to figure into the entertainment industry. They are working both sides of the streets. They are selling non-servile blacks to placate the black audience and at the same time showing stupid or amoral blacks or unrealistic blacks to satisfy the white audiences' assumptions about blacks."

Bob Peete, a black writer who worked on *The Bill Cosby Show* and was a story editor for *Good Times,* explains it another way: "There is a real difference between black and white humor. The chief distinction is that black humor is more attitudinal: it's not what you say, but how you say it. The attitude imparted to the line gets the laugh. For instance, if Redd Foxx is on camera and someone knocks at the door, Redd might say, 'Come in,' and the audience would crack up. Now 'come in' is obviously not a joke, but with Redd it can be funny. Richard Pryor does the same thing, he doesn't tell jokes. On the other hand, white humor is structured to a straight-line-punch-line format."

According to some black performers and writers, the disparity between creation and performance in a black sitcom adversely affects the quality of the material, which in turn almost assures the show's failure. "It's a self-fulfilling type situation," comments one writer. "White writers produce mediocre shows about blacks and, when they fail, decide that the audience doesn't want black shows. Therefore, fewer shows are produced."

The reasons for the dwindling number of black shows on television may or may not be that simple. It is clear, however, that television sitcoms are a virtual wasteland when it comes to authentic black humor—despite the work of Redd Foxx, Sherman Hemsley, Robert Guillaume, and Ja'net DuBois (of the defunct *Good Times*). Some black comedians, such as Richard Pryor, have refused to attempt molding their humor into the sitcom format. Since blacks are predominantly represented on television in sitcoms, a more authentic prime-time view of black style and attitudes seems extremely bleak.

One possible remedy for the situation has been suggested by comic actor Cleavon Little: "I've been doing pilots for years and they've failed, I think, because they've all had white writers, white producers, and white directors. If we had blacks doing those things—all of them—we could bring another kind of ethos, nuance, to the comedy. That hasn't been investigated. Let us try, control our own humor, and I'm sure you'd see a difference."

No network has yet agreed to this proposal. The results of such an experiment, however, may be revealed shortly in a new thirteen-part non-commercial series entitled *With Ossie and Ruby*. These half-hour shows, airing on PBS, star Ossie Davis and Ruby Dee and present a varied entertainment package featuring comedy, music, drama, and literature. Although Davis stresses that the show's focus is "the common landscape shared by all Americans," most involved guests and writers are of minority backgrounds. With its emphasis on vaudeville, blues, and jazz, on poets and dramatists such as the late Langston Hughes, the program's reception may well indicate whether television audiences are receptive to more authentic material by blacks and other minorities. Meanwhile, if the present trend continues on network television, the problem for many black viewers seeking more realistic reflection of their own culture during prime time may again become as it was for that Harlem bar's resident sage—a matter of imagination.

Study Questions: Gans

[?] *Do you agree with Gans's analysis of the underlying messages in America's news? Are there some messages or values that he claims underlie the news that you believe do not? If so, which ones? Do you perceive any underlying messages or values in news that Gans has overlooked?*

What lessons, if any, should a reporter learn from Gans's study?

Consider the section of this essay titled "Altruistic Democracy." How can stories about corruption, conflict, protest, and bureaucratic malfunctioning be reported except as deviations from an ideal, altruistic democracy? What are the alternatives?

Why do you think the news media give greater coverage to stories about violations of freedom of the press and censorship of libraries than they do to stories about violations of other constitutional protections, such as the civil liberties of radicals and persons accused of crimes?

Can you find newspaper stories that depart from the norms that Gans claims pervade the press? How or why do you think they got into the media? Why do you think these kinds of stories do not dominate the news?

Herbert J. Gans

THE MESSAGES BEHIND THE NEWS

A sociologist weighs the news and finds that it is neither neutral nor impartial in surveying American society

Journalism is, like sociology, an empirical discipline. Like other empirical disciplines, the news does not limit itself to reality judgments; it also contains values, or preference statements. This in turn makes it possible to suggest that there is, underlying the news, a picture of nation and society as it ought to be.

The values in the news are rarely explicit and must be found between

Herbert J. Gans is professor of sociology at Columbia University and the author of *The Levittowners.* This article is adapted from *Deciding What's News,* to be published in April by Pantheon Books.

the lines—in which actors and activities are reported or ignored, and in how they are described. Because journalists do not, in most instances, deliberately insert values into the news, these values must be inferred.

I shall employ a narrow definition of values, examining only preference statements about nation and society, and major national or societal issues. I also distinguish between two types of values, which I call topical and enduring, and I will analyze only the latter. Enduring values are values which can be found in many different types of news stories over a long period of time; often, they affect what events become news and even help define the news.

The list that follows is limited to the enduring values I have found in the news over the last two decades, although all are probably of far more venerable vintage; obviously, it includes those which this inferrer, bringing his own values to the task, has found most visible and important. The methods by which I identified the values were impressionistic; the values really emerged from continual scrutiny of the news. Some came from the ways actors and activities are described, the tones in which stories are written, told, or filmed, and the connotations that accrue to commonly used verbs, nouns, and adjectives, especially if neutral terms are available but not used. When years ago the news reported that Stokely Carmichael had "turned up" somewhere, while the president had, on the same day, "arrived" somewhere else, or when another story pointed out that a city was "plagued with labor problems," the appropriate values were not difficult to discern, if only because neutral terms were available but were not used. However, sometimes neutral terms are simply not available. The news could have called the young men who refused to serve in the Vietnam War draft evaders, dodgers, or resisters, but it rarely used the last term.

The enduring values I want to discuss can be grouped into eight clusters: ethnocentrism, altruism, democracy, responsible capitalism, small-town pastoralism, individualism, moderatism, order, and national leadership.

ETHNOCENTRISM

Like the news of other countries, American news values its own nation above all others, even though it sometimes disparages blatant patriotism. This ethnocentrism is most explicit in foreign news, which judges other countries by the extent to which they live up to or imitate American practices and values, but it also underlies domestic news. While the news contains many stories that are critical of domestic conditions, they are almost always treated as deviant cases, with the implication that American ideals, at least, remain viable. The Watergate scandals were usually ascribed to a small group of power-hungry politicians, and beyond that, to the "imperial presidency"—but with the afterthought, particularly following Nixon's resignation, that nothing was fundamentally wrong with American democracy even if reforms were needed.

The clearest expression of ethnocentrism, in all countries, appears in war news. While reporting the Vietnam War, the news media described the North Vietnamese and the National Liberation Front as "the enemy," as if they were the enemy of the news media. Similarly, weekly casualty stories reported the number of Americans killed, wounded, or missing, and the number of South Vietnamese killed; but the casualties on the other side were impersonally described as "the communist death toll" or the "body count."

Again, as in war reporting everywhere, atrocities, in this case by Americans, did not often get into the news, and then only toward the end of the war. Seymour Hersh, the reporter credited with exposing the Mylai massacre, had considerable difficulty selling the story until the evidence was incontrovertible. The end of the war was typically headlined as "the fall of South Vietnam," with scarcely a recognition that, by other values, it could also be considered a liberation, or, neutrally, a change in governments.

ALTRUISTIC DEMOCRACY

While foreign news suggests quite explicitly that democracy is superior to dictatorship, and the more so if it follows American forms, domestic news is more specific, indicating how American democracy should perform by its frequent attention to deviations from an unstated ideal, evident in stories about corruption, conflict, protest, and bureaucratic malfunctioning. That ideal may be labeled altruistic democracy because, above all, the news implies that politics should be based on the public interest and service.

Although the news has little patience for losers, it insists that both winners and losers should be scrupulously honest, efficient, and dedicated to acting in the public interest. Financial corruption is always news, as is nepotism, patronage appointments, logrolling, and "deals" in general. Decisions based, or thought to be based, on either self-interest or partisan concerns thus continue to be news whenever they occur, even though they long ago ceased to be novel.

Politicians, politics, and democracy are also expected to be meritocratic; the regular activities of political machines are regularly exposed, and "machine" itself is a pejorative term. Although the news therefore regards civil-service officials more highly than "political appointees," the former are held to a very high standard of efficiency and performance; as a result, any deviant bureaucratic behavior becomes newsworthy. "Waste" is always an evil; the mass of paperwork created by bureaucracy is a frequent story, and the additional paperwork generated by attempts to reduce the amount of paperwork is a humorous item that has appeared in the news regularly.

The news keeps track of the violations of official norms, but it does so selectively. Over the years, the news has been perhaps most concerned with freedom of the press and related civil liberties; even recurring local violations, school boards that censor libraries, say, have often become national news. Violations of the civil liberties of radicals, of due process, habeas corpus, and other constitutional protections, particularly for criminals, are less newsworthy. Another official norm observed by the news is racial integration. Because citizens are expected to live up to these norms altruistically and because the norms are viewed as expressions of the public interest, the violations of the legal and political right of blacks in the South were news even before supporters of the civil rights movement began to demonstrate.

While—and perhaps because—the news consistently reports political and legal failures to achieve altruistic and official democracy, it concerns itself much less with the economic barriers that obstruct the realization of the ideal. Of course, the news is aware of candidates who are millionaires or who obtain substantial amounts of corporate or union campaign money, but it is less conscious of the relationship between poverty and powerlessness, or of the difficulty that Americans of median income have in gaining political access.

The relative inattention to economic obstacles to democracy stems from the assumption that the polity and the economy are separate and independent of each other. Under ideal conditions, one is not supposed to affect or interfere with the other, although, typically, government intervention in the economy is more newsworthy and serious than private industry's intervention in government. Accordingly, the news rarely notes the extent of public subsidy of private industry, and it continues to describe firms and institutions which are completely or partly subsidized by government funds as private—for example, Lockheed, many charities, and most privately run universities.

RESPONSIBLE CAPITALISM

The underlying posture of the news toward the economy resembles that taken toward the polity: an optimistic faith that, in the good society, businessmen and women will compete with each other in order to create increased prosperity for all, but that they will refrain from unreasonable profits and gross exploitation of workers or customers. While monopoly is clearly evil, there is little explicit or implicit criticism of the oligopolistic nature of much of today's economy. Unions and consumer organizations are accepted as countervailing pressures on business (the former less so than the latter), and strikes are frequently judged negatively, espeially if they inconvenience "the public," contribute to inflation, or involve violence.

Economic growth is always a positive phenomenon, unless it brings about inflation or environmental pollution, leads to the destruction of a historical landmark, or puts craftsmen or craftswomen out of work. In the past, when anchormen gave the stock market report, even the most detached ones looked cheerful when the market had had a good day, assuming this to be of universal benefit to the nation.

Like politicians, business officials are expected to be honest and efficient; but while corruption and bureaucratic misbehavior are as undesirable in business as in government, they are nevertheless tolerated to a somewhat greater extent in the former. For example, the January 2, 1978, issue of *Time* included a three-page critique of government bureaucracy, entitled "Rage Over Rising Regulation: To Autocratic Bureaucrats, Nothing Succeeds Like Excess"; but a business-section story reporting that General Motors had sent refunds to the purchasers of Oldsmobiles equipped with Chevrolet engines was only one column long and was headed "End of the Great Engine Flap."

It is now accepted that the government must help the poor, but only the deserving poor, for "welfare cheaters" are a continuing menace and are more newsworthy than people, other than the very rich, who cheat on their taxes. Public welfare agencies are kept under closer scrutiny than others, so that although the news reported on the "welfare mess" in the 1960s it did not describe equivalent situations in other government agencies in the same way. There was, for example, no "defense mess," and what is "waste" in H. E. W. programs is "cost overruns" in Pentagon programs.

SMALL-TOWN PASTORALISM

The rural and anti-industrial values which Thomas Jefferson is usually thought to have invented can also be found in the news, which favors small towns (agricultural or market) over other types of settlements. At one time, this preference was complemented by a celebration of the large city and of the vitality of its business and entertainment districts; but the end of this period can be dated almost exactly by *Life*'s special issue on the cities, which appeared in December 1965.

For the last ten years cities have been in the news almost entirely as problematic, with the major emphasis on racial conflict, crime, and fiscal insolvency. Suburbs are not often newsworthy, despite the fact that a near majority of Americans now live in them, and they, too, have generally received a bad press. During the 1950s and 1960s, suburbs were viewed as breeding grounds of homogeneity, boredom, adultery, and other evils; since then, they have come into the news because they are suffering increasingly from "urban" problems, particularly crime, or because they keep out racial minorities.

The small town continues to reign supreme, not only in Charles Kuralt's "On the Road" reports for CBS News, but also in television and magazine stories about "the good life" in America. Stories about city neighborhoods judge them by their ability to retain the cohesiveness, friendliness, and slow pace ascribed to small towns, and during the period of journalistic interest in ethnicity, to the ethnic enclaves of the past.

Needless to say, the pastoral values underlying the news are romantic; they visualize rural and market towns as they were imagined to have existed in the past.

Small-town pastoralism is, at the same time, a specification of two more general values: the desirability both of nature and of smallness per se. The news dealt with the conflict between the preservation of nature and the activities of developers long before the environment and ecology became political issues; and, more often than not, the news took at least an implicit stand against the developers. The postwar developers of suburbia were seen as despoiling the land in their rapacious search for profits; that they were concurrently providing houses for people was rarely noted.

The virtue of smallness comes through most clearly in stories that deal with the faults of bigness, for in the news, big government, big labor, and big business rarely have virtues. Bigness is feared, among other things, as impersonal and inhuman. In the news as well as in architecture, the ideal social organization should reflect a "human scale." The fear of bigness also reflects a fear of control, of privacy and individual freedom being ground under by organizations too large to notice, much less to value, the individual. As such, bigness is a major threat to individualism.

INDIVIDUALISM

It is no accident that many of the characters in Kuralt's pastoral features are "rugged individualists," for one of the most important enduring news values is the preservation of the freedom of the individual against the encroachments of nation and society. The good society of the news is populated by individuals who participate in it, but on their own terms, acting in the public interest, but as they define it.

The ideal individual struggles successfully against adversity and overcomes more powerful forces. The news looks for people who act heroically during disasters, and it pays attention to people who conquer nature without hurting it: explorers, mountain climbers, astronauts, and scientists. "Self-made" men and women remain attractive, as do people who overcome poverty or bureaucracy.

The news often contains stories about new technology that endangers the individual—notably the computer, which is viewed anthropomorphically, either as a robot that will deprive human beings of control over their own lives or as a machine endowed with human failings, which is therefore less of a threat. In any case, there is always room for a gleeful story about computers that break down. The news has, however, always paid attention to the dangers of new technology: when television sets were first mass-produced, they were viewed as dehumanizing because they robbed people of the art of conversation; similar fears were expressed at the time of the institution of digit-dialing in telephones.

Conversely, the news celebrates old technology and mourns its passing, partly because it is tied to an era when life was thought to have been simpler, partly because it is viewed as being under individual control.

MODERATISM

The idealization of the individual could result in praise for the rebel and the deviant, but this possibility is neutralized by an enduring value that discourages excess or extremism. Individualism that violates the law, the dominant mores, and enduring values is suspect; equally important, what is valued in individuals is discouraged in groups. Thus, groups that exhibit what is seen as extreme behavior are criticized in the news through pejorative adjectives or a satirical tone.

For example, the news treats atheists as extremists and uses the same approach, if more gingerly, with religious fanatics. People who consume conspicuously are criticized, but so are people such as hippies, who turn their backs entirely on consumer goods. The news is scornful both of the overly academic scholar and the oversimplifying popularizer: it is kind neither to highbrows nor to lowbrows, to users of jargon or users of slang.

The same value applies to politics. Political ideologists are suspect, but so are completely unprincipled politicians. The totally self-seeking are thought to be consumed by excessive ambition, but the complete do-gooders are not believed. Political candidates who talk only about issues may be described as dull; those who avoid issues entirely evoke doubts about their fitness for office. Poor speakers are thought to be unelectable, while demagogues are taken to be dangerous. Those who regularly follow party lines are viewed as hacks, and those who never do are called mavericks or loners—although these terms are pejorative only for the politically unsuccessful; the effective loner becomes a hero.

ORDER

The frequent appearance of stories about disorder suggests that order is an important value in the news, but order is a meaningless term unless one specifies what order and whose order is being valued. Social disorder is generally defined as disorder in the public areas of the society. A protest march in which three people die would be headline national news, whereas a family murder that claimed three victims would be a local story. Disorders in affluent areas or elite institutions are more likely to be reported than their occurrence elsewhere. In the 1960s, the looting of a handful of stores on New York's Fifth Avenue received as much attention as a much larger looting spree taking place in a ghetto area that same day. Peaceful demonstrations on college campuses, especially elite ones, are usually more newsworthy than those in factories or prisons. But the major public area is the seat of government; thus, a trouble-free demonstration in front of a city hall or a police station is news, whereas that in front of a store is not.

Still, the most important criterion of worthiness is the target of the demonstration. The anti-war demonstrations of the past decade were covered as disorder stories because they were aimed at presidents. Likewise, the 1978 coal strike did not become a magazine cover story until it involved the president.

Beneath the concern for political order lies another, perhaps even deeper concern for social cohesion, which reflects fears that not only the official rules of the political order but also the informal rules of the social order are in danger of being disobeyed. Hippies and college dropouts of the sixties were newsworthy in part because they rejected the so-called Protestant work ethic; even now, drug use by the young, and its consequences, is in the news more than alcohol use because it signifies a rejection of traditional methods of seeking oblivion or mind expansion. Indeed, the news evaluates the young almost entirely in terms of the adult rules they are in the process of rejecting.

Moral disorder stories are, in the end, cued to much the same concern for social cohesion, particularly those stories which report violations of the mores rather than the laws. Such stories are based on the premise that the activities of public officials, public agencies, and corporations should derive from the same moral and ethical values that are supposed to apply to personal, familial, and friendship relations. Even if every political reporter knows that politicians cannot operate with the same ideal of honesty as friends, the failure of politicians to do so continues to be news. In the last analysis, the values underlying social and moral disorder news are the same, although the two types of news differ in subject and object: social disorder news monitors the respect of citizens for authority, while moral disorder stories evaluate whether authority figures respect the rules of the citizenry.

With some oversimplification, it would be fair to say that the news supports the social order of public, business and professional, upper-middle-class, middle-aged, and white-male sectors of society. Because the news emphasizes people over groups, it pays less attention to the institutionalized social order, except as reflected in its leaders; but obviously the news is also generally supportive of governments and their agencies, private enterprise, the prestigious professions, and a variety of other national institutions, including the quality universities. But here, too, always with a proviso: obedience to the relevant enduring values.

Nevertheless, the news is not subservient to powerful individuals or groups, for it measures their behavior against a set of values that is assumed to transcend them. Moral disorder stories can bid the elites to relinquish, or at least hide, their moral deficiencies. To be sure, the values invoked in moral disorder stories are themselves often set by and shared by these elites. The president's policies are not often viewed from the perspectives of, or judged by, the values of low-income and moderate-income citizens; corporate officials are even less rarely judged by the values of employees or customers; or university presidents, by the values of students or campus janitors. Instead, the values in the news derive largely from reformers and reform movements, which are themselves elites. Still, the news is not simply a compliant supporter of elites, or the establishment, or the ruling class; rather, it views nation and society through its own set of values and with its own conception of the good social order.

LEADERSHIP

If the news values moral and social order, it also suggests how to maintain them, primarily through the availability of morally and otherwise competent leadership. The news focuses on leaders; and, with some exceptions, public agencies and private organizations are represented by their leaders. In the past, magazine cover stories often reported national topics or issues in relation to an individual who played an instrumental or symbolic leadership role in them. When necessary, the news even helps to create leaders; in the 1960s, radical and black organizations functioning on the basis of participatory democracy sometimes complained that journalists would pick out one spokesperson on whom they would lavish most of their attention, thereby making a leader out of him or her.

Although several practical considerations encourage the news media to emphasize leaders, the news is also based on a theory of society that would argue, were it made explicit, that the social process, above all others, is shaped by leaders—people who, either because of their political or managerial skills, or personal attributes which inspire others, move into positions of authority and make things happen. A lengthy 1974 *Time* cover story that surveyed existing definitions of leadership concluded that most "emphasize honesty, candor, and vision, combined with sheer physical stamina and courage"; to which the magazine added that "courage without brains was [not] sufficient." A leader must also be strong and able to control subordinates; their moral failings and inefficiencies are a sign of weak leadership.

The foremost leader in America is the president, who is viewed as the ultimate protector of order. He is the final backstop for domestic tranquility and the principal guardian of national security, his absence from the White House due to resignation or death evoking fears of an enemy attack or possible panic by a now leaderless populace. Through his own behavior and the concern he shows for the behavior of others, the president also becomes the nation's moral leader. He sets an example that might be followed by others: should he permit or condone corruption among his associates or appointees, he is suspected of moral disorder. Finally, he is the person who states and represents the national values and he is the agent of the national will.

NEWS VALUES & IDEOLOGY

If the news includes values, it also contains ideology. That ideology, however, is an aggregate of only partly thought-out values which is neither entirely consistent nor well integrated; and since it changes somewhat over time, it is also flexible on some issues. I call this aggregate of values and the reality judgments associated with it para-ideology, partly to distinguish it from the deliberate, integrated, and more doctrinaire set of values usually defined as ideology; it is ideology nevertheless.

The para-ideology can itself be placed on the conventional spectrum, but not easily, since journalists are not much interested in ideology or aware that they, too, promulgate ideology. As a result, individual stories and journalists can span various parts of the spectrum, although their values rarely coincide with those on the far right or the far left. Even the news media as a whole, and the news, analyzed over time, are not easily classified.

In its advocacy of altruistic and official democracy, the news defends a mixture of liberal and conservative values, but its conception of responsible capitalism comes closest to what I would call right-leaning liberalism. On the other hand, in its respect for tradition and its nostalgia for pastoralism and rugged individualism, the news is unabashedly conservative, as it is also both in its defense of the social order and its faith in leadership. If the news has to be pigeonholed ideologically, it is right-liberal or left-conservative.

In reality, the news is not so much conservative or liberal as it is reformist; indeed, the enduring values are very much like the values of the Progressive movement of the early twentieth century. The resemblance is often uncanny, as in the common advocacy of honest, meritocratic, and anti-bureaucratic government, and in the shared antipathy to political machines and demagogues, particularly of populist bent. Altruistic democracy is, in other words, close to the Progressive ideal of government. The notion of responsible capitalism is also to be found in Progressivism, as is the dislike of bigness, the preference for craftsmanship over technology, the defense of nature, and the celebration of anti-urban pastoral society. Journalistic para-ideology and Progressivism are further akin in their mutual support of individualism, their uneasiness about collective solutions, other than at the grassroots level, and their opposition to socialism. Moreover, the preservation of an upper-class and upper-middle-class social order, like the need for morally and otherwise competent national leadership, has its equivalents in Progressive thought.

The Progressive movement is long dead, but many of its basic values and its reformist impulses have persisted. The news is reformist and its being so helps explain why it is not easily fitted into the conventional ideological spectrum. Of course, Progressive thought can be placed on that spectrum, although historians have not yet agreed whether the movement was liberal, conservative, or both. In any case, the news may be marching to a somewhat different drummer; and when journalists are unwilling to describe themselves as liberal or conservative, and prefer to see themselves as independents, they may be sensing, if not with complete awareness, that they are, as a profession, Progressive reformers.

Study Questions: Kervin

? *What position does Kervin take on the issue of journalistic objectivity? Do you agree with her view? Why or why not?*

Do you agree with Kervin that all American news media use the same frames or assumptions about reality in reporting the news? In justifying your response, use some stories that you find in various newspapers and television newscasts.

What are the major elements of the mediated picture of people and events in El Salvador that Kervin identifies? Which of these elements are likely to be more closely related to an American view of "reality" than to an El Salvadoran view?

In what ways does Kervin's article support the points made by Lippmann earlier in this section? In what ways does Kervin expand on Lippmann's points?

What does Kervin mean when she argues that " 'reality' is neither a fixed place or concept; it differs between ideologies and changes over time"?

If Julia Lesage, who is quoted by Kervin, is correct in the claim that people in different countries may interpret a picture in quite different ways, how can we determine what a valid or "correct" interpretation is?

How can Kervin's arguments explain the existence of the negative stereotypes of black people that Watkins points out in "Beyond the Pale"?

Denise Kervin

REALITY ACCORDING TO TELEVISION NEWS: PICTURES FROM EL SALVADOR

For pictures of a war, there seems to be very little shooting. Soldiers on either "side" of the conflict are generally seen moving down city streets and jungle paths, in training, or just standing around as if waiting for something to happen. Certain images, however, do carry the emotional impact normally expected of pictures from a battlefield: corpses lying by roadsides and piled in village squares; adults and children near the dead, sometimes mourning, but mostly just standing there, apparently impotent to do anything. A reporter in a voiceover explains that neither group of soldiers is winning and, after four years of fighting, the people of this land just want peace.

If a U.S. citizen thinks about the civil war taking place in El Salvador, he or she will probably conjure up images such as those above, seen on commercial television news programs. Without additional sources of news, not sought out by most viewers, the images and sounds coming from the three network news programs determine general conceptualization about issues such as the U.S. presence in El Salvador. Television news, therefore, is a powerful site of ideological representation, a locus of meaning-production that is hidden behind its seemingly neutral transferral of events in the world to the audience at home. What television news offers is not only particular recordings of events and people, but arguments about the world, certain ways of seeing reality. In the following pages, I will discuss how television news came to define "reality" within coverage of the civil war in El Salvador by the three commercial television networks from 1977 until 1982.

The power of television news resides in its apparent ability to present the world unchanged, its images and sounds assumed by the news audience to be "reality." Two factors account for television news being taken as a direct line into the world: images and the goal of objectivity, the two being related and mutually reinforcing. A handbook published by CBS News in 1958 sums up the advantage of television news for its viewers: "During a period of time you are there yourself to see what someone said or did."[1] News images are composed largely of iconic signs, generally decoded as mirrors of the world, making the gap between the sign and what it represents disappear, taking with it the signifying practice of newsworkers who produced the message. In this oneness of representation and being lies the basis (in part) of reality in television news. This reality and the societal perceptions upon which it is based are culturally-specific: while images are more universal than words, pictures are still stamped with a society's ideological preconceptions. As Julia Lesage points out in relation to film, the meaning of an image may differ between the United States and El Salvador: " . . . what a North American film audience may interpret as an image connoting 'poverty' may signify 'a farm family's daily life' in its country of origin."[2] Therefore, the "realistic" news images the audience sees of the conflict in El Salvador are bound to *our* society and may not be particularly illustrative of reality for the people of El Salvador.

The second factor involved in television news' realism is objectivity which, along with the images, determines the presentation of the world within the news. First, objectivity, as the separation of fact and value, is the entrusted mode of operation that society expects of newsworkers—from reporters in the field to videotape editors at network headquarters. By presenting facts devoid of opinions, the news supposedly allows members of the audience to make their own value judgments. This ideal of news from "nobody's point of view" must, of course, be operationalized, that is, newsworkers must have some practical idea of how objectivity is to be achieved. According to Gaye Tuchman's research into newswork, within the everyday news routines that have built up over time there are found "strategies of objectivity." Examples of such strategies include presenting evidence and using quotations from opposing points of view. Such routines provide known guidelines for doing newswork, easing the inherently chaotic nature of journalism. Use of these guidelines also acts as a protection for newsworkers against being edited, and can forestall charges of libel from unhappy newsmakers.[3]

Such objective routines derive in large part from the dominant positivist paradigm within our society, which holds that belief should come only after presentation of evidence. Television news does this in *what* it broadcasts—

the newscasts' words, but most concretely through its pictures, and in the image/sound interaction—and in *how* these sign systems are interpolated using objective strategies. For instance, a "balanced" report can mean the juxtaposition of pictures of a guerrilla leader and a member of the current government presenting their opinions about the latest incident defined as news. Besides such a general structural effect, strategies of objectivity also find expression specifically in a story's visuals. Examples of such strategies include placing the camera at a "neutral" distance from the subject of a shot (avoiding closeups and extreme long shots) and by setting the camera at eye level, not allowing high or low angles of the subject.[4]

Regardless of television news' claim of objectivity, and of the seemingly neutral language of pictures, news visuals are the end-product of news-workers' signifying practices. A camera is not simply turned on the world; images are chosen, recorded in certain ways, and juxtaposed within syntagmatic chains, based on certain codes. Taken as a whole, the news could be said to be based on a general code of realism, which would include strategies of objectivity as sub-codes. Realism, as a mode of representation, of *re-presenting* the world, belongs to our society as a whole, not just to newswork. We learn from birth to perceive in terms of these codes, while other cultures learn perception according to different sets of codes. For example, Sol Worth and John Adair found that Navajos taught only how to operate film equipment made movies about their world using codes not generally found in western cultures.[5] As a mode of representation, realism contains implicit assumptions about communication and technology, which affect how television news is viewed. Nicholas Garnham, discussing British documentaries, sums up American attitudes toward television news:

> This mode sees the act of communication as essentially passive and its tools, for instance the camera, as essentially neutral. It stresses the recording function of film or television rather than its manipulative and illusion-creating function. [. . . It assumes that] there is a real world out there and a subject/observer/voyeur who records the real world with the minimum intervention, who opens a window on the world.[6]

This "window on the world" is, of course, a window on a particular, ideological world. Any discussion about objectivity or a code of realism must deal with *what* reality is being examined. Both objectivity and the code of realism are based on ideological assumptions that are historically and socially situated. Objectivity is built upon a belief in a single, coherent reality "out there," beyond human manipulation, waiting to be revealed by an impartial camera through realist codes. However, "reality" is neither a fixed place or concept; it differs between ideologies and changes over time. Of course, within a single society exists an overriding system of explanations and assumptions that is taken to be reality by a majority of the people. This system is the dominant ideology, whose strength rests on its obviousness, its naturalized appearance as "the truth." Given that, television news does offer *a* "reality" to its viewers: it offers messages about the dominant ideology within our society. It is the duty of the newsworker, as a professional and as a member of a news organization, to give viewers an unbiased look at that reality. As Philip Schlesinger, in his book *Putting 'Reality' Together,* says, "The claim to be detached . . . is in fact premised on an uncritical and generally unarticulated commitment to the established order."[7]

Newswork is a process of encoding; journalists spend their time engaged in turning events in the world into messages for mass consumption. When newswork closely follows the objective criteria expected of it, when it essentially provides a direct line to our ideological reality, this work tends to disappear. Guaranteed by the dedication of news organizations to objectivity and made concrete through use of the code of realism, a news story implicitly says to a news audience, "What you see here is true, these people and their actions are all real in just this way." In other words, the closer newswork follows its mission of objectively reporting the world, the more the resulting signifying practice disappears from the attention of most viewers. Our reality may be a construct, but the tools used in its construction are naturalized to the point of invisibility. The news, therefore, occupies an interesting position within our culture because of the assumed symmetry of product and reality. While ideological work goes into a news story, the particular codes used to render the story "realistic" effectively conceal that labor. The pictures the audience sees of El Salvador are refracted through an invisible hegemonic lens. These images may therefore say more about assumptions in this country than about events taking place in El Salvador. . . .

What are these messages about El Salvador and what do they indicate about the role of the U.S. there? Over the last several years I have conducted research into how the war in El Salvador has been visually encoded on network television news, using a sample of 137 stories broadcast from 1977 until 1982. What I have found points to a remarkably consistent visual and ideological approach across time and across all three networks, resulting in a singular image and explanation of the El Salvadoran civil war. Some of the most important questions I have tried to answer in a systematic decoding of these news reports are:

- Which participants within the war are seen most often within the news stories and what are they shown doing?
- How are these people and others seen less often portrayed visually, particularly in terms of the code of realism?
- Do the coding choices affecting the images suggest implicit arguments or frames about the war in El Salvador and the U.S. presence there?

I analyzed my selected sample of news stories using an observational approach based on semiotic theory. Information about each report was encoded from videotapes and then tabulated using a computer. This part of my study provided a broad quantitative picture of what was happening within the coverage, such as whether low angles were being used in picturing the El Salvadoran military officers, or guerrilla soldiers were given the most closeups. The result was essentially a very close denotative reading of the news stories' visual system. The next step was to interpret the connotations associated with these pictures of a war and, lastly, to determine the ideological meanings within the news stories' mythic level, that is, what frames are at work within the coverage of El Salvador.

Turning first to the question of which subjects the audience sees the most in the stories, the answer must take into account both the frequency and duration of appearances. The subjects with the greatest number of appearances fall into exactly the same descending order across all three networks: anchors (seen in all the sample stories); El Salvadoran civilians; government soldiers; reporters; and corpses. In terms of how much of a network's total time each of these groups is on screen, this same order holds, except that on ABC and NBC civilians are seen slightly longer than the anchors. It would seem that ordinary El Salvadorans are very prominent within U.S. coverage of the war in their country. However, looking at the average durations for subjects' appearances at any one time in the reports, El Salvadoran citizens, while seen comparatively often, are allowed only a brief time on-screen. This same dichotomy holds true for government troops as well, which fall just behind civilians in both frequency and duration of appearances. The subjects allotted a greater duration at any one time are not the people who directly experience El Salvador's war, but rather newsworkers and those who make the decisions about that war: U.S. government officials (primarily the ambassador to El Salvador); El Salvadoran government officials; U.S. military advisors; guerrilla spokespersons; and El Salvadoran military officers. The overall effect of this handling of the different subjects within the coverage is that the El Salvadoran troops, the guerrilla soldiers, and the El Salvadoran people form a backdrop to the weightier treatment of those in power. As I will discuss below, the latter group tends to be "showcased" by the visual coding used in the news stories, while the former become more a part of the scenery than active participants in a civil war. Exceptions to this general approach to encoding are important, as I will show.

The difference between how those with and without power are seen in the news reports is also noticeable in the actions they perform. The actions noted in my study can be divided into active reactions to the war, displaying a certain amount of control over situations, or passive reactions, indicating that power actually rests outside the subject. In terms of television news, speaking for oneself (as opposed to being quoted, or talking without sound while a voiceover supplies narration) is a potent form of ideological power. Not surprisingly, the anchor and reporter do approximately 90 percent of the talking within all the news reports. The top five subjects talking on both ABC and CBS are exactly the same: reporter; anchor; U.S. government official; El Salvadoran government official; and religious member. NBC, on the other hand, while similarly having the reporter and anchor first and second, then lets people in the "other" category (mainly experts on various topics touched on in the stories), El Salvadoran citizens, U.S. government officials, and guerrilla leaders speak. The percentage of time each of these subjects talks is quite small, but must be compared to the other actions the subject performs. For example, on NBC El Salvadoran civilians speak about as long as those in the "other" category, approximately 2 percent of the total network time. However, for civilians, speaking only amounts to about 7 percent of their time on-screen, while "others" are seen speaking about a third of the time they are shown. Looking at speaking in these terms, once again U.S. and El Salvadoran government officials dominate the coverage, spending 40 percent to 70 percent of their time talking.

Second to speaking, figures having authority in the news stories are seen sitting, often as they talk under a voiceover. The anchor or reporter, of course, controls what is said, resulting in something of a loss of power for U.S. and El Salvadoran officials, yet these shots also show the subjects as being in positions of authority simply because they have the luxury *to sit.* In the coverage of El Salvador's war subjects mainly sit in meetings and at press conferences, discussing the future of that country. The people actually fighting and dying in the war rarely seem to sit. Primarily, guerrilla soldiers are seen moving through the jungle, engaged in training and other war-related activities. Government soldiers are shown walking, with a greater or lesser degree of purposefulness, as they patrol village and city streets. While the reports continually refer to the latest killings by the guerrillas, government troops, or death squads, little actual fighting is seen. Only the results of the killing are shown, in the form of corpses and the mourning of the El Salvadoran people, as I will discuss below.

The above information provided me with a general outline which I then wanted to fill in by studying the visual codes by which these subjects and actions are presented, particularly in relation to the code of realism. For example, not only do the anchors and reporters speak the most, they also get to address the camera, and therefore the viewers at home, directly. Observations about camera distance, angle, and movement (zooms, pans, tracks, and tilts), and the orientation of the subjects' bodies toward the camera were recorded. With some exceptions, the same subjects that are shown talking the most—newsworkers, U.S. and El Salvadoran government officials—are also shown closest to and most frequently facing the camera. According to Tuchman, camera distances in television news have attendant "social meanings."[8] For example, the accepted placement of a news camera, according to the code of realism, corresponds to distances at which one can discuss business, but not place a hand on the other's arm. Having the camera closer than this distance, which roughly corresponds to shots from a medium or waist-up shot to a long or full-body shot, works to "capture emotion at the cost of objectivity."[9] Using the same logic, shots further away than this general distance cause the subjects to be depersonalized, so that they cease to be individuals. Presumably the latter camera distance would still be acceptable to show crowds and would not seem to break the code of realism, as these shots would.

Within network coverage of the war in El Salvador, these rules are both followed and broken. For example, the anchors, reporters, El Salvadoran and U.S. government officials, and, on two networks, guerrilla spokespersons are consistently shown closer than the accepted "objective" distance. These subjects are also looking just past, or, in the case of the newsworkers, directly into the camera. Often these people have their names or titles superimposed under their image. These consistent patterns of encoding signify that these subjects deserve the audience's attention, are to be listened to, and should be seen as individuals with responsibilities and power. These are the subjects who talk to the audience, who describe what is happening and what ought to happen. This coding of anchors and reporters works to infuse these individuals' presence into the news programs, a coding choice which probably represents an attempt on the networks' part to gain product differentiation. This explanation cannot hold true for the similar coding choices made for the other authority figures cited above. Since such coding breaks with accepted practice, and it is unlikely that all camera crews have been issued the same shooting instructions (studies indicate that such overt orders have very rarely been forthcoming from the networks' higher echelons), the conclusion I came to is that newsworkers are relying on implicit codes existing within our society as a whole.

Contrast the above with the presentation of the subjects directly involved in the daily war. Both government and guerrilla troops are seen at the furthest distance presumably tolerated within the code of realism. El Salvadoran citizens are seen at that distance or even further away, being no more than bodies within large crowds, or distant figures wandering down village or city streets. Most of the time government troops are facing away from the camera; civilians and guerrillas are generally turned toward the camera, but the general use of long and extreme long shots negates any possible personalizing effect. Civilians and government soldiers are also shot using the greatest amount of camera movement. A technique often seen is for the camera to initially focus in a tight shot, then zoom out to a long or an extreme long shot often at a high angle, capturing the El Salvadorans within their environment, which, more often than not, bears traces of the latest fighting. The camera zooms in and out, pans and tracks to follow movements, tilts to observe actions, but rarely gets close enough for any length of time to turn these subjects into individuals. Seldom, if ever, speaking for themselves or identified by their names or occupations, these people do not seem to be distinct personalities. The guerrillas, government soldiers, and especially the El Salvadoran people largely exist only symbolically, as representatives of their groups. . . .

While ordinary El Salvadoran citizens figure prominently in the news reports as symbols for their group as a whole, there are instances when they are signified as individuals, times when the horror of the war within a particular life is made clear. At these points the code of realism is dropped entirely and these generally depersonalized figures become real human beings. Shown in close, touching distance, these people are seen mourning their dead: a mother wailing by the grave of her son, a man kneeling by the body of his brother. So, too, the audience is allowed closer in order to observe the dirty, often sick faces of children living in refugee camps among animals and garbage. The U.S. news audience sees the El Salvadoran people as *individuals* only during extremely emotional moments, the horrors of the war presented in human terms as the reporter in a voiceover speaks of the people as "caught in the middle" between left and right. The notion that the ordinary citizens of El Salvador inhabit a politically neutral zone, wishing only for peace, is one of the primary angles used within the coverage.

In general, the coverage of the war in El Salvador is consistent across time and across the three networks in how it visually treats the various groups involved. The code of realism is applied fairly strictly to those in El Salvador who are intimately familiar with the fighting: government troops, guerrilla soldiers and civilians. Figures of authority, as well as the newsworkers actually encoding the reports, generally merit a different code, one that focuses on them as individuals. The ordinary television news viewer probably reads images encoded using the code of realism as neutral, sees them as simply relaying "reality." Whether these same images would seem neutral to an El Salvadoran, raised within that culture's codes, is open to question. . . .

NOTES

[1]CBS, *Television News Handbook* (New York: McGraw–Hill, 1958), p. 17.

[2]Julia Lesage, "Films on Central America: For Our Urgent Use," *Jump Cut*, no. 27, July 1982, p. 16.

[3]Gaye Tuchman, "Objectivity as Strategic Ritual," *American Journal of Sociology* 77, No. 4, January 1972. See also Tuchman, *Making News* (New York: The Free Press, 1978).

[4]Tuchman, *Making News*, pp. 115–21.

[5]Sol Worth and John Adair, *Through Navajo Eyes* (Bloomington: Indiana University Press, 1972). See also Jan Deregowski, "Pictorial Perception and Culture," *Scientific American* 227 (November 1972): 82–88.

[6]Nicholas Garnham, "Television Documentary and Ideology," *Screen* 13, no. 2 (Summer 1972): 111.

[7]Philip Schlesinger, *Putting 'Reality' Together* (Beverly Hills: Sage Publications, 1979), p. 164.

[8]Tuchman, *Making News,* pp. 115–21.

[9]Ibid., p. 119.

Study Questions: Schmertz

? | *Does the fact that the demographic characteristics of journalists do not mirror those of the United States population as a whole reduce the probability that the news adequately serves the entire population? Why might the unrepresentativeness of journalists affect the quality of the news we get? Should anything be done about this unrepresentativeness? If so, what? Who should do it?*

Whether or not you agree that journalists are unrepresentative of the people, what are the advantages of thinking of them as representing us when they cover the news? What are the disadvantages?

With which of Schmertz's other criticisms of the news media do you agree? With which do you disagree? What are the bases for your opinions?

Schmertz blames the press for the low confidence the public has in government, churches, big business, schools, and other institutions. Do you agree that the news media are to blame? If so, what should be done?

The author offers, at least indirectly, a number of suggestions for improvement of the news media. What are they? How practical and useful is each suggestion?

Herbert Schmertz

THE PRESS AND MORALITY

If the public in this country were 95 percent white . . . 80 percent male . . . 93 percent college graduates . . . 78 percent earning more than

These comments were part of a debate amongst Herbert Schmertz, Mobil's vice president of public affairs, William Safire, columnist for *The New York Times* and Don Hewitt, executive producer of CBS's *60 Minutes.* The debate was moderated by WOR radio talk show host Sherrye Henry. It was part of a series of public policy discussions held at the John Drew Theater of Guild Hall in East Hampton, New York, during the summer of 1983.

$30,000 a year...and a full 50 percent professing no religion at all...then—just maybe—our leading journalists and broadcasters, the cutting edge of the media, could support their claim to be surrogates for the public.

By what right, then, does the press say, as Dan Dorfman has said, "To lie to the press on a public matter is, in effect, to lie to the people"? Or as my friend Don Hewitt has said of *60 Minutes,* "We've served as ombudsmen." Don says the program opens the window and hollers for the American people.

But I must disagree. There is nothing in the Constitution that says: For the purposes of this Constitution, the press is the same as the people. I looked again this morning. It's just not in there.

So what we have is a claim made by the press—on behalf of the public— when the press isn't anything like the people. I cited some data describing our leading journalists when I opened—and the data make the point— the media bear little resemblance, either demographically or philosophically, to mainstream America.

In fact, recent surveys such as that done by Professors Lichter and Rothman reveal that the views of America's leading journalists are frequently in direct opposition to prevailing American values. Sociologists characterize the perspectives of top media people as cosmopolitan and antibourgeois—about as far as you can get from Middle America without actually moving to East Hampton.

Even journalists themselves concede the vast difference. Daniel Schorr said it in *The Washington Post* recently: We're Not the Good Guys Anymore.

And against Don Hewitt's assertion of the ombudsman's role, consider what Charles Kuralt said in *The Los Angeles Herald Examiner,* "The best minds in television news are thinking more about packaging and promotion and pace and image and blinking electronics than about thoughtful coverage of the news."

Are these the journalists we want to empower as surrogates for the public? And I don't mean we, here . . . I mean We the People.

I say no.

We the People have chosen to build a democratic society. We elect those we want to represent us. No one elected the media to represent the public. To put it bluntly, they are self-appointed keepers of the public morals— as defined by themselves.

But so what?

Perhaps they are entitled to be the wardens of public virtue. Perhaps journalists have the mysterious power completely to repress their social attitudes, liberal perspectives, political biases, post-bourgeois goals . . . and actually sit in for each and every citizen as they examine the critical issues of the day in a cool . . . rational . . . intelligent . . . fair-minded fashion. . . .

You know, like *The New York Post* does.

Does anyone really believe that a media establishment in which the *Post* is highly successful—a member of the club—can then go before the people with a straight face and expect to uphold a claim that it is surrogate for the public—especially when the so-called responsible press sees the *Post* in action day after day and never says a critical word.

Or take a look at the media's practices and procedures . . . the way they can damage people without either indictment or trial. I'll skip right over the easy stuff, like *60 Minutes,* and talk about the painful stuff—meaning the abuses I have personally endured at the hands of these . . . surrogates.

(But before we leave the easy stuff, did you catch those out-takes from the Galloway trial: that phony spontaneous confession . . . the empty threats: See you on television . . . and the acting coach on the crew urging a witness, "Let me have a little reaction!" Good clean fun, all of it!)

Fun aside, when I think of surrogates, I think of false quotes. People who didn't say what they're alleged to have said. . . . Or, more commonly, who said it in a context where it didn't mean what the reporter says it means.

I think of unnamed sources—like all those mythical folk who told reporters there were fleets of mythical tankers lurking offshore during the 1973 oil embargo.

I think of the front-page headlines you get whenever you are accused—and that later story on page 123—or no story at all—reporting that the charges against you have been dismissed.

I think of the deals between reporters and the legislative or executive branches of government—cases in which reporters are secretly given government material in exchange for favorable stories about a government official. . . . Or the even worse cases, in which the press foments government action in order to make news of it—going to government agencies and telling them, "Here is some information. Start an investigation and then we'll cover it as news."

I think of all the times I've heard distant echoes of Joe McCarthy, cases where the reporter is waving this secret document, this hidden memo, this list he has . . . and he claims it's about you . . . and he wants you to answer questions about it . . . but he won't show it to you. It's a secret, he says. And if you answer that it must be stolen material, the reporter can respond—as *The Wall Street Journal* did to me—Well, we certainly didn't steal it!

I don't think there's any need to describe . . . for this crowd . . . the questionable values that afflict TV journalism—the slavery to ratings . . . the pandering to the lowest common denominator . . . the emotional presentation to entice a larger audience . . . the subversion of news values to entertainment values . . . the ruthless compression of facts to fit preordained timetables. I mean . . . that sort of thing isn't news to any of you, I'm sure.

But when I think of television, I think of special categories of abuse—

unnatural practices unique to the electronic media, such as rehearsing favorable interviews . . . such as editing techniques that make Mother Theresa look like Mommie Dearest . . . such as the thirty-second bite in which your one-hour interview is reduced to a cursory snippet that somehow manages to make your attacker's point . . . such as the made-for-TV demonstration . . . and finally, the true masterpiece of theater, the jacklighted ambush interview in which they spring out from behind the potted palm and—while the subject is stupified by the lights, camera, and clamor—get him to admit that he is really Idi Amin.

Is that ethical behavior?

I have found that the media don't like to discuss morality—especially their own, and especially not with me. They seem to feel that outsiders should not question the goodness or badness of what goes on in the press. But they rarely examine themselves, and this resolute failure of self-examination . . . this neglect of the press to cover its own errors and deficiencies . . . has provoked the new public skepticism about the rights and privileges claimed by the media.

Has the press measured up to this society's rules for civilized and ethical behavior? In my experience, they have not. The record is replete with instances in which the press has accused, prosecuted, convicted, and punished an individual with greater speed and severity than any court of law . . . and with absolute disregard for even minimum protection of the victim's civil rights.

In these instances, the victim never gets the chance to confront his accusers, to examine the documentary evidence used against him, to evaluate the sources of the accusations and evidence. Compounding all of this is the rabid haste to get into print. Then, afterwards, as those who have been convicted in the media's dock will testify, persuading an editor to give you the right to correct the record is most often impossible.

And, let's not forget the fact that the hallowed journalistic tradition of letters to the editor doesn't even exist on any of the three major networks' evening news shows.

And yet, the general mood of the media about this ethical problem is best summed up in a statement made by one of tonight's speakers, Don Hewitt, "Who am I to sit in judgment on other men of the press?"

So what is the answer? If the nation's communications media are at times capricious, vindictive, unreliable, or even unethical, is that something terribly important and significant? Should our society . . . should we, the people in this hall tonight, and others like us everywhere . . . should we be concerned about it? Does it matter?

I think it does. And I'll tell you why.

Let's begin with the fact that it's hard to find any institution in this country today that the people trust. They're not really very high on any group—be it government, the church, big business, the army, the schools, medicine, the family, marriage, the courts, you name it. I'd say that in the United States today we are going through a crisis of confidence.

Public confidence in these and other institutions is, in my opinion, at an all-time low because the public is poorly informed. I don't think they're getting fair, objective, accurate news—I think they're getting news infected by errors, prejudices, pressures to increase ratings and circulation, and the drive for greater power and salary. This criticism doesn't come just from business. Consider this indictment:

> The mass media often give a distorted view of life, so that often man does not know how to deal with that which is written. . . . The world of political journalism, of speculation, again showed itself to be superficial.

This is a recent statement by the Roman Catholic Primate of Poland, Jozef Cardinal Glemp. The result of all this distortion and superficiality is that the public is beginning to conclude our system is rotten and should be replaced.

If the public's conclusion about the corruption of the system is reached on the basis of bad information, and mis-information, the foundation of our society will have been threatened for no good reason beyond the narrow goals of the media.

That is why I urge the media to begin a process of self-examination that will lead to more responsible press and—yes—a freer press.

*S*tudy *Q*uestions: *T*homas

[?] *How do Thomas' and Schmertz's critiques of the press differ? How are they alike? Do they suggest the same or different solutions? Whose ideas for improvement are more likely to work?*

Do you perceive the liberal bias in the press that Thomas sees? What specific examples of it have you observed? What counter-examples have you found?

How effective do you believe Thomas' suggestions would be for improving the news coverage of religious conservatives, or of any other group?

In "Beyond the Pale," Watkins suggested that we would get more valid pictures of black people in the media if there were more blacks working in the media, constructing those images. Do you believe we would get more valid pictures of big business or of the Moral Majority if people such as Schmertz and Thomas were constructing the images of those groups for us?

Do Gans, Schmertz, and Thomas perceive the major values underlying news stories in our major media the same way? Where do they disagree? Why do you think they disagree?

Do all of the articles in this section of the book reflect agreement on the major problems of the news media? On what points do the authors agree? Are there some disagreements on what the problems are? If so, what are they? What position would you take on these issues? Why?

Cal Thomas

HOW TO CLEAN UP AMERICA: THE PRESS

There is a widely held belief in America that news reporters deliberately slant the news to reflect the liberal viewpoint. As a broadcast journalist for twenty-one years prior to coming to Moral Majority, I can tell you this is not true.

Instead, there has developed what is referred to by Tom Bethel of *Harper's Magazine* and Joe Sobran of *National Review* as a "beehive mentality."

There isn't a deliberate slant. There is a common mindset. The results are the same.

Bethel and Sobran note that bees in a hive don't "talk" to one another but they do communicate, and although they perform different tasks they all work toward a common goal.

Writes Sobran, "There is no need to posit an overarching conspiracy. The world collectivist movement goes forward. None of its constituent parts—communist, socialist, liberal—runs the whole thing; they don't even consciously cooperate, for the most part." They do not, however, sting one another!

When conservatives are in power, there is rarely a story reporting a speech by a conservative President or a bill passed by a conservative Congress that isn't immediately followed up with a comment from a liberal detractor. Such is not the case for liberal Presidents or liberal programs. Occasionally a conservative will be interviewed, but it is strictly a pro forma arrangement. Disagreements that are reported are usually between liberals and center on how much more should be spent on a government program and not how much less.

The press has done a horrible job in reporting the resurgence of moral values and conservative political clout. Were it a homework assignment, the press would receive an "F" and be required to take the course over again in summer school.

Thanks to the press, one of our major jobs has been to communicate to the public that Moral Majority is not responsible for everything that goes on in the country. Our name is being used generically, much as Jello is used to describe gelatin or Xerox for copying machines, Kleenex for tissue and Sanka for decaffeinated coffee.

NBC News recently reported a story from Wisconsin and Virginia on attempts by some local people to ban certain books from their public libraries. The reporter referred to the efforts as "Moral Majority" activities. When I called the reporter and challenged him, he said the name "Moral Majority" was in lower case letters. How is the public to make the distinction? The fact is, he knew very well what he was doing and the image he was trying to portray.

Journalism today, particularly broadcast journalism, displays a lack of depth. Today's trainee is tomorrow's network reporter. More and more we are learning of fabricated stories, such as *The Washington Post* scam involving a phony story about an 8-year-old boy supposedly hooked on drugs. The reporter, Janet Cook, resigned and the paper was forced to return the Pulitzer Prize.

Then there was *The New York Daily News* which carried a made-up story by its Belfast reporter designed to stir up sympathy in America for the IRA. The reporter was forced to quit. How many more of these type of incidents exist we may never know.

Fortunately we no longer have to rely exclusively on the commercial press to get our viewpoints across. The growth of special interest publications and the direct mail industry have given us the opportunity to speak directly to our people and to by-pass the commercial press which is, by and large, dominated by persons who share a similar world view. Nevertheless, the press can make it awfully difficult for us and they must be dealt with. To allow them to misrepresent our true views is to put ourselves in the position of fighting an extended pitch battle that will certainly keep us on the defensive, rather than on the offensive.

We need to be perceived through the press as responsible, law-abiding Americans who are simply trying to exercise the same rights the liberals exercised so well for so many years. We just want to be part of the pluralism they're always talking about, though they don't mean by pluralism what the dictionary means. They mean do it their way or at least allow them to do it their way and, if you don't, you're narrow minded, anti-intellectual and non-pluralistic. Often you can defeat this sort of logic with a smile, particularly when they refer to you as an Ayatollah!

So, how do you make an impression on the press and win a fair hearing? Don't expect to convert them to your point of view, but do expect them to be fair.

Never condemn an individual reporter, station or newspaper in public. That will immediately put them on the defensive and the merit of your argument will be muffled by their reflex action to protect their great institution. Praise or criticize principles, not people.

If you get "burned" in an interview, don't threaten never to talk with that reporter again. Learn from your mistakes and adjust your comments accordingly. Occasionally there are reporters who are simply out to get you and you may have to decline interviews with them. In such cases you should let the editor know that you'll be happy to speak with any other reporter on the staff and tell the editor why.

Rehearse before doing an interview unless you have a lot of experience. Get someone to ask you questions that are likely to come up.

Meet and take to lunch station managers, city editors, reporters and anyone else in positions of authority and influence at newspapers and broadcast stations. In these informal meetings you can be seen as a person who is not a fanatic, does not foam at the mouth and is reasonably articulate. Of course if you are a fanatic, do foam at the mouth and cannot put together a simple sentence, this technique will probably be counter productive for you!

People fear the unknown. They need to know that you are a responsible citizen, seeking to work within the law and are doing nothing more than exercising the rights guaranteed to you and to liberals under our Constitution. The idea that Jerry Falwell is forcing his views down the throats of millions of Americans is ludicrous. It means that those millions have no world view and no sense at all and that Falwell is a modern-day Pavlov who, upon the ringing of his bell, causes people to salivate and vote for conservatives. You and I know we are just expressing some widely held views and giving those views a platform they have been denied in the past.

It is important in meeting the press and, through them, the public, that you dress well. This is so simple it is often overlooked and it is to your advantage that you be properly dressed.

Take stock of your wardrobe. Many in the media believe we are illogical, neanderthal jerks who dress accordingly in "Goodwill" clothes. You may like polyester and leisure suits. Don't wear them to interviews or news conferences. If you're a woman, don't wear pants. Wear a dress that does not look "frumpy."

Men, don't wear white socks ever, except while participating in an athletic event or mowing the yard. Avoid white shoes and white belts, especially in winter. Buy some wool suits in black, grey or blue and get coordinated shirts and ties that are conservative. No prints, please. Go to a hair stylist and get a decent haircut. No burrs and please, no "greasy kid stuff." You don't want your image to speak for you in a negative way before you've had a chance to open your mouth.

If you hold a news conference, have the hotel or a private firm provide the refreshments for the press. I once attended a news conference in Washington where a pro-life organization was trying to save money. They provided a stained coffee pot from someone's home, some paper cups and cookies some of the women baked at home which were stacked on a single paper plate. The whole scene reeked of amateurism and was so treated by the few reporters who stayed. Break out the silverware, the china cups and saucers and the danish pastry. Go first class or don't go.

Don't be afraid of the press. Let me let you in on a little secret. Many reporters are dumber than you are. They ask predictable questions and rarely understand the answers. Many of them are experts at self-promotion, particularly the broadcasters. They're more interested in their careers than they are in accurately reporting the truth. Not all, but many.

Keep in mind we are fighting for our Constitutional right to speak and to be heard. If we can get our message across to the public, I am convinced they will respond because it is a sensible message and it is the right message.

Another piece of advice peripherally related to the press. Try to meet those people who are attacking you or who are opposed to your stands. These might include local preachers, public officials, etc. Most of Jerry Falwell's detractors have never met him, nor have they had the decency to call his office before launching attacks on his views or his faith. Call up these people who don't like you or what you are doing. Make an appointment and show them how responsible you are. They don't have to agree with you. Make the focus the issues you are addressing, not the "new right" or Moral Majority.

If you are a Christian, and your critic is, too, appeal to them on the basis of dividing the body of Christ and the importance of dealing privately and behind the scenes if a brother has offended you. You'll notice that Jerry Falwell does not attack or criticize Christian pastors in public, though many attack and criticize him. I believe he is being biblical and they are not. Such criticism allows the press to attack religious faith. You wouldn't think of holding a news conference to detail the differences and struggles and problems in your family. Why, then, should religious people hang their dirty linen out for all to see. These are family matters and should be dealt with in private and out of the public glare.

Usually in each town there is at least one Christian reporter or at least one who has a strong sense of fairness and of right and wrong, good and bad. Find out who it is and set up a meeting. I even discovered one at *The New York Times!* Now that he's met a real live official with Moral Majority, he'll be able to share with his colleagues at the *Times* what we're really all about. There can be a "fallout" effect from such an encounter.

You can also benefit from press criticism of your efforts. You're not always right and criticism is sometimes a good yardstick for self-measurement. Sometimes you do go off half-cocked and you ought to be doing things differently and more responsibly. The press can help you to see how others perceive the way you are doing things. Though that perception can often be wrong, it can also be right. Learn to be objective in assessing your goals and motives.

Section 6

MEDIA AS SHAPERS OF BEHAVIOR

Like the previous section, this one contains articles about the consequences of mass media. In Section 5, the focus was on media content—how media portray the world and the implicit assumption that people learn about the world from what they see (or do not see) in the media. In Section 6, the emphasis shifts to the audiences of mass-mediated content. The authors of the articles in this section are concerned with possible connections between what people see, read, or hear and their attitudes and, ultimately, their actions. Those connections often are assessed through empirical research. Some of the articles in this section report on research or describe methods used to learn about audience behavior. Others explore the social and behavioral implications of strategies used by media producers to enlarge audience size.

The section begins with James Atlas' overview of VALS, a controversial audience analysis system that uses lifestyle typologies, rather than traditional demographic categories, to identify target audiences for advertising. Atlas describes interviews with VALS's boosters and critics, concluding that the real significance of the VALS approach is a shifting emphasis from the sale of products or services to the promotion of consumption as a value in itself.

Charles Atkin, John Hocking, and Martin Block are concerned with magazine and television advertisements for alcoholic beverages and their relationship to teenagers' drinking. After reviewing research on that relationship, the authors predict that heavy exposure to advertisements, coupled with teenage susceptibility to persuasion, increases drinking. The researchers conducted a survey of teenagers' media use and drinking habits, and they found that exposure to advertisements is significantly associated with drinking and intentions to drink.

Jim Mintz looks at the often-ignored, "rock-'em-sock-'em" world of promotion, the business of catching the attention of an audience for media products. He is especially concerned with widespread, although controversial, attempts to attract viewers with suggestions that a television program contains sex or violence. Based on his analysis, Mintz postulates a future in which advertisers and promotion people directly determine the content of programs and not just the content of advertisements for those programs.

The section concludes with Daniel Linz, Edward Donnerstein, and Steven Penrod's study of the consequences of exposure to a series of movies depicting violence against women. The researchers found that men who viewed a large number of these violent films became rather callous to violence. They responded less emotionally to it, did not perceive it as being as violent as they did at the beginning of the experiment, and considered such films less degrading to women. After having been exposed to these fictional films, they also judged the victim of a violent rape less compassionately.

The articles collected in this section postulate a diverse array of media effects. None of the essays "proves" direct, causal links between media and attitudes or behavior, but each does demonstrate a rather solid basis for concern about potential or likely effects. Because such effects do not lend themselves readily to scientific control, and because people are not exposed to the media in isolation from the many other influences in their environment, we may never have absolute proof that media are harmful or helpful. Nonetheless, to take the position that media are just "bubble gum"—fun while the flavor lasts but harmless in the end—is naive and irresponsible. The media play too large and important a role in American life to be dismissed so easily. Furthermore, there is a substantial body of research that, when taken together, strongly indicates that the media sometimes are powerful influences on beliefs and the behaviors that spring from those beliefs.

Despite the fact that it will be a long time (perhaps forever) before we know for certain about specific effects of media on individuals, there are decisions we must make. Even with our incomplete understanding of what the media are doing to us, we go on watching television, raising new generations of media consumers, and buying advertised products. Issues of regulation and control—to which many of the study questions for these essays are directed—await resolution. To wait for government or science to provide definitive answers probably is to wait in vain. In any case, we cannot wait; all of us must cope with the media and their effects on a daily basis. *So, what will you do? How will you live with the media? Could you live without them? Why should it matter to you?*

S*tudy* Q*uestions:* A*tlas*

What does Atlas mean when he says that VALS is "a credo, an aesthetic"?

Do you believe that the lifestyle selling approach is effective?

What are the probable advantages to advertisers of aiming for a particular kind of audience, rather than simply trying for as large an audience as possible?

Can you cite evidence from your own examination of the media that advertisers are selling lifestyles as much as products and services?

Is the kind of research discussed by Atlas ethical? Is directing a sales pitch to conform to the values and lifestyles of a particular audience segment ethical? Why or why not?

Do you think the advertising industry's confidence in the VALS classification system is warranted? Why or why not? Considering Atlas' illustrations of each type, what role do stereotypes seem to play in VALS-based advertisements?

Into which of the VALS categories do you best fit? Do you believe you are influenced by the kinds of appeals Atlas says are appropriate for your category? Why or why not?

Do you believe adults can be meaningfully categorized into nine types, as the developers of VALS have done? If you were a major advertiser, would you buy this service? Why or why not? If your answer is no, would you change your mind if you found evidence that such information would help you direct your advertising more effectively?

If you were charged with developing an advertising campaign, would it help you more to know that potential purchasers were largely achievers; or would it help more to know that they were primarily professionals or skilled workers, between 35 and 50 years old, married, with children in school, and had incomes between $30,000 and $40,000 a year? What else would you like to know about your intended audience?

James Atlas

BEYOND DEMOGRAPHICS

How Madison Avenue knows who you are and what you want

In the late 1960s the advertising firm of Ogilvy & Mather introduced a campaign for Merrill Lynch Pierce Fenner & Smith that featured a herd of bulls galloping across a plain; the slogan was "Bullish on America." By 1979 the herd was gone, replaced by a lone bull that wandered through the canyons of Wall Street or huddled in a cave (where it "found shelter"). One ad, which ran in fourteen large-circulation magazines, from *Forbes* and *Institutional Investor* to *Esquire* and *Scientific American*, showed the solitary bull silhouetted on a mountaintop beneath a sunset out of Tintoretto. Imagination, instinct, and versatility were the traits stressed in the text. Young & Rubicam, the largest ad agency in America, had taken over the Merrill Lynch account and come up with a new slogan: "A Breed Apart."

The campaign worked. A follow-up survey showed that within eighteen months the company's recall score—the percentage of people who noticed and remembered a Merrill Lynch ad—went from eight to 55; its share of the market on the New York Stock Exchange was up two points. "There's nothing wrong with being bullish on America," Jim Walsh, the advertising manager of Merrill Lynch, said when I spoke with him not long ago at the company's offices on Lower Broadway, in New York City, " but it didn't reflect who we were and what we were becoming"—less a giant investment house than an innovative firm dedicated to serving the private investor. "We'd conveyed an image of stability and reliability," Walsh said. "Now we were looking to capture the upwardly mobile, the self-motivated."

The lone-bull motif had actually been Ogilvy & Mather's invention. The problem for Young & Rubicam was the "Bullish on America" theme: an appeal to a clientele with the herd instinct instead of to entrepreneurial investors who saw themselves as visionary capitalists and self-made men. "We all love to see America grow, but the heavy investor wants an investment firm that's going to help *him* get a big share of that growth," Dr. Joseph Plummer, the executive vice-president for research at Young & Rubicam, told an audience of business and communications students at the University of Illinois last year. "Our strategy shift to 'A Breed Apart' was clearly emotionally on track with the Achievers target audience."

The Achievers target audience? Plummer was "talking VALS"—refer-

James Atlas is an associate editior of *The Atlantic*.

ring to one of the consumer types identified by the Values and Lifestyles Program of SRI International, formerly the Stanford Research Institute, in Menlo Park, California. Devised by a group of market-research analysts associated with the institute, the VALS typology divides Americans into nine life-styles or types, which are grouped in four categories, based on their self-images, their aspirations, and the products they use. Survivors and Sustainers are in the Need-Driven category, which accounts for 11 percent of the population; I-Am-Mes, Experientials, and the Societally Conscious are in the Inner-Directed category, 19 percent of the population; Belongers, Emulators, and Achievers (the ones Merrill Lynch was after) are in the Outer-Directed category, 68 percent of the population; and at the very top of the VALS hierarchy are the last type, the Integrateds, a mere two percent of the population. "VALS is a classic research model," Plummer said one afternoon in his airy corner office, high in the Young & Rubicam Building, on Madison Avenue. "It's a whole new dimension for us. Before VALS, we didn't really have a sense of who the consumer out there was. Now we know how they live and what they buy—and why they buy it."

Until the 1970s, market research was dominated by "demographic segmentation": the classification of consumers by age, income, level of education, and other quantitative variables ("two-point-one children, 90 percent married, with three-quarters of a dog," as Plummer puts it). The seventies were a difficult period for the advertising industry. "There were a lot of things going against it," says William Meyers, the author of *The Image-Makers,* a forthcoming book about Madison Avenue. "You had a baby-boom generation that was cynical about the American dream, at least the way Madison Avenue portrayed it; a stagnant economy; and more women entering the work force, which cut into the captive housewife audience."

Not that hard times in the advertising business are like hard times anywhere else. What had been a $19.6 billion industry in 1970 was a $54.6 billion industry in 1980. Total advertising expenditures increased faster than the GNP. "In a time of generally stuttering economic growth, advertising enjoyed remarkable, almost giddy leaps upward," Stephen Fox writes in *The Mirror Makers,* a newly published history of advertising. But the much-heralded "creative revolution" that had swept through advertising in the sixties—the vodka bottle in the Wolfschmidt ad propositioning a tomato ("We could make some beautiful Bloody Marys together"); the Statue of Liberty modeling a Talon zipper; the Playtex commercial that featured a woman in a black evening gown walking a panther down the street ("Tames your figure like nothing else")—was over. "In less than a decade the creative revolution gathered, prospered, and then inevitably cycled away," Fox writes. "Nothing is more fragile than an advertising fashion."

In such a volatile climate VALS qualifies as a phenomenon with a long history. In six years it has grown from a modest in-house project at SRI to a two-million-dollar operation, billing each of its 151 clients up to $30,000 a year for access to its data. J. Walter Thompson and Doyle Dane Bernbach, *Newsweek* and *The New York Times,* Mitsubishi Motor Sales and Volvo of America, use it. Scarcely a week goes by without the unveiling of some new VALS-inspired campaign. A recent ad for *The National Geographic* that ran full-page in *The New York Times* carried the headline THE NATIONAL PSYCHOGRAPHIC above a text that declared: "According to VALS, 80% of our readers are in the three most desirable groups—Achievers, Societally Conscious, and Belongers." Potential advertisers knew what the terms meant. Dr Pepper has based its latest campaign ("Hold Out for the Out of the Ordinary—Hold Out for Dr Pepper") entirely on VALS. "As we see it, there is a new trend among the Inner-Directed, and a whole new realm opening up," David Millheiser, the brand manager for Dr Pepper, recently told a reporter from the trade journal *Marketing & Media Decisions.* "We currently see 30 percent of the young population as being Inner-Directed; it's the most rapidly growing segment. Our projections indicate Inner-Directeds will make up 60 percent of that population by 1990." So convinced were Dr Pepper's executives of this trend that they were willing to ignore ("turn off," in advertising parlance) the whole Outer-Directed market. "Those with an Inner-Directed interest will jump in," Millheiser predicted. "We must be differentiated from the mass-market products." . . .

What unified these papers was their reliance on the nine life-styles that make up the VALS system. Through the early seventies [Arnold] Mitchell had been working on various models that he hoped would be able to account for the influential "baby-boom" generation's peculiar notions about what constituted success. Finally, during a weekend in 1976, he hit upon the "double hierarchy," a bulb-shaped chart that illustrated two paths to the top of the VALS ladder: the I-Am-Me, Experiential, Societally Conscious (Inner-Directed) route, and the more conventional Belonger, Emulator, Achiever (Outer-Directed) route. Borrowing terms from David Riesman's classic of sociology, *The Lonely Crowd,* and the psychologist Abraham Maslow's five-tiered hierarchy of "needs growth," Mitchell devised elaborate portraits of these nine types, each intended to describe "a unique way of life defined by its distinctive array of values, drives, beliefs, needs, dreams, and special points of view."

The early VALS reports were highly speculative, and drew much of their data from the Bureau of Census, the Department of Labor, and other government agencies. There was no hard evidence that the VALS typology was reliable or that the types even existed. So the people at VALS devised a way to "validate" their hypothesis. The VALS 1980 Field Survey—"based on a national probability sample of households with telephones," according to Mitchell—used a questionnaire eighty-five pages long, on subjects ranging from "Attitudes" to "Media Habits," "Eating and Food Preparation," and "Household Inventory and Product Use." There were questions about respondents' sexual habits ("I like to think I'm a bit of a swinger") and general disposition ("I like myself pretty much the way I am"); how much television they watched and when; what kind of cleaning products they used; which brand of margarine they bought and why. There were questions about credit cards, checking accounts, mortgages, and IRAs; about waterbeds, decorator telephones, lawn furniture, cameras, and pets (did the respondents own "Hamsters, gerbils or mice," "Horses, donkeys, etc."?). Over a million "data points" were developed, Mitchell claims.

Administered to 1,635 subjects, the VALS survey yielded a vast archive of consumer lore: Sustainers drink more instant-breakfast products than any other group. Emulators read more classified ads. Belongers go bowling three times more than I-Am-Mes. Societally Conscious households score high in ownership of dishwashers, garbage disposers and food processors. Experientials attend fewer high school and college sports events than I-Am-Mes but just as many professional sports events. Achievers play golf, drink cocktails before dinner, and have a lot of credit cards.

Now that it had its own data base, VALS could offer clients not only its numerous reports but also profiles of specific markets. Among the many services listed in its latest brochure are "detailed quantification of VALS types in terms of demographics, attitudes, regional distribution, household inventories, activities, media habits, and consumption patterns for over 700 categories"; "access to special data tapes and print-outs, and VALS on-line computerized data bases"; and "a tailored system for classifying people into VALS segments in ways relevant to *your* interests." Beginning this year, clients interested in the whole package—and prepared to lay out $26,000—can enroll in the Leading Edge program, which qualifies them to receive the services listed above plus "bonus" reports and services. "We're into geo-demographic research now," Deborah Moroney, the manager of data services for VALS, told me. "Classification by Zip Code. You live on the Upper West Side, right?" (How did she know?) "10024? 10025? You're Bohemian Mix."

Subscribers can also avail themselves of "Getting Started with VALS" (known as "Program Element A"), a day-long "familiarization session" at SRI headquarters, which includes the screening of *American Portrait*, a documentary film about the VALS types. I saw it during a visit to Menlo Park last winter. I had read Mitchell's book and a good many of his papers, so I had a fairly clear idea of the VALS types, but the film enabled me to see actual representatives of each type and made the types more vivid.

American Portrait begins with the Need-Driven, Survivors and Sustainers, America's marginal classes. Estelle, an old woman shown knitting in her parlor, is a Survivor; she lives in a sparsely furnished apartment, scrapes by on Social Security, and hardly ever goes out. But at least her life possesses a certain dignity—unlike the lives of the Sustainers we see next, a seedy assortment of gamblers and touts interviewed at the race track on what somehow feels like a weekday afternoon. A burly Hispanic confesses that when money comes in he treats himself to a meal in a fancy restaurant; but he isn't going anywhere, and he knows it.

Need-Drivens are an ethnically mixed lot; Outer-Directeds (Belongers, Emulators, and Achievers) are distinctly American. Dave and Donna, a blond Belonger couple, are interviewed standing in front of their local church. Later on, in their kitchen, they explain their choice of neighborhood in theological terms: "This is where the Lord wants us to be." An older Belonger couple, Jessie and Ken (he's a retired career military man), pose before their split-level house and talk about patriotism. Belongers, the largest group in the VALS typology (they make up 38 percent of the population), are traditional, conformist; they're what used to be known as Middle Americans. "They get a job and they stick with it," the narrator says. "They find a product they like and they stick with that."

Emulators, ten percent of the population, are less conventional, and have a mildly dissolute aura about them—like the bartender in a Hawaiian shirt who won big at the craps table the night before and is already making plans to spend his winnings. You won't find him putting the money in an IRA. "Emulators are always on their way," the narrator explains. "They want the Achiever life but they haven't cracked the code." They do seem a pretty bewildered lot. "Where did these people get it?" Lenny, a door-to-door salesman, frets as he drives through a wealthy neighborhood marveling at the posh homes. "I mean, do they own a factory, or what?"

Achievers, 20 percent of the population, are the second-largest group and the richest. Ann-Marie and Steve, interviewed in their hot tub, are a typical Achiever pair. Steve is blunt, athletic, hearty; Ann-Marie, sipping a glass of wine, talks in a quiet, authoritative voice about her theory of interior design, the effort she makes to balance formality with a "personal touch." Ann-Marie and Steve have "the right stuff," according to the narrator; and so does John, an Achiever architect who has a Porsche. John worries that he works too hard and doesn't have many friends, but there's nothing he can do about it; he's driven. "You either win or you lose," he says. "Money is a way of keeping score."

To Rob Noxious, however (the name is Rob's own invention), money means "hatred and anger and resentment." Rob, a guitar-playing punk rocker who goes around in shades and sports an earring, is an I-Am-Me. Together with the Experientials and the Societally Conscious, he belongs in the Inner-Directed category. But Rob is a rebellious youth, angry and maladjusted; his identity, the narrator sums up reprovingly, is "I-Am-Not-My-Parents." Jody the Jogger, interviewed on the run, and Tyrone, a muscular young man engaged in "a search for peak experience," are among the Experientials, a more wholesome group. "I like a little excitement, a little adventure," Jody testifies. "I'm happy," Tyrone declares.

Inner-Directeds seem Californian; they backpack, do yoga, are into holistic medicine. But where Experientials and I-Am-Mes only focus inward, the Societally Conscious (11 percent of the population) are aware of social issues and active in politics. Andy, a bookseller with a penchant for sixties rhetoric about the excessive power of corporations, clearly was once a campus radical. He's still suspicious of politicians, but he's working within the system now, and his shop is doing well. Tom, another representative of the Societally Conscious, lives in a comfortable suburban home with his wife, Sherona, and their infant son; he's a lawyer for the Environmental Defense Fund. (Is it just a coincidence that the two Societally Conscious men depicted in *American Portrait*—dark-haired, bespectacled Andy and balding, bearded Tom—both appear to be Jews?)

The Integrateds, the last group shown in the film, represent the VALS ideal. Chris, a management consultant who wears a tie but keeps his shirt open at the neck, hopes to devote thirty or forty hours a month to "learning." So do Mel and Patricia, a writer and an artist with a lucrative clothing business. Mel wants to paint and compose music too, he says, strolling in a park with his arm around Patricia. Integrateds are both creative and prosperous; no wonder they're the smallest of the VALS groups.

Essentially what we're trying to do is to understand people," Brooke Warrick, who produced *American Portrait,* told me in Menlo Park. "Our goal is to identify constellations of underlying motives within American society." The atmosphere of the VALS headquarters supports his claim. Housed in the sprawling SRI complex, the corridor of plainly furnished offices has the informal feel of a college English department. The staff prides itself on being "heterarchical"—that is, without a lot of titles on the doors—and Societally Conscious. "Our goal is responsible consumerism," Warrick told me.

Though SRI has annual revenues of some $175 million, it is a not-for-profit organization, and the VALS program benefits from this status. I was curious about what happens to the profits. "Internally we look like a profit-making company," Warrick explained. But there is "an elusive difference." SRI has no stockholders, so profits are invested in research, "for the benefit of our clients." But surely VALS employees must get some share of the profits? SRI does offer "compensation incentives," Warrick admitted, and staff salaries reflect the program's success. Then what does "not-for-profit" mean? "It means we don't pay taxes."

On the wall of every staff member's office is a framed copy of the VALS "Mission Statement":

> The mission of the VALS program is to exert a positive and creative force in the evolution of the American culture. VALS aims to do this by acquiring, disseminating, and applying insights into how values can aid institutions and individuals to operate in a more humane, productive, responsive, and ethical way.

Specifically, VALS intends:

- To become a significant part of American business thinking
- To enhance public awareness of the role of values in social change
- To extend applications of VALS to non-business domains
- To contribute to SRI research, remain financially healthy, and operate for the enjoyment and personal growth of the staff.

VALS, then, is more than a market-research outfit; it's a credo, an aesthetic, a way of interpreting contemporary life. "Hegel says somewhere that the philosopher's task is to comprehend his time and thought," James Ogilvy, who gave up a job teaching philosophy at Williams to join VALS, said one afternoon in his office. "In the university I could not comprehend my time and thought. Here I can." The portable radio on his desk was turned to a classical-music station. In the corner was a Herman Miller chair. "My wife bought it for me," Ogilvy said. "It's supposed to remind me that it's okay to just sit around and read." . . .

Teresa Kersten, a VALS marketing consultant with a B.A. from the humanities honors program at Stanford, told me that *Reader's Digest* uses VALS when advising potential advertisers on how to reach its readership. Clairol was reluctant to advertise in *Reader's Digest*, "because they were convinced its readers were a bunch of stodgy, middle-aged housewives," Kersten said over lunch at the Bay Window, a cozy English tearoom near the SRI complex. "It's definitely an Outer-Directed audience, with a strong Belonger component, and the *Digest* had to show the advertiser how they could address that audience." *Reader's Digest* went to Clairol and interpreted two of its "product executions" for Nice 'n Easy hair coloring according to VALS. One was an Inner-Directed ad, more appropriate for, say, *Cosmopolitan;* the other was Outer-Directed, and fine for *Reader's Digest*. The Inner-Directed ad showed a woman in a slip, feeling her hair, enjoying the softness Clairol gave it. "She was focused inward," Kersten pointed out. "The whole ad was about how good the product makes you feel." The woman in the second ad was a traditional, Outer-Directed type: she was wearing a dress and makeup, and giving a testimonial.

Clairol ultimately decided on "a new creative," as Paula Byrne, the research manager at *Reader's Digest,* describes it, which ran in both magazines. It showed a fully dressed woman in profile, and it had the challenging tone that Inner-Directeds like and the endorsement that Outer-Directeds like. *Color and condition that should have been yours can be,* declares the new creative. *Make it happen. Sells the most. Conditions the most.* Outer-Directeds are reassured that Nice 'n Easy is popular, and Inner-Directeds feel in charge of their own lives. Make it happen.

For most of its clients VALS has done just that. Henderson Advertising, a firm in South Carolina that handles the Folonari wine account, knew that it should be going after Inner-Directeds, because VALS data revealed that they were the kind of people who drink wine and were "first-time users"—that is, willing to buy new brands. "They make their own judgments, take chances," Jack Shimell, Henderson's director of marketing services, says. "They'll go out and try something a little different." And they're casual about the wine they drink—which is why Pernell Roberts, the "spokesman" for Folonari, was shown in a recent Henderson's ad without a tie, grabbing the jug right out of the refrigerator. "ID's will drink jug wine," Shimell says. "They don't care if it has a cork or not."

When Recreational Equipment, Inc., an outdoor-gear retailer in Seattle, wanted to find out more about who was buying its products, it commissioned VALS to do a survey and learned that between 48 percent and 50 percent of its customers were Societally Conscious (versus a mere 11 percent in the country at large). So it designed a catalogue featuring models who bore vestiges of the counterculture—beards, moustaches, longish hair—and conducted an "environmental review" of its stores with an eye toward making them more congenial to those types. "Earth tones appeal to our customer base," Carsten Lien, the vice-president of Recreational Equipment, says, "and we know that Societally Conscious types process information well. They make highly informed purchase decisions, so we tend to offer a lot of information about our products." From VALS reports the retailer's marketing executives also knew, for instance, that skiing, a popular sport among eighteen-to-thirty-four-year-olds, is less popular among those with "maturing lifestyles"—people with families. Once they enter what Lien calls "the withdrawal mode," these people tend to buy more camping equipment than sports gear. "What VALS did," Lien says, "was give us a feel for the phases of people's life-styles as they go through life's conduit toward the grave."

Joseph Plummer, of Young & Rubicam, has used VALS on a number of campaigns. "You remember the 'Jell-O Is Fun' campaign?" he asks. "The woman who tells her family, 'I didn't make dessert. Instead, I made some fun'? Jell-O's a Belonger brand; it shows women in the provider role. So we got some Belonger women in here, and tried it out on them. They loved it." Thus the famous "Watch that wobble, see that wiggle" campaign.

Where did one come up with Belonger women? I wondered. "We found a town in the New York area that had a good sample of the more consumer-oriented VALS types, and did in-depth interviews. We talked to them, photographed them, photographed their homes. We questioned them about what products they used, and tape-recorded their answers. Then we analyzed our data and put together a series of consumer profiles based on VALS."

One couple Young & Rubicam interviewed were Holly and Bill, a management trainee and a designer who live in a Boise Cascade pre-fab but have put a lot of money into their living room. Holly and Bill are Emulators, and Emulators "spend where it shows," Plummer says (even if their sense of interior design is a little off; they've installed track lighting and a chandelier in the same room). They jog and play tennis, shop at Saks and Bloomingdale's, and read "Achiever life-style" magazines. They'd like to *be* Achievers, but they lack the Achiever style and the money to back it up.

What VALS offered, according to Plummer, was a new way for the "creatives" at Young & Rubicam to visualize the needs of Holly and Bill— or of Ruth, a Belonger who works as a secretary in her local church and has a flamingo on her front lawn; or of Carol, an Achiever executive who lives in a wealthy Connecticut suburb and buys only top-of-the-line brands because she doesn't like "the hassle of shopping around." VALS has made consumers less abstract. It has clarified "their needs, their lives, their lifestyles, and their experiences," and gives a sense of them as individuals rather than statistics.

Not everyone in the advertising business is so convinced. One complaint I have heard often is that the VALS types are contrived and artificial. "In reality, all of us have traits common to each of the eight types," John Hadley, the associate research director at Foote, Cone & Belding's Chicago office, wrote in 1982 in *On-Line*, the newsletter of Interactive Market Systems, a distributor of computerized media and marketing data. "One may have Belonger tendencies in a grocery store, Achiever tendencies in an auto showroom, and Emulator tendencies at a stereo dealer. VALS doesn't account for this possibility." For all its sociological complexity—the academic treatises on consumer values, the references to Maslow and Riesman, the fine distinctions among types—the VALS typology is still highly theoretical. It was "built from the top down," Hadley argued. "—developed conceptually by piecing together other theories rather than empirically from consumer data."

Another objection is that VALS isn't really comprehensive. Survivors and Sustainers are largely ignored (they're "extremely downscale typologies," one marketing consultant I spoke with explained). Nor are the main groups original. The affluent types correspond, more or less, to the conventional gradations of middle class (Belongers) and upper-middle class (Achievers and Societally Conscious). These types represent "a jazzed-up version of the all-American status ladder—with a heavy marketing orientation," Joan Kron observes in her book *Home-Psych: The Social Psychology of Home and Decoration*. Or, as Jim Walsh, of Merrill Lynch, puts it, "Some of 'em are ridiculous."

Then there's the matter of statistics. Is the VALS sample large enough to give a sense of the various types? Integrateds, the exalted two percent, are generally discarded as too small a group to consider in any meaningful way, and some of the other categories are marginal: I-Am-Mes constitute three percent of the population, Experientials five percent (though VALS consultants claim they're the fastest-growing type). "The samples suddenly fall apart when you break them down into all those groups," one marketing executive whose firm subscribes to VALS admits. "For the smaller categories you're talking about a few hundred people, and that's just not enough to work with."

To increase the data base, VALS consultants devised what they call the VALS Lifestyle Classification System, a highly abbreviated version of the original survey that consists of thirty statements—"I like to be outrageous"; "Just as the Bible says, the world literally was created in six days"—with which respondents are asked to agree or disagree. Clients can administer the new form to consumers and forward the results to Menlo Park to be classified into VALS types. (How they do it is "proprietary information," but the people at VALS claim that the short form yields virtually the same results as the longer one.) Since 1982 Simmons Market Research Bureau (SMRB) and Mediamark Research Inc. (MRI) have been including the new VALS form in their surveys, which encompass much wider samples than VALS uses; Simmons and MRI each poll 20,000 people annually. VALS clients who put up $12,500 for access to the SMRB/VALS or the MRI/VALS data base get a "VALS-coded" breakdown of which VALS types use their products. Instead of identifying its readers as, say, men from eighteen to thirty-five with incomes of about $25,000, *Penthouse* can say that it has "a strong franchise among Inner-Directed Males." (According to MRI/VALS, 46 percent of *The Atlantic*'s readership are Societally Conscious.)

Advertisers that appeal to an "upscale audience" can assume that Achievers, Experientials, and the Societally Conscious are their primary customers. The average Achiever—to resort to the old demographic profile—is forty-three years old, with 13.7 years of education and a median household income of $37,000; the average Experiential is twenty-seven years old, with 14.2 years of education and a median household income of $26,000; the average Societally Conscious is thirty-six, with 14.7 years of education and a median household income of $32,000. For a client interested in advertising a domestic wine, it's worth knowing that these three segments rank highest in domestic-wine consumption and read the most weeklies but are on the low end of the spectrum when it comes to watching television. The conclusion is obvious: forget television and concentrate on magazines.

Still, even agencies that have "gone on-line" with VALS recommend caution. "Magazines don't have those breakouts," Carla Loffredo, a vice-president and the director of media at the Marsteller agency, says. "And even if a magazine is predominantly one type, we still want to reach the others. Say we're marketing an antihistamine, and we know from VALS that more Achievers use antihistamines than any other type. We still have to address the Belonger segment; they're a major marketing type we can't ignore."

VALS is "one of many inputs," Loffredo says. "We use a little bit of everything"—and that seems to be the consensus among media buyers. "We use it along with demographics," Chet Bandes, a vice-president and the director of media research at Doyle Dane Bernbach, says. "Like any tool, you apply it where the marketing data makes sense." Chester Gore, the president of the agency that bears his name, says that VALS is "as good a single measure of who's out there as we have," but his advice to advertising directors contemplating a print campaign in a specific magazine is to take an issue home for the weekend and read it. "If you can't figure out who it's trying to reach, talk to the editor—and if you still can't, advertise somewhere else." VALS isn't the only way to interpret the consumer, John Hadley concluded in his *On-Line* article. "It is just a *different* and *additional* way."

American Portrait ends with a glimpse of the Stars and Stripes whipping in the wind while Aaron Copland's patriotic *Appalachian Spring* swells in the background and the narrator intones: "VALS helps us to see the America of tomorrow." Living in that America, at least as it is depicted in the VALS documentary, will require a good deal of money. The Societally Conscious Tom and Sherona can afford a big house on a quiet suburban street (even if he does work for the Environmental Defense Fund); Ann-Marie and Steve, the Achiever couple lolling in their hot tub, are clearly well off. As for the Integrateds Mel and Patricia, they're more interested in art than in material possessions—though even Mel concedes that "money makes thing easier."

These couples are in what Carsten Lien, of Recreational Equipment, Inc., calls "a buying mode." They're young and they have a lot of money to spend. It is primarily to their generation that VALS has addressed itself. "Forget the cult of youth," James Ogilvy says. "The Oedipal rebellion of the sixties is over. We're going from slay the father to protect the mother." In *The Nine American Lifestyles,* Arnold Mitchell predicts that Inner-Directeds, now 19 percent of the population, will constitute nearly a third by 1990. (This figure includes the Integrateds, a category that will grow from two to four percent.) In the "Renaissance" future, one of four that Mitchell posits and the one he believes in most, the 1980s will turn out to be the "Decade of the Real Thing"—a decade characterized by the quest for "the down-to-earth, the authentic, the direct, the honest, the unfrilly, the real." The number of Belongers will decline; Achievers and Emulators will react to the predominance of Inner-Directed values with a "new conservatism"; Experientials and the Societally Conscious will continue to express themselves through "artistic pursuits and single-issue politics." In the 1990s a new class of visionary Achievers—"a kind of person the United States has not yet known"—will emerge and eventually combine with Inner-Directeds to produce a more activist Integrated type.

How will these attitudes affect business in America? Some changes are visible already: a preference for low-tar cigarettes, decaffeinated sodas, foreign cars, low-alcohol beers and wines. But products are products, and there's no indication that the "graying counterculturalists," as William Meyers refers to the Inner-Directeds of the 1980s and 1990s in *The Image-Makers,* will be spending any less. The "bottom line," according to the VALS introductory brochure, is "how to apply values and life-style information in marketing, planning, product development, and other areas of business"—in other words, how to get across the message that it's okay to be a consumer again.

Study Questions: Atkin, Hocking, and Block

In the introduction to this article, the authors raise the question of whether beer, wine, and liquor advertising simply shifts brand preferences or whether it increases overall demand. Why should this question be of interest to citizens and officials concerned about advertising regulation?

According to the authors, Canada has banned the sort of lifestyle advertising of beer, wine, and liquor that Atlas discusses in the preceding article. What would you guess was the rationale for the ban on this particular kind of alcohol advertising and not all other kinds?

Considering the reasons, reported in this article, for why young people say they drink, what kinds of beer, wine, and liquor advertisements are likely to be most effective with this group?

How would you account for Atkin, Hocking, and Block's finding that advertising is relatively most important for liquor drinking and least important for wine drinking?

As the authors point out, a correlation between amount of exposure to advertising and amount of consumption of a product may mean that advertising increases the probability of drinking, that drinking increases the probability of attending to beer, wine, and liquor ads, or that both are related to some third factor. Do you agree with the author's analysis and conclusion that advertising is the most active force? Why?

How well do you believe these authors prove that advertising increases drinking among teenagers? Are there any weaknesses in their study?

> *Assuming the generalizations of this study are supported by future research, what, if anything, do you believe should be done? Should Congress ban the advertising of alcoholic beverages on radio and television as it did the advertising of cigarettes? Can you justify such banning in broadcasting if it is not banned in the print media? Would a legal ban on beer, wine, and liquor advertising in the print media be a violation of the First Amendment? Why or why not?*
>
> *Is your position on banning beer, wine, and liquor advertising consistent with your position on broadcasting deregulation?*

Charles Atkin, John Hocking, and Martin Block
TEENAGE DRINKING: DOES ADVERTISING MAKE A DIFFERENCE?

Those Young People Who Say They Have Seen More Television and Magazine Ads for Beer, Wine, and Liquor Generally Drink More or Expect That They Will Begin Drinking

In the climate of increasing research interest and regulatory controversy regarding the social impact of advertising, advertising for alcoholic beverages, especially as it influences adolescents, has been the focus of much attention. In 1976, hearings held by the U.S. Senate Subcommittee on Alcoholism and Narcotics raised policy-relevant questions concerning alcohol advertising effects. According to one of the committee members, Senator Hathaway, "many millions of American youth are bombarded every day with thousands of messages about drinking from hundreds of glamorous, friendly, healthy, adventuresome, sexy, even famous people telling them of the joys and benefits of drinking."(4) He raised the question, "How much of it is actually designed to encourage nondrinkers to start drinking, and to encourage moderate drinkers to drink more?"

His comments echo some of the same questions raised in the early 1950s in England by the Amulree Commission, which concluded that ad-

Charles Atkin is Professor in the Department of Communication, Michigan State University. John Hocking is Associate Professor in the Department of Speech Communication, University of Georgia. Martin Block is Associate Professor and Chairman in the Department of Advertising, Michigan State University.

vertising does not merely shift brand preferences, but tends to increase overall . . . product demand.(6) More recently, Canada's concern with effects of beer and wine TV commercials resulted in a 1981 ban on "lifestyle" advertising and ads that portray drinking as desirable behavior, and in 1979 Sweden also banned all domestic advertising of alcohol. In the United States, the U.S. Bureau of Alcohol, Tobacco, and Firearms and three other federal agencies commissioned the research project on the influence of alcohol advertising on young people that is reported in this article. Here, we focus on the relationship between exposure to alcohol advertising and drinking patterns of adolescents who are below the legal drinking age.

Mass media in the United States carry a massive amount of advertising for alcohol products.(1,4) In the late 1970s, popular magazines such as *Newsweek, People, Cosmopolitan, Sports Illustrated,* and *Playboy* presented at least a dozen liquor advertisements per month, and network television aired more than 5,000 beer commercials per year in programs often viewed by adolescents. Advertising of wines increased dramatically in all media during the past decade. By 1980, spending for alcohol ads in all media had reached almost one billion dollars. It is estimated that the typical teenager is exposed to about one thousand beer, wine, and liquor ads each year; indeed, exposure is greater for adolescents than for adults.(1)

Drinkers and drinking are portrayed in alcohol ads in a variety of favorable ways.(1) Characters in ads are primarily youthful, physically attractive, and well-to-do, and are often depicted as successful, manly or womanly, happy, adventurous, elegant, and sophisticated. Some ads feature celebrities, such as athletes and entertainers. Among the promised or implied benefits of drinking are social camaraderie, romance, escape, refreshment, social approval, and relaxation. Drinking is shown to be appropriate in a wide range of situations, and negative consequences of drinking are, not surprisingly, never depicted in commercial advertising.

Teenagers may be particularly receptive to this advertising. Early adolescence is a period of experimentation with alcohol, and by high school a majority drink at least once a month; almost half have become drunk, and one-quarter can be classified as problem drinkers. Reasons young people give for drinking include social acceptance and conformity, getting high, achieving a tranquilizing effect, escape, enhancement of manliness or womanliness, and taste.

A variety of learning theories can be used to explain how adolescents might be affected by repeated exposure to positive messages about alcohol. Leventhal(5) argues that young people are conditioned to accept alcohol advertising through jingles, sports associations, and identification with characters who display breeding and discriminating taste. He notes that advertising appeals may instigate the entirely new activity of learning to drink, may suggest new types of alcohol for trial by drinkers, and may provide ritualized ideas about the proper contexts for consumption. Hammond(3) suggests that ads appeal to young people because the messages stress their desired goals, such as good times, sex, and social acceptance. The ads may also contribute to the conception that drinking is a legitimate and normal activity in society. From Bandura's social learning approach, it can be inferred that the mere observation of mediated drinking may increase the observer's tendency to copy that activity. This is especially the case when the modeled behavior is portrayed as rewarding and pleasurable, as content analyses indicate is the case with alcohol ads. In one experiment, students who saw a model drinking heavily later tended to consume greater quantities of wine during a taste-testing exercise than those who saw a model drinking lightly or not at all.(2)

The uses and gratifications perspective is also suggestive. Since adolescents presumably have a strong need for information about a substance with which they are experimenting, they should be motivated to attend more frequently (relative to other age groups) to alcohol ads and acquire more ideas and images from the messages in these ads. In addition, those who are favorably inclined toward drinking may seek out advertising messages to reinforce those opinions.

Considering the Quantity and Enticing Quality of Alcohol Advertisements and the Susceptibility of Youthful Audiences, We Expected to Find Higher Levels of Drinking Among Those Most Exposed to Beer, Wine, and Liquor Advertisements in the Mass Media

To test for the predicted positive association between amount of [natural] exposure to alcohol advertisements and amount of reported alcohol consumption by teenagers, we used a correlational survey design. A questionnaire was used to ask teenagers about their drinking behavior, their exposure to alcohol advertising, relevant demographic information, and other possible communication influences. The questionnaire was administered to a sample of 665 teenagers from the seventh through twelfth grades in Michigan, California, New York, and Georgia. The sample was demographically typical in terms of sex (49 percent male, 51 percent female), race (84 percent white, 12 percent black, and 4 percent Oriental or Chicano), community size (18 percent large urban city, 30 percent medium urban city, 31 percent suburban or college town, and 21 percent small town or rural area), occupational status of parents (35 percent upper-middle-class, 39 percent lower-middle-class, and 26 percent working-class or lower-class), and church attendance (30 percent regular, 23 percent occasional, 25 percent seldom, and 22 percent never).

Half the sample received a questionnaire focusing on liquor advertising and consumption, while the other half was asked about beer and wine. For liquor, respondents were first asked [which magazines they read and how frequently. The frequency of reading each one was then weighted by the average number of liquor ads it carries a month. That is, reading magazines that carry many liquor ads was counted more heavily than reading magazines that carry few such ads.] Respondents were next asked to report the number of liquor ads they typically noticed when they read magazines and what proportion (from "none" to "most") of the ads they attended to for at least five seconds. Respondents were also asked the number of ads they remembered for each of six categories of liquor (e.g., gin, scotch). This measure was supplemented by a more concrete measure that involved photographs and brief verbal descriptions of nine specimen ads, in which respondents estimated how many times they had seen each of the displayed ads, how much attention they had paid (from "little" to "close"), and how many times they had seen other ads for each brand (from "none" to "many"). Measures of these responses were combined into an overall index of liquor advertising exposure.

For beer/wine advertising, the questionnaire featured parallel items asking about beer and wine advertising exposure. Respondents' access to ads was measured by the amount of television they viewed during prime time and sports programming (when most alcohol commercials are shown) and by how many magazines they read of those presenting beer and wine advertisements. Their attention to ads for beer and wine on television and in magazines was also tapped. Photos of specimen ads were used as for the respondents in the liquor group, and measures derived from these items were similarly combined into an overall beer/wine exposure index.

The other major set of items measured alcohol consumption. The questionnaire listed the names of the most popular brands of liquor or beer and wine. To minimize the respondents' possible apprehension about reporting illegal behavior (all were under the legal drinking age in their states), the questions focused on their attitudes toward the various brand names. The respondents were also asked to indicate which of these brands they "have personally drunk." . . .

A subsequent question asked, "Do you ever drink beer these days? If yes: What is the total number of beers that you drink in a typical week?" Six quantitative responses were provided, ranging from "none" to "25 or more." The item was repeated for wine. In the liquor form of the survey, the wording was, "Do you ever have mixed drinks or straight liquor drinks these days (for example, gin & tonic, rum & cola, tequila sunrise, screwdriver, scotch, bourbon, or amaretto)? If yes: What is the total number of drinks that you have in a typical week?"

Those respondents who indicated that they had never consumed a given type of alcohol were asked, "Do you think you will start drinking liquor (beer, wine) when you're older?"

For each type of alcohol, scores for the items measuring drinking of particular brands and total weekly consumption were summed into parallel "amount of drinking" indices for beer, wine, and liquor.

To account for the role played by influences other than advertising, the questionnaire asked respondents about other interpersonal and mass media factors that might be relevant to drinking. One set of items dealt with social encouragement to drink. In separate questions, respondents were asked to rate the opinions of their close friends, father, and mother, along a scale from "they want me to drink" to "they don't care" to "they don't want me to drink." Another set of questions asked respondents to estimate how often their parents and peers actually consume alcohol. Regarding parental influence, the index was constructed by summing responses to the following quesitons: "What do other people think about your drinking? Mark the opinion of each of these sets of people" (parents don't want me to drink = 1, parents don't care = 2, parents want me to drink = 3) and "How often do these other people drink alcohol?" (mother/father never drink = 1, drink sometimes = 2, and drink a lot = 3). The same procedure was used for peers. Other individual questions asked how often respondents viewed television characters consuming alcohol and how often they viewed public service messages advocating moderation in drinking.

The question of whether respondents in general underreported or overreported their alcohol consumption cannot be answered in the absence of direct observation. Some might want to brag, some might want to conceal, and others might simply have exaggerated perceptions or faulty memory. Two points are relevant: the consumption figures from national samples using a variety of methods tend to show similar results, and there is no reason to believe that teenagers with high versus low levels of advertising exposure differ in the validity of their reported drinking (and, of course, the crucial findings in the study are *relative* levels of drinking according to advertising exposure, not the absolute amount of drinking that occurs).

The Statistical Analysis Involved the Computing of Correlations Between All Predictor Variables and the Indices Representing Amount of Drinking

[The amount of drinking was correlated with the measures of each factor that might influence drinking, using special statistical techniques to eliminate the influence of other factors. These results are shown in Table 1. The higher the correlation, the closer the relationship between drinking and that particular influence shown along the left side of the table. The significant correlations, those that are unlikely to have been due to chance, are marked with an asterisk.

As Table 1 shows, exposure to advertising is significantly related to

Table 1

Standardized correlations between key predictors and amount of beer, wine, and liquor drinking

Predictor	Beer drinking	Wine drinking	Liquor drinking
Advertising exposure	+.20*	+.08	+.34*
Peer influence	+.43*	+.24*	+.26*
Parental influence	+.01	+.14*	−.05
Church attendance	−.09	−.01	−.12*
Sex (male > female)	−.16*	+.01	+.10
Age	+.16*	+.09	+.14*

* = significant

beer drinking. In fact, according to these results, it is second in importance only to peer influence, which showed the highest correlation. The correlations for sex and age were also significant. As expected, boys tend to drink more than girls and older adolescents more than younger adolescents. Neither parental influence nor church attendance is significantly related to beer drinking.

As the second column of figures in Table 1 shows, wine drinking by adolescents does not appear to be affected by advertising. The correlation between the two was not significant. The only important influences on wine drinking found are those from peers and parents.

According to the results of this study, advertising seems to have its strongest effect on the consumption of liquor by teenagers. Of the six possible causes tested, advertising was clearly the strongest. This can be seen in the last column of the table. Peers are the second most important influence on liquor drinking. The correlations of age and church attendance with liquor consumption are also significant, but not very high. The positive correlation for age means simply that older teenagers tend to drink somewhat more than younger ones. The negative correlation of church attendance with liquor consumption means that those who attend church more tend to be somewhat less likely to drink liquor.

In none of these analyses were the viewing of television characters drinking, viewing of public service announcements against drinking, social class, or community size significantly related to the probability or amount of teenage drinking.

To show the relationship between drinking and exposure to advertising more clearly, we divided our respondents in half, according to how much beer, wine, and liquor advertising they had been exposed to. So we had a high exposure and a low exposure group. Tables 2 and 3 show the percentage of each group who drink different amounts.

Table 2

Percent of respondents drinking beer and wine, by level of advertising exposure

	High exposure (n = 167)		Low exposure (n = 168)	
	Beer %	Wine %	Beer %	Wine %
Total number consumed per week:				
15 or more	5	0	5	0
5 to 10	11	1	5	2
3 or 4	10	2	9	2
1 or 2	20	18	10	12
None or never drink	54	79	71	83

Beer: significant; wine not significant.

Brands ever consumed:				
Budweiser	65		44*	
Michelob	55		38*	
Miller	67		47*	
Olympia	28		21	
Pabst	49		35*	
Schlitz	50		40	
Gallo		29		27
Andre		15		10
Paul Masson		15		14

* = significant.

	(n = 73) %	(n = 114) %	(n = 108) %	(n = 124) %
If never drank, plan to drink when older:				
Yes	20	26	11	18
Maybe	33	49	28	38
No	47	25	61	44

Wine: significant; beer not significant.

These results are consistent with those reported earlier. They show a significant effect of advertising on beer drinking, but a negligible effect on wine drinking. Sixteen percent of those in the high exposure group drink five or more bottles of beer a week, compared to only ten percent of the low exposure group. On the other hand, there is little difference between the two groups in wine drinking.

The results are even more striking when we look at the most heavily advertised brands of beer and wine. In every case, a greater percentage of the high exposure than the low exposure group drink more of these advertised brands of beer and wine. Although not all of the differences for

Table 3

Percent of respondents drinking liquor, by level of advertising exposure

	High exposure	Low exposure
	(n = 166)	(n = 164)
	%	%
Total number of straight and mixed drinks consumed		
per week:		
15 or more	2	1
5 to 10	7	3
3 or 4	12	5
1 or 2	24	18
None or never drink	55	73
Significant		
Brands ever consumed:		
Gordon's Gin	35	13*
Beefeater Gin	15	7
Smirnoff Vodka	38	18*
Wolfschmidt Vodka	16	9
Bacardi Rum	47	20*
Ronrico Rum	18	11
Chivas Regal Scotch	21	8*
Seagrams Whiskey	45	27*
Canadian Club Whiskey	36	15*
Jack Daniels	43	15*
Wild Turkey	23	11*
* = significant		
If never drank, plan to drink liquor when older:	(n = 66)	(n = 98)
	%	%
Yes	20	10
Maybe	39	26
No	41	64
Significant		

individual brands are significant, the consistency across all brands indicates that these differences clearly are not due to chance.

When adolescents who had never drunk were asked whether they plan to do so when they are older, the effect of advertising can be seen for both beer and wine. A larger percentage of the high exposure group said they planned to drink beer and wine when they are older. This difference was statistically significant only for wine. These results are shown on the bottom of Table 2.]

The cross-tabulations for liquor appear in Table 3. At least three drinks per week are consumed by 21 percent of those highly exposed to liquor advertising, compared to 9 percent of those less exposed. The proportion is also higher for each individual brand, each of which is regularly advertised in magazines. An average of 31 percent of the high-exposure group versus 15 percent of the low-exposure group say they have tried each of the 11 brands.

For the subset of adolescents who have not yet begun drinking liquor, the heavily exposed nondrinkers are more likely to indicate that they plan to drink in the future, by a 59 percent to 36 percent margin.

The Evidence from This Field Survey Indicates That Advertising Has an Influence on Drinking Behavior During the Adolescent Years

The relationship between exposure to ads and liquor drinking is strongly positive. There is a moderate association for beer, while the linkage to wine drinking is weak. Peer influence appears to play a bigger role in beer and wine drinking, while the contribution of advertising is relatively greater for liquor drinking. Advertising is more strongly related to both beer and liquor drinking than is parental influence, age, sex, church attendance, social status, or viewing alcohol in entertainment programming.

The limitations of this survey design require that caution be exercised in drawing causal inferences regarding advertising effects. Two key issues restricting definitive conclusions are spuriousness and direction of causality.

First, the association between exposure to advertising and drinking might be explained by [the fact that both are caused by some other factor or factors. The] analyses attempted to control for the most likely contaminating factors, such as sex, church attendance, and social encouragement. However, it is possible that certain unmeasured personality characteristics or attitudinal orientations might [lead to] both exposure and drinking. For example, dissatisfaction with life may motivate viewing of those TV shows carrying heavy beer advertising and also produce reliance on alcohol, or sexual liberalism may motivate reading of erotic magazines featuring liquor ads and also lead to consumption of alcohol. In addition, coincidental exposure to entertainment or informational content in magazines or on television may contribute to drinking behavior. Although the viewing of drinkers in TV programming was controlled for, reading of editorial content in magazines was not measured. A moderate positive correlation has been found between amount of alcohol advertising carried and favorability of articles dealing with alcohol in major magazines.(7) Thus, a portion of the exposure-drinking relationship could be spurious, although the statistical controls imposed in the analysis should minimize this problem.

Second, the direction of causality is in doubt, due to the lack of time ordering in the static design. Advertising is not necessarily the causal agent in the relationship. Heavier drinkers may be motivated to attend to alcohol advertising, so that the positive relationship may be due to drinkers seeking ads rather than ads stimulating alcohol consumption.

While it is plausible that this reverse causality might account for a portion of the association, several considerations suggest that advertising is the more active force.

First, of the two variables, exposure is more likely to be the antecedent one in the life cycle of the adolescent. Most young people will see numerous ads before the time they experiment with alcohol or become regular drinkers.

Second, exposure to advertising is seldom a highly motivated form of selective information seeking; people are often indiscriminately exposed to whatever ads they encounter while watching TV or reading through magazines, and the entertaining style of the advertising may attract more attention than the substantive nature of the product. Even if drinkers do seek reinforcement from advertising, this probably provides psychological support for continuing consumption, such that ads maintain or increase drinking behavior.

Third, the predispositions of those adolescents who have not yet started drinking seem to be affected by advertising. Many more of the highly exposed nondrinkers express an intention to drink in the future, compared to less-exposed adolescents. Since they have not yet performed the behavior presumed to motivate selective exposure, the reverse causal sequence is an unlikely explanation for the relationship.

In conclusion, the survey evidence shows that exposure to alcohol advertising is significantly associated with drinking behavior and intentions. Furthermore, it appears that the relationship is primarily explained by advertising influence rather than reverse causation or [other factors not considered in this study].

REFERENCES

1. Atkin, C. and M. Block. *Content and Effects of Alcohol Advertising.* Springfield, VA: National Technical Service (PB–82123142), 1981.

2. Caudill, B. and G.A. Marlatt. "Modeling Influences in Social Drinking: An Experimental Analogue." *Journal of Consulting and Clinical Psychology* 43 (1975): 405–15.

3. Hammond, R. "Statement to Hearing Before the Subcommittee on Alcoholism and Narcotics." In *Media Images of Alcohol: The Effects of Advertising and Other Media on Alcohol Abuse.* Washington, DC: U.S. Government Printing Office, 1976.

4. Hathaway, W. "Opening Statement." In *Media Images of Alcohol: The Effects of Advertising and Other Media on Alcohol Abuse.* Washington, DC: U.S. Government Printing Office, 1976.

5. Leventhal, H. "An Analysis of the Influence of Alcoholic Beverage Advertising on Drinking Customs." In *Alcohol Education for Classroom and Community Drinking,* edited by R. McCarthy, pp. 128–46. New York: McGraw-Hill, 1964.

6. Levy, H. *Drink: An Economic and Social Study.* London: Routledge & Kegan Paul, 1951.

7. Tankard, J. and K. Pierce. "Alcohol Advertising and Magazine Editorial Content." *Journalism Quarterly* 59 (1982): 302–5.

Study Questions: Mintz

[?] *What does the title of this article mean? What is a "hot sell"? Do you believe there is anything wrong with this practice? Why? How do you explain the success of the "hot sell"? What does that success say about our society?*

What are the major techniques used to mislead viewers about the amount of sex and violence in a program?

Is this type of misleading promotion different in any essential way from advertising that makes you believe a patent medicine or an automobile has properties that it does not?

Are there analogous types of misleading promotion for other forms of mass communication such as books and movies? Cite specific examples.

Should government regulate misleading promotions like those discussed in this article? Are there better ways to handle the problem? If so, what are they? Or do you believe any type of control would be a mistake, that advertisers and promoters should have "poetic license"?

Why are television promos especially important in attracting television audiences? Are other forms of advertising and promotion for television programs likely to be as effective? Why or why not?

Do you see evidence that Mintz's concluding prediction already is coming true?

Jim Mintz

THE HOT SELL

How TV turns on the viewers

Sprawled across two full pages of *TV Guide* is a young blond woman with her skirt hiked up. A bare-chested man, stroking her thigh, leans down for a kiss. Below this steamy scene, ad copy introduces the characters for a new television show, but it's hard to tell if the blond is the one with the tag line, "always on the prowl," or the one who "demands performance."

Jim Mintz is a writer living in New York City.

This is how Steve Sohmer, NBC's chief of promotion, kicked off the campaign to entice viewers to watch *Bay City Blues,* last fall's new show by the creators of *Hill Street Blues.* Sohmer's strategy was to obscure the show's plot--about a small-town baseball team—and give it a sexy image. This is called a "hot sell" in the promotion biz, and nobody does it better than Sohmer. You know how it goes: six-and-a-half seconds of fast action, with a breathless script—"A night of passion threatens to destroy a dream!" or, "Watch as Joe and Sunny inch closer and closer to their affair!"

The show's creators at MTM Productions were aghast. Before they saw the lurid *TV Guide* spread, they had hoped NBC's ads for their show would feature spectacular outfield plays and fans standing for "The Star Spangled Banner."

"There was no basis in the scripts" for NBC's promo ads, says a *Bay City* writer. "They were completely misleading." Another MTM insider confides that *Bay City*'s executive producer, Steven Bochco, complained to Sohmer, "We know the audience likes illicit sex, but that's not the show we're doing."

The *Bay City* promo provides just one example of what many in Hollywood consider a trend. "The networks have gone promo crazy," says Leonard Goldberg, one of television's most successful producers. "The shows they are advertising don't really exist."

Hot promotion frequently works wonders for a show's ratings, but it seems to have backfired for *Bay City Blues.* The series, which critics favored, is now off the air after less than a season, a flop in the ratings. It may have fallen victim to a crazy network gospel: The image of a prime-time show is more important than its substance.

The leading apostle of this creed is Steve Sohmer, despite his inability to sell *Bay City* and NBC's other recent bombs. Sohmer was an obscure young advertising executive until a few years ago, when the networks suddenly became convinced that enough promotional hype—the hot sell— can turn any new show into a hit. Now he and the other network marketing men, Roy Polevoy at ABC and Mort Pollack at CBS, have been put in charge of selling shows as if they were bottles of hair tonic. None of the three seems to mind which producers' toes he crunches along the way.

Steve Sohmer is a tough, self-confident, fast-talking 42-year-old New Yorker. He says, slowly, "Hype . . . is not . . . a dirty word."

"Steve is a great huckster," says Lou Dorfsman, who unobtrusively made CBS's promos for 20 years before Sohmer came along. "He would unzip his fly to win."

Seven years ago, when Sohmer quit his own ad agency to head CBS's promotion operation, he didn't even own a TV set. But he had something more valuable—the marketing savvy to sell J.R. Ewing's devilish grin (not to mention the "Who Shot J.R.?" cliffhanger) and help make CBS's *Dallas* the top show in television. With Sohmer's assistance, CBS regained its first place among the networks in 1980, boasting seven of the eight top-rated shows.

Two years later, NBC lured away the whiz-kid of promotion with a staggering deal—including a $250,000 salary, a $75,000 bonus for running the annual network affiliates meeting (according to *Variety*), extraordinary "creative freedom" to direct and broadcast without interference from above, and an opportunity to take over programming duties in addition to promotion. Sources also report the network promised to work with Sohmer as an independent producer after he leaves NBC.

Networks are willing to pamper promo experts because their on-air house ads have proven the best way to get audiences to "sample" the premiere of a new show. Dull promos mean low sampling and a dead show. A hot 10-second promo for a movie, aired constantly, can send its ratings up 25 percent—often meaning the difference between a hit and a failure.

Normally a behind-the-scenes showman, Sohmer takes his bows at NBC affiliates meetings. Regardless of recent ratings, the affiliates cheer lustily for him. Network staffers tell the story, perhaps apocryphal, of NBC chairman Grant Tinker watching his affiliates fawn over Sohmer. "I think this guy wants my job," Tinker remarked to then-president Robert Mulholland—who replied, "I think he already has it."

Talking from behind the cigar that appears permanently appended to his left hand, Sohmer comes on like the announcer in one of his brash on-air promos. He says things like, "When Mr. T turns it on, you know the sparks'll really fly." He chain-smokes cigars, snuffing out one stubby Macanudo as he fiddles with the cellophane around a fresh one.

Network secretaries find the custom-tailored Sohmer glamorous, from his blue eyes to his dazzling gold-and-diamond bracelet and maroon Rolls Royce. Network writers appreciate his love of Shakespeare, fine wine, and haute cuisine. And local TV executives are simply amazed—at how he finds a limo while everybody else at a convention boards the bus, or how he shows up at a weekend meeting with a beautiful young actress on his arm. One of Sohmer's closed-circuit speeches to affiliates captured his "imperial" style, according to an observer. The network Barnum was escorted into camera range by several "scantily clad" ladies, "like a Hawaiian king."

Sohmer loves beautiful women and has dated a succession of blonds since his divorce several years ago. (Since then he has dropped 100 pounds from his six-foot frame; he now weighs 200 pounds.) Sohmer, though, is no party animal; his dates can expect to spend most evenings in front of his living room's three television sets comparing prime-time shows.

Glamorous women are also the stuff of his promos, along with suggestive come-ons. The announcer insinuates: "Mickey goes all the way—to get a plumber . . . from one hotbed of excitement to another . . . Laura moves in with Remington and the place explodes . . . Manimal's passion for a wolfwoman really lights her fire . . . tonight on NBC."

There are television veterans who wouldn't mind seeing the hot-sell promos vanish from the tube. ABC's chief speechifier, network president James Duffy, has spoken out against misleading promotion but isn't situated at the right point in the organization chart to stop them. "The shows aren't sleazy," Duffy says, "so why do we need the sleaze look?"

"Promos today are tremendously aggravating. They're mind pollution," says leading New York ad man George Lois, a network promo-maker in the 1950s. "They're all of a very similar style—boom-bang graphics with no attempt to emphasize substance." Steve Sohmer's promos, in Lois's view, represent the worst of the new style. "He appeals to the most visceral thing, thinking all guys want is tits and ass. That becomes the image of the network, and I can't believe that's what NBC wants."

Sohmer's approach, however, is exactly what NBC went after. "They courted Sohmer and gave him a totally free hand," says Leonard Goldberg, who once headed programming at ABC. "Sohmer at CBS was controllable; he reported to people. I think NBC went too far—the people selecting the shows have to control promotion: otherwise, the tail is wagging the dog."

Sohmer's critics say he went out of control during one Emmy awards broadcast. George Lois calls it "one of the most revolting nights in the history of television." It was NBC's turn to televise the awards ceremony, and when the network won most of the Emmies, Sohmer turned the usually non-partisan event into an on-air victory party. As NBC's Emmies accumulated, Sohmer inserted live promo spots from around the country congratulating his network. Seeing the promos on monitors in the auditorium, the Hollywood audience hissed its disapproval, whereupon an NBC functionary scurried to turn off the monitors.

The promotion backfired, and NBC had to face complaints about its manners when it should have been free to revel in its successes. "Most people associated with the show thought it was in poor taste," says a source in the National Academy of Television Arts and Sciences, sponsor of the awards. The Academy's board of governors was said to be "displeased with NBC's self-aggrandizement," and to have appointed a committee to make sure it never happens again.

Sohmer, who recalls that Tinker also "wasn't particularly happy" about the Emmy show, is unrepentant, except to concede that the promos came out "heavy-handed." "We essentially apologized," he says, "[but] I still think doing live promos during the Emmies is a brilliant idea." He admits to one mistake: "If the promos hadn't been fed back into the [Hollywood audience's] room, everybody would've said it was cute."

In comparison to Sohmer's handiwork, the promos of 25 years ago were wallflowers—nothing more than a card frozen on the screen for 15 seconds, carrying a utilitarian message like "NEW NIGHT FOR *FATHER KNOWS BEST*," with a network logo and a still photo of the stars.

Lou Dorfsman, Sohmer's predecessor at CBS, still keeps a deck of these oversized promo cards within a few feet of his desk. Dorfsman is a graphic designer, not a marketer or a promoter. He translated the refined taste of CBS president Frank Stanton into the widely admired CBS "look," but his promo spots were short on hype. "We simply helped people find the shows they liked," he says. Dorfsman made only a few hundred on-air promos a year (perhaps one-twentieth of today's number), and CBS aired them only during time that advertisers didn't want. His sell, if it can be called that, was usually soft. The promo for the *Jack Benny Program,* one of Dorfsman's favorites, showed a vase of flowers with a violin sound track of Benny's theme, "Love in Bloom." When the vase broke, the announcer said, "Tune in tonight and maybe he won't play."

Dorfsman the Gentle was deposed at CBS, his network's ratings demolished, his low-key, classy approach repudiated—all by Fred Silverman, head programmer at ABC.

Silverman had pioneered a new skill, finding what he called "the heat" in a television show and blasting viewers with it repeatedly.

"Fifty percent of success is the program and 50 percent is how the show is promoted," Silverman has said. Using quick video editing, his staff produced fresh spots for each episode, hiking the number of spots produced from 300 to 1,600 a year.

Silverman proved the power of hot, heavy promotion for the first time in 1976, during ABC's broadcasts of the winter and summer Olympics. He used frequent promos of popular sports events to attract a huge audience and then packed the sports broadcasts with promos for *The Captain & Tenille* and the rest of his prime-time lineup. "That was the turning point," says ABC's James Duffy. In the following season's ratings, ABC knocked CBS out of first place for the first time in more than 15 years. "The promo launch really helped," Duffy recalls. "We exploded."

Dorfsman observes, somewhat bitterly, "the whole point of ABC's Olympics was to use the nice fresh audience for all their prime-time crap."

CBS brass understood little of the revolutionary progression Silverman was transplanting from the advertising world: The more promotion, the more viewers sampled a new show, the more kept tuning in week after week. Dorfsman remembers CBS chairman William Paley asking, what if promos get our shows good sampling, and then the audience doesn't like the shows—won't that be embarrassing?

That was the relatively innocent marketing scene Sohmer entered in July 1977. For the previous five years, he had run Steve Sohmer Inc., which made slide presentations to advertisers on behalf of *Newsweek* and other publications.

At CBS, he began by imitating the on-air promo that ABC had used so effectively. The content of the modern promo, says Sohmer, had been invented several years earlier by Harry Marks, his counterpart at ABC.

Marks isn't shy about telling how ABC developed the smarmy hype that has become the standard for U.S. television. First, he says, "we threw out the cliché copy like 'Join the madcap merriment tonight,'" and hired an announcer who could say, "The *Lo-o-o-o-o-ove Boat.*" For an unwatched new show called *Baretta* "we had the announcer talk street-talk," and jazzed up the detective's image with quick shots of his swagger, his laugh, his undercover disguises. Further, ABC superheated the ads with action scenes that weren't actually in the shows being promoted; this tactic would be considered improper today. "We used a stock reel of car crashes and explosions until Broadcast Standards said it was false advertising," says Marks. *Baretta*'s ratings shot up among teenagers, who lifted the show's overall score from 14.3 to 21.1 and ensured its success. Even when it used snippets of actual action and dialogue from a show, ABC pressure-cooked its promos. "We'd look for the hot, provocative quotes," says Marks, "and we would always take them out of context." "For *Charlie's Angels*, of course, we used as much flesh as we could, but we would also tease the audience with Farrah Fawcett-Majors saying, 'I haven't had my photo taken nude since I was six years old.'" Adds Larry Sullivan, another ex-ABC promoter, "Sure we tease them. We sell the possibility of tits and ass and the possibility of violence."

For years, until recently, the networks refused to clutter their air-time with ads for more than one product per 30-second spot, but they didn't seem to mind hyping five of their own programs in the same 30 seconds. At ABC, Marks bundled four together in 20-second blocks. ABC's announcer (then and now), Ernie Anderson, quick-changes his voice to suit each plug. He once did a block promo combining five seconds for *Donny and Marie* and five seconds for a movie about the Munich Olympics killings. "And it worked," says Marks. *Roots*, a high point of 1970s programming, was also the greatest sell ever by Fred Silverman and Harry Marks. "There was promo gold in *Roots*," says Marks, referring to the brutal images of slavery, but there was "lots of trepidation" at ABC about how the audience would react. So the mini-series was sold as the heartwarming saga of an American family, with Chicken George jumping over a fence at the end of every promo. Silverman gave Marks's team much of the credit for the *Roots* success.

In other ABC shows, there was so little "promo gold," so little heat, according to Marks, that Silverman's staff had to tell producers, "We need promo material even if you have to insert it." Promo people recall a Silverman underling ordering a bar scene re-shot so that a woman, not a man, would be drenched in beer, revealing a fair amount of anatomy under a wet T-shirt.

"I've heard lots of horror stories about network promotion in the 1970s," says Sohmer. "ABC went from third place to first with that rock-

'em-sock-'em world of overstatement. But CBS was the last place on earth you'd see that." Nevertheless, Sohmer's CBS had to compete in the rock-'em-sock-'em world, and Lou Dorfsman's low-key traditions had to be broken. Sohmer's assessment of the history of the promo: "Lou Dorfsman invented TV promotion, Harry Marks perfected it, and I, if I did anything, made it a business." CBS doubled Sohmer's staff of promo writers, tripled the promotion budget, and loaded the airwaves with the results. One of his writers remembers, "Before Sohmer, everybody disdained promotion, like they'd never dream of asking anyone to watch their wonderful programs."

Sohmer chafed somewhat at CBS's conservative style. He wasn't allowed to use the word "lovers" in a promo, and he told a reporter that CBS, unlike the other networks, prohibited the use of double entendre and violence. Sohmer did, however, manage to air Loni Anderson, the curvy blond of *WKRP in Cincinnati,* purring, "This is Jennifer, reminding you not to touch that dial—or anything else."

Dorfsman's idea of a good promo in the 1970s had been to find a little scene and let it play for 30 seconds, to give a feel for the show. Under Sohmer, says a writer, "There were monumental changes. It was cut, cut, cut—quick lines and gags to support the announcer's words." Whenever *All in the Family*'s swinging kitchen door hit Edith, or Archie emitted a raspberry, it made the promo. In the search for punchy material, Sohmer admits, "We ruined a lot of *M*A*S*H* jokes." (Eventually executive producer Burt Metcalfe prohibited him from using clips from the show's second half.) It may not have been subtle, but Sohmer's fast, funny approach helped *Lou Grant* and a number of other new shows catch on.

Sohmer closed the promo gap and helped make CBS competitive again, but within a year, *Washington Post* critic Tom Shales renamed CBS "the Clutter Broadcasting System." He decried the network's "punchier, harsher, more abrasive" promos as "an ecological slur not unlike billboards on a highway."

"Steve did lots of tasteless, brash shit," says Dorfsman, who still works at CBS. "But we climbed out of the cellar and he should get some credit for it."

This year, Sohmer and company will make 8,000 on-air promos, using time that in advertising terms would be worth up to $400 million. Increasing numbers of the spots, at all times of day, attempt to lure viewers to NBC's low-rated daytime soap operas—a program category that Sohmer himself oversees as well as promotes, along with Saturday-morning and late-night programming. . . . He takes credit for transforming *A-Team*'s Mr. T from "that scary guy in *Rocky,* a monster" into a tough but good-hearted star. "I saw his cuteness," Sohmer says. Overall, NBC's heavily promoted made-for-TV movies have jumped ahead of the other two networks' films in the ratings. And a number of Sohmer campaigns, such as the NBC News "Go Where the News Is" spots are widely regarded as imaginative and classy.

Years ago, a western was promoted with a scene of one cowboy pushing the head of another cowboy toward a campfire. Today, network censors nix such outright violence. NBC's rules allow guns to be fired in promos but prohibit showing who gets hit. But if violence is off limits in promos, that leaves only one way to heat up a show's image. As NBC programmer Brandon Tartikoff once said, "If you can't have Starsky pull a gun and fire it 50 times a day on promos, sex becomes your next best handle."

"Does she or doesn't she?" Sohmer says, "That's the best way to make promos." Ads for NBC's *Jennifer Slept Here,* for intance, usually raise the possibility that something sexy is about to happen between blond bombshell Ann Jillian and her 14-year-old co-star, Joey. When Joey's facing his first date, Jennifer purrs, "Practice on *me.*" It's a perfect two-second bite out of the show, Sohmer explains, because it reaffirms the sitcom's premise that Jennifer helps Joey grow up. "She's saying, 'practice your social skills on me,'" Sohmer explains, with a straight face.

Though he inherited some of ABC's editing tricks and brash style, Sohmer says the Wild West atmosphere of the seventies has given way to a more businesslike approach. "Those days are over." NBC is too big a company, with too much dignity, "to take a chicken and call it a gorilla." He acknowledges that NBC's promos sometimes take lines out of context, the copywriting trick that Harry Marks perfected at ABC. He says he only does it "for fun," however, not to distort.

But here's what Sohmer did with a *Bay City Blues* promo:

Announcer: "Tonight, Frenchy tries out and blows it, but his wife pinch hits."

(Cut to his wife, Judy Knuckles, and male stranger in a bedroom.)

Judy: "There's lots I'll do for my husband."

(Cut to stranger, facing Judy.)

Stranger: "You're fantastic."

Despite the promo's clear implication, Judy had refused to sleep with the guy. In the show, his line, "You're fantastic," followed a speech from Judy putting him down and asserting her loyalty to her husband. "We were trying to build her up as somebody with integrity," says a *Bay City* writer. A viewer who saw that promo "might be disappointed by not seeing the payoff and disgusted at what was attributed to the characters."

"Why would I want to make Judy Knuckles look not nice?" asks Sohmer. He doesn't remember the promo well, but denies vehemently that it could have strayed from the "spine" of the show. "We don't make things appear as they're not, period. If you imply something and then don't show it, you lose the audience in two minutes."

Apparently, the audience did falter. The series was canceled. One can only speculate about the ratings the program would have attained if it had corresponded more closely with its promos.

In the case of *Bay City Blues*, producer Steve Bochco wouldn't have been the one to give in. "It would [have been] like talking to a goddam wall," Sohmer imagines. But with other series, it has occurred to Sohmer to intervene more actively. Consider the NBC adventure show *Gavilan*, which came and went two seasons ago. Sohmer's crew concocted promos featuring "a series of women in various stages of undress whispering 'Gavilan' through moistened lips," according to the show's creator, Tom Mankiewicz. "I was totally appalled. Gavilan was a loner, not a lover." When producer Leonard Goldberg complained, Sohmer told him. "Your show should be like my promos."

More recently, Sohmer collaborated for the first time with the like-minded Fred Silverman—in a marriage presumably made in ratings heaven—and their offspring is *We've Got It Made*. Silverman's series concerns a beautiful, buxom blond named Mickey who moves in as the maid for two "cute guys" and makes their girlfriends hideously jealous. The guys leer shamelessly, providing a wealth of footage for suggestive promos.

After a hot and heavy campaign, the show opened with a huge—32 percent—share of the audience. No misrepresentation was necessary to heat up the promos. *We've Got It Made* doesn't deal in incidentally sexy plots; the program is *about* sexual tension, Sohmer says.

"It wouldn't surprise me," observes an ABC executive, "if Freddie had said to NBC, 'Here's a hot concept and here's a hot way to sell it.'" Visions of the promos may even have come first in Silverman's mind. He won't comment on such speculation: Sohmer says he himself "saw the show's commerciality" and thought up the promos. In any case, it would be hard to find a sitcom situation better suited to the hot sell.

Media historians may some day footnote *We've Got It Made* and its network kin as examples of a breakthrough form of entertainment derived from advertising. Soon after they appeared, the television industry recognized producers as bothersome middlemen, and eliminated them along with traditional pretensions to artistic creation. Throwing off years of oppression, the true masters of audience manipulation were put in charge, and Steve Sohmer was free at last.

The Hustling of Prime Time

Every week, CBS shortens *60 Minutes* by one to put in promotional spots. That is premium air-time which, if sold commercially, would go for $400,000. Altogether, during a year, the networks set aside the equivalent of $1 billion in commercial time in a never-ending campaign to draw us to their programs. They know that the best way to sell television is through television. Watch for these tricks of the promoter's trade:

Divide and Conquer   Ever since ABC did so for *Roots*, the networks have fashioned separate promos for different audiences. A prime-time show often has three distinct "sells": to women during the daytime, to kids early in the evening, and to men during sports broadcasts. During soap operas last year, ABC included special lines calculated to draw women to *Hardcastle & McCormick*: The announcer described the young hero as "one hunk of American male," and a clip of tape had the hunk himself saying, "I'm hot." For ABC stations in big cities, the network prepared promos picturing the hero of *Tales of the Gold Monkey* as a wise-cracking Humphrey Bogart type. For small towns, he was a new John Wayne.

"Counterpromote" the Competition   The word was that CBS's Navy series, *Emerald Point N.A.S.*, would appeal to women, what with all those dazzling uniforms. So NBC set out to cripple *Emerald Point*'s premiere by attracting women to its made-for-TV movie that night, *Sessions*. Instead of emphasizing the bawdy aspect of the prostitution storyline, NBC's promos showed the prostitute crying, trying to explain herself. NBC beat CBS in the ratings, and *Emerald Point* never recovered.

Repeat and Repeat Again   Network promoters aim to run enough promos to plug each program to a viewer eight to 10 times, in the hope that repetition will awaken the desire to tune in. But repetition can also trigger rage in viewers. During last year's World Series, ABC saturated its commercial breaks with ads for *Nighthawks*, a movie starring Sylvester Stallone. Inning after inning, game after game, fans heard Stallone growl his hottest line, "I'm gonna kill that stinking pig!"

Let the Announcer Do the Selling   Five seconds of interaction among a program's characters are too much. Better to show mere moments and add a tease by the announcer. For *Hotel*, the announcer begins, "It's not easy being a beauty queen." A female then delivers the sizzler, "He likes to touch me." Announcer: "Everything has its price."

Nothing Beats Sex and Violence   In a talk to colleagues in the Broadcast Promotion Association last year, Steve Sohmer praised the CBS promo for the film *Murder Me, Murder You*: "It turned an ordinary cops-and-killers movie into a sensational 36 share." CBS had opened its promo with quick shots of various female chests while the announcer drooled, "31 delicious flavors of deadly double-dip delight." It ended with guns firing at the viewer, a switch-blade popping open and a tortured girl pleading, "Nooo!" "Double dip indeed!" Sohmer chuckled after screening the promo. The next season, Sohmer's copywriters used the "double dip" gag in a sexy ad for NBC's *We've Got It Made.*

Study Questions: Linz, Donnerstein, and Penrod

What cautions or qualifications do the researchers place on their findings? Do you think the effects of these films would have been different if they had been viewed in a movie theater or on a home television screen rather than under laboratory conditions?

What were the effects of viewing a large number of films in which there was violence against women? What are the practical implications of the authors' findings?

Linz and his colleagues argue that dampened emotional response to actual aggressive situations may be just as important an effect of exposure to aggressive films as lowered resistance to one's own aggression. Do you agree with their argument?

Under what conditions are men more affected by violent films?

What do the authors mean by "disinhibition"? Why should viewing many aggressive films have a disinhibiting effect?

Who were the subjects of this experiment? Do you think their demographics could have had any effect on the findings? Do you think female students would have given responses similar to those reported in the study? Would they respond differently to any of the questions asked by the researchers?

What precautions did the researchers take to assure ethical selection and treatment of their human subjects? Why were these precautions necessary?

What are some theoretical explanations for the effects found for violent and pornographic films? Which of these explanations do you find most persuasive?

Do you believe that the kinds of effects found for these films should concern us? Why? If you believe they should, what course of action do you suggest? Who should do what?

Daniel Linz, Edward Donnerstein, and Steven Penrod

THE EFFECTS OF MULTIPLE EXPOSURES TO FILMED VIOLENCE AGAINST WOMEN

Men Who Viewed Five Movies Depicting Violence Against Women Came to Have Fewer Negative Emotional Reactions to the Films, to Perceive Them as Significantly Less Violent, and to Consider Them Significantly Less Degrading to Women

Much concern has been expressed over what is perceived to be an increasing trend toward the portrayal of brutality against women in the media. Some individuals contend that the continual portrayal of women in film and other mass media as victims of sexual assault and other violent acts encourages the battering and sexual harassment of women in real life (21). Laboratory investigations of the effect of media portrayals on aggression against women have generally shown that exposing men to such portrayals results in more negative attitudes about women and increases in aggression against them (24). The study reported in this article attempts to extend previous research by exposing men to five commercially released, feature-length, R-rated movies that depict violence against women and then measuring the impact of this exposure on judgments made about the victim of a violent sexual assault.

Malamuth (22) first pointed to the possibility that aggressive-pornographic stimuli might increase aggressive behavior against women. In his study, male subjects viewed aggressive or nonagressive pictorials in *Penthouse* magazine that had been judged to be equally sexually arousing. The aggressive stimulus depicted the rape of a woman with some suggestion that the woman became sexually aroused by the rape. The nonaggressive stimulus depicted mutually consenting sex. Half the subjects were also given a communication designed to reduce inhibitions against aggression in which

Daniel Linz is a research psychologist at the University of California, Santa Barbara; a research associate with the UCLA Center for the Study of Women; and a lecturer in the Department of Psychology and the Communication Studies Program at the University of California, Los Angeles.

Edward Donnerstein is chairman of the Communication Studies Program at the University of California, Santa Barbara.

Steven Penrod is an associate professor of psychology at the University of Wisconsin-Madison.

the experimenter said it was "okay" to behave as aggressively as they wished. Following exposure to these stimuli, subjects were insulted by a female confederate and then given the opportunity to give her an electric shock. Those males who were exposed to the aggressive pornography and also received the disinhibitory communication delivered significantly more electric shocks than the others.

Donnerstein (11, 12) conducted similar studies using short pornographic film clips. In one study (12), male subjects were either angered or treated in a neutral manner and then exposed to a non-aggressive pornographic film, an aggressive-pornographic film, or a neutral film. After viewing the films, subjects were given the opportunity to aggress against either a male victim or a female victim, both confederates of the experimenter. The results indicated that the combination of exposure to aggressive pornography, a high level of pre-exposure anger, and pairing with a female victim resulted in the highest level of aggressive behavior. However, even nonangered male subjects exposed to violent pornography showed significantly higher levels of aggression when paired with a female victim. Additional experiments (14) have demonstrated that exposure to aggressive-pornographic films with what has been characterized as a "positive" outcome (i.e., the victim apparently enjoys being roughed up or becomes sexually aroused while being raped) will increase subjects' subsequent aggression against a female even when the subjects are not angered. Exposure to aggressive-pornographic depictions with "negative" outcomes (in which the victim is seen to abhor the experience) does not appear to result in greater levels of aggressive behavior against women by nonangered subjects, although the effect is still found for angered subjects.

Donnerstein (13) has also investigated the independent contributions of violent and pornographic content to aggressive behavior against women. Male subjects were angered by either a male or female confederate and exposed to one of four types of film: arousing nonaggressive-pornographic, aggressive-pornographic, aggressive only (in which a woman is taunted at gunpoint by a man, tied up, and slapped around), and neutral. Subjects' self-reports and physiological data demonstrated that the aggressive film was seen as significantly less sexually arousing than either the pornographic or aggressive-pornographic films. For subjects whose inhibitions were lessened by their being angered by a female and then being presented with a female target to aggress against, the aggressive-pornographic film produced the highest level of aggressive behavior. It is interesting, however, that subjects exposed to the nonpornographic aggressive film also exhibited significantly higher levels of aggressive behavior than subjects who saw either the neutral or nonviolent pornographic films. But these effects, and similar effects reported elsewhere by Donnerstein (13), occurred only for males who were first angered by the experimenter.

These Findings Can Be Explained by Two Interrelated Psychological Processes: Stimulus-response Association and Disinhibition

Berkowitz (6,7) has proposed a stimulus-response association model which assumes that the film viewer reacts "impulsively" to certain stimuli in the environment. Confronted with the appropriate stimuli, an individual who is predisposed to react aggressively—either because his inhibitions have been weakened due to his being angered first or because he has vicariously or directly learned that pleasures or rewards arise from his actions—will respond in an aggressive manner. In this view, pornographic and nonpornographic films or other stimuli that depict male aggression against females will become associated with aggressive responses to which the individual is predisposed. When the individual is placed in a situation in which cues associated with aggressive responding are salient (i.e., a situation involving a female victim) and in which he is predisposed to aggress because he is disinhibited (i.e., angered), he will be more likely to respond aggressively because of the stimulus-response connection previously built up through exposure to the films.

This account is compatible with Bandura's explanation of aggressive behavior, which emphasizes factors other than anger as contributors to the disinhibition process (2). Emotional reactions that may inhibit an individual from engaging in a particular behavior can be eliminated in several ways. For example, an individual may learn vicariously through the observation of a model viewed in a violent film clip that aggressive acts do not result in negative consequences and may even lead to positive ones (1, 2). When males are exposed to positive-outcome aggressive-pornographic films that depict women becoming sexually aroused from violence, then, they may come to "learn" that women enjoy this type of treatment. This account would also explain why negative-outcome aggressive pornography does *not* result in aggressive behavior among nonangered or nonpredisposed subjects.

Research focusing on modeling suggests that disinhibition may occur despite the fact that a violent depiction is shown with a negative outcome. Subjects' emotional reactions to certain behaviors can be reduced or eliminated when they observe models engaged in those behaviors. In a clinical situation this may allow a patient to engage more easily in a previously anxiety-provoking activity (3, 4). To the extent that aggressing against another is anxiety-provoking (5, 19, 20), the negative emotional arousal associated with an aggressive response may inhibit subjects' behavior. Continued exposure to films depicting models engaged in aggressive behavior—in this case, violence against women—may lead to a reduction of this associated anxiety. By this reasoning we might expect that prolonged exposure to *either* negative- or positive-outcome aggressive pornography, or even to aggressive portrayals that are completely void of pornographic content, will result in greater aggressive behavior subsequent to film viewing. Thomas (31), for example, demonstrated that male subjects exposed to a 15-minute aggressive film subsequently delivered more electric shock to a confederate and exhibited lower average pulse rates than control subjects both before and after delivery of the shock.

Desensitization to filmed violence through repeated exposure may affect people in ways other than predisposing them to actual aggression. For example, adults and children exposed to a condensed version of a television detective program exhibited lowered emotional sensitivity (measured by galvanic skin response) to films of real-life aggression, as compared to control subjects (33). These findings are consistent with those of previous studies indicating that children exposed to an aggressive television program were less likely than those who viewed an equally exciting control film to intervene in a fight between two other children (15, 32).

These Studies Suggest That One Consequence of Dampened Emotional Reaction to Filmed Violence Is a Failure to Respond Emotionally to, and Perhaps a Failure to Intervene in, an Actual Aggressive Situation

This effect may be just as important as the reduction of inhibitions against personally engaging in an aggressive act. In the real world, aggression is a low-frequency event. In the typical grade-school classroom, for example, there may be one or two aggressive children, with the other class members either the victims of aggression or, more likely, bystanders to aggressive acts. As adults, although we may be unlikely to engage in aggressive acts ourselves, we may witness actual aggression (e.g., an entire apartment building may hear the husband in a single apartment physically abusing his wife), and we are sometimes asked to evaluate victims of aggression (e.g., we might be asked to serve as jurors in a case involving violent assault).

Most previous research on aggressive pornography (e.g., 11, 12, 13) has involved brief exposure to filmed violence. This exposure apparently has been lengthy enough to enable subjects to learn vicariously that women might enjoy sexual violence, if the outcome of the film is "positive," but not if it is "negative." After more lengthy or graphic exposure to negative-outcome aggressive-pornographic materials or to aggressive-nonpornographic materials, however, we might find a level of disinhibition equal to that found in subjects who either have been angered or have observed a model whose aggressive behavior is rewarded. The purpose of the study reported here was to expose subjects to a relatively large dose (approximately two hours a day for five days) of filmed aggression against women that had negative consequences, to see whether such a desensitization effect would occur and to test the possibility that it would "spill over" into subjects' later reactions to a physically injured rape victim.

We hypothesized that male subjects' prolonged exposure to filmed violence would result in a systematic reduction in emotional reactions to the violent films. On the first day of viewing, we expected subjects to indicate a high degree of anxiety and depression which would, by the last day of viewing, be significantly lower. We also hypothesized that, as subjects became less anxious and emotionally upset by the violent content of the films, they would report the films to be more entertaining and enjoyable, since they would no longer associate them with a negative state of arousal. Viewing extremely violent movies is probably a relatively novel behavior for most subjects, and so their attitudes toward such materials may be ill formed and rather ambiguous. As their initial feelings of anxiety dissipate with each exposure, subjects may infer that they are enjoying the material more, because they are no longer negatively aroused. Once subjects are emotionally "comfortable" with the violent content of the films, they may evaluate the films more favorably in other domains as well. Thus, material originally found to be offensive or degrading to women may be evaluated as less offensive or degrading with continued exposure.

A reduction in the level of emotional arousal or anxiety should also blunt subjects' awareness of the number of violent scenes or amount of violence in the films viewed. Rabinovitch, Markham, and Talbot (26), for example, found that children who had seen a violent television episode were less likely later to identify violent scenes in a set of stereoscopically presented slides containing pairs of violent and neutral scenes. We hypothesized that a reduction in anxiety should serve to dissipate sensitivity to emotional cues associated with each violent episode and thereby reduce subjects' perceptions of the amount of violence in the films. Consequently, by the end of an extensive exposure period, subjects should perceive the films as less violent than they had initially.

Our final hypothesis was that the subjects' judgments about a victim of violence in another context would be affected by their desensitization of filmed violence. Specifically, we expected that individuals who have been emotionally desensitized through prolonged exposure to films depicting violence against women should show less emotional reaction to the plight of an actual female victim of violence. Confronted with the victim of a violent rape, desensitized subjects should exhibit less sympathy toward her and judge her as less severely injured than a control group of subjects who have not been exposed to violent films.

The Experiment Was Conducted in Four Phases: an Initial Prescreening, a Film Viewing Session, a Simulated Rape Trial, and an Extended Debriefing

Fifty-two males recruited from the engineering, computer sciences, and psychology departments at the University of Wisconsin–Madison completed the Symptom Checklist-90 (10) in the psychology department. The SCL-90 is a 90-item self-report symptom inventory designed to reflect the psychological symptom patterns of psychiatric and medical patients. Scores on the hostility and psychoticism subscales were used as screening variables to eliminate from the sample anyone suspected of a predisposition toward aggression. Since the second phase of the study involved prolonged exposure to violent materials over several days with no debriefing until the final day, we feared that overly aggressive subjects might ruminate over and perhaps imitate certain scenes from the films. Previous research (23) has suggested that individual predispositions toward hostility and psychoticism may be related to a stated willingness to rape among college-age males. Consequently, we decided to accept no one for participation in our study if his hostility score was high. Three males were eliminated from the original pool by these criteria. The psychoticism subscale scores for all subjects were extremely low, with nearly all subjects scoring 0.

The eligible males were then contacted by phone and told that a film evaluation study was being conducted in the communication arts department. They were informed that they would be required to view six films over five consecutive days (two films on the last day) and would receive a payment of $3 per film plus a bonus of $22 once all films had been viewed and the debriefing session completed. Those who indicated that their schedules permitted them to attend all sessions were then informed that they would be viewing commercially released R-rated films that might contain explicit sex and/or violence. At that point they were again given the opportunity to decline participation. It is important to note that in all cases, subjects who declined to participate did so when first informed about the time commitment involved rather than when informed about the content of the films.

Twelve subjects from those interviewed were randomly assigned to view the R-rated violent films. An additional twelve males were recruited as control subjects from among those who had declined to participate due to scheduling difficulties. The control subjects were asked to report to the communication arts department for a single hour session, which involved viewing a videotape and completing a questionnaire.

Subjects viewed five films, one per day, for five consecutive days. Because we were interested in making comparisons between first- and last-day reactions to the films, the twelve film-viewing subjects were further divided into two groups. Seven of the subjects saw the first and fifth films in one order, while the remaining five subjects saw them in reverse order. The first group saw *Texas Chainsaw Massacre* on the first day; the second group saw *Maniac* on the first day; on the fifth day the two were reversed. The intervening films, presented in random order to both groups, were *I Spit on Your Grave, Vice Squad,* and *Toolbox Murders.* All of these films have been commercially released, and some have been shown on campus or on cable television. Each film contains explicit scenes of violence in which the victims are nearly always female. While the films often juxtapose a violent scene with a sensual or erotic scene (e.g., a woman masturbating in the bath is suddenly and brutally attacked), there is no indication in any of the films that the victim enjoys or is sexually aroused by the violence. In nearly all cases the scene ends in the death of the victim.

After viewing each film, subjects completed the Multiple Affect Adjective Checklist (38), which yields anxiety, depression, and hostility or annoyance subscale scores. The MAACL consists of 132 adjectives describing an affective state. Subjects were directed to mark an "x" in boxes describing how they feel "now—today." Next, subjects completed a questionnaire on which they rated, according to several scales, the extent to which the film they had viewed combined sex and violence, was violent (i.e., bloody, gory without being sexually violent), was degrading to women, and was enjoyable. Subjects were also asked to record the number of scenes they found to be offensive.

On the last day, after viewing the fifth film, subjects were informed that the sixth and final film had not arrived. They were then introduced to a representative from the law school who told them that members of their department were pretesting a rape trial documentary; since the film to be viewed by the subjects had not arrived, would they agree to watch the law school documentary? At that point the control subjects were brought into the room and were seated with the experimental subjects.

All subjects watched a videotaped reenactment of a complete rape trial, including all trial elements (opening statements, direct and cross-examination of witnesses, closing arguments, judge's instructions.) The case, derived from the transcript of an actual rape trial, involved a man and woman who originally encountered one another in a bar. The man is claimed to have followed the woman from the bar in his car, pulled her car over on the road by impersonating a police officer, persuaded her to get into his car, and driven to an abandoned factory lot where the sexual assault allegedly occurred. During the course of the trial the victim alleged that the defendant had struck her in the face; this testimony was corroborated by a physician witness. After the trial, subjects completed a questionnaire on which they indicated their verdict and assessed the defendant's intentions and the victim's resistance, responsibility, sympathy, unattractiveness, injury, and worthlessness.

Next, those subjects who had viewed the five films were extensively debriefed, in two stages. First, subjects viewed a videotaped statement in which the first two authors explained the purpose of the study and alerted subjects to the possibility that they could become desensitized to the violent content of the movies. Second, it was pointed out that because many of the scenes in the films involved a juxtaposition of sex and violence, subjects might begin to confuse the pleasurable reactions they had had to the sexual portion of the scene with the violent portion, with the result that their feelings about the violence might change in a more positive direction.

Finally, subjects were assured that in no way do women enjoy, seek, or deserve to be victims of sexual or nonsexual violence. The experimenters remained in the room for as long as necessary to answer questions about the study. Two days later subjects reported for a final debriefing session, participating in a group discussion led by a clinical psychologist in which they were encouraged to share their reactions to the movies and later meeting with a clinical psychologist to discuss their reactions to the films. Two months later, subjects completed a follow-up mailed questionnaire that again assessed their feelings about participation in the research and probed for any residual detrimental effects.

The Comparison of Subjects' Moods and Judgments about the Films Revealed a Number of Changes Between the First and Last Days of Film Viewing

[As will be recalled, the presentation of the films had been counterbalanced on the first and last days, with intervening films presented in random order. A statistical test revealed significant differences between subjects' scores on the first and last day for the depression subscale of the MAACL (mean drop from 21.42 to 18.50) and for the anxiety subscale (mean drop from 12.91 to 9.75). The difference between first- and last-day scores on the hostility subscale was nonsignificant.

Table 1 presents the items comprising each of the film evaluation scales, with the first- and last-day means, the item-to-total correlations, and the overall measure of internal consistency. As a conservative measure of reliability, coefficients were computed on scores from the first day rather than the last day, when subjects would presumably be more consistent in their evaluations of the films. Scales were derived for the first and last days, and mean differences were tested. There were significant differences between subjects' scores on the first and last days on three of the four measures. After viewing all five films, they perceived them as significantly less violent, less degrading to women, and more enjoyable. Their perceptions that the films contained much sexual violence also declined, but this change was not significant.

Table 1

First- and last-day individual item mean scores, items-to-total correlations, and reliability coefficients of items contained in film evaluation scales (n = 10)

	Items-to-total correlation (n = 10)	First day	Last day
		(n = 12)	
		mean	mean
Perception of sex and violence (reliability = .63)			
1. Overall to what extent did sex and violence occur together in this film?	.34	2.58	1.91
2. Of the violent scenes (if any), how many also contained sexual content? (This may include intercourse, rape, simple nudity, or other suggestive scenes.)	.73	2.45	1.72
3. How many scenes involved the rape (sexual assault) of a woman?	.12	1.16	1.25
4. Did this film portray violence toward women in a sexual context?	.70	2.08	2.50
Perception of violence (reliability = .79)			
1. Overall how much violent behavior was portrayed in this film?	.57	6.91	6.16
2. Thinking about the movie as a whole, how many violent scenes did the film contain?	.34	4.42	3.91
3. How graphic was the violence in this film?	.57	6.90	5.45
4. How bloody or gory was the violence in this film?	.33	6.66	4.83
5. To what extent do you think the violence will come to mind in the next 48 hours?	.71	4.17	3.00
6. To what extent did the scenes of violence in the film make you look away from the screen?	.15	3.67	3.16
7. Did this film portray violence toward women *but* not in a sexual context?	.36	6.58	6.16
8. Did this film portray violence toward men *but* not in a sexual context?	.72	4.92	4.83
Degrading to women (reliability = .74)			
1. How degrading is this film to women?	.59	4.50	2.41
2. This movie was: (1) uplifting; (7) debasing.	.59	5.75	5.66
Enjoyment (reliability = .52)			
1. This movie was: (1) not entertaining; (7) entertaining.	.35	2.25	3.08
2. Overall, do you enjoy this type of film?	.35	1.64	2.36

Table 2 presents scores on the rape trial evaluation scales and the reliability coefficients for each scale. When the judgments of subjects who had seen the violent films were compared to the judgments of comparable subjects who had not seen the films, it was found that the former judged the rape victim to be significantly less injured and less worthy. There was also a consistent, although], nonsignificant, trend among the mean differences. The subjects who had viewed the films showed a tendency to assign greater responsibility to the victim for her sexual assault and to judge her as having resisted her assailant less. They also indicated slightly less sympathy for the rape victim than control subjects.

Table 3 presents the correlations between the final day's scores on the film evaluations, postfilm mood evaluations, and post-trial evaluations. As predicted, there was a significant relationship between the enjoyment ratings of the films and anxiety and depression scores: subjects who were less anxious and less depressed at the conclusion of the last film also rated the material as more enjoyable.

The pattern of correlations also revealed a high degree of association between how subjects perceived the films on the final day of viewing and their judgments of the rape trial. Subjects who perceived more violence in the films on the final day (subjects who were not as desensitized to the violence) attributed less responsibility to the victim for her own assault, showed her more sympathy, judged her to have made a greater attempt to resist her assailant, and ascribed more intentionality to the defendant. A similar pattern of associations can be observed between subjects' last-day enjoyment of the films and their judgments of the number of offensive scenes with their perceptions of how responsible, worthwhile, and attractive the victim was.

Of the other correlations in Table 3, only the (negative) relationship between enjoyment and number of offensive scenes was even marginally significant ($r = -.42$). . . .

As We Had Predicted, Prolonged Exposure to Filmed Violence Lowered Emotional Reactions to the Material, with Subjects Significantly Less Depressed and Anxious on the Final Day of Viewing and More Likely to Enjoy the Films

Subjects' perceptions of the violence portrayed in the films also changed over the five days. The films were perceived to be significantly less violent by the last day of viewing (although not significantly less violent sexually). Ratings of how degrading the film was to women and of its offensiveness were also significantly lower by the last day.

We also found a tendency for the desensitization to the filmed violence against women to "spill over" into subjects' judgments of a female victim in another context. Men who were exposed to the large doses of filmed violence against women judged the victim of a violent assault and rape to

Table 2

Items-to-total correlations and reliability coefficients of items contained in rape trial scales (n = 12)

	Items-to-total correlation
Defendant intention (reliability = .73)	
1. Generally how responsible was (the defendant) for the sexual assault of (the victim)?	.41
2. (The defendant) pulled the victim's car over with the intention of sexually assaulting her.	.71
3. (The defendant) deliberately followed (the victim) after she left the tavern with the intention of raping her.	.52
Victim resistance (reliability = .71)	
1. (The victim) was found to have sexual intercourse against her will.	.55
2. The victim resisted (the defendant's) advances.	.55
Victim responsibility (reliability = .81)	
1. Generally, how responsible do you think (the victim) was for her own sexual assault?	.71
2. The defendant was only responding to (the victim's) advances.	.66
3. (The victim) should have foreseen the possibility of danger by getting into (the defendant's) car.	.35
4. (The victim) was responsible for her own sexual assault because she acted like she was personally interested in (the defendant).	.79
5. (The victim) was responsible for the incident because she did not resist when (the defendant) kissed her.	.52
6. (The victim) was responsible for her own sexual assault because she enticed (the defendant) in the bar in the first place.	.43
Victim sympathy (reliability = .57)	
1. After hearing the facts of the case, I felt some pity for (the victim).	.81
2. I felt sorry for (the victim) at the conclusion of the trial.	.18
3. Hearing the facts of the case caused me to be very sympathetic toward (the victim).	.20
Victim unattractiveness (reliability = .78)	
1. I felt (the victim) was:	
(1) likable; (9) unlikable	.28
(1) attractive; (9) unattractive	.66
(1) friendly; (9) unfriendly	.73
(1) pleasant; (9) unpleasant	.75
(1) appealing; (9) unappealing	.17
(1) an enjoyable person; (9) an unenjoyable person	.62
Victim injury (reliability = .48)	
1. Hearing the facts of the case led me to believe that (the victim) experienced severe emotional upset as a result of being sexually assaulted.	.20
2. How certain were you that (the victim) suffered a very severe injury to her face?	.34
3. In your opinion how severely was (the victim) injured?	.37
Victim worthlessness (reliability = .75)	
1. When thinking about (the victim) my thoughts are predominately: (1) very positive; (9) very negative.	.60
2. I felt (the victim) was: (1) valuable; (9) worthless.	.60

Table 3

Correlations between final-day film evaluations, rape trial evaluation scales, and MAACL scores (n = 12)

	Perception of violence	Enjoyment	Number of offensive scenes	Degrading to women
Final-day postfilm mood evaluations (MAACL)				
Anxiety	.34	−.51*	.18	−.02
Depression	.26	−.69***	.22	−.08
Rape trial evaluations				
Victim responsibility	−.65***	.40*	−.63***	.06
Sympathy for victim	.61**	−.42*	.37	.12
Victim injury	.58**	−.04	.32	.15
Victim worthlessness	−.48*	.41*	−.54**	−.27
Defendant intention	.68***	−.45*	.22	.04
Victim unattractiveness	−.23	.64***	−.43*	.06
Victim resistance	.64***	−.28	.08	.09

*marginally significant
**significant
***highly significant

be significantly less injured and evaluated her as generally less worthy than the control group of subjects who saw no films.[1] Finally, subjects who rated the material as less offensive or violent and more enjoyable by the last day of viewing were much more likely to judge the victim as more responsible for her own sexual assault and the defendant as less responsible. Subjects who reported seeing fewer offensive and violent scenes on the last day also judged the victim as offering less resistance to her assailant and felt less sympathy for her. Greater enjoyment of the material on the final day was also correlated with attributions of greater victim responsibility and less defendant intention and with a significant tendency to rate the victim as a less attractive and less worthy individual.

These findings add strength to the mounting evidence (15, 26, 32, 33) that sustained exposure to filmed violence may lower sensitivity to victims of violence in other contexts. The findings are also consistent with a more recent study (36) which suggests that, after reading a newspaper account of a convicted rapist, subjects exposed to relatively large amounts of pornography presenting women in degrading or demeaning circumstances recommended reduced sentences for rapists.

The expected positive intercorrelations between enjoyment of the films and perceptions of how degrading and violent they were did not emerge, however. Nor was emotional arousal (as indexed by anxiety and depression) a significant predictor of degradation scores or perceptions of violence. This suggests that changes in subjects' perceptions of violence over time may not be directly influenced by reduced anxiety and depression, as we had hypothesized. Nor were subjects' judgments about a rape victim directly moderated by these variables. On the other hand, this does not rule out the possibility of an *indirect* relationship between emotional desensitization and judgments of the victim that is moderated by *enjoyment* of the films. Indeed, the pattern of correlations (significant correlations between anxiety, depression, and enjoyment and a significant correlation between enjoyment and victim derogation in the rape trial) suggests that this may be the case. However, the small number of subjects in this study prohibits the use of a causal modeling approach that might elucidate these relationships.

The changes over time in subjects' perceptions of how violent and degrading the films were might be accounted for by a more fundamental process of classical conditioning. Nearly all the films used in this study contained scenes of violence against women in a sexual or erotic context. Immediately before a woman is brutally assaulted in many of the films, she is seen disrobing, masturbating, engaging in sexual intercourse, sunbathing, etc. During and after her assault, the cues associated with those presumably mildly arousing, pleasing scenes are juxtaposed with the violent images. For example, in one carefully crafted scene (from *Toolbox Murders*), the background music that accompanied a scene in which a woman masturbated is reintroduced during a violent assault scene. Additional cues, such as the victim's nudity as she attempts to escape the assailant after the first assault and the eroticized portrayal of the dead victim as a "pin-up" style photograph at the end of the scene may have the effect of classically conditioning sexual arousal to a violent scene. Previous research (27, 28) has demonstrated that sexual arousal can be conditioned to previously neutral stimuli (such as articles of clothing) by presenting photographs of the neutral articles immediately prior to sexually arousing photographs. More favorable evaluations of scenes of violence against women may have been created by presenting scenes of rape or other violence immediately prior to normally arousing scenes. A sufficient number of pairings of this sort, across a lengthy exposure period, may result in subjects' judging scenes previously rated as extremely violent or degrading as less so.

The increasingly positive evaluations of filmed violence that accompany prolonged exposure may also be moderated by a misattribution process. Studies of misattribution of arousal have pointed to the fact that labels for arousal may be quite malleable (29, 35). Subjects may become mildly sexually aroused by the erotic portion of the films and, while still experiencing residual arousal as the scene turns violent, misattribute this arousal to the violence. Subjects finding themselves in this state after several viewings may perceive the films to be less violent and less degrading to women.

In addition to conditioning and misattribution, a third process may account for changes in perceived violence and degradation with repeated measures. Berkowitz (8) has suggested that, as observers encounter violent scenes again and again, other related aggressive ideas are more likely to be activated. These newly activated ideas may either facilitate aggressive responding (i.e., ruminations involving situations in which aggression is rewarded or justified) or inhibit aggressive responding (i.e., thoughts about the negative or punishing consequences of aggression). Viewers' ratings of how enjoyable or degrading the films were may be influenced by the extent to which they perceived the film aggressors to be rewarded for or somehow justified in their violent behavior. If the female victims of violence are seen as deserving their plight (i.e., as sexually promiscuous or "too liberated"), other thoughts concerning justifiable aggression may be simultaneously activated, serving to move subjects' evaluation of the material in a positive direction. They may feel less anxious about the violence and evaluate it as less degrading to women because it is associated with other morally justified or otherwise positively portrayed acts of aggression.

Of course, these processes are not mutually exclusive. All or some of them could account for the desensitization effects found here, and future research could profitably be directed toward better understanding of these mediating processes.

Finally, it is necessary to mention several limitations of this study, some of which are endemic to all laboratory studies of aggression. First, subjects were asked to participate as mock jurors and evaluate the rape victim and her injury almost immediately after they had been exposed to the violent films. It is possible that the effects observed were only short-term ones. A longer time interval between the last film exposure and evaluations of the rape victim might attenuate the current findings. Indeed, some theorists (e.g., 8) have agreed that nearly all effects observed after exposure to violent media are short-lived, due to the temporary nature of related aggressive thought activated immediately after exposure. Future research should vary the time interval between movie viewing and dependent measure tasks.

Second, many laboratory studies of pornographic materials (including this one) employ procedures that may render findings inconclusive (16, 17, 25, 30, 37). It is possible that the cover story we provided subjects concerning their participation in the rape trial was not believed, particularly by students who had taken one or more psychology courses. Since only minimal precautions were taken to ensure that students did not talk to one another about the films they were viewing, it is possible that the findings were in some way invalidated. Little is known about the relationship between subjects' naiveté and their responses in experiments. However, available research (18) suggests that greater knowledge of the experimenters' intentions in laboratory studies of aggression actually serves to suppress aggressive responding rather than enhance it. Thus, our findings may actually underestimate the effect of the films. This, coupled with the fact that most of the subjects were not psychology students and may not have been acquainted with typical psychological laboratory procedures, suggests that our findings may be robust.

NOTES

[1] As noted earlier, there were also nonsignificant but consistent differences between subjects who had been exposed to the violent films and control subjects on judgments concerning the defendant's intention and the victim's resistance, responsibility, sympathy, and attractiveness. It is possible, as one reviewer has noted, that larger differences might have been found if the topic under study had been one in which subjects were less likely to be apprehensive about personal evaluations from the experimenters. Berkowitz and Donnerstein (9) have noted, for example, that the available empirical evidence (e.g., 34) on evaluation apprehension among subjects in the laboratory suggests that people taking part in psychological experiments are inclined to be restrained in attacking their victims if they suspect that the researcher is interested in their aggressive behavior. Because of this, whatever high levels of aggression are obtained often come about in spite of subjects' attempts to present themselves favorably. In this study, subjects in the violent film condition may have been unwilling to make a socially undesirable evaluation of the victim, deliberately dampening their responses in expectation of the experimenter's scrutiny— particularly if they suspected the real purpose of the rape trial task.

REFERENCES

1. Bandura, A. *Aggression: A Social Learning Process.* Englewood Cliffs, NJ: Prentice-Hall, 1973.

2. Bandura, A. *Social Learning Theory.* Englewood Cliffs, NJ: Prentice-Hall, 1977.

3. Bandura, A., E.B. Blanchard, and B. Ritter. "The Relative Efficacy of Desensitization and Modeling Approaches for Reducing Behavioral, Affective, and Attitudinal Changes." *Journal of Personality and Social Psychology* 13 (1969): 173–99.

4. Bandura, A. and F.L. Menlove. "Factors Determining Vicarious Extinction of Avoidance and Behavior Through Symbolic Modeling." *Journal of Personality and Social Psychology* 8 (1968): 99–108.

5. Berger, S. "Conditioning Through Vicarious Instigation." *Psychological Review* 69 (1962): 406–56.

6. Berkowitz, L. "Some Determinants of Impulsive Aggression: Role of Mediated Associations with Reinforcement for Aggression." *Psychological Review* 81 (1974): 165–76.

7. Berkowitz, L. "Aggressive Humor as a Stimulus to Aggressive Responses." *Journal of Personality and Social Psychology* 16 (1970): 710–17.

8. Berkowitz, L. "Some Effects of Thoughts on Anti- and Prosocial Influences of Media Events: A Cognitive-Neoassociation Analysis." *Psychological Bulletin* 95 (1984): 410–27.

9. Berkowitz, L. and E. Donnerstein. "External Validity is More Than Skin Deep: Some Answers to Criticisms of Laboratory Experiments." *American Psychologist* 37 (1982): 245–57.

10. Derogatis, L.R. and P.A. Cleary. "Confirmation of the Dimensional Structure of the SCL-90: A Study in Contruct Validation." *Journal of Clinical Psychology,* 1977.

11. Donnerstein, E. "Aggressive Erotica and Violence Against Women." *Journal of Personality and Social Psychology* 39 (1980): 269–77.

12. Donnerstein, E. "Pornography and Violence Against Women." *Annals of the New York Academy of Sciences* 347 (1980): 227–88.

13. Donnerstein, E. "Erotica and Human Aggression." In *Aggression: Theoretical and Empirical Reviews,* edited by R. Geen and E. Donnerstein. New York: Academic Press, 1983.

14. Donnerstein, E and L. Berkowitz. "Victim Reactions in Aggressive-Erotic Films as a Factor in Violence Against Women." *Journal of Personality and Social Psychology* 41 (1981): 710–24.

15. Drabman, R.S. and M.H. Thomas. "Does Media Violence Increase Children's Tolerance of Real-Life Aggression?" *Developmental Psychology* 10 (1974): 418–21.

16. Gross, L. "Pornography and Social Science Research: Serious Questions." *Journal of Communication* 33, no. 4 (1983): 111–14.

17. Harre, R. and P.F. Secord. *The Explanation of Social Behavior.* Oxford: Basil Blackwell, 1972.

18. Kruglanski, A.W. "The Human Subject in Psychology Experiments: Fact and Artifact." In *Advances in Experimental Social Psychology* 8, edited by L. Berkowitz. New York: Academic Press, 1975.

19. Lazarus, R.S., J.C. Speisman, A.M. Mordkof, and L.A. Davison. *Psychological Monographs* 76 (34, whole no. 553), 1962.

21. Leidholdt, D. "WAP and NOW Protest 'Pieces.'" *WOMANEWS* 4, no. 10, November 1983.

22. Malamuth, N. "Erotica, Aggression and Perceived Appropriateness." Paper presented at the 86th annual convention of the American Psychological Association, Toronto, September 1978.

23. Malamuth, N. "Factors Associated with Rape as Predictors of Laboratory Aggression Against Women." *Journal of Personality and Social Psychology* 45, no. 2 (1983): 432–42.

24. Malamuth, N. and E. Donnerstein. "The Effects of Aggressive Pornographic Mass Media Stimuli." In *Advances in Experimental Social Psychology* 15, edited by L. Berkowitz, 1982.

25. Orne, M.T. "On the Social Psychology of the Psychological Experiment: With Particular Reference to Demand Characteristics and Their Implications." *American Psychologist* 17 (1962): 776–83.

26. Rabinovitch, M.S., J.W. Markham, and A.D. Talbot. "Children's Violence Perception as a Function of Television Violence." In *Television and Social Behavior,* edited by G.A. Comstock, E.A. Rubinstein, and J.P. Murray. Vol. 5. Washington, DC: U.S. Government Printing Office, 1972.

27. Rachman. S. "Sexual Fetishism: An Experimental Analogue." *Psychological Record* 16 (1966): 293–96.

28. Rachman, S. and R.J. Hodgson. "Experimentally Induced 'Sexual Fetishism,' Replication and Development." *Psychological Record* 18 (1968): 25–27.

29. Schachter, S. and J. Singer. "Cognitive, Social, and Psychological Determinants of Emotion." *Psychological Review* 69 (1962): 379–99.

30. Strickland, L.J., F.E. Aboud, and K.J. Gergen, eds. *Social Psychology in Transition*. New York: Plenum, 1976.

31. Thomas, M.H. "Physiological Arousal, Exposure to a Relatively Lengthy Aggressive Film and Aggressive Behavior." *Journal of Research in Personality* 16 (1982): 72–81.

32. Thomas, M.H. and R.S. Drabman. "Toleration of Real-Life Aggression as a Function of Exposure to Televised Violence and Age of Subject." *Merrill-Palmer Quarterly of Behavior and Development* 21 (1975): 227–37.

33. Thomas, M.H., R.W. Horton, E.C. Lippencott, and R.S. Drabman. "Desensitization to Portrayals of Real-Life Aggression as a Function of Exposure to Television Violence." *Journal of Personality and Social Psychology* 35 (1977): 450–58.

34. Turner, C.W. and L.A. Simmons. "Effects of Subjects' Sophistication and Evaluation Apprehension on Aggressive Responses to Weapons." *Journal of Personality and Social Psychology* 30 (1974): 341–48.

35. Valins, S. and R.E. Nisbett. "Attribution Processes in the Treatment of Emotional Disorders." In *Attribution: Perceiving the Causes of Behavior*, edited by E.E. Jones, et al. Morristown, NJ: General Learning Press, 1972.

36. Zillman, D. and J. Bryant. "Pornography, Sexual Callousness, and the Trivialization of Rape." *Journal of Communication* 32, no. 4 (1982): 10–21.

37. Zillman, D. and J. Bryant. "Pornography and Social Science Research: Higher Moralities." *Journal of Communication* 33, no. 4 (1983): 107–11.

38. Zuckerman, M. and B. Lubin. *Manual for the Multiple Affect Adjective Check List*. San Diego, CA: Educational and Industrial Testing Service, 1965.

Section 7

MEDIA AS SHAPERS OF INSTITUTIONS

When most of us think about the media, we think about the various ways we use them, the benefits that we gain from them—such as information and enjoyment—and sometimes the negative impact that they have on us or on our children. Seldom do we think about their larger impact, the ways they alter the institutions that are important to our lives: our political system, religion, and sports, among others. The purpose of this section is to help you see the institutional changes being wrought by our communications media. The views of the authors presented in this section provide some special vantage points from which you will be able to clearly perceive the interactions between media and institutions.

The section begins with excerpts from David Halberstam's monumental study of CBS. The excerpts describe the role of media coverage of the Vietnam War and the relationship between the media and the presidency. Halberstam recalls the escalation of presidential-media interaction in the Johnson years, as well as the Nixon-Agnew antagonism for the media. Halberstam takes us through the years of Walter Cronkite's ascendency as a national agenda-setter and into the Watergate years. From Halberstam's description of people and events, we learn about pressure and competition within a news organization and about how it responds to political pressure from the outside. Ultimately, the picture Halberstam draws of the relationship between the presidency and the media is of intimate interdependency, inevitable conflict, and mutual influence.

The next two articles are about the effects of media upon the electoral process. Ralph Whitehead, Jr., shows how direct mail has become a mass medium. His focus is the 1982 elections, which generated the largest wave of political direct mail in American history. He describes the formula for direct mail campaigns that hold a reader's attention through carefully

319

controlled revelation of information and emotional appeals. Whitehead illustrates the operation of the formula in campaigns by groups from all parts of the political spectrum.

Timothy Wirth and George Watson focus on television. Their article takes the form of a debate between a member of Congress and a network vice president over whether networks should project the winners of elections before polls are closed. The debate hinges not so much on whether such projections influence voters as on the ethics pertinent to the problem and what should be done about it.

Another pair of articles addresses the media's power to confer status upon an issue or an individual. The topic is familiar, but we offer it with a twist. Instead of looking at the extremes to which people go to attract and direct media attention, these authors discuss what happens when celebrities become political figures. Donald Kaul asserts that well-known actors have an unfair advantage when they speak out on political issues or become candidates for public office. By contrast, Mark Dowie and Donald Talbot see celebrity status as a distinct disadvantage in the political arena. Dowie and Talbot report on an event they characterize as a "gangland slaying"—the cancellation of the *Lou Grant* television series after the program's star, Ed Asner, openly criticized American policy in El Salvador. Dowie and Talbot show how the series fell victim to complaints and threats of product boycotts by politically conservative organizations. Network officials stated that the decision to cancel the series resulted directly from fallen audience ratings. However, the authors produce evidence that programs whose stars publicly take issue with the government, especially programs with politically potent content, are likely to feel the ax.

Robert Abelman and Kimberly Neuendorf direct our attention away from politics and toward religion with their study of televangelism. These authors conducted a content analysis of major religious, social, and political themes addressed in "Top-30" religious television programs. The authors assert, among other things, that the popular charge of overt political activism by religious broadcasters is unfounded. However, the researchers point to the money-raising success of religious television as evidence that its persuasiveness is powerful. By implication, Abelman and Neuendorf's research suggests that the probable impact of the electronic church on traditional religion and other institutions needs to be carefully considered.

The impact of television on sports is easier to document, as Neil Amdur's article demonstrates. He traces the growth of televised sports and examines the medium's effects on uniform designs, game rules and even the creation of new sports. He also looks at its effects on people involved in sports. Amdur considers the roles of economics, aesthetics, and technology in the "takeover" of sports in America by television.

The effects of the media on institutions such as elections and sports are relatively easy to see because these influences often are observable in the media themselves. The real trick is to determine whether such influences on our time-honored institutions are for good or for evil. One way to approach the problem is to identify motivations for institutional change in relation to the media. *Who is likely to benefit most from a change? What benefits will be derived? By whom?* The answers to these questions can then be weighed against the integrity of the institution. *What benefits will be lost? By whom?* Change almost always involves trade-off and compromise. We must decide where the line between acceptable and unacceptable compromise resides. This line can serve as a baseline for deciding whether media influence on an institution should go unchecked.

Such is the reasoning that ought to precede consideration of questions including what should be done to control media influence and by whom? Action-oriented as Americans are, we easily grow impatient with the reasoning process. Meanwhile, the rapidity with which our society is changing under the influence of mass media fuels our eagerness for solutions. Clear thinking and decisive action on problems such as those discussed in this section make for tough assignments. *Is it not time we gave them their due?*

Study Questions: Halberstam

[?] *In what ways did the media affect the Vietnam War and the Watergate affair? How did the media affect the Lyndon Johnson and Richard Nixon presidencies? Should the media have this sort of influence? If not, how would you suggest they report about people and events without influencing them?*

When journalists take on an assignment, as Walter Cronkite took on the Vietnam story, should they begin by accepting our government's position, or should they begin by questioning our government's position? Is it possible for a journalist to be too suspicious or too critical of government?

Based on the evidence Halberstam presents, was Walter Cronkite justified in reporting that the Vietnam war did not work and that the United States should get out? Is it appropriate for a journalist to use his or her special access to the media to advise the government in this way? Or is it a journalist's job to stick to reporting the facts?

Should a president and the White House staff try to control or manipulate media coverage of the president, as Halberstam claims occurred in Nixon's administration? What are the arguments for this practice? What are the arguments against it? Why do you think presidents are so preoccupied with the media? Why do they attack the media so frequently?

> *What strictures upon the free speech of news reporters and editors does Halberstam reveal? Assuming Halberstam's description is accurate, how do you explain Salant's and Paley's positions regarding Watergate reporting? Do you think their positions were justified? Why or why not?*
>
> *How much independence from other parts of the media (including top management) does Halberstam think a news department needs? If you were in William Paley's shoes during the Watergate era, would you have acted differently from the way he did? Do you think a large news organization should give free reign to reporters and editors? Assuming that the organization's managers wanted to do so, what factors might justify reducing newsworkers' freedom?*
>
> *To whom do you believe the free press portion of the First Amendment refers; that is, who should have the freedom to make decisions about what is published: reporters, editors, publishers, or stockholders of the newspaper or broadcasting company?*

David Halberstam

CBS: THE POWER AND THE PROFITS

. . . Cronkite Goes to Vietnam, 1965: If This Isn't World War II, What Is It?

When Walter Cronkite decided to go to Vietnam in the summer of 1965, he had successfully resisted an ill-advised attempt by his own company to displace him, and he was the senior journalist of the most important broadcast news medium in the world.

In those days Vietnam was a consensus war, and Cronkite was television's consensus newscaster. But in Saigon on that trip, his best qualities seemed to haunt him. He symbolized an American tradition of good faith and trust—and these characteristics were about to become casualties in Vietnam. He was inclined to take without question the word of men who had titles and positions. Often these were from World War II, men who had been his peers then and who were his peers now. It was a generational situation: he shared not just their perceptions but their seniority. They were four-star, he was four-star. They had to know what they were doing because he knew what he was doing. It was a danger of the journalist as superstar: instant access to the top of the ladder before doing hard grounding in the field, finding out the difference between what was going on out there and what the top brass said was going on, and *why* there was such a difference.

When he went to Vietnam in 1965, Cronkite was not an objective man but a centrist man, and there is a difference. In his own mind he was objective, a middle-of-the-road containment man. The government's position, which he accepted, was not necessarily objective or legitimate, but it represented the center. He did not doubt the corruption and weakness of the South Vietnamese government, and he did not expect to see democracy flower in the Mekong Delta, but he had been conditioned to the rhetoric of a generation—indeed, he had helped push some of that rhetoric in long CBS documentaries on American air power, and in coverage of those great American space shots. He did not feel at ease with the people who were attacking the conventional wisdom, and when he arrived in Saigon in 1965, he did not like the cynicism and brashness of the younger correspondents. (From time to time he remembered, not entirely with pleasure, his own brashness during World War II.) Morley Safer, who was then CBS Saigon bureau chief, tried to put Cronkite in contact with younger officers, men who were in touch with the day-to-day reality of the war, but it was an uphill struggle. The Air Force, on which Cronkite had done those sympathetic documentaries in the 1950s, reached out to him and showed him all its finest toys and newest weapons, and he simply could not go against the past. He knew almost intuitively how hard to look, and how hard not to look. It was important that in his own mind he was not violating his objectivity by accepting unquestioningly the government position. Rather, at the time of the 1968 Tet offensive, he challenged the government position, and he was aware then of a departure from objectivity.

He was also, whatever his own sympathies, the man who, as managing editor of the CBS *Evening News,* ultimately passed on the reporting of the younger, critical reporters from Vietnam. And while the nightly CBS report from Saigon had faults—lack of air time, lack of cumulative meaningful texture, an emphasis on blood and bang-bang in film—it nonetheless stood out. Some of the American military people called CBS the Communist Broadcasting Station. But by journalistic consensus, the two best television reporters of the war were CBS's Safer and his younger colleague, Jack Laurence.

Consensus Newsman Turns Against the War

What television did slowly but surely with this particular war was to magnify its faults and brutalities, and to show, as the Safer film from Cam Ne proved, that you could not separate civilian from combatant. That was part of it. The other part was the way television had speeded the pace of life in

America. Everything had to work faster—even war—and as bench mark after bench mark of victory predicted by the architects passed without victory, the war seemed to drag on. Everything now, because of television, was part theater, and the Vietnam War was becoming a drama with an unhappy ending which had played too long. Slowly the consensus began to change, and as it did television began to change, too, becoming more doubting, more mistrusting. And so Walter Cronkite, the man of consensus, changed as the nation changed. Walter Cronkite was always acutely aware of his audience and its moods; he was very good at leading and being led at the same time, at once a good reporter and a good politician.

At the time of the Tet offensive, early in 1968, Lyndon Johnson and his war policy were extremely vulnerable. Cronkite returned to Vietnam to do his own special broadcast; he was in effect covering a very different war. He was uneasy; he knew that he was stepping out of his natural role. He had carefully avoided revealing his real opinions and feelings on the *Evening News,* and there was no doubt that even people who agreed with what he was about to do would have a new kind of suspicion about him— Walter was somehow not quite so straight anymore, not so predictable. He was very good at anticipating the reaction; he knew that Huntley-Brinkley, particularly because of Brinkley, were already perceived as being more editorial than he was, and that serious implications rode on that perception. He talked it over with various producers at CBS and with Dick Salant, head of CBS News, and they agreed what whatever misgivings they had, their shared sense was that if you were the signature figure of a serious news organization, your obligation was to cover a major story at a time when it was confusing and dividing the nation.

With that encouragement, but not without a good deal of reservation, Cronkite went to Saigon at the time of the Tet offensive. It was an Orwellian trip, for Orwell had written of a Ministry of Truth in charge of Lying and a Ministry of Peace in charge of War, and here was Cronkite flying to Saigon where the American military command was surrounded by failure and trying to sell it as victory. He and his producer, Ernie Leiser, traveled together, and they had trouble landing in the country. All the airports were closed. They finally reached Saigon, a city at war. Cronkite wanted the requisite briefing with General William Westmoreland, and that was truly Orwellian: pressed fatigues, eyes burning fiercely, the voice saying that little had happened, almost surprised that Walter was there, though of course it was fortunate that he had come, since Tet was such a great victory. Exactly what the Americans wanted.

Then Cronkite headed north with Leiser and Jeff Gralnick, his favorite young producer, who had just come to Saigon as a correspondent. They tried to get into the Khe Sanh, which was undergoing very heavy fighting, but no one would write the insurance policy; it was too dangerous. So he went instead to Hue. Just the day before, Westy had said that the battle was over. But it was clear that no one had bothered to tell the North Vietnamese; and the Marines were fighting desperately to retake Hue. The younger CBS men were impressed by the sight of Cronkite striding right into the center of the street fighting: The old war horse, they thought, takes all the risks. But it was a crucial moment for him, because for the first time he saw the credibility gap, face front.

He was shocked, not so much by the ferocity of fighting, but because to his mind the men in charge of the war were not to be trusted. Even his way of leaving Hue was suggestive. There were exceptional precautions, extra weapons aboard (having had the U.S. Embassy in Saigon overrun on the evening news was bad enough, but if the American mission lost the best-known newscaster of the day in a city which it had allegedly just pacified . . .), and the plane carrying, along with the famous commentator, twelve dead GIs in body bags.

They stopped at Phu Bai on the way back to Saigon, and Cronkite met with his old friend General Creighton Abrams. Abrams was then the deputy commander, scheduled to replace Westmoreland eventually. He was candid with Cronkite about the dimension of the catastrophe, the degree to which the command had been taken by surprise, and the impact of it. Here was the number two man in the American command—close to, but free of responsibility for, the debacle—confirming Cronkite's own doubts and sounding like one of the much maligned American journalists in Saigon, and explaining how and why the mission had been so blind. From there Cronkite returned to Saigon to meet with his CBS colleagues. He was, thought those who worked with him, very different on this trip, introspective and disturbed, searching for answers. Usually Cronkite prided himself on his objectivity, on his detachment and his lack of involvement. An event was an event and nothing more.

The last night he had dinner with a group of correspondents on the roof of the Caravelle Hotel, and he kept asking, again and again, How could it have happened? How could it have happened? Peter Kalischer, the senior and most knowledgeable of the correspondents, spoke strongly: It has been happening for years, there were lies from the start, we had been building on a false base, we were essentially intruders in Vietnamese lives. Later Cronkite went up to the roof of the Caravelle with Jack Laurence, the youngest and probably the most anguished of the CBS reporters. He was twenty-six when he arrived; his reporting had been distinguished by a human dimension, and he seemed to catch the feel of the young American GIs better than other television correspondents did. Cronkite and Laurence stood on the roof and watched the artillery in nearby Cholon, and Laurence felt a certain resentment. He didn't like the breed of older correspondent who observed the war from the Caravelle roof, armchair generals who watched the shells and did not know or care where they landed. He and his contemporaries preferred on their days off to sit in their rooms and get stoned on pot. He did not know if this was less or more moral, but it allowed him on occasion to forget the war and the bodies.

Cronkite, who was trying to measure the distance on some of the artillery rounds, must have sensed this resentment, because he talked to Laurence, not so much as a senior correspondent to a junior one, but almost as a father to a son. He said he was grateful to Laurence and the other reporters who had risked so much day after day for the news show, and he understood how frustrated a younger man could become with the bureaucracy of journalism and what seemed like the insensitivity of editors. He had undergone similar frustrations in World War II, the difficulty of communicating with older men thousands of miles away who were not witnessing what he was witnessing. Laurence was touched, and felt that Cronkite had been changed by what he had seen.

Cronkite did a half-hour news special, which he insisted on writing himself—which was by itself unusual. This was the period when the Johnson Administration was seriously considering a commitment to Vietnam of 200,000 more troops. He said that the war didn't work, that more troops would not turn it around, and that we had to start thinking of getting out. These were alien and hard words for him, but he did not feel he could do otherwise. He was ready for it and the country was ready for it; he moved in part because the consensus was moving, helping to shift the grain by his very act. Other forces were at work: Eugene McCarthy and Robert Kennedy challenging Johnson out front; Defense Secretary Clark Clifford leading a reassessment from within the Administration. But Cronkite's reporting did help change the balance. It was the first time in American history that a war had been declared over by a commentator. In Washington Lyndon Johnson watched and told his press secretary, George Christian, that it was a turning point; that if he had lost Walter Cronkite he had lost Mr. Average Citizen. It solidified his decision not to run for re-election. He had lost his consensus. Cronkite, hearing of what Johnson said, tried on future occasions to bring the subject up when he was with Johnson; but Johnson knew the game, and, when the question was raised, took off on long tirades against the press in general and the press's sinister betrayal of the national interest in particular.

The Dick Nixon Show: The Message Is That the Medium Stinks

The Nixon Administration was even more preoccupied with television than its predecessors. Richard Nixon himself was obsessed by television, perhaps because he scored an early coup (the Checkers speech) on it, and was later a victim of it (the debates with Kennedy); perhaps because he sensed that if he controlled it he could make it show the Nixon he wanted to be and not the Nixon he was. In the Nixon years, television was not just a means but an end. Those who opposed him on it became his real opposition. He struggled to control his exposure. Unsure of who he was, Nixon was obsessed by exterior definitions of himself. His was a television White House; it was dominated by Bob Haldeman and his people. Haldeman came from the world of the manipulative arts, not from the world of politics. Haldeman paid close attention to television. He knew after which prime-time shows it was advantageous to schedule a presidential broadcast, and which ones never to break in on. In 1968 Haldeman devised the campaign tactic of scheduling only *one* appearance a day that could be filmed, on the theory that if the network producers had a choice of film for two or more Nixon campaign appearances, they would always pick the least flattering one. Therefore, schedule Nixon tightly, control the environment, and give the networks the film *you* want, not what they want. It was Haldeman, too, who, during the chaos of the 1968 Democratic convention in Chicago (kids, cops, pols, blood, all in the street, and all on television), made sure that Nixon was on a boat and out of reach of a camera so that there could be no connection, not even subliminal, in the public mind between Nixon and that kind of politics. Once they were in the White House, more time and energy of more key White House people was spent deciding when and how to get the President on television—and how to keep potential adversaries off—than in dealing with the Congress or the Democratic opposition.

By comparison with Nixon and his aides, previous Presidents had pressured the networks with kid gloves. Now there was an orchestrated assault upon the integrity of the network news divisions, an attempt to put them on the defensive and to reduce public respect for them.

CBS News was the strongest of the three networks, and the theory was that if CBS was bent, the other two would follow. Early in the conflict between the Nixon Administration and the media, Walter Cronkite called it a conspiracy. At the time, Joe Wershba, an old Murrow hand, had congratulated Cronkite on his response to Agnew, but said that he was bothered by the word "conspiracy"; wasn't that too harsh a word? A few years later, as more evidence began to come out from Watergate, including a memo on NBC by Larry Higby of Haldeman's staff which said that the aim was to destroy the institution, Wershba apologized to Cronkite.

Nixon dispatched Vice-President Spiro Agnew to attack the press in general and the networks in particular ten days after he announced his policy of Peace with Honor. He intended to sell his policy with as little negative or pessimistic analysis as possible. Americans would think they were getting both peace and honor in Vietnam, even if neither was in fact, under the conditions set by Nixon, attainable. But the selling of the policy was more important than the policy. He had, in singling out the networks and unleashing Agnew upon them, picked up the scent of the networks' vulnerability. For a decade they had been, if not the cause, at least the bearers, of bad and jarring news: racial conflict, a terrible war, and protest against a terrible war. Kill the messenger.

To many Americans, the old verities about America still lived: America was good, and the less said about the bad, the better. The Nixon-Agnew onslaught against the media was more successful than most telelvision executives like to admit. Nixon drew blood, and people in television were newly sensitive to the issues raised. Yes, the networks would carry bad and unsettling news when it was warranted, but there was a subtle drop-off in their aggressiveness in seeking it out, and a new defensiveness about their reporting. At CBS in the early 1970s, for example, Charles Kuralt's reports on roving around America became easier to include in the news show. Kuralt had been doing his charming bits of Americana for some time; now there was an intensified effort to find Kuraltlike human interest stories— good stories, but stories that did not jar people's nerves. There was even a word for them at CBS—"HI," Human Interest—and the word was, *get more HI*. At the height of the Nixon-Agnew pressure, Bill Paley decided to drop instant analysis after presidential speeches. Later it was reinstated. CBS did not back down on really important issues under the attack (or remove Dan Rather from the White House beat, which was a prime Nixon priority). But it made sure that with the bad news, the abrasive or critical reporting, there was a certain amount of sugar coating. TV correspondents as good guys. If not lovable, at least likable.

The Nixon Administration's war on the networks had a second front. That was a subtle but deliberate attempt by the administration to turn the outlying affiliate stations against the network news divisions in New York. The Nixon men saw their strongest, most centralized rival for power and political opposition in network television. They set out to do something that Kennedy and Johnson had never tried—to decentralize the networks, provoke regional pressure from the affiliates on home-office news questions. They had discovered that the affiliates were the soft underbelly of the networks. The affiliate station owners tended to be Republicans, but there was more than party politics to this effort. There were social and cultural aspects of it: the local station owners were businessmen; they were closer to the local chamber of commerce outlook than to any notion of a journalistic tradition; and they were not from New York. They did not like the contemporary counterculture in its various manifestations, especially not when the networks covered it and, by covering it, encouraged it. In any showdown between the traditionalist values, or the allegedly traditionalist values, of the Nixon Administration and those of the CBS newsroom, the affiliate owners were by inclination and instinct on the side of the Administration.

In 1970, CBS planned to put on a small, frail show called *The Loyal Opposition,* designed to compete with presidential use of television—four half-hour shows in an election year. The Nixon people roused the affiliates against it; they brought so much pressure that the show was canceled abruptly after only one viewing. Herb Klein, the nice guy of the Nixon Administration press operation, quietly worked the boondocks, taking the "good cop" approach. He was not, like Agnew, looking for headlines, but rather stirring up the natives against network news, encouraging the affiliate owners to protest the kind of coverage that alien forces in New York were subverting them with—the impudence of Dan Schorr and Dan Rather, the lack of patriotism of the Saigon bureau. (Dick Salant, head of CBS News, spent two days arguing a committee of affiliate representatives out of the idea that they should visit the Saigon bureau, shape it up, and express their displeasure with its reporting. The suggestion originated in the White House.)

There was no doubt that the Nixon Administration found a receptive response among affiliate owners: the things Nixon disliked, *they* disliked. They began to put a constant pressure on the news show, particularly against Dan Schorr, and most of all against Dan Rather. The Administration hit a sensitive nerve. The affiliates had a powerful lever against the less than mighty news department: the power not to take CBS programs. Indeed, right after the 1974 tangle between Rather and Nixon at the Houston meeting of the National Association of Broadcasters, CBS officials went to their affiliates' meeting and had to defuse a major recall move against Rather.

In 1972, Richard Nixon campaigned for the presidency by being President, as incumbents usually do. He had learned the lessons of the 1970 off-year election when he made a number of hard-sell campaign appearances as if he were running for sheriff. His ultimate 1972 campaign weapon was his trip to China. Whatever history was made, he played it as political theater, hour on hour of picture postcards of China, Nixon with Mao and Chou and a cast of 800 million exotic extras. Campaigning. The networks had bitten all the way for that one, covering it exactly as Nixon had planned, perhaps a little more so. Senior network news executives smuggled themselves on planes as sound technicians. One Nixon aide thought it was as if there were two Republican conventions that year, the first in China, the second in Miami.

Even so, the Nixon people took few chances with the second, and real, Republican convention. They studied how the networks had covered previous national conventions, and they broke the code and wrote their own scenario. They knew when the networks took breaks, and how long the breaks lasted, so that if there was something they wanted to slip by quietly, they were ready to use the network commercial breaks as a cover. They had the convention timed to the second. They doled out a roster of young attractive Republican comers and stars to all networks as the convention wound on. All of it went according to script, according to schedule—balloons to be let off at exactly the right moment. Then someone got hold of the schedule, but even that didn't really cause any bother. All of it was perhaps boring, but better boredom than the chaos of earlier conventions. Control was of the essence.

CBS Covers Watergate . . . Reluctantly

At one point during the 1972 campaign, Gordon Manning at CBS News suggested to Walter Cronkite that he call the President personally to see if he could set up some kind of exchange or interview: Cronkite Meets the President, Nixon Faces Walter. "And," said Manning, "don't take Ziegler on the phone. Go directly to The Man." So Cronkite called the White House and twice Ziegler called back, but Cronkite refused to take the calls. Finally Nixon himself came on the phone, and Cronkite said, "You know, there are all these issues, and you yourself have said that the choice has never been so clear, and I wonder if you could come on the show so we could talk about the differences." The implicit understanding was that McGovern would get an equal shot. Nixon's immediate reaction (both Manning and Cronkite were impressed by how acutely he was attuned to the media, and knew how to deflect something he didn't want to do) was, "I'd love to, but what will I tell Howard Smith and Jack Chancellor?"

But there was that fall, always in the background, hovering like a dark shadow, Watergate: the issue that would not go away. A third-rate burglary, the Administration said. It was dismissed, put aside, ignored, overlooked, but it would not go away. That was partly because reporters Bob Woodward and Carl Bernstein of *The Washington Post* kept finding connections between the Watergate burglary and successively higher levels of the Administration. It was also because among aficionados of American politics there was a sense that Richard Nixon was a man who trusted no one in politics and who accordingly ran his own campaigns, handled all details himself. But it was a story that was extremely difficult to get a handle on. Watergate exposed a great deal about politics and the presidency; it also exposed the weaknesses of the news media: the news media, and television particularly, were reactive, they did not initiate things. They liked things to happen right smack out there in front—a debate in the Congress, a courtroom trial—so that they could describe them. Less risk. Less initiative. They did not like to investigate, and in particular they did not like the idea of pursuing a journalistic investigation of someone as powerful as the President of the United States.

CBS was not alone in this. NBC, which also had a strong news staff, was ambivalent about Watergate, unsure of how hard to ride it, and wary that it might blow up in everyone's face. NBC's Washington reporters complained about troubles they had with their superiors in New York, and a lack of enthusiasm for Watergate stories. In the spring of 1973, Carl Stern of NBC, a lawyer as well as a first-rank reporter, learned that E. Howard Hunt, one of the Watergate plotters, was blackmailing the White House and threatening to tell all. It was an important story; Stern immediately went on NBC radio with it. (Radio now is virtually unedited; a reporter calls the radio desk, tells what he has, and gives a rough estimate of time to be saved: none of the corporate filters that reach into television these days inhibit radio). The story went out quickly over NBC radio, and it turned out to be the most important news story that day. Stern thereupon called the television news desk and explained what he had for the *Nightly News* broadcast, and that he had already used it on radio. But the executives of the *Nightly News* wanted no part of Hunt's blackmail; NBC television was afraid to broadcast what NBC radio was doing.

Watergate was a bottled-up story, covert instead of overt. It was a very easy story not to see, not to cover, and not to film. During the campaign, when Woodward and Bernstein were writing some of their most important stories—the middle of September to Election Day—NBC devoted a total of only 41 minutes and 21 seconds covering Watergate, and ABC gave it 42 minutes and 26 seconds. Even that coverage was more often than not perfunctory. The Democrats and Larry O'Brien Charged; the Republicans Answered. Of the three networks, only one covered Watergate with any enterprise or effort, and that was CBS.

The decision at CBS to do two major Watergate reports in the fall of 1972 began with a decision to do a long study on the wheat deal. From the start, the Soviet wheat deal had offended Walter Cronkite's old-fashioned values. He told his associates late in the summer that there was something wrong with the wheat deal, and that this was going to be the Teapot Dome of the Nixon Administration. Cronkite's strength on the *Evening News* is that he wears two hats, that of anchorman and that of managing editor, and he can, within the limits and as long as he doesn't push too hard too often, get what he wants on the show. In this case he wanted the wheat deal. It was not a story which television could do easily. There were few opportunities for film, and CBS, like the other networks, lacked the inclination to do serious investigative reporting. Television liked what was on the surface, and was made uneasy by what was beneath the surface.

Cronkite assigned Stanhope Gould, a talented young CBS producer. His graphics and his illustration of the story were exceptional. The wheat story in fact was infinitely complicated. Even in the best newspaper it was the kind of story that sent puzzled readers back to reread the preceding paragraphs before it all came together. For television it posed comparable problems, but the CBS team was able to put it all together. The strength of the report was that it broke out of the language of networkese—that short, hard, semi-wire-service exposition—and tried to do something intricate in a short time by nuance and implication. The normal television way would have been to show lots of film of wheat fields, the wind rippling through them, as background for a few bland narrative sentences. But this time CBS concentrated on explaining about exports and commodities and apparent conflicts of interest, returning to Cronkite to explain that story, once, twice, and then three times. At one point Cronkite came out of his chair to point to some graphics, and the audience had to know it was important. *Walter would not have come out of his chair for just anything.* It was a triumph for CBS News, a reversal of the normal order whereby print leads and television follows.

The CBS executives and Cronkite were encouraged to take a try at some Watergate special reports. In the summer of 1972, the word to members of the Washington bureau who had wanted to go all out on Watergate had been no, it was not a television story, they would wait on events. Now suddenly, with the election approaching, CBS tried to parachute into Watergate. Gordon Manning of CBS had worked in years past at *Newsweek* with Ben Bradlee, now *The Washington Post*'s editor. Manning (as Agnew might have suspected) called Bradlee to ask for the *Post*'s help on the story: to turn over sources, or, even better, its documents. Bradlee had answered in a way that would have surprised Agnew: Manning could bleep off, there would be no help, there would be no documents, indeed, there *were* no documents. And when Stan Gould of CBS went to see Bradlee, he came away with the very strong impression that Ben Bradlee, very much like Agnew, did not like network newsmen. In fact, Bradlee knew that he and his two *Wunderkind* reporters were skating on thin ice, and he was supersensitive to the charge of collusion and conspiracy. So the CBS team came down from New York, and, though reporters like Schorr and Rather were energetic, the story was derivative, putting together what had been in the *Post,* and crediting other sources, mostly the *Post*'s. It was a very difficult journalistic decision to make: it was all there, and yet very little was there. Gould was telling his superiors that is was an important story, and that though they did not have sources of their own to confirm it, it all smelled very bad. *The Washington Post* and *Time* and the *Los Angeles Times* were pushing it hard, and the White House denials were very odd, very carefully phrased. But if CBS went with it, like it or not, they were going to be in bed with the *Post.* That is not unusual—it is accepted journalistic practice for the networks to run stories that have appeared only in the *Times* or some other publication, giving the proper credit—but this would be dicier. In effect, the decision was to do *The Washington Post* story or do nothing.

They decided to go. Part one was the espionage itself, the break-ins plus Segretti and the spying operation. It ran slightly more than fourteen minutes. Fourteen minutes was the real breakthrough, more, even, than the content. An entire news show, less commercials and pauses, consumes only twenty-two minutes. The effect is that all news items are equal, and equality is enforced by brevity—everything runs two minutes or less. Three minutes for the apocalypse. Four minutes if it's an American apocalypse.

Now here were *fourteen* of twenty-two precious minutes going to Watergate. It was as if the *Times* had played only one story in an entire daily edition. It was very strong reporting.

When he screened the show in New York, Cronkite was immediately enthusiastic, although not everyone else was pleased. Sandy Socolow, the producer of the show, was furious at Gould: first, because of the length (Gould had pulled off a Walter-Mitty-like triumph against the New York producer system; he had usurped virtually the entire news show); second, for being so late. It came in on Friday, ten days before the election. Gould, Socolow realized, had presented him with a virtual fait accompli.

There was another unhappy CBS executive: Dick Salant, president of CBS News, who had attained his job not because he was a creative, original newsman, but because he was a lawyer and a corporate figure. He was expert in the *implications* of news—what it might mean legally and politically. He stood between the forces coming down from the executive levels of Black Rock (the new 36-story CBS building) and the forces pushing up from the newsroom. Salant, during the Nixon years, had come through to the newsroom as a man of considerable integrity. He had understood what was important about CBS News, and shepherded it through a difficult time; he loved the news business, for which he was not trained, and despised the law, for which he was. As he had gotten closer to retirement he had seemed to those around him an increasingly liberated man. When John Ehrlichman demanded the head of Dan Rather—that Rather be transferred away from his White House assignment—Salant not only laughed Ehrlichman off, but deliberately leaked the information to print reporters as a means of securing Rather's job and zinging the Nixon White House. But now, reading Gould's script, Salant was clearly upset: "—do we really have to go with this? . . . isn't this quite long? . . ." He could sense the problems ahead, and that they would not be pleasant ones. But Gordon Manning was ready to go, and Socolow, still privately irritated with Gould, was backing his man (it was now news against corporate pressure). Besides, they had the most important of all CBS News forces going for them, Walter Cronkite. Fourteen minutes it was, and fourteen minutes it would be. There would be a part two, to be scheduled.

Chuck Colson Finds the Chairman's Number

The show was aired on Friday night, October 27, 1972. It had television's impact and authority. Though CBS was extremely careful to credit *The Washington Post* as a source, and equally careful to carry White House denials, there was no doubt about the special force of the report: this much time on a national news show, Walter Cronkite's stamp of approval on it—if that's what Walter said, that's the way it was:

CRONKITE: At first it was called the Watergate caper—five men apparently caught in the act of burglarizing and bugging Democratic headquarters in Washington. But the episode grew steadily more sinister—no longer a caper, but the Watergate affair escalating finally into charges of a high-level campaign of political sabotage and espionage apparently unparalleled in American history. Most of what is known of the Watergate affair has emerged in puzzling bits and pieces, through digging by the nation's press and television newsmen. Some of the material made public so far is factual, without dispute—those men caught in the act at Watergate, for instance. Some is still allegation, uncovered by the press but as yet legally unsubstantiated. We shall label our sources carefully as we go along. But with the facts and the allegations, we shall try tonight to pull together the threads of this amazing story, quite unlike any in our modern American history . . .

Among those who watched the show that Friday night was Charles Colson, the White House's chief television monitor, generally felt to be the cobra of the operation. He was deputized by Nixon to deal with the networks, the bad cop to Herb Klein's good cop. Colson was a man, in those days before he found Jesus, full of swagger and a touch of the bully; he was often described in newspapers as being a tough ex-Marine. Colson's reports back to the White House starred Chuck Colson: Colson telling off people, network executives cringing as Colson laid down the law. Nixon delighted in all this. It was nice work if you could get it, for Nixon was obsessed by what the networks were doing, and there was no way Colson could lose. If he described network officials showing great timidity as he handed down the line, Nixon loved it. And if he reported flashes of network courage, vague life signs, then there was all the more need for a Colson at the White House. Heads he wins, tails you lose.

Chuck Colson watched that Friday night, and he was quick to the phone. The Nixon White House was not going to stand for reporting like this. He had visited the network officials earlier that year. Frank Stanton, who had grown accustomed to dealing with the big boys himself, encouraged calls from Colson; if there was something wrong with CBS News, just call Dr. Stanton, and they would talk. Stanton's position, oft expressed to the newsroom, was that he was simply protecting its interest, taking the heat. But some CBS newsmen were not so sure that this was his sole intention. They wondered whether this was a wise way to deal with people in power, particularly the Nixon people; they would have preferred that protests about their reporting come directly to them. Stanton's way of operating meant that the news division never knew what the White House was saying and doing, or whether the CBS corporate structure was bending and trading off. There was irony here: in the last few years of his tenure at CBS, Frank Stanton was regarded as being, willy-nilly, the inheritor of the Murrow-era credo; CBS news people regarded him, variously, as being shrewd, intelligent, protective, and devious, and they were uneasy about the dualities of his role.

As it happened, Colson, seeing the long CBS Watergate report, made his first call to Stanton, who was out. Mrs. Stanton was on a long-distance call to a friend. The White House operator cut in to announce that the White House was calling, and would Mrs. Stanton get off the phone. She did, with a feeling that there were crude people in power these days. She tried to reach her husband and missed him a couple of times; by the time she got him, it was too late. Colson had already gone to Bill Paley, who had *also* encouraged White House calls. When Stanton realized that Colson had called Paley, he became a little nervous. He had a sense of what was in store, and that Paley was not ready for it; that he, Stanton, had shielded Paley too long, and that Paley might be particularly vulnerable to such calls. It was just before the 1972 election; Nixon seemed a sure winner, and a landslide winner to boot. Charles Colson found in William S. Paley a very willing listener.

Colson told Paley, in language they taught in the Marine Corps, that this was the most irresponsible journalism he had ever seen, that it was pure McGovern work. The CBS people, he said, were pretending to be journalists but were in effect working for George McGovern. He said it was much too long, that it was too close to the election, that it was all old stuff, and old stuff which had been lies to start with; CBS was just using *Washington Post* stuff, and CBS would live to regret it.

Shortly thereafter, William S. Paley summoned Richard S. Salant. By Saturday Paley had made almost exactly the same charges to Salant, with one exception. He did not say where they came from, and he did not mention the White House or Colson. In the gossipy world of television news, the word got around that the White House had complained, that Paley was furious, that he had ripped Salant apart, and that part two of the Watergate show was in jeopardy. The next Monday morning Paley and Salant went back and forth again and again. They had had sessions like that before, but never so long. The position of each had a certain fragility. Paley liked to have it both ways with the news department. He liked to keep it reasonably contained and minimize how obstreperous it was, yet he liked to be able to say to outsiders that he never told the news department what to do, and that he left it to its own devices. Salant, in turn, was not Paley's man. Salant had come first from the law firm which handled the CBS account. In the complicated corporate structure of CBS, he was Frank Stanton's man, and he admired and esteemed Stanton, which meant that he did not necessarily like or esteem Paley, since he picked up some of Stanton's prejudices and attitudes, and Stanton and Paley had fallen out over the question of Stanton's succeeding Paley as CBS's chief operating officer.

Stanton was not at these sessions, which was odd, although at the meetings Paley again and again associated Stanton with his position. Stanton never talked with Salant in those days, didn't tip off his own feelings about the first show, nor let Salant know the crucial missing ingredient: that all these meetings with Paley had been precipitated by one call from the White House. This of course placed Salant in an ambivalent position—he was dealing with his own organization, which was reacting to pressure, but he did not know that there was pressure, or what its nature was. He could not tell whether these remarkable long sessions with Paley reflected Paley's genuine feelings, or whether Paley was responding to someone else. He was at the center of it, but he was in the dark.

Salant, good lawyer that he was, ordered a list of the *other* long news segments CBS had run on the *Evening News,* to prove that this report was not unique. He was buttressed there. But at base he was puzzled by Paley's insistence and firmness: this was unlike the Chairman; the attention span and the effort that he was putting into these two shows were different from any other confrontation they had ever had. Gradually, as Paley began to ask more and more about the second segment, Salant found the key. Paley had almost certainly made a promise to somebody that there would be no part two, and he was trying in as genteel a way as he could manage to order the news department not to run it, without actually giving the order. That was what all this confusing bullying and repetition in their long sessions was about.

Those who were working with Salant at the time thought that he had left Paley's office on Monday morning visibly shaken. This was just before the screening of part two. It was one of those moments when everyone in the room was aware that he was no longer just a newsman, that outside considerations were playing a role, and that the corporate presence was breathing heavily. The decisions were no longer entirely those of the news division. The second report was scheduled for the same length as the first one, about fourteen minutes. It wound up at eight minutes. This one had a sequence on laundering money in Mexico—again, a subject that was difficult enough to explain in print, let alone on television. But Gould had come up with illustrative graphics, and Rather was there explaining the importance of Haldeman and Chapin and Mitchell, somehow bringing it all very close to Richard Nixon. The report ended with Cronkite saying that the story was important, and that the White House denials were not very convincing.

The meeting on the second segment included Salant, Socolow, Manning, Paul Greenberg (Cronkite's executive producer), and Gould, who had produced the two segments. Cronkite did not attend. The smell of trouble was in the air, and Gordon Manning had decided to hold Cronkite out of battle, as a one-man reserve battalion. Salant was strong for cutting back. It was too long, he said; besides, a great deal of it was repetitious. Then Salant said a very odd thing: "I hope I feel this way because I'm a fair and honest newsman." It was an oblique remark, but he was suggesting that he did not even know his own feelings, and that there was now so much pressure on him that he hoped the reasons he was stating were his own, not Paley's, and not, dear God, those of Richard Nixon or Chuck Colson. Then he brought up a report that Dan Schorr had done during Labor Day weekend. The Schorr report had been on laundering money, and Salant wanted to know how this new story was different from Schorr's. (One difference was that a weekend news report, particularly on a Labor Day weekend, when no one is presumed to be paying attention to the news, is different from the Cronkite news. A weekend report is hit or miss, and the audience accepts it or rejects it; but the *Evening News* is CBS, it has the imprimatur of Walter Cronkite, it means that what comes over the air is true and real and semiguaranteed. Take it seriously.)

Salant had the text of the old Schorr story, and they began to compare them. Other executives in the room had forgotten about the earlier report, or, like most CBS listeners, had never heard it; they shook their heads, thinking that Salant was one smart lawyer son of a bitch, how did he ever remember that one, what a great argument to take to the news department. Gould argued strenuously on behalf of the second report, pleading that it not be cut, that it was new, that Watergate needed above all to be summed up, not nickel-and-dimed, that the *time*, and indeed, the repetition, were crucial. Everyone at CBS, Gould argued, was hearing the same thing from Middle America, that Watergate was too complicated to understand. This was a journalistic failure, he said, and in particular it was a failure of network news departments who were charged with reaching the great mass audience and helping it understand such things. Manning and Socolow also argued for the story. Manning emphasized that this report had been promised to the CBS audience on the air, and he said that it would ruin morale in the newsroom if it was dropped or severely cut. But there was also a sense in the room that limits were once again being set, and the corporation was reentering the game.

Socolow was charged with taking the old Schorr script and removing overlap and repetition, and then cutting the second report down to size. Socolow told his wife that night that he and his colleagues might be out of jobs the next day. But he managed to cut the story from fourteen minutes; he showed it to Cronkite, who bought it.

Gould was furious. As far as he was concerned, the script had been gutted. As far as he was concerned, they had backed down to pressure. Even if the words were similar, the graphics were much weaker.

Cronkite took the script to Salant, who approved it—Well, let's go, but this may be it.

Paley was furious, in a special rage after it was broadcast. He and Salant went around one more time, and he made clear what he felt: this must never happen again. But it was done, or almost done.

Epilogue: A Few Character Studies

A few days after the 1972 election, when the Nixon Administration was riding its highest, when the President was talking to his aides about how they were really going to get their enemies this time, Chuck Colson called Frank Stanton. This Administration was not going to play gentle games anymore. No more Mister Nice Guy. The Nixon Administration knew who its friends were and who its enemies were, and it was going to bring CBS to its knees on Madison Avenue and Wall Street. The CBS stock was going to collapse. When Richard Nixon got through with CBS, there was going to be damn well nothing left. They were going to take away CBS's five owned and operated stations (a major source of CBS's wealth). "We'll break your network," Stanton heard him say. On he went, with a litany of what the Administration was going to do to CBS. Stanton was not surprised, but he was upset. There was a dimension of fury and arrogance to Colson's harangue that, even from this Administration, was chilling. If a CBS reporter had found a top Nixon aide making similar threats to the head of U.S. Steel or General Motors, it would have become the lead story that night. But Frank Stanton, who had come to love the news department but also loved to lobby, said nothing: he was not about to challenge the Administration. Later, long after the Nixon Administration was on the defensive and coming apart, he put his account of these confrontations in an affidavit.

There were several other footnotes to CBS's two Watergate shows. A few days after they ran, Katharine Graham of *The Washington Post* happened to see Bill Paley at a party. Until then she had felt that the *Post* was covering Watergate pretty much alone, and that no one else was joining the fight. But now, in her view, CBS was with the *Post,* and to her mind that meant that Bill Paley and she were together. CBS had enlarged the story, given it a national constituency, and more muscle. So she ran over and kissed him. "You saved us," she said. He seemed to freeze just a little bit. It was precisely what he did not want to hear.

The day that Frank Stanton retired, in the spring of 1973, a small party was given for him. It was not an occasion he looked forward to. He was privately very bitter about how his career at CBS had wound up, and about the trouble between him and Paley. He did not, in fact, want to retire. So the party was kept small, just a few old friends who had fought some of the same battles at CBS. It happened by chance to be the day that all the Nixon people fell out of the tree: Mitchell, Haldeman, Ehrlichman, Dean. And Stanton, usually so correct, proper, and reserved, turned to a friend. The ferocity of his words, and the language, shocked his old friends: "I hope they get that little son of a bitch Colson, too."

At the time that Watergate broke open, William S. Paley was in China, far from the flood of news that the top ranks of the Nixon Administration were either resigning or being indicted. Paley, traveling with Gordon Manning, got back to Hong Kong, where a huge stack of *The New York Times* was waiting for them. On the way back to America Paley read them, one after another. He said very little as he read, just occasionally sucking in his breath. A light gasp or two. After several hours he turned to Manning and asked how it could happen. These were all educated men. They had all been to law school. How could it have happened? Manning said it was simple.

"Why?" asked Paley.

"Because they lacked character," said Manning.

There was a long pause. "I guess you're right," Paley said.

But he evinced no regrets for having taken the Administration's side against the news division's on Watergate. Indeed, those who knew Paley well were sure that by the time he got back to America he was already congratulating himself for having had the courage to stand up to all that pressure from those terrible people. The Murrow-Paley tradition, he must have thought, still lived. He was the one who had made sure that they ran those two fine reports right before the election. Sure enough, when this reporter went to interview him about other matters, Paley got the subject over to Watergate and he seemed to expand with pride: CBS had done what no one else had done on Watergate; it had stood alone, had taken *The Washington Post*'s local story and made it a national story, and he, Bill Paley, was very proud of it.

S*tudy* Q*uestions:* W*hitehead*

| ? | *In what sense or senses is direct mail "the underground press of the eighties"? How is direct mail "underground"? According to Whitehead, is this new underground press more partisan or less partisan than most newspapers and broadcasting stations in this country? Does Whitehead think the development he describes is good or bad? What do you think about it?*

How does Whitehead explain the spectacular increase in the use of direct mail in political campaigns?

In what ways and for whom does direct mail aid communication during an election campaign? In what ways and for whom does direct mail harm communication during a campaign?

> *If you are interested in politics (as we hope you are), what advantages do you gain from direct mail? What advantages do you gain when the statements of candidates or parties are filtered through the regular news media?*
>
> *In what sense can we view direct mail as part of the "demassification" of the media—appealing to specialized rather than general audiences? How effective is direct mail at this?*
>
> *On the basis of what you read in this article and your own analysis, do you believe direct mail is more important for mainstream groups or for groups that do not command the support of a large portion of the population?*
>
> *For what kinds of messages do you believe direct mail is most effective? Does direct mail have any limitations, other than those mentioned in response to earlier questions?*
>
> *Looking closely at a direct mail appeal you or someone you know has received, does it follow the formula Whitehead describes? How might you explain any deviations you discovered from that formula?*
>
> *Are the popular mass media becoming more like direct mail or less? In what senses?*

Ralph Whitehead, Jr.

DIRECT MAIL: THE UNDERGROUND PRESS OF THE EIGHTIES

With little notice, the 1982 elections set off the largest wave of political direct mail in American history. Hundreds of millions of letters flooded the nation's mailboxes to tout both candidates and causes. In the four weeks before election day, the flow of political mail rose to more than fifteen million pieces a week. Thus, the mail's weekly circulation figures, so to speak, were half again as great as those of the country's largest daily newspaper, *The Wall Street Journal*.

Since the election, moreover, the direct-mail experts, and the political forces they serve, have been working quietly to shape a new wave of appeals, tied this time to the 1983 action in Congress and the electoral prospects

Ralph Whitehead, Jr., is a professor of journalism at the University of Massachusetts, Amherst. This article was made possible in part by a grant from the Elmer Davis Memorial Fund.

for 1984. Consequently, after this current respite, the mail sacks will begin in a few weeks to bulge once again.

The prime purpose of much of this mail is to prompt its readers to give money to an office-seeker, an interest group, or a political party. But this is no longer the sole purpose of the mail. Today, it is also acting in American politics as an alternative medium. Its power lies chiefly in its ability to tell its readers what they wouldn't otherwise know and to cast this information in a compellingly readable form. For its millions of steady readers, political mail plays a crucial role in forming opinion. To do this, moreover, it must do its work apart from and even in opposition to such journalistic conventions as balance and objectivity.

Richard Parker, a political activist in the sixties who is now a direct-mail consultant to such clients as Senator Edward Kennedy and the California State Democratic Party, describes this new role simply: "The mail is the underground press of the eighties."

As a rule, political mail conforms to a strict editorial formula. Tested by experience, and used by liberals and conservatives alike, this formula is designed to seize the reader's attention and then to hold it through what often will be four to six pages of single-spaced copy. This persuasive text weaves its arguments-for-action from two disparate elements: raw emotion and hard information.

In order to grab the reader in the crucial instant after a letter leaves its envelope—that crucial instant when the recipient may decide to sail it into the trash—its opening lines play to the emotions, usually to the sense of fear or alarm:

"What I'm about to tell you is so shocking, so threatening that you may not believe it!" begins a letter signed by Roger Staubach, the former quarterback for the Dallas Cowboys, and sponsored by Morality in Media. "But I can't let another day go by without alerting you to the danger that may invade your home."

Senator Edward Kennedy, in a letter soliciting funds for his 1982 Senate campaign: "I want to share with you a deeply troubling and alarming attack, something to date only a few others have seen. It comes from a curious letter I received, and it disturbs me. . . ."

Terry Dolan of the National Conservative Political Action Committee: "Have you ever considered television to be a threat to our free way of life? Well, the misuse of television by the liberals who control our news media makes it a real danger."

A save-the-dolphins letter from Greenpeace: "Along the shore, they were starting to feed the bodies of the dolphins into mechanical shredders. It's difficult to describe the revulsion. . . ."

Once the formula has engaged the reader by playing on his emotions, it uses information in much of the rest of the text. The nature of the information varies, of course, depending on the nature of the appeal and of the organization or individual who is sending it. Usually, the information is based on at least a measure of reporting and research. What's more, it generally is factually accurate, even if the facts are used to advance highly partisan arguments and interpretations.

The letters sent by many issue groups, for example, will discuss their policy concerns or report on their strategic plans, as well as on the moves made by their adversaries. The American Civil Liberties Union's mail often reports on its cases in the lower courts, provides state-by-state briefings on civil liberties efforts, and monitors such abuses as censorship campaigns in Virginia, Illinois, and New York. One recent ACLU letter devoted half of its space to a report on the Georgia town of Kennesaw, where a law was passed to require a gun in every home and ammunition in every gun. A Planned Parenthood letter offers brief reports on four different legal actions the group is pursuing to secure abortion rights. Environmental groups commonly use their mail to report on their local efforts, as do gun-control organizations, the National Organization for Women, and other groups.

At the other end of the political spectrum, a letter sent out not long ago by a group calling itself Americans Against Taxpayer Funding of Groups Allied With Hayden and Fonda offered a detailed breakdown of how many federal community-action dollars have gone to eight different grass-roots activist groups. The letter took pains to push the dollar total right down to two decimal places: $2,655,076.56. The trouble is, the letter neglected to do a similarly scrupulous job of actually tying Tom Hayden or Jane Fonda to at least three of the groups.

Letters are often loaded with facts and statistics which the writer uses to support the unsupportable. For example, a New Right letter mailed by a group called Leadership Action provides a grim statistical portrait of American public schools: "Boys and girls, 10, 11, and 12 years old, attack, rob and even kill their teachers. In the past 15 years, unwed teenage pregnancies have risen 76 percent. Drug use among teenagers under 18 years has risen 205 percent since 1968. And if that's not bad enough, government spent six times more tax dollars on schools in the last sixteen years but test scores have dropped dramatically." What, the letter seems to be asking, is the remedy for all these ills? School prayer, of course.

One of the conventions of these letters, as it happens, is The Striking Fact. Usually slammed home in a single sentence, this bold but documented assertion is designed to fuse emotion and information for maximum impact. A Kennedy letter: "The new military budget calls for spending more money—$89.7 million—for military bands than the entire budget proposed for the National Endowment for the Arts." A riposte for Citizens Organized to Replace Kennedy: "If Kennedy and the liberals keep spending wildly, by the year 2,000 a $75,000 house will cost over $2,400,000!"

Information counts just as much as emotion does in the formula for political letters. "Emotion will grab the reader, but once you've grabbed 'em, you've got to hold 'em," explains Tom Mathews, a partner in the liberal direct-mail firm of Craver, Mathews, Smith & Company. "To hold 'em— to get into their heads far enough to get them to take an action step—you have to use information. Here's what's happening in this country. Here's how our cause or candidate can help. Here's how *you* can help."

Richard Viguerie, the direct-mail impresario of the New Right, is credited with first using letters as a medium rather than merely as a fund-raising trigger. For eighteen years, Viguerie has used the mail as an explicit alternative to what he sees as a liberal monopoly in the media mainstream. "It's not that the media presents [sic] the news in a partisan way, it's that they present the positive side of liberal causes, liberal issues, liberal personalities and, for the most part, ignore conservative causes, conservative issues, and conservative personalities, or present them in an unfavorable manner," Viguerie wrote in 1980 in *The New Right: We're Ready to Lead.* "However, there is one method of mass commercial communication that the liberals do not control—direct mail. . . . You can think of direct mail as *our* TV, radio, daily newspaper and weekly newsmagazine."

Frank O'Brien, who handled the direct mail for Ralph Nader's Public Citizen before stepping into a similar role two years ago for the Democratic National Committee, says that his own experience has confirmed Viguerie's insight.

"At the DNC, we got into the mail for the money," O'Brien recalls. "As we were working with it, we lifted our head one day and said, 'Hey, we've got a lot more than just a fund-raising tool here.'" As O'Brien sees it, liberal groups and candidates used to mail, say, a hundred letters for funds, and only care about those two or three recipients who sent in a check. "Viguerie has been just as concerned to communicate to the other ninety-seven or ninety-eight," O'Brien goes on. "So liberals used the mail to pay the bills while conservatives used it to move the country."

In the eighteen months leading up to the 1982 elections, the DNC flattered Viguerie by imitating him. It ran a sustained mail campaign on Social Security. Its target was Democratic voters of modest means, with addresses in or on the edges of America's cities. "We went to older blue-collar couples, told them of the threats to Social Security, and assured them the Democratic Party would stick up for their benefits," says O'Brien. The letters asked for donations, but the DNC needed only enough money for the mailings to pay for themselves. (They did this and more: 80,000 people joined the party's donor rolls, contributing $1.2 million.) "The reason why twenty-five percent of the voters surveyed by NBC on election day cited Social Security as their prime concern is partly because we sent letters to ten million likely voters and said: 'On election day, your prime concern should be Social Security,'" concludes O'Brien.

Other experts on direct mail also see it as an alternative to conventional journalism, but don't share Viguerie's ideological view of its function.

"We've lost our old American tradition of a hard-hitting partisan press," argues William Schneider, a public opinion analyst for the *Los Angeles Times* and *National Journal* who has studied extensive interviews with people who regularly respond to letters on such issues as women's rights and the environment. "This leaves millions of people without a choice or a vehicle, and they see these qualities in direct mail. Two themes recur in the interviews: People like to see an argument, a point of view, what they think of as straight talk. They also like the information in the letters. It lets them follow the action in the women's movement or environmental legislation in a way that they can't through the regular news."

"There's no conscious conspiracy in the media, but journalism does bring an unconscious filter to its work, and this creates a hunger in people for what the mail can do," argues James Lucier. He is an aide to Republican Senator Jesse Helms of North Carolina, who is a guiding spirit of the Congressional Club, a political action committee with a strong fund-raising record. Earlier, Lucier backed up James J. Kilpatrick in writing pungently conservative editorials for the Richmond *News Leader*. "Journalism," Lucier says, "is caught up in formal and rationalistic conventions, so it comes across to most people as an exotic world with a strange language. A letter is a way to . . . get directly at people and what concerns them."

The rise of mail as a medium reflects two other changes as well. One is the broad shift from mass media to tailored and targeted media: from general-interest to special-interest magazines, and from broadcasting to narrowcasting. A letter is as tailored and as narrowly cast a medium as we can use today. The other is the change in our forms of political action. With the decline of party organizations, and with the media now providing people with most of their political information, more and more Americans have managed to become armchair activists. The mail makes it easier—and more interesting—to follow the political action, and easier to form political judgments. Whether people send in their $10 or $25, or express their views to friends, or simply vote the way the letter writers want them to, the mail is helping them to be participants in the political process.

Study Questions: Wirth and Watson

[?] | *Should the Federal Communications Commission bar television networks or stations from projecting election winners before all polls close? Is there any other action you would support that might reduce the possible impact of such projections on voting turnout in western states? Or is this a matter with which the government should not be concerned?*

> *From the point of view of broadcasters and politicians, is there an essential difference between broadcasters doing something because of government pressure (of the sort being exercised by Representative Wirth) and doing it because it's the law? Why might the former be preferred by both groups?*
>
> *Watson implies that the media are justified in broadcasting or publishing any reliable information they have. He says their job "is to report and not withhold news." Do you accept Watson's position when it comes to forecasting election winners before everyone has voted? Do you accept his position in other cases, no matter what effect this information might have?*
>
> *Does the competition among networks that Wirth and Watson mention have more positive or more negative impact on election coverage? On other news coverage?*

Timothy Wirth and George Watson

SHOULD TV STOP PROJECTING ELECTION WINNERS?

Timothy Wirth

Representative Wirth, why do you feel the TV networks should curtail projections of winners until polls close?
A democratic society is successful only if people participate in it, and we have very clear evidence that early projection of election returns tends to discourage some of the people from voting.

I was at a polling place in Colorado in 1980 where people stepped out of voting lines and went home after the TV networks projected President Carter the loser. Early projections have an impact not only on national results but also on local contests. I don't understand how the networks can arrogate to themselves the right to decide the outcome of an election before all the votes are in.

Timothy Wirth is a Democratic Representative of Colorado.

George Watson is Vice-President of ABC Network News.

What's the difference between traditional public-opinion polls and the projections made by the networks?
People understand that polls before an election are nothing more than opinions. But after the voting has started, the projections of networks are reported and heard as facts, as if the election were over.

In Iowa this year, one network projected Mondale the winner at 8:12 P.M. and another at 8:18 P.M., even though no voting in the caucuses was allowed until 8:30 P.M. at the earliest. Later, in the New Hampshire presidential primary, the networks carefully couched their predictions. But they still, in effect, projected the winner in 7 P.M. newscasts, even though the last polls didn't close until 8 P.M.

TV-news people say projections are a necessary part of the press's role—protected under the Constitution—of keeping the public informed—
The First Amendment is not the issue. The news media's exercise of good judgment is. To their credit, several news organizations back in 1979 knew there were American hostages in the Canadian Embassy in Iran, but they did not report this.

The question is: What public good is served by the networks' mad rush to be first with a projection, presumably to improve their TV ratings? Who cares whether a network makes an election projection at 8:12 P.M. or at 8:18 P.M.? Nobody but the network and its competitors.

Do you want Congress to act to change the situation?
I would not like Congress to mandate when the networks can project. That could violate the First Amendment. Instead, the networks should exercise voluntary restraint. Why should the nation change its electoral mechanism and voting hours because of cockamamie pressures in the media?

Do you favor state laws that prohibit interviews with people as they leave polling places?
If the networks refuse to cooperate, they're going to see a whole variety of actions taken by local governments. The overwhelming majority of Americans are very unhappy with the networks' interference with the electoral process.

George Watson

Mr. Watson, why do you feel the networks are justified in projecting election winners before the polls close?
Our job is to report and not withhold news. But we never project election results until polls are closed in a given state and reliable information on the outcome is available.

In a national election, when state polls have closed on a winning number of electoral votes, then the President has been elected. Only in a landslide election does a problem arise, when voting in the East determines the outcome before everyone has finished voting in the West.

Studies show that when the networks made early projections in 1980, from 1 to 3 percent of the voters decided their vote didn't matter and stayed away from the polls. Didn't this harm the democratic process?
The evidence that people stay away from the polls because of news reports is very thin and inconclusive.

The fact is that in 1980 fully 86.8 percent of Americans who were registered did vote. That's an extraordinarily large percentage for any democracy. The problem for our democracy is that fully 60 million Americans are not registered to vote and are, in effect, engaged in a boycott of voting.

Critics say the networks should not conduct what amounts to a separate TV-sponsored election by interviewing voters leaving polling places—
We use exit polls very cautiously. They provide very useful information about why people vote as they do, and they have become an extraordinarily reliable indicator of how elections are going to turn out.

At ABC News, we do not, however, use exit polls to project the winner of any state election until the polls are closed in that state.

It has also been charged that the practice of projecting winners stems largely from competition among the networks—
Well, we do not regard competition as a game. It's a precious component of a free press. And, as Churchill said about democracy, competition among news organizations may be the worst system, except for all the others. While competition might lead to excess on occasion, it usually invigorates our free press with a healthy rivalry to get the news right and to get it first.

What is your attitude toward Washington State's prohibition against exit interviews within 300 feet of the polling places?
We strongly oppose it, and we have joined with several other news organizations in a suit to overturn the Washington law, arguing that it is an unconstitutional abridgement of freedon of the press.

Can anything be done to prevent voters in states where polls are open from being influenced by news reports of results in states where polls have closed?
One solution is that the polls should close at the same hour in all states. That would eliminate the problem in Far Western states.

Study Questions: Kaul/Dowie and Talbot

? *Why does an actor such as Ed Asner have so much influence? Do you agree with Donald Kaul's humorous assessment? Is there wisdom beneath those satiric words, or is he just pulling your leg?*

The Asner case raises the difficult issue of whether actors who play highly credible television or film characters should take advantage of their characters' credibility to advocate political positions. What is your opinion on this issue? Should actors have less freedom of speech than bankers, teachers, or carpenters?

Is the Asner case different from that of an actor who plays the role of a physician doing commercials for over-the-counter medications? How so?

Was CBS right or wrong to cancel the Lou Grant *series when its star became controversial because of his political activities? Were advertisers right or wrong to remove their commercials from the show when Asner became so controversial? Why? If you were president of CBS, how would you have handled this case? If you were investing $10 million for advertising to promote a new product, would you want that advertising associated with a show or an actor with whom a lot of people were angry?*

Should a major communications firm be as susceptible to influence by pressure groups as CBS apparently was in this case? If so, how can it keep employees from being overly timid about public issues? If not, how else can the public exert influence on the giant communications industries?

Do you agree with Dowie and Talbot that the political right in this country has been more effective at grooming celebrities for political leadership than the left has been? What evidence do you have for your agreement or disagreement?

What relationship do you see between the Asner case and the cases discussed by Halberstam?

Donald Kaul

MORGAN FAIRCHILD, VP?

Conservatives are jumping all over Ed Asner, television's "Lou Grant," for speaking out on the issue of El Salvador. Grant came to Washington with several of his colleagues—including "Pa Walton" and "Johnny Fever" of *WKRP*—to launch a fund-raising drive for medical aid to the people of El Salvador.

Asner, who is the president of the Screen Actors Guild and who seems to be laying groundwork for a political career, took the opportunity to say things like, "I'm trying to get this country to stop its *gringo* participation in the fate of El Salvador or change its age-old non-attention to the problems of Central America, which are true land reform and true democratic practices."

That really made the right-wingers mad. They greeted his pronouncement with hoots of derision, jeering at the notion that an actor might be looked at as a serious spokesman on serious issues.

To tell you the truth, I kind of agree with them.

Not that I think we should muzzle people like Asner. It's a free country; he can say what he wants. But I don't see any reason to pay him any special attention.

Actors are not particularly thoughtful people, nor are they, as a rule, well-read. (I remember being shocked, once, to read Laurence Olivier's admission that he never read books; just plays.) They tend to be sensitive, insecure types with the sometimes magical ability to pretend they are something they are not and to read speeches prepared by others with an illusion of conviction.

Were I seeking people from whom to get advice about the real world, I would rank actors, as a group, behind doctors, lawyers, bankers, professors, newspapermen, foremen in body shops, welfare mothers, bus drivers and bartenders. Just ahead of disc jockeys.

Which is not to say that some actors are not intelligent, well-informed citizens or that Ed Asner isn't one of them. That's not the point.

The point is that Asner has an unfair advantage when he speaks out on an issue, for he speaks not merely as Ed Asner but also as Lou Grant, that tough, lovable, no-nonsense guy on the TV show. I doubt that you would be seeing him as a spokesman for a view if he were famous for playing a rotten millionaire on a prime-time soap opera.

The sad fact is that the American public is fast losing its ability to discriminate between dream and reality. There are a lot of yokels out there who watch the tube and actually believe that what is happening to the characters they see is happening to the actors themselves.

Some will say that this trend has found its ultimate expression in the presidency of Ronald Reagan. He is, after all, an actor who has been taken seriously. (It's either that, or the presidency is being taken lightly; I'm not sure which.) But he is only the beginning of what we have to look forward to.

Reagan uses the skills he learned as an actor to good advantage, but his professional image was not so dominant as to confuse voters. They knew they were voting for Ronald Reagan, not some character he was identified with.

But what if Alan Alda or Carroll O'Connor were to run for office. Would we be electing Hawkeye Pierce and Archie Bunker, or Alda and O'Connor? I don't want to find out.

Do you want Charlton Heston as your secretary of defense, wearing a breastplate and a helmet with feathers? Do you think Burt Reynolds would make a terrific secretary of transportation? Robert Young a great secretary of health and human services? John Houseman a distinguished secretary of education? Morgan Fairchild a nifty vice-president? (Although, admittedly, Miss Fairchild would bring a certain welcome candor to that office. She was recently quoted as saying, "I've had to take some bad parts, but it's better than hooking on the side.")

I happen to agree with much that Ed Asner says on the subject of El Salvador, but ignoring him is a small price to pay to uphold the sound principle of keeping actors in their place—Never-Never Land.

Mark Dowie and David Talbot

ASNER: TOO HOT FOR MEDIUM COOL

The killing of *Lou Grant* was more like a gangland slaying than the work of a lone assassin. William Paley, the octogenarian don of CBS, may have given the final nod (he certainly could have stopped it); but New Right hitmen like Jerry Falwell, Charlton Heston, Representative John Le-Boutillier and Lynn Bouchet, as well as TV advertisers like Kimberly-Clark and the Peter Paul Cadbury Company, all pulled triggers on an assortment of deadly weapons that put *Lou Grant* in the grave. And the murder was carried out in full view of liberal Hollywood bystanders, who, with few exceptions, put up not a whimper of protest.

We'll examine the evidence against this line-up of suspects. But first, the motives.

Lou Grant was not just another imbecilic stretch of air time. No other TV series so consistently confronted the major issues of our day, from nuclear war to corporate malfeasance to the reign of torture in foreign countries. Even when episodes dealt only with newsroom policy, the show was somehow tweaking the nose of power or poking a finger of ridicule at one sacred cow or another. Sometimes the program pulled punches; sometimes it turned preachy or maudlin—twin dangers of social-issue melodrama. But is was the only network series that week in and week out acknowledged what producer Gene Reynolds calls "the clash of ideas."

The principal attraction of the show was probably the ensemble of newsroom characters, each of whom had a distinct and developed identity, and the idealized image of work life they projected. The staff of the *Los Angeles Tribune* was composed of decent, hard-working and intelligent professionals who managed to find time in their demanding schedules to share some laughs and look out for each other. It was the kind of office where we all wanted to work.

At the center of this ensemble was Lou himself, the gruff but tenderhearted city editor who has been a popular television fixture for 12 years. Actor Ed Asner created this character in *The Mary Tyler Moore Show,* fleshed him out in the *Lou Grant* show and then did something quite remarkable and generous with him: Asner donated his burly and eminently likable persona to a string of worthy causes—the PATCO (air traffic controllers) strike, the Screen Actors Guild, various First Amendment battles, the Democratic Socialist Organizing Committee (though Asner says, "People who call me a socialist know more than I do") and, most explosive of all, the victims of El Salvador's rampaging military.

The reaction from the Right was, in the words of *Lou Grant* cocreator Allan Burns, "swift, continuous and excessive." Not since Jane Fonda took a stand during the Vietnam War has a Hollywood celebrity come under such withering fire. Asner was in some ways even more offensive, more threatening to conservatives than Fonda, because his TV show brought him into American living rooms every week and because his public image was more engaging than Fonda's, who is still trying to shake off the damaging—and sexist—epithet "strident."

For honest, levelheaded Lou Grant to speak out against U.S. involvement in El Salvador's bloodbath was simply too much for the Right. The bleeding-heart sentiments of the TV show were bad enough; much worse, however, was to have a TV character whose credibility was probably only a notch or two below Walter Cronkite's lash out against Reagan administration policy. The goal, then, was to destroy Lou Grant, to assassinate Ed Asner's lovable character so that the man inside the role could not speak so convincingly. Their success was stunning. Says Burns: "I've never seen anybody transformed so quickly from being everyone's favorite uncle to a Communist swine."

Finally, of course, Asner lost not just the character he had spent 12 years developing, but his show. After a memorable run, which garnered it a wallful of awards and an abundance of prestige, *Lou Grant* was abruptly terminated by CBS and consigned to rerun oblivion. Asner, once one of the network's most favored employees, had only 48 hours to vacate his offices on the CBS lot in Los Angeles.

ANATOMY OF A MURDER

The official line handed out by everyone at CBS is "Ratings, not politics, killed *Lou Grant*." But this story is so full of holes that even network officials have a hard time sticking to it in private. The show did suffer some ratings slippage in its last season, dropping from a 32 percent market share to a 27 percent share. But none of the CBS executives we interviewed considered this a disastrous decline—just a "little disconcerting," in the words of CBS Entertainment Division West Coast president Bud Grant.

Other long-running shows such as *The Waltons* and *Little House on the Prairie* have been revived after they began to lose steam—by beefing up their promotion budgets and making dramatic changes in their story lines. (Mary Tyler Moore could have looked up Lou during a visit to L.A., rekindling their special relationship for an episode or two.) And shows with considerably worse ratings have been kept on the air. . . .

CBS could never publicly admit that ratings are not the entire *Lou Grant* story, because to do so would be to concede that the network responds to political pressure—something it has always denied, from the blacklisting days of the 1950s to the present. But it is difficult to avoid this conclusion.

Soon after Asner's Washington, D.C., press conference, at which he announced plans to send medical aid to victims of the Salvadoran junta, CBS headquarters in New York began receiving a flood of mail threatening boycotts against *Lou Grant* sponsors unless the show was pulled off the air.

Lynn Bouchet of the Center for Inter-American Security (CIS), a right-wing, Washington, D.C.-based think tank, estimates that his organization alone triggered 5,000 letters to CBS with a poisonous direct-mail letter sent out to the 70,000 member-supporters of CIS. "If you liked Jane Fonda, you'll love Ed Asner," said the letter, which was signed by Representative John LeBoutillier (R.-New York). "Where Jane Fonda gave aid and comfort to the Communist enemy, Ed Asner gave that and $25,000."

Thousands of other letters came into CBS from irate Moral Majoritarians, fired up by a direct-mail appeal from Jerry Falwell. "Ed Asner says President Reagan's Communist enemies are his friends," wrote the electronic evangelist. "Are we to stand idly by while ultraliberal actors like Ed Asner arrogantly insult the president of the United States at a press conference for all the world to see?"

Panic quickly spread through the ranks of these sponsors, some of which also began receiving angry letters. Kimberly-Clark was the first to dump *Lou Grant*, explaining that it was concerned about Asner's public statements on El Salvador. This—as well as the fact the Kimberly-Clark has holdings in El Salvador—has been widely reported in the press.

But *Mother Jones* has learned that Kimberly-Clark was not the only *Lou Grant* sponsor that responded to the pressure. Vidal Sassoon, the maker of hair-care products, began to wilt after receiving only 13 letters. A worried Sassoon personally wrote CBS seeking a "solution to this unfortunate situation." Fretted the hair stylist-entrepreneur: "We, by sponsoring the show, did not wish to embroil ourselves in a political controversy. We do not feel we should be pressured into withdrawing our sponsorship. But on the other hand, we do not wish to have our products suffer because of an unfortunate association with a political issue."

Peter Paul Cadbury, the candy manufacturer, decided to drop *Lou Grant* after receiving only "six to ten" letters. "It seemed like a lot to us," a company spokesperson told *Mother Jones*. The letters, he added, expressed "our personal feelings—we support the president."

Sponsors were not the only ones to pull their backing from the show. There was trouble among some CBS affiliate stations as well. On March 1, John Amos, head of the American Family Broadcast Group—owners of a string of television stations in the South and Midwest—popped onto the TV screen immediately before that night's *Lou Grant* episode to deliver a startling denunciation of the show's star:

> Ed Asner has become, we feel, the self-appointed secretary of state of America, especially as relates to El Salvador. Contrary to our policy there, he has spoken out in favor of Communist rebels and is raising money here to be sent to the rebels in El Salvador.
> The liberal Left in this country, for which Asner appears to be a spokesman, is trying to paint our actions in El Salvador as another Vietnam. The difference between these situations is the difference between night and day! Vietnam was on the other side of the world . . . while El Salvador is just two steps from being next door to us.

The broadcasting executive suggested that Asner keep his opinions to himself, like "the great lady and great actress," Bette Davis, and pointed out that Ronald Reagan gave up his acting career to "serve the people."

CBS moved swiftly to spare its sponsors and affiliates further embarrassment. On May 6, it announced the show's cancellation. According to a story circulating at MTM, the company that produced *Lou Grant*, the order to kill the show came at the last minute directly from Paley, the network's perennial chairman, after the show had been rescheduled for the new season. "The imperial Paley got pissed off at Ed for not playing the game," says an MTM writer. "He probably thought, 'We pay Asner a fortune. Why isn't he a team player? He's agitating in the Screen Actors Guild for more money for actors, making statements about El Salvador. We've got to cut him loose.'"

CBS vice-president David Fuchs confirmed that Paley was indeed at the meeting during which the controversial decision was made. Fuchs went on to insist, however, that "it was not a single-vote decision, and Asner's politics had nothing to do with it."

But according to a CBS official we questioned at the network's convention, *Lou Grant*'s fate was determined the moment Asner held his press conference on El Salvador. "When Asner made his comments," says the official, "it became inevitable the network would have to cancel the show. He left us no choice."

ASNER AGONISTES

Why did Ed Asner risk his TV show and his career by speaking out on such a volatile issue as El Salvador? "I just got tired of being angry and not speaking my mind, of always walking on eggshells," he told us during a lengthy interview in the CBS office from which he would soon be evicted. On the walls, between the photos and memorabilia from *The Mary Tyler Moore* and *Lou Grant* shows, hung emblems of his political commitment: a bumpersticker ("In El Salvador, U.S. Guns Kill U.S. Nuns"), a PATCO picket sign, a photo of Asner addressing a Social Security rally. "You know," he continued, "I've played it carefully ever since I've been in show business. I've been selective in picking issues. During the Vietnam War, I was too busy toeing the line to get involved."

But Asner felt compelled to jump into the El Salvador fray. He agreed to speak at the fateful press conference after an emotional meeting with two Catholic nuns, who described to him the horrors of the war. In the middle of the press conference, while he was fielding some surprisingly hostile questions from reporters, Asner suddenly realized, "I just stopped walking on eggshells. And I felt a great sense of relief."

Some friends and associates of Asner's felt he had taken on more than he was prepared for, not only with the El Salvador issue but also in the Screen Actors Guild, where he came under immediate attack from Reagan crony Charlton Heston and other conservatives as soon as he took over the

Guild presidency. "After the press conference," says Allan Burns, "[producer] Gene Reynolds and I went to Ed and told him, 'These people are playing hard ball—they're out for your head.' I felt he lacked the sophistication to see who he was playing against."

Asner concedes that he could have been a better tactician in countering the assaults from the Right. "I could have staged a more carefully orchestrated media campaign. I am an emotional creature, and too infrequently I bring my brain into things ahead of my heart. I have never been a leader. Courage," he added quietly, "unless it's effective, means shit."

Asner emphasized that he has no regrets about taking a stand. Throughout our interview, he seemed downcast, answering questions in a slow and subdued manner as he sought to make sense of all that had befallen him. The one moment his voice became passionate was when he talked about the urgency of the El Salvador issue. "Think of it: for a few dollars more—like the Clint Eastwood movie—our country is backing a government which is involved in disfigurations by acid, and in cutting off the heads of lovers and stuffing them inside the women . . . The die is cast: I can't back off on El Salvador now."

How badly has Asner's career been damaged? He is trying to finalize a deal with NBC to play Jacobo Timerman in a TV movie based on *Prisoner Without a Name, Cell Without a Number,* the newspaper publisher's account of his torture and imprisonment at the hands of the Argentine military. But this project—like other acting possibilities—remains up in the air. "I would be a fool to say I'm not concerned," he said. "I want to keep acting and having the wonderful choice of roles I've had so far. Whether I could interest a network in another TV series at this point is doubtful. But they probably would not be adverse to casting me in a TV movie, since that's a one-shot deal and it's much harder for pressure groups to mobilize against."

Asner is concerned not only about his career but also about the "chilling effect" that the CBS cancellation and his treatment at the hands of the Right will have on the Hollywood community. "What is happening to me will discourage others in TV from speaking out. The level of fear is rising. I see it on other performers' faces when they see me. Some of them are afraid to be around me; they get sweaty palms when I walk into the same room. I think it's a combination of delight that they're not me and guilt that they haven't done anything."

HOLLYWOOD LOCKJAW

One of the most disturbing aspects of the *Lou Grant* affair is the wall of silence in Hollywood that greeted Asner's downfall. Asner has many closet supporters in the entertainment industry, but shockingly few who are willing to go public. After dozens of phone calls to various Hollywood luminaries known for their liberal views, *Mother Jones* could find only three who were willing to comment on the Asner controversy—actors Robert Redford, Jane Fonda and Mike Farrell, costar of the TV series *M*A*S*H.* "I am concerned about the future of free speech and creative expression in this country," said Redford in a prepared statement. "There is an alarming pattern developing . . . I don't know about the *Lou Grant* situation specifically. But blacklisting, if that's what is happening, is hard to trace and I think it's worth looking into. I certainly feel that Ed Asner has every right to speak his mind."

"I fully realize the political ramifications when someone in this industry takes controversial positions and suffers the consequences," said Fonda in her statement to *Mother Jones.* "Whatever one thinks of Asner's fundraising on behalf of medical aid to El Salvador, he shouldn't be subjected to McCarthy-like attacks and character assassinations because of it. I respect Ed Asner as a humanitarian and I'm grateful for his guts."

But the rest of Hollywood is ducking and running for cover. Even MTM, the TV company for which Asner has worked for the past 12 years, seems to be divorcing itself from the beleaguered actor. Steven Bochco, executive producer of the MTM show *Hill Street Blues,* which many say is the only bold and innovative series left on television, declined to comment on the demise of *Lou Grant.* A spokesperson for the company explained that it would be "self-serving" for Bochco to make a public statement about another MTM show. According to Asner's assistant, Terry Behimer, MTM even "held up our outgoing mail" after the cancellation.

Asner's predicament also raises serious questions about the way the Left treats its celebrities: constantly beseeching them to lend their names and support to causes, and then failing to give them adequate protection when they become overly exposed. Celebrities, as Jane Fonda once pointed out in a book interview, can serve an important political function in a country that spends so much of its time plugged into the media. But, she added, undoubtedly thinking of her own plight in the early 1970s, "These people must be cared for, and tended to, and encouraged a great deal, because they are extremely vulnerable. They must not be led down garden paths, taken in directions where they don't want to go, pushed too far and too fast, or anything like that."

After CBS announced the cancellation, an assortment of progressive groups and unions—many of which have benefited from Asner's support and the show's coverage of issues—organized two demonstrations outside CBS' main studio in Los Angeles. The demonstrations, which turned out between 600 and 1,000 people, made an important statement to CBS, and the network also came under fire from Ralph Nader's broadcasting reform group. But when it comes to mounting intensive, well-organized, long-term pressure campaigns against the media, the Right is way out in front.

Most progressive groups, says Norman Fleishman, "simply don't understand the value of mass letter-writing to network officials." Fleishman is the director of a group called Microsecond, which is trying to raise the Hollywood community's awareness about the dangers of nuclear war. It was after attending a Microsecond seminar that *Lou Grant* writers scripted an episode about nuclear war—the final one before the show's cancellation was announced.

For activists like Fleishman, who have been working for years to influence TV programming by educating writers, producers and actors, the loss of *Lou Grant* was a particularly severe blow. "*Lou Grant* made a magnificent contribution," he says. "At a time when the human race is on the brink, TV is the most effective tool for raising public consciousness. Entertainment is the only way to reach masses of people. There are scores of writers and producers who are dying to do these kinds of relevant shows. But instead, it looks like the networks are going right back to the bouncy, bouncy crap—the jiggle shows."

The Right has always been aware of the political significance of Hollywood celebrities. "Joe McCarthy and the other blacklisters were correct," observes Fleishman. "If you want to do the most damage, go after the entertainment people."

The Right is also adept at grooming celebrities for political leadership—the charming storyteller who currently occupies the White House being the most notable example. Perhaps the final lesson of the *Lou Grant* affair is that progressives simply need a more effective celebrity strategy if we want to continue to get our ideas into the spotlight.

Study Questions: Abelman and Neuendorf

[?] *Is the religious programming found today on American television, radio, and cable representative of this country's religions? Why or why not?*

Do you side with the supporters or the opponents of the electronic church? Are television, cable, and radio proper media of communication for churches? Assuming that these are proper media for churches, are televangelists using them appropriately? Are there any changes you would suggest?

Table 5 in the article shows that health-related issues are the most prevalent problems discussed on these religious television programs. How do you explain that? Do you believe that is also the most prevalent problem discussed in traditional churches? If not, how do you explain the difference?

> What else do you conclude from the information presented in this article? Do any of the data reported in the tables surprise you?
>
> What are the advantages and disadvantages of apportioning free time to religious broadcasters (as was once the practice), as opposed to selling time to religious groups in the way it is sold to other advertisers (today's practice)?

Robert Abelman and Kimberly Neuendorf

HOW RELIGIOUS IS RELIGIOUS TELEVISION PROGRAMMING?

Seventy-five Percent of Programming Content Has a Religious Theme, While Only Two Percent Is Overtly Political—and Solicitations Average $190 Per Hour

Television evangelist Billy Graham says he "can preach to more people in one night on TV than perhaps Paul did in his whole lifetime" (8, p. 16). Indeed, while estimates place the lifetime listenership of Jesus Christ at no more than 30,000 people, millions of Americans tune in every week to the "electronic church" (6). The propriety of this popular on-the-air worship is a hotly debated issue and one of increasing concern to the traditional clergy. According to Dean Colin Williams of the Yale Divinity School,

> The breadth of the Gospel is not reflected in the narrow compass of the electronic church of TV. Electronic evangelism allows itself to become constricted by the medium and it becomes a consumer religion of instant gratification. . . . It doesn't help people to think . . . . It draws upon people's feelings of disappointment and alienation (7, p. 67).

Similarly, church historian (and Lutheran pastor) Martin E. Marty suggests that televised religion is weaning adherents away from the traditional local churches: "The electronic church threatens to replace the living congregation with a far-flung clientele of devotees to this or that evangelist" (9, p. 26). He further suggests that "the [TV] church is fostering in our midst a completely private 'invisible religion' [which] is—or ought to be—the most feared contemporary rival to church religion" (5, p. 6).

Robert Abelman and Kimberly Neuendorf are Assistant Professors in the Department of Communication, Cleveland State University. The research reported in this article was funded by a grant from Unda-USA, Washington, D.C. The authors wish to thank Patrick DiSalvatore, Diocese of Cleveland.

In opposition, TV preacher Pat Robertson of the Christian Broadcasting Network, which owns four UHF television stations and five FM radio stations and operates 71 regional call-in centers and CBN University, defends religious programming:

> To say that the church shouldn't be involved with television is utter folly. The needs are the same, the message is the same, but the delivery can change. . . . It would be folly for the church not to get involved with the most formative force in America (7, p. 67).

Billy Graham also maintains that

> TV evangelism is clearly enlarging the realm of religious influence, not narrowing it. TV preachers touch the hearts of shut-ins, night workers, the very old, the very young, tenement dwellers—people often cut off from the comforts of a local church. Its real converts are coming not from traditional churches, but from commercial TV, whose diet of secular programming leaves viewers starved for spiritual nourishment. Gradually, TV religion is evolving into a TV alternative (5, p. 8).

The political and ideological ramifications of the debate regarding religious programming have been most visible in TV producer and writer Norman Lear's nationwide battle with the Moral Majority. In an effort to raise funds to combat TV evangelism, for example, Lear claimed that "the ability of moral majoritarians to shape public attitudes and to influence the climate of public debate is unprecedented and poses an enormous danger" (9, p. 24). According to Lear, contemporary religious programs are highly conservative and political and have "overpowered America's airwaves with their messages of hostility, fear, and distrust." Hadden and Swann's review of religious programming (6), however, suggests that not all of the top syndicated religious programs are conservative and that not all of the conservative programs are political. Given the prevalence of this fare, its large audience, and the heated debate about its purpose and function in the United States and overseas, there has been surprisingly little systematic, quantitative exploration of the content of the electronic church.

The Purpose of this Article Is to Identify, Document, and Trace Some Major Dimensions of the Themes and Topics of Religious Television Fare

The single criterion used to select a topic for examination was our judgment of whether that topic might have potentially significant social implications. That is, if presented in certain amounts and forms, is the topic likely to have social effects on issues of some significance to broadcasters, policymakers, religious leaders, and viewers?

The analysis reported here includes five classes of information: (a) reference to and attitudes toward a variety of social, political, and religious topics; (b) proper name reference to people, places, and groups; (c) composite portrayals, or themes, of the programs' social, political, and religious content; (d) reference to social, political, and religious problems and whether or what kind of solutions to these problems were offered; and (e) appeals for and uses of money and an account of the types of products offered in the programs.

To determine which religious programs are the most prevalent, we first obtained a stratified random sample of forty U.S. towns and cities from U.S. Census information. The sample was stratified by size of the town or city: 10 towns with a population of less than 20,000 persons; 10 cities with a population of 20,000–100,000 persons; 10 cities with a population of 100,000–1,000,000 persons; and the 10 most populated cities in the United States.[1]

To arrive at the sample of programs, we examined the issues of *TV Guide* for the two-week period June 11–June 24, 1983, for each of the 40 cities, as well as consulting *Broadcasting/Cable Yearbook* for any religious cable channels carried that were not listed in *TV Guide*. This process yielded a total of 698 different programs (18,845 episodes). We selected the "top 30" of these programs for analysis, based on an index composed of (a) the frequency with which the program was aired in the forty cities during the sample period, (b) the number of different markets in which the program was available, (c) the length of the average episode, (d) the number of different cable and broadcast stations on which the program was available, and (e) the total number of households, both broadcast and cable, capable of receiving the program. All index components were calculated for the sample cities and were standardized before inclusion in the index.[2] Three cancelled programs could not be included, so the final sample consisted of 27 programs.[3] Using a random sampling of off-air programming (where available) and tapes provided by the religious institutions that produced or distributed the programs, we selected three episodes of each, resulting in 81 episodes.[4]

A team of three coders participated in the analysis of themes and topics. During an initial session, the coders were introduced to the scope and purposes of the project, the methodology, and the variables and coding categories. Practice sessions were supervised and each coder's responses were discussed; when coders had completed several practice sessions, they independently viewed and coded the same set of episodes until intercoder reliabilities reached .80 for all categories. After this point, each program was viewed by a single coder. Periodically (every 10–15 episodes), coders analyzed the same program to provide a reliability check, each of which exceeded the .80 level.

Each episode of every program was divided into five-minute segments in order to facilitate analysis. At the end of each segment, a coder used a prepared checklist to indicate whether a topic had been mentioned, and if so whether it had been treated disapprovingly, neutrally, approvingly, or had been debated. A particular topic was coded only once per five-minute segment, regardless of how much time it actually consumed. For each five-minute segment, the overriding focus, or "theme," to which the majority of topics were related was coded as either social, political, or religious. Although a topic in a given category might have an orientation associated with one of the other two categories—for instance, a social topic might have a political orientation—we made the assignment to a particular category if the other ramifications of the topics were not discussed or explicitly addressed. Topics were not considered mutually exclusive.

Overall, a Wide Variety of Social, Political, and Religious Topics Is Discussed, with Death, Communism, and God Leading the Respective Categories

Social topics entail discussions of or references to human society, the interaction of the individual and the group, or the welfare of human beings as members of society. As seen in Table 1, death and dying is the social topic referred to most, accounting for 151 individual references or approximately 19 percent of all social topics. The function, content, and impact of the broadcast media accounts for 6 percent of all social topics; when references to the print media are added, the media account for almost one quarter of all social topics. The institution of marriage is also a common topic; related topics such as divorce and family violence are infrequently referred to, as are women's rights/issues, minority rights/issues, and ethnic/racial prejudice.

The majority of social topics are dealt with in a neutral manner. In general, when an evaluative judgment is made, disapproval is expressed for such things as crime, violence, abortion, and sexual behavior in general. Approval is indicated for such issues as women's and minority rights, marriage, education, and the print and broadcast media. Very few social topics are the subject of debate.

Political topics entail discussions of or references to local, national, or international government structure, the conduct of management, and acts of or against a government or a political system. As seen in Table 2, there are very few direct references to political topics in our sample. Several topical subjects are not mentioned at all (i.e., gun control, nuclear power, sex education); "timeless" issues are the most frequently discussed. General politics accounts for approximately 17 percent and communism for approximately 15 percent of all political topics.

When political issues are discussed, they are dealt with in a neutral manner about half the time. Evaluations are typically conservative (i.e., in favor of strong and ready armed forces, prayer in public school, and Rea-

Table 1

Frequency and treatment of social topics

	Disapproval	Neutral	Approval	Debate	Total
Crime	15	20	—	1	36
Aging	1	26	2	1	30
Death and dying	29	112	7	3	151
Scientific findings (citing of research)	1	4	4	—	9
Mass media—print	5	52	14	—	71
Mass media—nonprint (television, radio, film)	8	80	43	2	133
Contraception	—	—	—	—	—
Homosexuality	2	5	—	—	7
Women's rights/issues	—	15	2	1	18
Minority rights/issues	—	5	5	—	10
Ethnic/racial prejudice	3	2	—	1	6
Violence (nonfamily)	20	16	1	—	37
Violence (family)	5	7	—	—	12
Sexual behavior (heterosexual)	12	14	1	1	28
Euthanasia	1	1	—	—	2
Abortion	19	5	—	2	26
Pornography	3	3	—	1	7
Divorce	5	14	—	1	20
Marriage	2	61	13	4	80
Education	1	42	36	4	83
Other	4	18	29	2	53
Total n	136	502	157	24	819
Total %	16.6	61.3	19.2	2.9	100

ganomics; against relations between the United States and the U.S.S.R., communism, and [to a minimal extent] the environmental movement and busing). However, the expressed viewpoint of these programs, collectively, is one against war and (again, to a minimal extent) nuclear arms.

Religious topics entail discussions of or references to the service, structure, function, or faith of organized or unorganized individuals dedicated to an adherence to God or the supernatural. As seen in the listing of religious topics in Table 3, God, Jesus, and the Bible are the most frequently mentioned topics. Also as expected, topics that oppose the traditional religious doctrine (i.e., the theory of evolution and atheism) are given little attention. Heaven is mentioned more than hell. However, sin is referred to more frequently than the act of being purged of sin (i.e., being "saved" or "born again").

Religious topics are treated neutrally less often than either social or political topics. Not surprisingly, God, Jesus, the Bible, faith, heaven, creationism, missionaries, being "born again" and "saved," and healing are

Table 2

Frequency and treatment of political topics

	Disapproval	*Neutral*	*Approval*	*Debate*	*Total*
Armed forces	—	13	2	—	15
Gun control	—	—	—	—	—
Death penalty	—	—	1	—	1
Prayer in public schools	—	—	2	—	2
Reaganomics	—	3	—	—	3
Welfare	—	1	1	—	2
Nuclear armament	1	4	—	1	6
Nuclear power	—	—	—	—	—
Environmental movement	1	—	—	—	1
Third world	—	9	—	—	9
Sex education	—	—	—	—	—
Busing	1	1	—	—	2
Religious freedom (e.g., Russian Jews)	—	1	1	—	2
Relations between U.S. and U.S.S.R.	5	1	—	—	6
Current wars	3	4	1	—	8
Potential wars	3	—	—	—	3
Communism	9	10	—	1	20
Politics (in the U.S.)	—	11	6	6	23
Other	7	13	8	3	31
Total n	30	71	22	11	134
Total %	21.9	51.8	18.2	8.0	100

spoken of approvingly; Satan, sin, and atheism are not. Religions other than the speaker's are more readily disapproved of or debated.

To Quantify Additional Social, Political, and Religious References, Coders Listed Verbatim Any Direct Reference to Proper Names of Places, Persons, or Groups

In terms of explicit references to persons, groups, and places, the emphasis is overwhelmingly domestic but surprisingly nonreligious. Of the total of 725 geographic locations mentioned, 75 percent are in North America. More proper name references are made to nonreligious persons and groups than to those with an explicit religious affiliation. Of all the references (excluding geographic locales), 31.5 percent are to social persons and groups, 12.5 percent are to political persons and groups, 20.1 percent are to religious persons and groups, and 35.9 percent are to "other" persons and groups. Consistent with the social topics analysis reported earlier (see

Table 3

Frequency and treatment of religious topics

	Disapproval	Neutral	Approval	Debate	Total
Supernatural (astrology, witchcraft)	9	5	1	—	15
God	1	163	381	6	551
Jesus	2	146	276	1	425
Satan	70	48	1	—	119
Hell	11	21	—	—	32
Healing (by an agent of God)	1	31	66	3	101
Sin	52	98	—	—	150
Second Coming of Christ	—	19	14	—	33
Armageddon	1	7	—	1	9
Being "born again"	—	24	29	1	54
Being "saved"	—	44	40	—	84
State of Israel	—	20	—	—	20
Missionaries to foreign countries	1	11	26	—	38
Missionary programs in U.S.	—	8	10	—	18
Other religions (than that of speaker/ program)	12	30	3	5	50
Theory of evolution	4	1	—	—	5
Creation	—	20	8	—	28
Atheism	3	5	—	—	8
Heaven	1	61	25	—	87
Faith	1	70	45	1	117
Bible as a text	—	233	81	1	315
Other	8	47	244	6	305
Total n	177	1112	1250	25	2564
Total %	6.9	43.4	48.8	1.0	100

Table 1), mass media institutions garner significant attention, with proper names of such institutions being the most frequently occurring social referents.

Not surprisingly, the overriding focus or theme of each five-minute portion of each program was religious rather than social or political (see Table 4). Nonetheless, approximately 25 percent of the segments did *not* have a religious theme, with 2 percent focusing on political issues and 23 percent on social issues. The likelihood of the program having an overall religious theme is largely determined by its type (e.g., talk, drama, sermon). In programs offering sermons or presenting revival meetings (e.g., "Jimmy Swaggart"), almost all of the content has a religious theme, while religious

Table 4

Social, religious, and political themes by program type

	All programs %	*Preaching/ revival* %	*Talk* %	*Drama* %	*Music/ variety* %	*Magazine* %
Social theme	23	5	16	76	5	46
Religious theme	75	92	83	24	95	40
Political theme	2	1	1	—	—	14

Note: Percentages total down columns.

dramas (e.g., "Another Life") place the greatest emphasis on a social theme, compared with other programs. Religious programs in a magazine format (e.g., "Real to Reel") offer a more even mixture of themes.

Problems Entailing the Discussion of or Reference to Human Conflict and/or Turmoil or Questions of a Practical and/or Theoretical Nature Were Frequently Raised—and a Solution Suggested

The list of problems in Table 5 is neither all-inclusive nor mutually exclusive, but is highly representative of the problems posed in the sample programs. If, in the course of the five-minute unit of analysis, an issue was presented as both a topic and a problem, it was coded as both and included in both this analysis and the earlier analysis of topics. Some of the included items are always problems by definition—health problems, psychological problems—while others might be discussed in some contexts as a general topic and in others as a problem requiring a solution. The proposed solutions to these problems were coded into the categories of God or Jesus, watching the program, making a financial donation to the church, human means, a combination of God and human means, or no solution offered.

Table 5 reveals that health-related issues are the most prevalent problems, followed by religious and psychological problems and problems associated with a physical handicap. God or Jesus is the most often mentioned solution to problems, followed by human means. God or Jesus is much more likely than human means to be mentioned as a solution to physical handicaps and to psychological, health, substance abuse (alcohol, drugs, tobacco), and religious problems. Man is most likely to be the proposed solution to problems associated with abortion and money matters.

A comparison with the social topics in Table 1 shows that some issues were not always discussed as problems. For example, pornography was

Table 5

Frequency of problems by types of solutions proposed

	None given	God	TV	Money	Man	Man and God	Other	Total
Health problem	45	61	—	—	23	—	4	133
Handicap	15	49	—	—	6	—	1	71
Alcohol problem	19	18	—	—	7	—	—	44
Tobacco use	1	5	—	—	2	—	—	8
Drug problem	24	21	—	1	8	—	—	54
Sexual problem	6	2	—	—	2	—	—	10
Abortion	4	3	—	—	13	—	—	20
Pornography	3	1	—	—	1	—	—	5
Divorce	9	3	—	—	—	—	—	12
Psychological problem	20	38	5	—	16	5	—	84
Family violence	4	—	—	2	1	1	—	8
Suicide	6	7	—	—	2	1	—	16
Financial problem	12	10	—	—	25	—	—	47
Unemployment	9	3	—	1	4	1	—	18
Religious problem	11	47	2	1	26	2	2	91
War	9	3	—	—	3	—	—	15
Racial/ethnic conflicts	1	2	—	—	6	—	—	9
Other	18	18	2	—	42	5	2	87
Total n	216	291	9	5	187	15	9	732
Total %	29.5	39.8	1.2	0.6	25.5	1.5	1.2	100

discussed 7 times, 5 of them as a problem; divorce was discussed 20 times but was considered a problem only 12 of these times; sexual behavior was a topic 28 times and a problem 10 times; family violence was a topic 12 times and a problem 8 times; abortion was discussed 26 times and was considered to be a problem 20 times. Thus, some controversial issues are not always overtly presented as "social ills" in need of change or solution.

The Frequency with Which the Programs Appeal for Money Was Explored by Examining (a) the Types and Cost of Religious Items Offered for Purchase and (b) the Frequency with Which Donations Are Requested, the Amount of Money Requested, and Statements Regarding the Purpose of the Requests

The types and cost of various items offered for sale during the programs in our sample were assessed. Items were divided into the categories of Bibles, other books and pamphlets, display items (e.g., buttons), magazines and newsletters, and tapes and/or records. Only those requests specifying a dollar amount (79 percent) have been included in the average dollar values reported.

Within the 81 episodes of our sample, there are 59 offers of materials for purchase. Nearly half (46 percent) of these advertisements offer the Bible and other books. When a specific amount of money is requested for the purchase of a Bible, the average is $191.91. The average cost of "other" books is $139.69. Other items present a wide range of purchase prices: display items cost an average of $148.57 each; the average price for religious records and/or tapes is $31.08; and subscriptions to magazines or newsletters cost an average of $2.00 each.

Only eight of the fourteen televangelists in the sample programs offered items for purchase.[5] Jerry Falwell offered the greatest variety of items, including Bibles, books, display items, magazines, and tapes/records. The cost of these items, averaged collectively across the three sample episodes, was $1,671.00 per hour.

All in all, during the average five-minute interval of religious programming, $8.95 is explicitly requested in return for offers of books and other materials. In our entire sample, $6,123.17 was asked for in offers of materials.

Programs often request funds without offering any tangible products in return. Excluding appeals for funds that did not specify an amount, this type of appeal still constitutes 65 percent of all appeals for money. The purposes stated for the appeals can be categorized as: purchasing air time, paying production/distribution costs, spreading the gospel/evangelizing, helping the needy, supporting a specific building project, supplying educational activities, helping the sick, and "other."

Within the 81 episodes of our sample, there are 38 explicit appeals for specific amounts of money for various causes. Approximately 42 percent of these requests indicate that the funds will go toward educational activities. The average request is for $173.93.

Although they are relatively infrequent, appeals for funds to keep a program on the air request the most amount of money, averaging $233.00 per request. The average request for production/distribution costs, on the other hand, is $35.00.

Building projects are the justification for requests averaging $138.33; requests to help those who spread the gospel average $30.00; requests for helping the needy average $15.00; and requests for helping the sick average $127.50.

Only six of the fourteen televangelists in the sample made explicit appeals for contributions to their particular ministry. They include, in hierarchical order of the amount of money requested, Jerry Falwell, Jack Van Impe, Oral Roberts, Jimmy Swaggert, Robert Schuller, and Fred Gottier. The primary justifications offered were educational activities (57 per-

Table 6

Explicit requests for money by program type, per hour and per episode

	Average request in sales		*Average request in donations*		*Total request for money*	
	per hour	*per episode*	*per hour*	*per episode*	*per hour*	*per episode*
Preaching/revival	$182.16	$130.07	$138.62	$98.98	$320.78	$229.05
Talk	26.44	21.05	87.20	69.44	113.64	90.49
Drama	0.00	0.00	0.00	0.00	0.00	0.00
Music/variety	22.56	18.62	68.08	56.19	90.64	74.81
Magazine	22.28	21.67	30.00	29.17	52.28	50.84
All shows	107.42	75.59	82.10	57.78	189.52	133.37

cent), buying air time (24 percent), and building projects (10 percent). Less than one percent of all solicitations were to go specifically toward spreading the gospel.

In total, during the average five-minute interval of religious programming, $6.84 is explicitly requested for church projects. In our entire sample, $4,679.93 was requested in contributions. Considering requests for donations *and* offers for products, an average hour of religious programming includes requests for $189.52 (see Table 6).

Table 6 also offers a breakdown of requests for money per hour and per episode, by program type. Overall, preaching/revival programs request the most money per hour, with talk shows a distant second. Religious dramas make no financial requests. Both music/variety and magazine programs request more per hour in donations than they do in the offering of products for sale. On a per episode basis, preaching/revival programs again request the most money, the majority from offers of products. Most of the requests per episode on talk shows are for donations.

While a fee is usually requested for an item, free items are also offered. On the average, 1.0 free items are offered per episode (1.4 per hour).

Our Data Suggest that the Popular Criticism Regarding the Presence of Overt Political Activism in Religious Programming Is Relatively Unfounded

The collective and overriding theme of the majority of these programs is, indeed, religion. The only exceptions to this pattern were religious dramas and magazine-type programs, where social themes predominate. Religious topics receive the lion's share of discussion within the programs. Political topics receive little discussion, and only two percent of all program content has an overriding political emphasis.

However, social issues are rather prevalent in religious programming.

Approximately 23 percent of program content has a social theme, with more explicit references to proper names within a social realm than to either political or religious persons and groups. More often than not, however, social topics are dealt with in a neutral manner.

Political topics, on the other hand, are often not presented neutrally; when this is the case, there tends to be a conservative, yet antiwar, viewpoint. The criticism that religious television programming promotes conservatism and aggression (9) is only partially supported by our findings, while Hadden and Swann's (6) suggestion that not all religious programming is conservative and not all conservative programs are political is borne out.

One of our most interesting findings, given the fact that mass media are common targets of political and social leaders, is that mass media are quite frequently discussed—and approved of—in these programs. This may reflect less a view generally held in religious circles than the media dependence of the "electronic church." In particular, television is a major source of revenue for many of the televangelists and thus is more likely to be praised than condemned. After all, television is the medium through which solicitations amount to an average of $189.52 per hour. If the average viewer watches only two hours of religious fare each week, as has been suggested is the case by survey data (4), he or she will be solicited for an average of $19,710.08 in the course of a year. This figure will of course vary according to the type of religious programming viewed, with viewers of dramatic programs the least likely to be the target of appeals for money and viewers of preaching/revival programs exposed to requests for an average of $33,361.12 per year. Considering that in 1980 the top four programs collectively took in over a quarter of a billion dollars (6) and that, in 1982, the Jimmy Swaggart Ministry alone collected over $60 million (3), these solicitations appear to be highly effective as well as pervasive.

It is not within the scope of our investigation to suggest the possible impact on viewers of the content analyzed in these sample programs. However, if religious programming is as successful in influencing social, political, and religious beliefs as it is in gathering contributions from its viewership, then many of Norman Lear's and Martin Marty's concerns regarding religious television's persuasiveness and usurpation of the living congregation are worth consideration.

NOTES

[1] Information regarding the sample cities employed in this investigation can be obtained from the authors.

[2] Information regarding the sample programs, including a demographic profile of their viewership, can be obtained from the authors. An index of availability was employed to gather the sample programs rather than ratings information, because the cost of national ratings figures was prohibitive.

³ "Real to Reel," produced and distributed by Unda-USA, was included in our sample although it was not one of the "top" programs."

⁴ The Religion in Broadcasting (RIB) Project at Cleveland State University conducted content analyses in the following areas: (a) a demographic profile of individuals appearing in the programs; (b) an analysis of the political, social, and religious themes and topics explored in each program; (c) an interaction analysis of verbal exchanges between individuals appearing in the programs; (d) an analysis of the communicative style of individuals engaging in sermons and other monologues; and (e) a measure of the amount, type and direction (i.e., male to female) of physical contact among individuals in the programs. Only the second analysis is reported here. A summary of research findings from each analysis appears in Abelman (1).

⁵ For a more extensive review of the quantity of requests for contributions by televangelists, see Abelman and Neuendorf (2).

REFERENCES

1. Abelman, R. "Ten Commandments of the 'Electronic Church.'" *Channels* 4(5), 1985.

2. Abelman, R. and K. Neuendorf. "The Price of Piety in the 'Electronic Church.'" Unpublished manuscript, Department of Communication, Cleveland State University, 1984.

3. *Frontline: Give Me That Big Time Religion.* Public Broadcasting Service program, telecast June 1984.

4. Gerbner, G., L. Gross, S. Hoover, M. Morgan, and N. Signorielli. "Religion and Television: A Summary." Paper presented at the International Communication Association Conference, San Francisco, 1984.

5. Graham, B. "The Future of TV Evangelism." *TV Guide* 31, no. 10 (1983):4-8.

6. Hadden, J. and C. Swann. *Prime Time Preachers.* Reading, Mass.: Addison-Wesley, 1981.

7. Hemphill, P. "Praise the Lord—and Cue the Cameraman." In *Television Today: Readings From TV Guide,* edited by B. Cole. New York: Oxford University Press, 1981.

8. Littell, J.F. Ed. *Coping with the Mass Media.* Evanston, Ill.: McDougal, Littell, 1976.

9. O'Brien-Steinfels, M. and P. Steinfels. "The New Awakening: Getting Religion in the Video Age." *Channels* 2, no. 5 (1983): 24-62.

Study Questions: Amdur

[?] *Why does television carry so many sporting events? What do you suppose are the demographics of people who watch or listen to a lot of broadcast sports? How do you know?*

How have professional and college sports changed because of television? Have those changes hurt or improved sports for those who attend live events? For the athletes involved?

> *What does Jennings Bryant mean when he says that the television sports audience sees a "packaged reality"? Should that concern anyone else?*
>
> *What problems does Amdur claim television has created for sports? What benefits has it created? Are there ways we might keep television's benefits for sports while reducing or eliminating its negative effects? If so, how?*
>
> *Are there some societal advantages to a major "shared experience" among Americans, such as the Olympic telecasts discussed by the president of ABC Sports? What does he mean by a "shared experience" in this context?*
>
> *How do you explain why some sports—such as football, tennis, basketball, and golf—have become so popular on American television, while others— such as soccer, racketball, and volleyball—have not?*
>
> *Do you think there is a connection between any of the problems of college sports (for example, illegal recruiting, snap courses without educational benefits, altered transcripts) and the large amounts of money involved in television coverage of college sports?*

Neil Amdur

THE CHANGING FACE OF SPORTS

The television dollars foster new perceptions

The sports and business officials from South Korea listened intently to the presentation from the American cable television executives—$750 million for the exclusive American rights to the 1988 Summer Olympics was a realistic figure to expect from a network, they were told.

They were also told that a pay television package, offering 19 straight days and 24 hours of Olympic activity for $200 a household, might generate as much as $1.8 billion just from the United States for the South Koreans.

No decision has been reached on how the Seoul Olympics will be sold or packaged, but there is no doubt that the final figures will be large and that television, as never before, is the most powerful force in sports. In addition to bankrolling established leagues and sports organizations and new ventures such as the United States Football League, which will play its first games in the spring, television has altered the texture, perceptions and images of American athletics.

Last Saturday, with just five days notice, the University of Houston shifted the starting time of its homecoming football game with Arkansas from 7 P.M. to 11:30 A.M. local time for a national television appearance. Traditional campus homecoming activities, such as parades, barbecues and alumni meetings had to be hastily rescheduled, but Houston and Arkansas received $140,000 each from CBS, and the other seven schools in the Southwest Conference divided an additional $340,000 from the appearance.

"I don't know a single university that would have resisted the $140,000," said Dr. Garth Jowett, the director of the school of communications at Houston. "Maybe Harvard and Yale, but then they wouldn't have gotten $140,000."

Thirty years ago, posting inning-by-inning scores of afternoon World Series games in the windows of barber shops, gas stations and bars was as much a ritual as the office pool and radio play-by-play of the games. In this year's World Series between the Milwaukee Brewers and the St. Louis Cardinals, five of the seven games were played after most Americans had left the office, during prime-time television hours that competed for viewer attention with movies, situation comedies and entertainment specials.

The current deadlock between the owners and players in pro football is entwined with television's ever-growing financial roots in the sport.

"Television has been a blessing for the owners and players in that they prospered from it," said Pete Rozelle, the commissioner of the strike-troubled National Football League. Mr. Rozelle successfully negotiated a five-year, $2.1 billion contract with the three commercial television networks last winter. "But it can be a mixed blessing, too," Mr. Rozelle said, "because it's partially responsible for the problem we have now."

On sheer numbers alone, televised sports have grown significantly. Since 1972, NBC's program allotment to sports has increased 42 percent; last year, the network programmed 468 hours of sports. According to research statistics from the A.C. Nielsen Company, the three commercial networks programmed 1,303 hours of sports in 1981, up from 1,075 in 1975. Not included in last year's figures were the continuous hours of programming on ESPN, the 24-hour all-sports cable network; other cable channels, and local independent stations that have contracts with professional teams.

This year, Home Box Office, a cable service, televised almost as many same-day hours of Wimbledon and the United States Open tennis championships as NBC and CBS. Golf tournaments have raised additional funds and expanded their coverage by selling the first two days of their events to cable or subscription services and holding the last two days for networks.

LESSER-KNOWN SPORTS SHOWN, TOO

"Television is now bringing to the American public an ever-increasing diversity of sports programming," said Representative Timothy E. Wirth, Democrat of Colorado, who as chairman of the House telecommunications subcommittee has conducted various hearings into the financial and social consequences of sports on television. "With a development of specialized cable TV services, such as ESPN, sports on television no longer means just baseball and football but now means less widely known sports such as karate and fencing as well."

What the viewer actually sees, however, according to Dr. Jennings Bryant, is "packaged reality." Dr. Bryant, who is the chairman of the communications department at the University of Evansville in Indiana, says "packaged reality is not the reality of the stadium or arena. It's what the producer and director, by their shot selection and pictures and the addition of commentary, create. It's a sports entertainment event rather than a sports event."

Several studies by Dr. Bryant and Dolf Zillman, the director of the Institute for Communications Research at Indiana University, have confirmed the visual and auditory impact television can have.

In one study, published earlier this year in the *Journal of Communication,* a group of about one hundred college students listened to dubbed commentary of a routine tennis match between two veteran players, Torben Ulrich and Sven Davidson.

The students were asked to watch as they normally would. Then they were asked to evaluate the event by reporting their feelings about the match in terms of how they enjoyed it and how intense the competition was. One third of the group listened to the commentary in which the players were reported to be good friends; one third heard commentary describing the players as bitter enemies; a third group heard commentary in which the relationship between the two players was not specified.

The results of the study, Dr. Bryant wrote, showed that viewers who perceived the competitors as hostile found the telecast more interesting, exciting and enjoyable.

"Although the play was unaltered," Dr. Bryant said, during a recent interview, "altering the commentary was sufficient to alter fans' perception of the event."

"The more you integrate drama and the more you attribute personal rivalry to two sides," says Elihu Katz, a professor of sociology and communications at the University of Southern California, "the more involvement you get from the viewer."

In a recently completed study, Dr. Bryant compared the descriptive, dramatic and humorous commentary during six randomly selected NFL telecasts on the three networks from the 1976 season with six games from last season. The conclusion: descriptive commentary had decreased slightly and dramatic commentary had increased thirty percent, with a clear trend toward more "player-versus-player conflict."

"Viewers' expectations of sporting events have changed because of television," Dr. Bryant said. "Because TV has to rely on dramatic elements that often have to do with high risk, giving all and violence, the event on television is different from what is unfolding on the field."

Edwin Diamond, the director of the New Study Group in the department of political science at Massachusetts Institute of Technology, points to the switch to more attractive, tighter-fitting uniforms, the liberalizing of rules in many sports and the focusing on Olga Korbut and Nadia Comaneci in Olympic gymnastics, a relatively obscure sport, as further examples of television's ability to rearrange reality.

In the pre-television days, football used to be a compact, dense game of three yards and a cloud of dust," Mr. Diamond said. "Now the game has been opened up to meet the interests of television—to make it more visual so the guy at home can follow it easier. It's become a highly visual game. The changes in costumes and rules came, I'm convinced, to meet the needs of television."

TV BECOMES SPORTS PARTICIPANT

The proliferation of sports has also changed the way television has done its job. In pursuit of technical innovations, networks have recruited the Goodyear blimp, installed television cameras in stock cars and used wireless microphones on football and basketball coaches, runners and outriders at thoroughbred race tracks. Refinements in editing, replays from a variety of camera positions, slick graphics and lighter, more mobile cameras have resulted in additional technical improvements. "For many people, watching Dr. J flying through the air for a dunk is not as exciting as watching the rerun of the dunk," said Dr. John Ledingham, an associate professor at the University of Houston, who was referring to Julius Erving, the Philadelphia 76ers forward. "And the athletes have caught on to the theory that they're show-business people."

The public's fascination with replays is one reason why many arenas and stadiums have installed large scoreboards equipped with slow-motion and rerun capabilities.

"It clearly produces a different kind of expectancy in the event itself for the viewer," said Dr. Bryant. "The spectator who goes to the stadium now may not find it as thrilling because the production is less satisfying than television."

Mr. Diamond says many "urbane, sophisticated" viewers willingly arrange their eating, sleeping and social schedules around major televised events such as the World Series, the Super Bowl or a heavyweight fight. Tennis fans have gotten up at 9 A.M. on the East Coast in recent years (earlier in other sections of the country) for NBC's live telecast of the men's singles final at Wimbledon. Last year, a major international mile race was run at 11:15 P.M. in Oslo to accommodate Saturday afternoon television in the United States.

Television's reluctance to embrace the World Hockey Association, American Basketball Association, World Football League and World Team Tennis was the primary factor behind the collapse of those leagues. In an October 1980 survey that preceded the formation of the United States Football League, Frank N. Magid Associates, a survey research firm, concluded that the single most important finding in its study was that 71.3 percent of the 600 respondents who were contacted and identified themselves as pro football fans had said that they "would watch" USFL games on television from March to July.

According to league sources, a number of prospective owners declined to commit until they were assured that the league had firmed up an agreement with ABC. The decision to hire Chet Simmons as its first commissioner underscored the USFL's ties to television. Mr. Simmons served as president of NBC Sports and president of ESPN, in addition to having guided ABC in its original coverage of the American Football League.

"A lot of sports exist because of television," said Mr. Simmons, who already has an ESPN contract for the USFL in addition to the lucrative ABC deal. "Before the 1972 Olympics, gymnastics was an obscure sport in the United States where kids tumbled on mats in high-school gyms. Now, you look at the sports anthology shows on the three networks, and you've got gymnastics events on almost every week."

Roone Arledge, the president of ABC News and also ABC Sports, says the success of the Olympics as a television event is due to the "shared experience" among American viewers. "It's like a whole nation sitting down to read a book together," said Mr. Arledge, whose network paid $225 million for the rights to the 1984 Los Angeles Olympics. In 1968, the rights for the Mexico City Games went for $4.5 million.

Mr. Arledge says "exclusivity" and the ability to "mass-market" is what has expanded television's horizons. Simply tying up the television rights to a specific sports event heightens its appeal.

No vehicle better dramatizes the rearranging of reality and the marriage among television, sports and the viewer than "Monday Night Football." It was initiated by ABC in 1970, after CBS and NBC, secure with their prime-time programming, rejected the idea as too speculative. Many ABC affiliate stations also opposed the idea, fearing that the network might drop college football.

"It was a gamble on ABC's part," Mr. Arledge said. "I scared them into it. I showed them what would happen if they didn't take the package. The NFL would have gone with an independent network, and ABC could have lost 100 stations."

The first Monday night telecast on September 21, 1970, which featured the Cleveland Browns against the Joe Namath-led New York Jets, drew a respectable 19.4 rating and 34 percent share of audience.

For the tired office worker finishing his first day of the work week, the bright lights of a stadium bouncing off football helmets became a social retreat, fueled by diverse, sometimes controversial commentary and neatly edited halftime highlights of Sunday games that occurred thousands of miles apart. Instead of becoming an afterthought to the weekend, "Monday Night Football" created its own showcase, ate into the entertainment shares of movies, restaurants and theater and ultimately spun off prime-time pro football telecasts on other nights such as Thursday.

Last year, in its twelfth season, the series enjoyed record ratings. The first Monday night game of this fall—Dallas versus Pittsburgh—was the highest-rated Monday night season opener ever.

"Monday Night Football" helped expand the NFL's viewing audience. A national telephone study conducted for NFL Properties in 1980 by the Pacific Select Corporation, a San Francisco-based sports marketing and consultant firm, revealed that women made up 38 percent of pro football's television audience.

INDOOR SOCCER AND KICK-BOXING

Matt Levin, who founded Pacific Select in 1971, sees new sports such as indoor soccer and kick-boxing as entertainment extensions of the television influence. The fragmentation of dollars into regional cable markets has spawned successful regional sports enterprises. "There's an insatiable hunger for sports programming in regional markets," said Levin. "And we are still in the growth phase of this production and programming."

"What I see happening in the eighties is a much greater fragmentation of sports on television and a specialization of audiences, in much the same way as what happened to magazines," said Dr. Michael Real, professor of telecommunications and film at San Diego State University. "With magazines, you had some of the general-interest national magazines suffer, but the specialty magazines continue to do well. I live in Del Mar, California, and I can see the Chicago Cubs now more often than as a kid in Chicago because WGN carries them, and WGN is picked up on cable. So I can remain a Cub fan, even living on the West Coast."

Bob Wussler, a former president of the CBS television network and the former president of CBS Sports, who is now executive vice president of Turner Broadcasting Systems Inc., said survey operators see the eighties as a "decade of stay-at-homes," with television and its various forms playing the major part in sports.

"Ultimately," Mr. Wussler said, "we're heading for a situation where most professional sports will be available for some form of pay television from 50 to 75 miles of the stadium. This will have to affect the future of sports and televised sports."

In looking toward the future, "Cablesports" reported: "Because interest in teams and sports tends to be heavily regionalized, except for football, many sports lend themselves more to regional television than to network television . . . Cable and over-the-air subscription television have significant opportunities to tap this highly developed, regional interest in the eighties. To do so will take ingenuity, entrepreneurial leadership and some moderately deep financial pockets."

Section 8

MEDIA AS SHAPERS OF THE FUTURE

Fromm the specifity of effects on behavior in Section 6, we took a step backward in Section 7 to get a longer view of media effects. In this section, we take a step forward as we attempt to peer into the murky mists of our media future. From this new vantage point, not only may we gain a glimpse or two at the future of media and their potential impact, we should also get a clearer view of the past.

Erik Barnouw's 1976 forecast of a world revolutionized by communications technologies is useful to study, despite its being no closer to realization today than it was in 1976. He provides a historical perspective for the key social issues of technological change and clarifies the human problems associated with such change. A major question he raises is whether technology developers should be responsible for the social implications of their inventions or whether such problems should be left to the "software people." Another important question for you to consider is whether Barnouw's forecasts are wrong or merely premature.

Marshall McLuhan had an answer for such questions. That answer is the main theme of the first chapter of his *Understanding Media,* which we have excerpted. McLuhan claims the medium itself is the message, implying that even inventors need a social conscience. Another idea McLuhan popularized is that media are extensions of the human senses. This idea underscores the related notion that media themselves have meaning and significance; in other words technologies have social impact independent of the particular content they carry.

One suggestion before you attack McLuhan: read him as you read a poem. Don't always take him literally. Consider much of what he says as a series of metaphors, and think of all the interesting and useful ways you can interpret them. In short, use McLuhan as a stimulus for your own thinking about mass media, not simply as a source of information that you merely must understand. In a sense, we do this when we read or hear anything; we must construct meanings from the words and visual images we get from any author. With McLuhan, our creative role in the construction of meanings simply may be more obvious because the stimuli we get from him are so unusual.

Gail Pool provides a concrete illustration of how technological development in one medium can impact another. She describes attempts by magazine publishers to learn from history so as not to repeat it. The communications revolution brought on by television happened largely without participation by the magazine industry. In cable television, magazine publishers now see a way to secure some of the medium's advertising potential for themselves. Their optimism is based upon the cultivation of specialized audiences (magazines' traditionally successful approach) for cable television shows. As magazines position their shows between the mass appeal of broadcast television and the narrowly specialized magazine, Pool predicts we will see an increase in magazine-style programs.

Leslie Woodhead, a British television producer, gained the perspective he needed to peer into the future of European television by making a documentary series on the history of world television. In his essay, he worries about the dominance of American programs in the world television market; and—as the BBC contemplates experimentation with advertising— he worries about deteriorating program quality. Woodhead sees his own future, as it were, in the American "deregulated, satellite-interconnected" present. Acknowledging the genius of some American programs, he worries nonetheless that competition for advertising dollars necessarily lowers the quality of most programs.

One of *The Village Voice*'s film critics, J. Hoberman, sees tendencies in many recent popular movies that may foretell a much more menacing future. According to Hoberman, stereotypical portrayals of the enemy, the hero, and of America result in Hollywood films that are "transparently fascist" in inspiration or in effect. These motion pictures, then, not only entertain us, but also interpret us to ourselves—bringing out the darker sides of our psyches—and, perhaps, painting a picture of our possible future. This is a future in which America becomes more chauvinistic, more antagonistic, with more of an "us against the world" mentality. It is this set of characteristics that Hoberman labels "fascist."

The collection ends with a more positive vision of our communication future: L. S. Harms's account of the evolution of communication orders from preconversation to conversation, literacy, mass media, and a "new communication order." He analyzes each order's assumptions about communication's role in society, asserting that there can be too much communication for human good, as well as too little. Harms describes a future driven by the assumptions of the new order. He envisions a horizontally structured communication arrangement. It is in contrast to today's vertically oriented structure, which enables only a few people to speak to the many. He lays out a communication bill of rights, suggestive of the policy implications of the new order.

From our vantage point in the midst of the mass communication order, the world Harms describes is difficult to imagine. That task of imagination may be less difficult, though, if we examine history and note especially the many ideas and assumptions that we take for granted today that once seemed outrageous or unrealistic. Such an idea as standard time zones was deemed an impractical dream in the nineteenth century. Today, it is simply an "ordinary idea," part of our world that we just take for granted. It masquerades as "common sense" so that we will not question its assumptions; it is part of our "world view" or "ideology." We need ideology much as we need one of its components, the stereotype. We have to make assumptions about the world as a basis for action. If we never stopped asking, "Is the ground I see really solid?" we would never take a step. Just as we need to interrogate, or question, our stereotypes to reveal their hidden assumptions (as we discussed in Section 5), we also need to ask questions that force ideological assumptions into the open.

Once, people "knew" the earth was flat. The ideology of the earth's flatness kept people from venturing too far from home, kept them ignorant of vast amounts of information, and kept them fearful of the unknown. In the 1960s we "knew" that routine space travel, even interstellar travel, lay just ahead, for the Soviets if not for us. Now we can see that many practical and political problems stand between us and interstellar or inter-galactical travel; and we have learned that some of our assumptions about the integrity of our space program were erroneous. Studying history gives us the benefit of hindsight. From Christopher Columbus to Sally Ride, history also teaches that to challenge dominant assumptions takes enormous courage.

Authors such as Hoberman, as well as Kervin, Johnson, and Lewis from other sections, ask you to question dominant assumptions (the pre-vailing "common sense") about media. Some brave people, like Harms, have freed themselves of the ideology of mass media sufficiently to question openly the current system and to postulate a whole new system lying beyond it. Their visions are at once exciting and distressing. They present you with a choice: you can accept the media world as it "is," or you can join the ranks of those who are critical of the existing system and work for a new order. You can participate in shaping the future of your public commu-nication environment. This is so because once you know that it is possible to see beyond your culture's assumptions—to see beyond ideology—you are free.

Study Questions: Barnouw

> Are the social implications of new technologies identified by Barnouw in 1976 clearer now than they were then?
>
> Peter Goldmark, once the head of CBS Laboratories, predicted over a decade ago that the new communications technologies would be "democratizing," that they would lead to "unprecedented government-citizen dialogue." Has that happened? If so, how? If not, why not?
>
> As Barnouw points out, many of the great benefits of the new techologies predicted today also were predicted for television, radio, and the movies when they were new. Is the prediction more likely to come true today?

Why are the questions Barnouw raises about gatekeeping and privacy so crucial? What are the advantages for consumers of concentrated authority in this case? What are the advantages of dispersed control?

Barnouw quotes Ithiel de Sola Pool as indicating that it is bad that the same fads, the same scandals of the week, the same ball scores, and the same entertainments exist throughout the United States. Why is that bad? Are there any benefits to society when people have such common experiences? Does Pool predict that our new technologies will make people's experiences more similar or more different? Do you agree with him?

What advantages of two-way communication does Barnouw suggest? Do any means of two-way communication exist today? Are they producing those benefits?

Do you think the determination of how technologies should be adapted and used by and for people should be left to the software folks? Why or why not? Why do you think Barnouw refers to the hardware man *and the software* people?

Which developments Barnouw discusses have come about? Which ones have not? Identify as many reasons as you can that communications technology development has occurred more quickly on some fronts than on others.

What does the last sentence in the article mean?

Erik Barnouw

SO YOU THINK TV IS HOT STUFF? JUST YOU WAIT

Don't look now, but your television set is about to be replaced by something more up-to-date. As with many giant steps in technology, it will involve ideas that science-fiction people have been picturing for decades—in fact, for a century or so. Now, at last, in diverse laboratories and field tests, their visions are turning into practical hardware. The ingredients seem to be right at our hands.

Erik Barnouw, long-time professor of dramatic arts at Columbia, is now a Woodrow Wilson Scholar at the Smithsonian. He is author of *Tube of Plenty: The Evolution of American Television* (Oxford).

Your television set, your stereo, your telephone are really quite primitive—"tom-toms" compared to what is now possible and inevitable, according to Peter C. Goldmark, the far-sighted retired chief of CBS Laboratories, responsible for many electronic breakthroughs.

A factor behind the euphoria is a development relating to cable television. This system has long been able to deliver twenty channels or more—
a versatility impossible to over-the-air television—so far not at a sensational
profit. Now it is about to be expanded further, in a fashion: it may soon
offer a choice of hundreds of channels, along with another dramatic op-
tion—two-way communication, the chance to talk back.

The key to all this is a mysterious "optical fiber," now emerging from
the laboratory. This glass fiber looks like a thin violin string. Laser beams
can travel through it and—incredibly—carry innumerable streams of communication simultaneously in both directions. Combine this virtuosity with
various "miracles" already familiar to us—computers, satellites, cassettes,
facsimile transmission—and what do you have? A "telecommunications"
revolution, it would seem. What its social implications may be, is not clear.
To Goldmark, it will be a momentous "democratizing" development, involving an unprecedented government-citizen dialogue. Others see it as
opening a new era in education. Still others see it as a breakthrough for
minority interests of all sorts, offering them a diversity of special channels.

There are also less optimistic opinions, but problems of use, in the view
of most telecommunications technicians, are for later. They themselves are
developing the "hardware." "Software" problems can be settled in due time
by writers, teachers, performers, producers, graphic artists, musicians and
so on—the software people, as they are known in telecommunications language. (Software people don't seem to care for this term. In fact, hardware
and software people tend to be kept apart by their vocabularies. But let us
set this problem aside and see what the hardware people have in mind.)

It goes like this. In one wall of your room will be a telescreen. It will
be able to bring you a wide range of images and sounds and data, via push-
button controls. In the first place, you can summon up current events,
drama offerings, game shows, athletic contests—not unlike your current
television choices. But you may also decide to see a classic film which a
computerized switching system can call forth from an archive. Or you may
decide to take a university course, prepared and stored in an electronic
repository; each lesson, as and when you need it, can be summoned by
your push buttons. When ready, you can order the exam: question after
question will appear on your telescreen, to be answered by push button,
and the sequence will be climaxed by your grade, which will at once be
recorded somewhere in a data bank.

For intensive study you may want some information on paper rather
than on the screen. Pushing the right buttons, you can bring it spilling out
in the form of a "printout." Your income tax forms may reach you in the
same way—unless that primitive business is abolished for an entirely new

system, to be mentioned presently. Your daily newspapers may also reach you in this way.

Instead of conversing with a computer you may prefer to talk to a human being—your daughter in St. Louis, for example. There seems no reason why the telephone function, including sight, should not be incorporated in the telecommunications system. Thus you and your daughter will be able to speak to each other while each appears on the other's screen. For conference calls, split-screen arrangements can be used, so that face-to-face business conferences can involve representatives of widely scattered offices, even on several continents. Much business work can be done at home, with instructions, reports, and statistics transmitted electronically— via words or visual display or printout, or a combination of them. The insanity of rush-hour travel may gradually pass into history.

One of the most irrational of modern logjams, the postal system, may also yield to tomorrow's telecommunications. The telescreen engineer sees every home or office as a "terminal." The well-equipped terminal of the future will be able to send, as well as receive, official documents and letters.

It is assumed by most telecommunications futurists that some of the choices available via your push-button (digital) controls will be free—sponsored by advertisers or available as a government service—while others will involve payment. Tuning to an opera performance will probably involve a fee. For a university course you will likewise be charged something, corresponding to current tuition fees. The method of payment will probably be made as painless as possible. The act of tuning may simply deduct the fee electronically from your bank balance. Perhaps, as you tune, an appropriate WARNING will appear on your screen—like the highway phrase, LAST EXIT BEFORE TOLL.

One of the forces propelling telecommunications toward a new era is the computer. Data banks are already, of course, a reality for insurance firms, banks, law enforcement agencies, health agencies; access to such data banks is available over long distances via cable or microwave or satellite. A Milwaukee hospital, about to perform an emergency operation on a patient from Los Angeles, can get the patient's computer-stored medical history in seconds. A New Orleans newspaper, instead of trying to maintain its own massive newsclipping "morgue" on international events, can purchase access to *The New York Times* computerized morgue or information bank. An FBI agent investigating a case in Albuquerque can instantly check fingerprints and other data in Washington computers. One computer can feed its data to another. In telecommunications scenarios, computers are constantly talking to each other.

In all such communication transactions, the term long distance is losing much of its meaning. When television programs or documents or data are transmitted by satellite, 3,000 miles involve no greater difficulty than 300 miles. In phone calls of the future, with two-way video in color, distance may no longer be a cost factor.

Thus the ingredients of the revolution are with us: their wider use seems certain to affect home and office, business and pleasure, information and persuasion, student and teacher, citizen and government, in ways that may be startling. Optical glass fiber is based on cheap and plentiful silicon, whereas coaxial cables use scarce, expensive copper. The difference may hasten the wiring of communities throughout the world. What the scientist foresees is that the virtuosity of the fibers, combined with that of satellites and computers and electronic recorders, will tend to integrate various communication systems and purposes into an extraordinary multichannel, interactive communications world: communication of one to one, one to many, many to one, many to many.

CAN FUTURE HARDWARE NEEDS BE MET?

So confident are scientists of this development that intensive meetings have already been held to work out details, to anticipate what hardware may be needed. Meetings have been held in the United States under the auspices of the National Research Council, sponsored by a consortium of government departments—Commerce; Health, Education and Welfare; Housing and Urban Development; Transportation—with participation by representatives of the Federal Communications Commission, the U.S. Postal Service, and the White House Office of Telecommunications Policy. All feel that the impending communications revolution may radically alter the context of their work. And all to the revolution for answers to their increasingly pressing problems.

The scientists brought together in such meetings are from diverse fields, representing television, telephone, telegraph, aerospace, computer and other industries. They see their interests converging—but also clashing. Thus the emerging telecommunications visions involve a power struggle, which will be, in fact, a continuation of struggles almost as old as the Republic.

The wiring of the world really began with telegraphy. In the United States this invention was soon seen to offer, along with rich blessings, some dangers. "What hath God wrought?" Samuel Morse had asked, clicking the first intercity message. For a time the answer seemed to be: monopoly power.

By the 1870s Western Union, absorbing small companies, had a web of wires reaching 37 states and nine territories. As the only such system, it could charge monopoly rates, but its leadership found other—and more lucrative—keys to wealth and power. Representative Charles A. Sumner of California charged in 1875 that sudden changes in market prices were repeatedly withheld from San Francisco until insiders had made a killing. Control of the flow of information could yield bonanzas.

With the invention of the telephone by Alexander Graham Bell in 1876, the monopoly position of the telegraph began to suffer erosion: information acquired an alternative channel. Western Union tried to throttle the competition with patent litigation, but failed to do so.

By the 1900s AT&T (American Telephone and Telegraph) was so wealthy that it could, with one $30 million check, buy control of Western Union. But by this time the nation had learned something of the dangers of monopoly control, especially in communications, and the sale was halted by antitrust action. The two wire systems remained as competitive elements, along with another rival, Postal Telegraph. This was a private company, formed in 1882, having nothing to do with the postal system; it simply decided to call itself "postal" because the word had become an anti-monopoly rallying cry. The company became especially active in communications abroad, and these activities eventually metamorphosed into ITT (International Telephone and Telegraph Corporation).

EARLY INVENTIONS SHRINK THE WORLD

Meanwhile, still another information channel had made an appearance: wireless, which became radio, which gave birth to electronics, which in turn bred the computer. In the laboratory, Edison's electric lightbulb turned into the electronic vacuum tube, and this helped lightbulb manufacturers such as General Electric, Westinghouse, and Western Electric (an AT&T subsidiary) to assume gigantic stature in electronics and radio.

During World War I their assembly lines produced quantities of electronic war material. The war dramatized the unique abilities of radio as a communications instrument, and this led in 1919 to formation of RCA (the Radio Corporation of America)—in which General Electric, Westinghouse and AT&T became controlling partners. Again a dangerous communications monopoly seemed to be forming, but antitrust pressures eventually dissolved the partnership, and made RCA independent of its creators.

Although RCA was organized as an international message service, its energies were soon redirected by the eruption of the broadcasting mania, which between 1920 and 1922 brought more than 500 stations to the air in the United States.

For a short time, all broadcasting stations performed independently, producing their own programs—a clearly irrational arrangement. Stations could be linked into networks by the use of connecting wires. AT&T, Western Union and Postal Telegraph all vied for this interconnection role. AT&T won the struggle. With the formation of NBC in 1926 and of CBS in 1927, AT&T became their sole means of interconnection. Some observers thought this posed the danger of a new power concentration, but once again a new element was to alter the situation.

With the dawn of the space age after World War II, the communication satellite emerged as an alternative means of interconnecting radio and television stations, as well as cable television systems, computer networks and other such systems. This brought the name Western Union back into the interconnection sweepstakes: by 1976 the Public Broadcasting Service was contracting with Western Union International for satellite interconnection to replace or supplement AT&T cables. And ITT had reentered the situation when it joined with RCA, AT&T and Western Union International in the formation of COMSAT (the Communications Satellite Corporation), to provide the world with international linkages.

All these, along with aerospace and computer interests, are behind the telecommunications visions in the laboratory, think tank and seminar. They are coplanners, but also rivals.

Who will be the gatekeepers of the evolving system? Will authority be dispersed, or concentrated? Will the multiplicity of channels provide a rich diversity of choice, or only seem to? Who will decide what treasures are to be stored in the electronic archives available to your push buttons? Our whole history teaches us that these are crucial questions. More recent history confronts us with still further questions. Will the right of privacy survive the telecommunications revolution and its network of data banks? For the moment such questions remain unanswered, and unanswerable. The current focus is on hardware miracles.

Meanwhile, dreams of things to come lure us on. They offer a heady mixture of possibilities. Ithiel de Sola Pool of the Massachusetts Institute of Technology points out that nowadays an average family, settling down for an evening, generally has three television network programs to choose from. This has been, he feels, "a powerful force toward conformity. Whereever one goes in the United States, the same fads, the same styles, the same scandal of the week, the same ball scores, the same entertainments are on people's lips." He feels that in contrast the emerging technology can then help to "individualize people rather than homogenize them."

He predicts: "Increasingly, communications devices will be adapted to individualized use by the consumer where and when he wants, on his own, without the cooperation of others; he will use machines as an extension of his own capabilities and personality, talking and listening worldwide, picking up whatever information he wants."

Pool apparently feels that Man himself will be changed by the emerging technology. "For the computer promises to make it possible to interrogate and inanimate data base with the same ease and success with which we now ask questions of a friend or colleague. . . ." He sums up: "A picture begins to emerge of a society ever more individualized in its interests and tastes."

The added factor of two-way "interactive" communication seems invaluable to Pool, as to others. Replacing an era in which "the citizen hears but is not heard," they see an era of citizen feedback. The economist Harold J. Barnett feels this factor will be especially important to local politics, restoring the "community ethos" which mass-audience television has helped to undermine. The factor is also considered important in "telemedicine," a subject of endless futuristic scenarios. These picture the physician examining and interviewing remote patients via telecommunications. A patient need not be brought to the electrocardiograph: the telecommunications system can provide the link.

The two-way factor will also be important in the use of special shoppers' channels. The buyer at home will be able to survey available merchandise, then place orders and authorize payments.

The possible impact of telecommunications on finance is particularly intriguing. The financial world is drowned in waves of paper—currency, checks, stocks, bonds, bills, orders, accounts—that flow endlessly from office to office via messenger or the postal system. That all this is obsolete is being shown by computer networks. "Computers and wire," writes Barnett, "are moving us to a cashless society." Payments will flow over the telecommunications system. In the computerized financial world, taxation may even be simplified by diverting to the government small fractions of all individualized transactions.

In the magazine *Science,* Edwin B. Parker and Donald A. Dunn describe the system of the future as a "combined library, newspaper, mail-order catalog, post office, classroom, and theater." It will resemble current television, yet change it radically. "Broadcast television is like the passenger railroad, taking people to scheduled places at scheduled times." Tomorrow's wired system is expected to be "like a highway network, permitting people to use their television sets in the way they use their personal automobiles; they may be able to select information, education, and entertainment at times and places of their own choosing." This will presumably foster "equal social opportunity in the United States."

We should recognize that new technology readily evokes rosy expectations. Possible blessings are more easily glimpsed than problems, and are more gratifying to contemplate. As we have seen, visions of the wired world have been with us ever since the invention of the telephone. As early as 1882, an artist pictured a woman shopping via television, and another taking a course via television. In the early 1900s, the motion picture was expected to have many of the same effects predicted for telecommunications—wide dispersal of knowledge, equalization of opportunity, strengthening of democracy and of international understanding. Broadcasting, at the very hour of its birth, was expected to have similar effects. The first issue of *Radio Broadcast,* launched early in 1922, predicted that broadcasting would

> . . . elicit a new national loyalty and produce a more contented citizenry. . . .
> . . . the government will be a living thing to its citizens instead of an abstract and unseen force. . . .
> . . . at last we may have covenants literally openly arrived at. . . .

. . . elected representatives will not be able to evade their responsibility to those constituents who put them in office. . . .

. . . the people's University of the Air will have a greater student body than all the rest of our universities put together. . . .

That same year a former Secretary of the Navy, Josephus Daniels, joined in the sanguine predictions: "Nobody now fears that a Japanese fleet could deal an unexpected blow on our Pacific possessions. . . . Radio makes surprises impossible." Magazine articles of the day featured such titles as "How Radio is Remaking the World" and "Radio, the Modern Peace Dove" and "Ether Waves vs. Crime Waves."

TELECOMMUNICATION MAY IMPROVE OUR LIVES

Were they wrong, or are some of these predictions only premature and about to come true in a new "telecommunications" phase of the electronic epoch?

In the already large and growing literature on the wired world of tomorrow, a persistent theme relates to transportation. For it is expected that "message movement" will eventually replace much "people movement"—thus relieving our glutted transportation system, easing problems of the use of energy and improving the quality of our air.

Again and again we are told that the "symbolic interchange" offered by telecommunications can and must replace a large percentage "of the physical encounters now serviced by physical travel." We will become telecommuters, teleshoppers and televoters. In the view of Dr. Gerhard J. Hanneman of the Annenberg School of Communication, University of Southern California, all this can lead to a more rational distribution of the population and ease the current pollution crisis.

But what will all those people be doing—those human beings who no longer need to stir from home, who will save endless hours of mass transport and be blessed with leisure? What will they do with their lives? What will their lives mean to them?

At this point, the hardware man invokes the software people. *They* are to enrich the citizen's life with a vast assortment of video services and packages: entertainment, education, art, culture. But the software man tends to be baffled by the assignment.

It seems to software people that the hardware specialist loves smoothly functioning equipment but does not love people, who are messy and disorganized. Why else would he devise these scenarios which always seem to eliminate people—or at least keep them out of the way, at home?

The root of all art is the fantasizing characteristic of human beings, by which they cope with the pressures and perplexities of their lives. Art serves the artist—and the audience, when art succeeds—as interpretation, clarification, redemption. What pressures will haunt the telecommunications viewer of tomorrow? What fantasies from the studios of software will fruitfully engage his attention, ease his tensions, keep him content before the telescreen and push buttons? The hardware emerging from our laboratories is truly miraculous. Designing the software may prove to be far more difficult.

Will there perhaps be a special channel for "appoved revolutionary activities"?

Study Questions: McLuhan

[?] *Does Marshall McLuhan agree with the one-time head of NBC and RCA, David Sarnoff, that "the products of modern science are not in themselves good or bad; it is the way they are used that determines their value"? If not, do you agree with Sarnoff or McLuhan? Why?*

McLuhan coined many interesting aphorisms. What do you think each of the following ones might mean? Do not assume that there are right or wrong interpretations. Simply see how many interesting and useful interpretations you can conceive.

- *The medium is the message.*
- *The content of any medium is always another medium.*
- *The greatest of all reversals occurred with electricity, that ended sequence by making things instant.*
- *The American stake in literacy as a technology or uniformity applied to every level of education, government, industry, and social life is totally threatened by the electric technology.*
- *The effects of technology do not occur at the level of opinions or concepts: . . . [the major effect is to] alter sense ratios or patterns of perception steadily and without any resistance.*
- *We become what we behold.*
- *Print created individualism and nationalism in the sixteenth century.*

What are the major questions about the structure, functions, or impact of the mass media that McLuhan's conception of mass communication—or your interpretation of his conception—raises?

Has McLuhan caused you to think about mass communication or the media in any different ways than you did before?

How does his view of mass communication affect debates over the impact of media violence and pornography?

Give an example, from your own experience, of a communication medium whose impact is independent of its content.

What theory or theories of the individual and of the society seem(s) to underlie McLuhan's way of thinking about mass media?

Marshall McLuhan

THE MEDIUM IS THE MESSAGE

In a culture like ours, long accustomed to splitting and dividing all things as a means of control, it is sometimes a bit of a shock to be reminded that, in operational and practical fact, the medium is the message. This is merely to say that the personal and social consequences of any medium—that is, of any extension of ourselves—result from the new scale that is introduced into our affairs by each extension of ourselves, or by any new technology. Thus, with automation, for example, the new patterns of human association tend to eliminate jobs, it is true. That is the negative result. Positively, automation creates roles for people, which is to say depth of involvement in their work and human association that our preceding mechanical technology had destroyed. Many people would be disposed to say that it was not the machine, but what one did with the machine, that was its meaning or message. In terms of the ways in which the machine altered our relations to one another and to ourselves, it mattered not in the least whether it turned out cornflakes or Cadillacs. The restructuring of human work and association was shaped by the technique of fragmentation that is the essence of machine technology. The essence of automation technology is the opposite. It is integral and decentralist in depth, just as the machine was fragmentary, centralist, and superficial in its patterning of human relationships.

The instance of the electric light may prove illuminating in this connection. The electric light is pure information. It is a medium without a message, as it were, unless it is used to spell out some verbal ad or name.

This fact, characteristic of all media, means that the "content" of any medium is always another medium. The content of writing is speech, just as the written word is the content of print, and print is the content of the telegraph. If it is asked, "What is the content of speech?" it is necessary to say, "It is an actual process of thought, which is in itself nonverbal." An abstract painting represents direct manifestation of creative thought processes as they might appear in computer designs. What we are considering here, however, are the psychic and social consequences of the designs or patterns as they amplify or accelerate existing processes. For the "message" of any medium or technology is the change of scale or pace or pattern that it introduces into human affairs. The railway did not introduce movement or transportation or wheel or road into human society, but it accelerated and enlarged the scale of previous human functions, creating totally new kinds of cities and new kinds of work and leisure. This happened whether the railway functioned in a tropical or a northern environment, and is quite independent of the freight or content of the railway medium. The airplane, on the other hand, by accelerating the rate of transportation, tends to dissolve the railway form of city, politics, and association, quite independently of what the airplane is used for.

Let us return to the electric light. Whether the light is being used for brain surgery or night baseball is a matter of indifference. It could be argued that these activities are in some way the "content" of the electric light, since they could not exist without the electric light. This fact merely underlines the point that "the medium is the message" because it is the medium that shapes and controls the scale and form of human association and action. The content or uses of such media are as diverse as they are ineffectual in shaping the form of human association. Indeed, it is only too typical that the "content" of any medium blinds us to the character of the medium. It is only today that industries have become aware of the various kinds of business in which they are engaged. When IBM discovered that it was not in the business of making office equipment or business machines, but that it was in the business of processing information, then it began to navigate with clear vision. The General Electric Company makes a considerable portion of its profits from electric light bulbs and lighting systems. It has not yet discovered that, quite as much as AT&T, it is in the business of moving information.

The electric light escapes attention as a communication medium just because it has no "content." And this makes it an invaluable instance of how people fail to study media at all. For it is not till the electric light is used to spell out some brand name that it is noticed as a medium. Then it is not the light but the "content" (or what is really another medium) that is noticed. The message of the electric light is like the message of electric power in industry, totally radical, pervasive, and decentralized. For electric light and power are separate from their uses, yet they eliminate time and space factors in human association exactly as do radio, telegraph, telephone, and TV, creating involvement in depth. . . .

In accepting an honorary degree from the University of Notre Dame a few years ago, General David Sarnoff made this statement: "We are too prone to make technological instruments the scapegoats for the sins of those who wield them. The products of modern science are not in themselves good or bad; it is the way they are used that determines their value." That is the voice of the current somnambulism. Suppose we were to say, "Apple pie is in itself neither good nor bad; it is the way it is used that determines its value." Or, "The smallpox virus is in itself neither good nor bad; it is the way it is used that determines its value." Again, "Firearms are in themselves neither good nor bad; it is the way they are used that determines their value." That is, if the slugs reach the right people firearms are good. If the TV tube fires the right ammunition at the right people it is good. I am not being perverse. There is simply nothing in the Sarnoff statement that will bear scrutiny, for it ignores the nature of the medium, of any and all media, in the true Narcissus style of one hypnotized by the amputation and extension of his own being in a new technical form. General Sarnoff went on to explain his attitude to the technology of print, saying that it was true that print caused much trash to circulate, but it had also disseminated the Bible and the thoughts of seers and philosophers. It has never occurred to General Sarnoff that any technology could do anything but *add* itself on to what we already are.

Such economists as Robert Theobald, W. W. Rostow, and John Kenneth Galbraith have been explaining for years how it is that "classical economics" cannot explain change or growth. And the paradox of mechanization is that although it is itself the cause of maximal growth and change, the principle of mechanization excludes the very possibility of growth or the understanding of change. For mechanization is achieved by fragmentation of any process and by putting the fragmented parts in a series. Yet, as David Hume showed in the eighteenth century, there is no principle of causality in a mere sequence. That one thing follows another accounts for nothing. Nothing follows from following, except change. So the greatest of all reversals occurred with electricity, that ended sequence by making things instant. With instant speed the causes of things began to emerge to awareness again, as they had not done with things in sequence and in concatenation accordingly. Instead of asking which came first, the chicken or the egg, it suddenly seemed that a chicken was an egg's idea for getting more eggs.

Just before an airplane breaks the sound barrier, sound waves become visible on the wings of the plane. The sudden visibility of sound just as sound ends is an apt instance of that great pattern of being that reveals new and opposite forms just as the earlier forms reach their peak performance. Mechanization was never so vividly fragmented or sequential as in the birth of the movies, the moment that translated us beyond mechanism into the world of growth and organic interrelation. The movie, by sheer speeding up the mechanical, carried us from the world of sequence and connections into the world of creative configuration and structure. The message of the movie medium is that of transition from lineal connections to configurations. It is the transition that produced the now quite correct observation: "If it works, it's obsolete." When electric speed further takes over from mechanical movie sequences, then the lines of force in structures and in media become loud and clear. We return to the inclusive form of the icon.

To a highly literate and mechanized culture the movie appeared as a world of triumphant illusions and dreams that money could buy. It was at this moment of the movie that cubism occurred, and it has been described by E. H. Gombrich (*Art and Illusion*) as "the most radical attempt to stamp out ambiguity and to enforce one reading of the picture—that of a man-made construction, a colored canvas." For cubism substitutes all facets of an object simultaneously for the "point of view" or facet of perspective illusion. Instead of the specialized illusion of the third dimension on canvas, cubism sets up an interplay of planes and contradiction or dramatic conflict of patterns, lights, textures that "drives home the message" by involvement. This is held by many to be an exercise in painting, not in illusion.

In other words, cubism, by giving the inside and outside, the top, bottom, back, and front and the rest, in two dimensions, drops the illusion of perspective in favor of instant sensory awareness of the whole. Cubism, by seizing on instant total awareness, suddenly announced that *the medium is the message*. Is it not evident that the moment that sequence yields to the simultaneous, one is in the world of the structure and of configuration? Is that not what has happened in physics as in painting, poetry, and in communication? Specialized segments of attention have shifted to total field, and we can now say, "The medium is the message" quite naturally. Before the electric speed and total field, it was not obvious that the medium is the message. The message, it seemed, was the "content," as people used to ask what a painting was *about*. Yet they never thought to ask what a melody was about, nor what a house or a dress was about. In such matters, people retained some sense of the whole pattern, of form and function as a unity. But in the electric age this integral idea of structure and configuration has become so prevalent that educational theory has taken up the matter. Instead of working with specialized "problems" in arithmetic, the structural approach now follows the linea of force in the field of number and has small children meditating about number theory and "sets." . . .

If the criminal appears as a nonconformist who is unable to meet the demand of technology that we behave in uniform and continuous patterns, literate man is quite inclined to see others who cannot conform as somewhat pathetic. Especially the child, the cripple, the woman, and the colored person appear in a world of visual and typographic technology as victims of injustice. On the other hand, in a culture that assigns roles instead of jobs to people—the dwarf, the skew, the child create their own spaces. They are not expected to fit into some uniform and repeatable niche that is not their size anyway. Consider the phrase "It's a man's world." As a quantitative observation endlessly repeated from within a homogenized culture, this phrase refers to the men in such a culture who have to be homogenized Dagwoods in order to belong at all. It is in our I.Q. testing that we have produced the greatest flood of misbegotten standards. Unaware of our typographic cultural bias, our testers assume that uniform and continuous habits are a sign of intelligence, thus eliminating the ear man and the tactile man.

C. P. Snow, reviewing a book of A. L. Rowse (*The New York Times Book Review,* December 24, 1961) on *Appeasement* and the road to Munich, describes the top level of British brains and experience in the 1930s. "Their I.Q.'s were much higher than usual among political bosses. Why were they such a disaster?" The view of Rowse, Snow approves: "They would not listen to warnings because they did not wish to hear." Being anti-Red made it impossible for them to read the message of Hitler. But their failure was as nothing compared to our present one. The American stake in literacy as a technology or uniformity applied to every level of education, government, industry, and social life is totally threatened by the electric technology. The threat of Stalin or Hitler was external. The electric technology is within the gates, and we are numb, deaf, blind, and mute about its encounter with the Gutenberg technology, on and through which the American way of life was formed. It is, however, no time to suggest strategies when the threat has not even been acknowledged to exist. I am in the position of Louis Pasteur telling doctors that their greatest enemy was quite invisible, and quite unrecognized by them. Our conventional response to all media, namely that it is how they are used that counts, is the numb stance of the technological idiot. For the "content" of a medium is like the juicy piece of meat carried by the burglar to distract the watchdog of the mind. The effect of the medium is made strong and intense just because it is given another medium as "content." The content of a movie is a novel or a play or an opera. The effect of the movie form is not related to its program content. The "content" of writing or print is speech, but the reader is almost entirely unaware either of print or of speech. . . .

Today when we want to get our bearings in our own culture, and have need to stand aside from the bias and pressure exerted by any technical form of human expression, we have only to visit a society where that particular form has not been felt, or a historical period in which it was unknown. Professor Wilbur Schramm made such a tactical move in studying *Television in the Lives of Our Children.* He found areas where TV had not penetrated at all and ran some tests. Since he had made no study of the peculiar nature of the TV image, his tests were of "content" preferences, viewing time, and vocabulary counts. In a word, his approach to the problem was a literary one, albeit unconsciously so. Consequently, he had nothing to report. Had his methods been employed in 1500 A.D. to discover the effects of the printed book in the lives of children or adults, he could have found out nothing of the changes in human and social psychology resulting from typography. Print created individualism and nationalism in the sixteenth century. Program and "content" analysis offer no clues to the magic of these media or to their subliminal charge.

Leonard Doob, in his report *Communication in Africa,* tells of one African who took great pains to listen each evening to the BBC news, even though he could understand nothing of it. Just to be in the presence of those sounds at 7 P.M. each day was important for him. His attitude to speech was like ours to melody—the resonant intonation was meaning enough. In the seventeenth century our ancestors still shared this native's attitude to the forms of media, as is plain in the following sentiment of the Frenchman Bernard Lam expressed in *The Art of Speaking* (London, 1696):

> 'Tis an effect of the Wisdom of God, who created Man to be happy, that whatever is useful to his conversation (way of life) is agreeable to him . . . because all victual that conduces to nourishment is relishable, whereas other things that cannot be assimilated and be turned into our substance are insipid. A Discourse cannot be pleasant to the Hearer that is not easie to the Speaker; nor can it be easily pronounced unless it be heard with delight.

Here is an equilibrium theory of human diet and expression such as even now we are only striving to work out again for media after centuries of fragmentation and specialism.

Pope Pius XII was deeply concerned that there be serious study of the media today. On February 17, 1950, he said:

> It is not an exaggeration to say that the future of modern society and the stability of its inner life depend in large part on the maintenance of an equilibrium between the strength of the techniques of communication and the capacity of the individual's own reaction.

Failure in this respect has for centuries been typical and total for mankind. Subliminal and docile acceptance of media impact has made them prisons without walls for their human users. As A. J. Liebling remarked in his book *The Press,* a man is not free if he cannot see where he is going, even if he has a gun to help him get there. For each of the media is also a powerful weapon with which to clobber other media and other groups. The result is that the present age has been one of multiple civil wars that are not limited to the world of art and entertainment. In *War and Human Progress,* Professor J. U. Nef declared: "The total wars of our time have been the result of a series of intellectual mistakes . . ."

If the formative power in the media are the media themselves, that raises a host of large matters that can only be mentioned here, although they deserve volumes. Namely, that technological media are staples or natural resources, exactly as are coal and cotton and oil. Anybody will concede that society whose economy is dependent upon one or two major staples like cotton, or grain, or lumber, or fish, or cattle is going to have some obvious social patterns of organization as a result. Stress on a few major staples creates extreme instability in the economy but great endurance in the population. The pathos and humor of the American South are embedded in such an economy of limited staples. For a society configured by reliance on a few commodities accepts them as a social bond quite as much as the metropolis does the press. Cotton and oil, like radio and TV, become "fixed charges" on the entire psychic life of the community. And this pervasive fact creates the unique cultural flavor of any society. It pays through the nose and all its other senses for each staple that shapes its life.

That our human senses, of which all media are extensions, are also fixed charges on our personal energies, and that they also configure the awareness and experience of each one of us, may be perceived in another connection mentioned by the psychologist C. G. Jung:

> Every Roman was surrounded by slaves. The slave and his psychology flooded ancient Italy, and every Roman became inwardly, and of course unwittingly, a slave. Because living constantly in the atmosphere of slaves, he became infected through the unconscious with their psychology. No one can shield himself from such an influence (*Contributions to Analytical Psychology*, London, 1928).

Study Questions: Pool

[?] *Marshall McLuhan asserts that the content of one medium is always another medium. In what senses, if any, does Pool support that claim?*

In what ways are cable and magazines alike? Does cable television serve the same functions for some people that magazines do for others?

What might magazine publishers gain from a liaison with cable? What might cable systems gain from an association with magazines? What might magazine readers and cable viewers gain?

What are the potential dangers to magazines from an association with cable such as Pool describes?

Has the marriage of magazines and cable been successful? If so, where and how? Do you believe any of the ideas suggested in this article will prove successful? Why or why not?

What factors limit how narrowly a cable system can focus its narrowcasting?

Gail Pool

CAN MAGAZINES FIND HAPPINESS WITH CABLE?

These are hard times for purists who like their media straight. Newspapers are on video, photographs are on disc, and not only are books being made into movies, movies are being made into books. One of the more recent media linkups involves magazines and cable. During the past year, cable subscribers have been exposed to programs derived in one way or another from a wide variety of magazines, from *Family Circle* to *Playboy*. Like much of what is happening in cable today, these programs are something of a dress rehearsal for the future. The shows are being carefully scrutinized by publishers, programmers, and advertising agencies. And the question is not how they are playing in some distant Peoria (which may not yet have cable); what matters are the ratings on Madison Avenue.

In turning to cable, magazine publishers are trying to keep history from repeating itself. About ten years back, television helped force out mass circulation magazines such as *Life* and *Look* by offering advertisers mass audiences no print medium could hope to match. Magazines that survived, and thrived, did so by tailoring material to special-interest audiences, offering advertisers not numbers but depth: the consumer really interested in their particular products.

Now cable with its numerous channels has the potential of offering that same narrowing capability. Once again an electronic medium is threatening to plunder the advertising base of magazines. And many editors and publishers, convinced that the magazine industry shouldn't have let television pass them by, are determined this time not to miss the boat. As Carey Winfrey, director of video development and marketing for CBS Publications, remarks, "We don't know the way the future is going, but anyone who doesn't experiment in some way is making a mistake."

Gail Pool is a writer who lives in Cambridge, Massachusetts.

But then, a lot of magazines that *are* experimenting are also making mistakes, unsure perhaps why they're in video in the first place. Monia Joblin, director of programming at USA Network, comments: "Everyone wants to be in on video—they're afraid not to be. But what they do depends on their vision of how to use it. To create a new market base? For promotion? And some magazines may not have a vision."

One basic vision is promotion. From cable's point of view, a magazine title is a known quantity that will draw viewers, and some magazines have gone on cable mainly in the hope of boosting circulation. *Family Circle,* for example, helped create 55 half-hour programs for a series, *It's a Great Idea,* based on its "Great Ideas" magazines, which ran first on the Satellite Program Network and then, for greater exposure, on the Christian Broadcasting Network. Like the publications, the programs featured projects in crafts, decorating, making Christmas gifts. To execute the projects, however, the viewer really needed the magazine—which was, of course, advertised on the shows.

But as a marketing vehicle *It's a Great Idea* was cost-effective for *Family Circle* only because it didn't cost the magazine anything. An independent producer underwrote the programs, for which, as it happens, sufficient advertising never materialized.

Even though cable advertising revenues will rise as more homes are hooked up, few publishers and fewer video programmers believe that a cable program can be primarily a promotional vehicle for a magazine; a program has to hold its own as a good show. But good programming is not easily come by, as anyone who has watched cable's meager offerings can testify. Cable programmers see themselves as up against an economic catch-22: cable hasn't yet got the programs that would lure the viewers who would lure the advertisers who would provide the capital that would create the programs that would lure the viewers, and so forth.

Into this programming gap sprang the notion that magazines could be of use because they "have editorial." It's a nice phrase, but what does it mean in regard to cable? Is it subject knowledge? But subject specialists exist outside the magazine world—in business, in academia. Even in the area of home interest, Julia Child cooked and Jim Crockett gardened without the backing of a magazine. Moreover, editors of special-interest magazines are seldom themselves specialists, and neither, for the most part, are their writers. Finally, as any video programmer will tell you, magazine articles, however skillfully written, are not video programs. And yet the notion of some transferrable editorial expertise persists, perhaps mainly on the magazine side.

At Meredith Corporation, Bruce Boyle, publisher of Meredith Video Publishing, interprets editorial in this sense as information. He sees Meredith, with *Better Homes and Gardens* and 38 other special-interest periodicals, with its book line and its book club, as a source of extensive material, already organized, that can be converted into video format. But while these informational resources may be useful in certain video applications (such as Meredith's educational videodisc "Understanding Your Body: A Woman's Guide From Better Homes and Gardens"), current cable programming makes it questionable whether information in any serious form is really what cable wants from magazines. Most cable programs are neither educational nor documentary; the service programs offer helpful hints, not the makings of serious analysis. This is true even of the better-produced shows. "Money Matters" on HBO, for example, bills itself as "entertaining information" from *Money* magazine. And it is. A recent segment on supermarket tactics was an eye-opener for the shopper and delightful to watch. But the information was on the level of "tips." What about information that isn't fun?

The answer to this question will become clearer if and when a greater number of serious magazines becomes involved. The fact that few "thought magazines" have been involved to date suggests that, in some people's minds at least, thoughtful information and video are a less than perfect match.

On television, of course, serious information has been subjected to the same entertainment pressures as lightweight information—witness the news. Bernie Shusman, a vice-president of Post Newsweek Video, thinks that cable is more open to experimentation. His exceptionally ambitious show, *Newsweek Woman,* a 25-minute weekly program associated with *Newsweek* and based in part on its editorial contents, runs on Hearst/ABC's *Daytime.* Four to four-and-a-half minutes may be allowed for a segment on, say, the Equal Rights Amendment, 25 minutes for runaway children, and 10 minutes for El Salvador. This makes for a leisurely pace that Shusman likes, but which he concedes will not be tolerated if cable gets into the ratings racket. Shusman sees *Newsweek Woman* as a news show in its own right, not a literal translation of the magazine.

Jim Perkins, president of Hearst/ABC Video Services, dismisses the notion that you can *do* a magazine on television, or that magazines contain an enormous amount of material just waiting to be converted into video. The resource that Hearst magazines have offered his programming service is not editorial content, but the proven ability of their editors to fashion publications to serve particular audiences.

This perception goes to the heart of the magazine-cable relationship. Magazines have learned to build special-interest audiences, to focus on subjects that will attract advertisers. These are skills cable needs, and magazines, in a sense, might serve as business consultants, providing cable services with marketing expertise.

That magazines have chosen to get involved *as magazines* is in part a defensive posture. As Bob Birnbaum, a consultant in publishing, management, and marketing who has specialized in electronic publishing, says, "After all, if you can launch a cable show from a magazine base, why can't you also launch a magazine from a cable base?" And this has already begun to happen. The program *Alive and Well,* a 2-hour weekday series featuring advice on how to keep fit, has spawned a magazine, *Alive and Well,* published by Bristol-Myers with the help of *American Health Magazine.* If it finds an audience it may expand, and, with its video exposure, offer fierce competition to existing health magazines. This is the sort of threat that magazines are trying, by early involvement, to forestall.

Of course, at this point all threats are hypothetical. No one knows whether narrowcasting on cable will work. Given the relatively small audience for cable—roughly twenty-five million households—and the fragmentation of that audience, only broad narrowcasting is feasible, such as women's interest programs on Hearst/ABC's *Daytime,* or the health features on the Cable Health Network. One of the few successful special-interest shows is *The American Baby Magazine Cable TV Show.* Based on *American Baby* magazine, which has a controlled circulation of expectant and new parents, the program has sufficiently targeted its audience to attract sponsors and is turning a small profit. But success as defined by *American Baby* is simply the ability to draw advertising. As with all of cable, no one knows yet who is watching the show; viewers have had no input.

What input viewers will have in the future is unclear. Some people hopefully predict that viewer choice—either by subscription or pay-per-view—will create a range of shows comparable to the range of magazines: from the glossy *(Omni)* to the plain and unprofitable *(The Nation).* But few people in the magazine or cable world share this vision. The consensus is that the unavoidably high cost of quality video will require advertising support. In fact, some people in the business believe that even advertising support will not make magazine-scale narrowcasting feasible. Harold Levine, chairman of the advertising agency Levine, Huntley, Schmidt and Beaver, says, "You can produce a good magazine for three hundred to four hundred thousand people and make money, but the economics makes it impossible on cable."

Moreover, while magazines can squeak by with low profits, or none at all, there is little enthusiasm in the cable business for no-profit programs. As for pay-per-view, it is likely that the industry, convinced that viewers won't spend money to "watch" a magazine, will reserve this form of payment—if and when it arrives—for spectacles, sports, and other special events.

The real point is that both cable and magazine people want advertising for the handsome profits it can yield, and that advertisers will almost surely in the end support the right kind of magazine-style programs. Special-interest magazines can offer advertisers detailed information about prospective audiences: what they earn, eat, wear, how they vote, how often they make love. Interactive cable could provide even more audience data than magazines can, along with the proven effectiveness of video advertising—an unparalleled combination. Already publishing and advertising consultants talk excitedly about advertising within a context (e.g., ski equipment on a ski show), which would avoid television's awkward shifts from drama to detergents. They talk of infomercials, the electronic equivalent of advertorials, in which advertiser-sponsored material, while briefly acknowledged as such, is presented in an editorial format. And they talk of cable as a brand-new medium, meaning, of course, a brand-new advertising medium.

Magazines will have a hand in carving out special markets on cable. Paul Caravatt, of Caravatt Communications, a program packager, is developing several magazines for cable, among them *Blair & Ketchum's Country Journal.* There is to be nothing revolutionary about *Country Journal*; as with all his shows, Caravatt says, he will "keep to what video does best: personality and how-to." What is innovative is his pursuit of a hitherto untapped video market: upscale rural dwellers. And whether or not Caravatt's *Country Journal* succeeds will depend as much on how upscale rural dwellers shape up as a market as it will on the quality of the show.

So what do magazines *qua* magazines gain from their involvement with cable? People speak about synergy, about ideas from the programs feeding back into the publications. One wonders whether they will be entertaining ideas. And whether magazines are really hard up for ideas. The truth is, improving magazines was never the point of the exercise.

An editor who does see a synergistic relationship between magazines and video is Nick Charney. But for Charney, editorial director of *Psychology Today* and of *Videofashion Monthly* (a videomagazine without a print base), the promise lies in video, not cable. He sees innovative videomagazines becoming feasible through the use of videocassettes and videodiscs. Cable, he fears, may repeat television's formulaic programming and inhibit creativity. Indeed, this may be the least harm it can do. Given its economic structure, cable, at least for now, may prove still more damaging to magazines.

Few publishers are eager to discuss the dangers of their involvement in cable. Advertising executive Harold Levine thinks many magazines are going to get burned—some by financial losses in a medium that may not be profitable for 5 to 10 years, others by lending their names to mediocre video programs and thus damaging their reputations. He also sees magazines undermining their own credibility as advertising media. Implicit in the "we couldn't beat 'em so we're gonna join 'em" attitude is magazines' acknowledgment of video as a more effective advertising medium than print.

But perhaps the greatest danger for magazines lies in the dominant role that advertising will almost certainly play in magazine programs on cable, and the effect that will have on special-interest magazines that may already be overly influenced by advertising concerns.

For cable, perhaps even more than for magazines, "special interest" is a marketing concept. There is a common misconception that the phrase means just what it says: that if there are enough people interested in collecting pebbles, there is room for a magazine called *The Pebble Collector*. This isn't quite true. A special-interest idea becomes potentially profitable only if it is associated with identifiable—and therefore advertisable—consumables: precisely what do pebble collectors buy, and can the providers of those goods and services afford to advertise? Can readers afford to buy special pebble-collecting shoes?

But despite the importance of advertising in magazine publishing, editors have tried to adhere to an ethic of editorial independence. Even magazines created on the basis of marketing studies claim *reader* interest. And there are subscribers, after all, to counterbalance the power of advertisers.

Editorial independence has always been precarious in television, and whatever may be true in the future, it is not affordable now in cable. Programmers are not secretive about this. Monia Joblin of USA Network says, "We have to put on programming that advertisers want to pay for." Cable Health Network's vice president for programming, Loreen Arbus, describes a new consumer-oriented health show as "helping the viewer without attacking the marketplace or its products."

The editorial independence of many magazines is already badly strained by their desire to please advertisers, and getting involved with cable is unlikely to put new backbone into publishers and editors. Video's high cost will increase magazines' need for revenues. And in competition with video "entertainment," "personality," and "how-to" programs, how will magazines fare? Will advertisers be willing to come in twice? On what basis will it be worth their while? How far will magazines go to hold on to their advertisers? When does information become advertorial?

For all the talk about what cable will do to magazine markets, there has been little talk about what cable will do to magazines themselves. How dismal if cable succeeds only in diminishing the range and depth of our magazines; if, despite the proliferation of media, and the mix-and-match of media forms, we face an increasing lack of real choice, a sameness to what we hear and see; if cable programs and magazines come to resemble each other by a reductive process, and in all of them we learn how to cook our (Marval) turkeys, fix our (Ford) cars and travel well (with American Express). Magazines might think twice about catching that boat.

Study Questions: Woodhead

Why would an East German, such as the official Woodhead quotes, be so vehemently critical of Dallas? *Is his criticism justified?*

Why do you think American programs are so popular with foreign audiences, even in countries that have extensive production industries of their own?

According to Woodhead, why do some governments prefer telecasting programs from the U.S. and other developed countries rather than having their people produce more of their own?

What does Woodhead see as the strength and uniqueness of American television production? What does he see as its weaknesses?

Why does he think the American style will dominate television in the future? What is the presumed relationship between competition for advertising dollars and deteriorating program quality that makes Woodhead fearful of the future of television in his own country? Do you think his fears are justified?

Leslie Woodhead

YANK TV: A NICE PLACE TO VISIT, BUT ...

For two years I've wandered the planet with film crews and fellow producers on an improbable venture. Our mission: to boldly go where no man has been crazy enough to go before—into the archives and memories of television to make a 13-hour documentary history of the medium worldwide. Granada Television calls the series *Television,* and aired it this winter in Britain. In the United States, public television is raising money to show the series later on.

The assignment appeared to be redeemed only by the dotty grandeur of its pretension. From Novosibirsk to Rio, television people smirked when they heard what we were attempting. My American friends in particular

---

Leslie Woodhead, an executive producer with Granada TV in Great Britain, has worked on documentaries and docudramas for more than 20 years.

knew from the outset what I've since discovered about the fatal labyrinths of copyright clearances, the profound hoarding instincts of slow-moving film archivists wherever they may be, and the life-consuming longueurs of a telex dialogue with broadcasters in Lagos or Manila. But for all the frustrations, it's been fun.

It has also given me a rare chance to reexamine my outsider's notions about American television, both from viewpoints out in the world, and from up close. In visits to America as a documentary producer over the last 20 years, I've always watched American television in a distracted kind of way in overheated motel rooms and with busy American television people in busy offices. Nevertheless, like most Brits passing through, I've been hypnotized, seduced, and worried, in equal measure, by what I saw.

For what it's worth, my closer acquaintance with American television has, on the whole, greatly increased my respect and admiration for some of the programs it makes. At the same time, I feel an ever-deepening alarm about the context in which those programs have to be produced. As a producer working within the protection of British television, with its still-surviving public-service ethic, I don't envy my American counterparts. I suspect we have seen our future in their deregulated, satellite-interconnected present, and I worry.

In a remote village in India, in a context that couldn't be farther from the American, we watched the making of an extraordinary and fiercely relevant drama, written and acted by villagers, and recorded on new Japanese video gear by a local TV station. The subject was wife-burning, the terrifying practice of murdering by fire a young bride who failed to bring sufficient dowry to her new family. The peasant girl who played the bride told us she believed the program would help educate villagers to change their ways.

At last it seems that cheap production using new lightweight equipment is breaking the economic equation that long dictated a diet of *Bonanza* and *I Love Lucy* instead of domestic productions in the Third World.

We discovered repeatedly that audiences prefer programs made in their own countries, when they can get them. Japan was once a mass-importer of American television, but now makes 95 percent of the programs it airs. The domestically made *Underground Executioner*—a samurai drama about a humble policeman who disposed of 1,500 evildoers in an ingenious orgy of vigilante extermination—wows the Japanese audience, while *Dallas* trails far behind.

But despite this new twist, we found the familiar story of the American television empire elsewhere. In the Philippines, which still imports some 80 percent of its prime-time schedule from the United States, we found ourselves watching *The Incredible Hulk* alongside people living in cardboard houses. "It's escapism," said an American Jesuit priest who's been involved for 30 years in Philippine broadcasting. And the regime likes it that way: "They don't want anything that will get people thinking about the way things are here right now. If the drama comes from New York or Hollywood, it's just far enough away that it's not going to rock the boat."

Dallas, the same soap opera that flops in Japan, is a big hit with viewers in East Germany, if not with government officials there. It comes over the Berlin Wall from the West. The drama chief of East German television doesn't mince words: "It's a very perfect, conventional, businesslike, propagandistic, cleverly made series which is unfortunately very much capable of affecting a manipulation of the consciousness of viewers to the advantage of the imperialists. So it is immensely dangerous." The East German counterattack is pitiless: They schedule Robert Redford movies against the West German nightly news.

In West Germany, we talked with an independent producer who has kinder words for American drama. Peter Marthesheimer, the man who brought the American miniseries *Holocaust* to the German audience, says it had a profound impact, unleashing a national debate about the Nazi horror in a way nothing else had done. He told us he'd seen many programs about the Holocaust on German television that had "more accuracy, more brain, and more delicacy." But he said, "This was the first time I was moved in my stomach; the other times I had been moved in my head."

The reason he gave was, for me, striking: "I don't care whether the methods are cheap or highbrow or lowbrow. They're the traditional Hollywood means of telling a story. You don't look from the outside at other people going into the gas chamber. You go for yourself." As a fellow European I hear what the man says. Unashamed enthusiasm for telling a harrowing human story that is rooted in strong but simple characters—which is the Hollywood way—still works for a mass audience. British critics may have derided *The Thorn Birds* but a BBC audience of tens of millions tuned in to watch it. There's an American ease with sentiment and melodrama that would disturb a European program-maker, but wins the attention of a European viewer.

Over the course of two years we observed at close hand the paradox of American television, the greed machine that makes some of the world's best programs. We relished the making of the *Astro Hypnotists,* a public-access show on Manhattan Cable; we filmed the *M*A*S*H* exhibit at the Smithsonian Institution in Washington, where perishable popular drama lives on as some kind of television icon, and we watched a big team at ABC make a marvelously sophisticated documentary about John F. Kennedy.

It's the sheer pace of most American television that assaults a British viewer. One executive told us that Americans have "the attention span of a pregnant gerbil." (In Japan, a producer told us that television rhythms have so saturated Japanese schoolchildren that teachers must introduce a joke into the lessons every 15 minutes to hold their students' attention.) But my initial distaste for American fast-food television was modified by two experiences during our research.

One occurred on a Saturday evening in October 1983 as we watched the final editing stages of the *ABC News Special Presentation* documentary on President Kennedy. Executive producer Pamela Hill had pulled together four teams of producers and editors, a much larger group than we'd be accustomed to using in Britain, for a film quite unlike anything we make. Its pace must have been three times as fast, but at the same time the teams' precise attention to details of image and sound gave the whole thing a genuine lyrical energy. It was my first real awakening to an American way of television, a style and pace that is, I think, authentically American and very powerful, owing little to the more leisurely expositions of European factual TV.

Our time spent with *Hill Street Blues*' impressive production team was the other telling contradiction of the cozy and widespread British assumption that American television is often simply more frantic and less complex. The moon was still out when I had breakfast with *Hill Street*'s senior writer, David Milch. I was reminded that Americans work harder than we do, and made abruptly aware how intelligent and committed to good work a team producing popular action telly-films can still be. "Appealing to a broad audience and maintaining quality need not be mutually exclusive ambitions," he told me, "if you tell good stories that identify drama in the rhythms and processes of people's lives." A few days later I sat in on a lecture Milch gave to student writers at UCLA. He rolled and twitched through torrents of talk like a cross between rock singer Joe Cocker and polymath Jonathan Miller. He was genuinely affecting as he urged students to "make vital the formula" and to "gain access to your own imaginations" while "abandoning the pleasures of virtuosity." To a British eye, *Hill Street* itself is another vivid demonstration of an American way of television quite without European parallels, full of pace and allusive energy. The series also demonstrates how rapidly a mass audience of alleged "pregnant gerbils" can become accustomed to decoding a very sophisticated set of television messages.

Of course *Hill Street* is not typical of the American network schedule. No one who has spent time in the splendid Museum of Broadcasting in New York reviewing, for example, the live drama of the 1950s, can fail to experience a sharp sense of loss. The best of those dramas from America's Golden Age of Television still rank among the best work ever done on television. It's the variety and original flavor that impresses the most.

And it's the blurring and loss of that flavor that seems all too evident in today's nightly brawl to win the ratings. Even David Wolper, who produced the landmark mini-series *Roots*, admitted disarmingly, "I thought the subject would make money." Fred Friendly explained: "The problem with television in this country is that commercial television makes so much money doing its worst that it can't afford to do its best."

What alarms me, as a producer for British commercial television, is that I can detect signs that our television institutions may be moving towards an alignment of forces more like the American. Granada and the other regional broadcasters that comprise Britain's ITV network have had a monopoly on television advertising for almost 30 years. The prospect of competition for advertising is our ultimate fear, and not solely for parochial corporate reasons. Most of us are convinced that whatever quality British television has achieved has been derived in large measure from the fact that neither the BBC nor ITV has had to adjust program standards to fight for the biggest audience and advertising revenue. We have never had to select and schedule programs in the knowledge that the loss of a single ratings point could cost our network $50 million per year. As a result, Granada can make *Brideshead Revisited, The Jewel in the Crown,* and *Television,* without regard to getting the maximum audience.

The American experience has special relevance for us today because Prime Minister Thatcher recently declared an interest in the possibility of partially funding the BBC through advertising. All of us in British commercial television wish the BBC success in its lobbying instead for an increase in the viewers' license fee that supports it. This is not just because we admire the BBC or wish our friends there a prosperous 1985.

In our filming we also sighted illustrations of the proliferation of satellites that is bringing America nearly unregulated competition for audiences. A young man named Mark Gordon has built a receiving dish from a kit and hung it out the window of his 23rd-floor apartment in the South Bronx. He doesn't regard his antenna as a threat to broadcasting quality, but as a way to liberate his viewing. Feeding directly from satellites in orbit 22,300 miles out in space, the antenna allows Gordon to bypass traditional broadcasting, ignore national boundaries, and receive as many as 300 channels of television from all over the world. "I wanted to prove to the industry," he told us, "that I can do something like this, and anybody else can do something like this." Point taken, Mark—although as far as I could see most of your channels seemed to be offering that old familiar diet.

We also talked with Alma, widow of Philo T. Farnsworth, one of the inventors of television. She recalls an early meeting with one of his backers, who demanded, "When are we gonna see some dollars in this thing, Farnsworth?" So the first picture he showed them was one of a dollar sign.

---

*S*tudy *Q*uestions: *H*oberman

?   *Many observers, including Hoberman and McLuhan, have suggested that artists tend to be ahead of their time, painting a vision of our future long before that future comes. Do you agree or disagree with that suggestion?*

Does Hoberman persuade you that many recent and contemporary films indicate that America may be becoming more fascist? What in his arguments do you find persuasive? What do you find unpersuasive?

Can you perceive the same fascist tendencies in many movies today that Hoberman does? If so, is it possible that these tendencies are a sign that our society is becoming more fascist? Or are these movies signs of fascist tendencies only to the degree that they are the kinds of movies "that a potentially fascist culture would be expected to produce and enjoy"?

How does Susan Sontag, as discussed in this article, characterize fascist films and fascist aesthetics?

Does Hoberman persuade you that the movies tend to make war seem a beautiful, holy mission?

What, if anything, is wrong with showing highly patriotic Americans massacring foreigners who have invaded our shores? Why does Hoberman criticize the glorification of war and promotion of American patriotism?

Assuming Hoberman's analysis is valid, what, if anything, should be done about such films as the ones he describes?

Why do you believe movies such as Rambo *have become so popular at this particular historical moment?*

J. Hoberman

THE FASCIST GUNS IN THE WEST

Are movies like Red Dawn *and* Rambo *just good, clean American fun, or is Hollywood developing its own brand of fascism?*

If the decline of the Western deprived American movies of what was once their preeminent ideological mode, ideology itself has scarcely vanished. Not since the Nixon-era cop-and-vigilante cycle has the action film become so blatant an arena for political wish fulfillment. In the early seventies, however, the demons were American. These days they strike from the outside.

J. Hoberman is a film critic for the *Village Voice* and a contributing editor for *American Film.*

Given the current climate, it now seems remarkable that as recently as 1983, *Octopussy* employed James Bond's first Russian antagonist in two decades. With the informal detente of the mid-sixties, Russians were supplanted by Chinese or East Germans as screen villains—and, in films and television series like *The Russians are Coming! The Russians are Coming!* and *The Man from U.N.C.L.E.*, they even appeared in a sympathetic light. These days, the only good Russian is a dead Russian—or a defector. Either way, Main Street is the enemy's goal, infusing movies as otherwise disparate as *White Nights* and *Red Dawn*, *Moscow on the Hudson* and *Invasion U.S.A.* with a backbeat of paranoia and an undercurrent of narcissism.

Something besides Spielbergism must have been happening over the past few years, and there should be a way to describe the Manichaean moral scheme, vengeful patriotism, worship of the male torso, and rabid emotionalism of recent Sylvester Stallone vehicles or those bizarre military scenarios that postulate either a Soviet occupation of America or a second Vietnam. Last summer, critic David Denby created a minor flap in the letters column of *New York* magazine by terming *Rambo* and *Red Dawn* "fascist" films. Readers wrote in accusing him of glibness and ignorance, as well as confusing fascism with anticommunism.

Denby replied that, although neither film was fascist in "the textbook sense of celebrating a dictatorial government of extreme nationalist tendency," both displayed a mixture of demagogic resentment and messianic promise (not to mention bellicose patriotism) that reminded him of European fascism. "Made in the wake of an American military defeat, *Red Dawn* and *Rambo* try to exorcise that defeat, as did Hitler after Germany's defeat in World War I, with theories of betrayal (the 'stab in the back') and with goofy rituals of purification—the drinking of deer's blood . . . in *Red Dawn*, the experience of torture in *Rambo*. Purification leads to renewal—a new type of American superkiller."

"It's possible," Denby concluded, that "we're seeing the stirrings of incipient fascism—a distinct American variant combining paranoia, military fantasy, and a style of individualism so extreme as to be pathological. If readers can come up with a better term, I'll gladly use it." (So far, he reports, they haven't.)

Nurtured on post–World War I chaos, European fascism was an authoritarian, anti-democratic, profoundly militaristic, and violently nationalistic movement—at once a reaction to Soviet communism and a response to the worldwide economic crisis. In Germany and Italy, fascist ideologues spouted theories of imperial expansion and racial superiority. Their mystical world view projected a Manichaean struggle between the powers of light and darkness. But megalomaniacal architectural plans and glorified neoclassical sculpture aside, there was very little that could be considered fascist art. Was there such a thing as a fascist film?

Historically, the official fascist cinema was distinguished more by what it didn't say than what it did—although German fascism was acutely movie-conscious. (Goebbels dreamed of producing a Nazi *Battleship Potemkin*, where Hitler even went so far as to credit the cinema, along with radio and the automobile, for his victory.) Even so, except for a few overtly political films like Leni Riefenstahl's staged documentary *Triumph of the Will,* the viciously anti-Semitic *Jud Suss,* the sort of wartime melodrama parodied in *Kiss of the Spider Woman,* and an occasional Führer-type biopic, the Reich's motion picture production was geared toward escapist romances and comedies. The same was true of fascist Italy and Franco's Spain.

But if D.W. Griffith's inflammatory, white supremacist, pro–Ku Klux Klan masterpiece *The Birth of a Nation*—a favorite of Hitler's and Goebbels', as well as the first film to use melodrama for propagandist ends, and, in this sense, the structural precursor for *Red Dawn* and *Invasion U.S.A.*—can be termed protofascist, over the years there have been a handful of Hollywood films that seem transparently fascist either in their inspiration or in their effect.

Released in early 1933, *Gabriel Over the White House,* which was produced (and reportedly written) by William Randolph Hearst, was a virtual call for an American Mussolini: After a near-fatal car accident, the new president of the United States assumes divinely mandated dictatorial powers. Declaring martial law, he conscripts the unemployed, summarily executes the nation's gangsters, and strong-arms the powers of Europe into paying off their war debts. Cecil B. DeMille's 1933 *This Day and Age*—in which a mob of "5,000 stalwart youths," outraged by a wealthy man's evasion of a murder charge, proudly disdain due process to elicit his confession at a torchlit midnight tribunal—was clearly influenced by the "moral purity" of Hitler's boyish storm troopers.

The President Vanishes, released in 1934, was a more benign version of *Gabriel*—with an American president forced to employ some extraconstitutional powers to combat a right-wing militarist threat. Seventeen years after the Hearst opus, the ruler of the universe again intervened in American politics in *The Next Voice You Hear,* starring James Whitmore and the future Nancy Reagan, which had God commandeering the airwaves to endorse the American way of life, stress the importance of regimentation, and underscore a faith that authority (be it the radio, the police, the factory boss, or the church) is always right.

The movies Denby terms "fascist"—as well as various Chuck Norris and Arnold Schwarzenegger vehicles—need to be seen in the context of *Star Wars* fun (the revival of military spectacle), Spielberg feelgood (the valorization of childish fantasy), ghostbusting insouciance (what—me worry?), and the reactionary racial and sexual politics of *Indiana Jones and the Temple of Doom* on the one hand and *An Officer and a Gentleman* on the other. Rather than fascist, these films are, perhaps, as Robin Wood recently wrote of *Star Wars* and *Rocky*, "precisely the kinds of entertainment that a potentially fascist culture would be expected to produce and enjoy."

In a sense, both Denby and Wood are transposing the methodology and thesis of Siegfried Kracauer's 1947 book *From Caligari to Hitler* to contemporary America. Kracauer analyzed the German silent and early sound cinema in terms of its emerging fascist themes—the submissive longing for a strong leader, the purity of the mountains versus the tawdriness of the cosmopolitan city, the increasing obsession with military history. (During the final three years of the Weimar Republic, no fewer than eight films were produced on the German "war of liberation" against Napoleon.)

Rather than recall a glorious past, however, our born-again war film is concerned with alternative universes and (as yet) undeclared wars. Three battlefields—Main Street, outer space, and contemporary Vietnam—haunt Hollywood. If the representation of conventional (or intergalactic) combat is comforting in an age of potential atomic annihilation, the dramatization of victory in Vietnam has a kind of lunatic piquancy, symbolizing the restoration of a lost national honor. For, John Wayne and the Green Berets notwithstanding, the Vietnam War has had an odd history in American films. Almost from the beginning, movies wished the war over. Vietnam films were far less obsessed with battlefield sacrifice than with the plight of the returning veteran—using him as either the scapegoat for or the redeemer of a guilty society.

The implication of *Uncommon Valor*, released in 1983 and coproduced by John Milius, was that the grunts had been sold out on the home front—and then "spat upon" when they returned. With its emphasis on patriarchal authority, mutilated genealogy, and male rites of passage, *Uncommon Valor* took the lead in visualizing Indochina as the site of America's symbolic castration. Unlike *Apocalypse Now* or even *The Deer Hunter*, it offered itself as a clear-cut exorcism of the shame and dishonor of American defeat.

Although some critics, notably Pauline Kael, scored *Uncommon Valor*'s underlying racism—Kael cited the "exultant, patriotic American music" that burst forth during the climactic massacres of the film's "little yellow-peril targets"—most praised it as a solid, old-fashioned action flick. When it came to the subtext, audiences were definitely more alert: *The New York Times* quoted one patron leaving the theater, who explained: "We get to win the Vietnam War." This fantasy recalls the softer vision of redemption offered by *E. T.*, *Close Encounters of the Third Kind*, and the comic version of Armageddon in *Ghostbusters*. (The compensatory nature of the new American war film is aptly demonstrated in the fantasy underlying *Let's Get Harry*, a Tri-Star film currently in production. Here, according to the studio press release, some "small-town factory workers" strike back at the South American terrorists who have kidnapped their friend. What's startling, of course, is that many more American factories than factory workers have been forcibly relocated to the Third World.) There is a strikingly solipsistic quality to current American patriotism. As the 1983 conquest of Grenada and the 1984 Olympics demonstrated, Reagan-era chauvinism celebrates itself; it thrives very well, and perhaps even better, in the absence of a clear-cut opposition. So it should come as no surprise that current action heroes exhibit an individualism bordering on the psychotic.

One need only compare *Rambo, Invasion U.S.A.,* or *Commando* with such World War II films as *Air Force, Bataan,* and *The Story of G. I. Joe* to see the change in emphasis from selfless teamwork to glorification of a supernaturally endowed, barely human *Übermensch*. Stallone and Norris make Clint Eastwood's Dirty Harry look like Adlai Stevenson (which suggests that the source of Eastwood's current appeal is nostalgia). Arnold Schwarzenegger, who had his first major role in the ubiquitous Milius's mock-Nietzschean *Conan,* a pulp paean to Hyborian Age militarism, appears to have carved out a career playing humanoid killing machines.

These two trends, the implacable hulk and the Vietnam exorcism, converged first in two Norris vehicles—*Missing in Action* (a more simpleminded version of *Uncommon Valor*) and its prequel, *Missing in Action II*—and then, with world-historic force, in *Rambo: First Blood, Part II,* a film endorsed by no less an authority than Ronald Reagan. As Susan Sontag wrote in her 1974 essay on the Nazi director Leni Riefenstahl, fascist films are concerned with "the rebirth of the body and of community, mediated through the worship of an irresistible leader." Box-office figures tell us they don't come any more irresistible than John Rambo.

Sontag's analysis of the fascist world view, deduced from Riefenstahl's films and photographs, takes on a particular resonance in the light of *Red Dawn, Rambo,* and *Rocky IV*. For Sontag, fascist films are "tales of longing for high places, of the challenge and ordeal of the elemental, the primitive; they are about the vertigo before power, symbolized by the majesty and beauty of mountains." Fascist aesthetics "flow from (and justify) a preoccupation with situations of control, submissive behavior, extravagant effort, and the endurance of pain; they endorse two seemingly opposite states, egomania and servitude." If *Red Dawn* is founded on the "longing for high places" and the "ordeal of the elemental," both *Rambo* and *Rocky IV* are notable for Stallone's fusion of suffering and megalomania.

Fascist ideology is also characterized by the emphasis on the physical and instinctual over the intellectual ("thinking with the blood," as Goebbels put it), attitudes Stallone has taken as his own. "What I try to do is interpret the longing of the everyday proletariat, the blue-collar man," he explained to *Rolling Stone.* "I think the intelligentsia should understand that this country now is functioning on emotional energy more than intellectual energy." He confided to another reporter, "I don't work these things out intellectually. I go by intuition, my emotions."

It's striking that *Red Dawn* and *Rambo* (not to mention *Rocky IV, Missing in Action,* and *Invasion U.S.A.)* emphasize the purification of their heroes. The chaste atmosphere of *Red Dawn* is matched by Chuck Norris' imperviousness to sex in *Missing in Action,* while the presence of a beautiful female guide in *Rambo* is less a pretext for eros than for revenge. "The fascist ideal," Sontag has noted, "is to transform sexual energy into a 'spiritual' force, for the benefit of the community."

In eighties America, this becomes a paranoid loyalty to the self. Rambo's complaint, after all, is that his country has failed to love him (and all MIAs) as much as he loves it. Decked in the accoutrements of patriotism as they are, neither Rambo nor Rocky is an endorsement of the status quo. Indeed, there is a powerfully nihilist aspect to Rambo's climactic assault on the computer bank that presumably planned his mission. (This fear of technology is reasserted in *Rocky IV.) The Terminator,* on the other hand, is nihilistic to the other extreme, introducing an implacable, murderous robot as a not-so-covert anti-hero.

It is often forgotten that fascism began as a protest movement. Before taking power, fascists attacked every aspect of the existing order—from profit-hungry businessmen and treasonous liberals to myopic intellectuals and grubby politicians. Significantly, Stallone sees himself as transcending current political discourse. "I'm not right-wing. I'm not left-wing. I love my country," he told *The New York Times.* "I stand for ordinary Americans, losers a lot of them. They don't understand big, international politics. Their country tells them to fight in Vietnam? They fight." This statement articulates a potent mixture of obedience and rage. Stallone has admitted that should he elect to make a *Rocky V*, the fighter "would have to go into politics, which seems to be the natural extension."

If Stallone is the noble savage of the new patriotism, Milius is the mode's leading theorist. Indeed, Milius, who has called himself a "Zen fascist," shows signs of having read Sontag's essay. Not only does *Red Dawn* open in the clouds like *Triumph of the Will,* the film's radical subservience of love to patriotism, marked lack of religion, naked hatred of politicians, and subliminal backdrop of Alpine purity set it apart from traditional Hollywood agitprop and relate it to the mythology of right-wing German nationalism.

What gives *Red Dawn* an additional exotic twist is Milius' transposition of a Third World liberation struggle to deepest Colorado. Milius is in love with the idea of guerilla warfare, right down to its fashion accessories— by the end of the movie, his high school quarterback-turned-freedom fighter is wearing a homemade burnoose. Huge chunks of *Red Dawn* are reversals of scenes from *Apocalypse Now*—originally written by Milius— with Americans enacting the role of Vietcong partisans and Russians playing the part of American invaders.

"Every single thing in *Red Dawn* is taken from the stories of Russian and Yugoslav partisans during World War II or from the Vietcong," Milius told an interviewer, emphasizing an identification that is all but pathological. Almost a decade earlier, he had used a similar equation to describe his relationship with the New York film critics: "I'm a Castro fighting in the hills against those fraudulent, narrow-minded, bigoted, and destructive people." Along with the desire for revenge and vindication, the post-Vietnam exorcisms are striking in their solipsistic identification with the erstwhile victor. By Milius' logic, the richest, most powerful nation on earth becomes something like an underdeveloped victim. America has been invaded, America is under occupation; Americans must engage in guerilla struggle.

That neither Milius nor Stallone served in Vietnam in no way mitigates the militarism of their films. On the contrary, playing at war becomes a substitute for the real thing. Describing Milius' attitude on the set of *Conan*, Arnold Schwarzenegger recalled that the director "promised us this shooting was going to deal with dirt and pain. That's exactly what we got." Milius, he continued, "runs a set like an army. So that's the feeling everyone had— that this wasn't a movie, it was a battle."

Walter Benjamin, who saw in fascism the introduction of spectacle into politics, noted that "all efforts to render politics aesthetic culminate in one thing: war." In his essay, "The Work of Art in the Age of Mechanical Reproduction," Benjamin quotes the futurist-turned-fascist Filippo Tommaso Marinetti in what could be an ecstatic review of *Rambo* or *The Terminator:* "War is beautiful because it initiates the dreamt-of metalization of the human body. War is beautiful because it enriches a flowering meadow with fiery orchids of machine guns. War is beautiful because it combines the gunfire, the cannonades, the cease-fire, the scents, and the stench of putrefaction into a symphony."

Perhaps the most fascistic aspect of the Stallone-Milius axis is its faith in the regenerative, if not hygienic, powers of war. The very title *"Red Dawn"* implies a rebirth, while *Rocky IV*'s Las Vegas sequences are meant to parody American decadence. *Invasion U.S.A.*, too, makes much of America's supposed moral weakness. "Look at them—soft, decadent. They don't understand the nature of their own freedom," say two Soviet agents on a beach near Miami. What shuts them up is the gunfire of Chuck Norris' symphony.

Rambo, Red Dawn, et al. play to the vengeful, authoritarian, nihilist component of the audience. Yet the only mass movement they address (so far) is that of moviegoers, and in this sense they can't really be termed fascist. But what would we call it if the Japanese or Germans were to suddenly engage in a flurry of World War II victory films or the Soviets to release melodramas in which the steroid *Übermensch* of *Rocky IV* repelled an American invasion of their sacred motherland?

Study Questions: Harms

? What is the "new communication order" to which Harms believes the new technologies could bring us? What assumptions underlie that order? Why does Harms believe that a new communication order is being mandated at this time?

What does Harms seem to think are humans' communication needs? What would you add to Harms's list?

Of all of these needs, which are not now being met adequately? What kinds of communication technologies or changes in the way we use technologies might help meet those needs?

Harms claims there can be too much as well as too little of various kinds of communication. On what does he base that claim? Do you agree? Why?

Why does Harms believe that two-way communication is so vital? Why does he think horizontal communication will dominate in the new communication order? What are the advantages and disadvantages of a horizontal communication system for the contemporary world?

How does Harms support the claim that we cannot ask books and most other mass media questions? Can you think of counterarguments that support the claim that we can interact with books and other media? What different ways to interact with a medium can you imagine?

What characteristics must a communication medium or a communication system have for you to be able to ask questions and get useful answers from it?

How is each of the communication rights Harms discusses related to the availability of different communication technologies?

Do Harms's three communication rights exhaust what you believe to be important for the ideal society? Are there other important communication rights? Are any of the rights listed by Harms irrelevant?

L. S. Harms

FROM WHAT? TO WHAT?

For perhaps half a million years, the core of human communication was ordinary, informal, face-to-face conversation. Today, when taking into account the totality of human communication, we note with renewed interest that at least half of human communication continues to be informal conversation. In our small world we observe that only through conversation do human communicators everywhere create and invent new ideas and share and use old ones. We acknowledge that many of the most important of these ideas cannot be reduced to writing. When taken together, these ideas constitute the ordinary but essential knowledge of a cultural group and, increasingly, of world society as well.[1] Ordinary knowledge exists in cerebral memories. It often does not get stored in artificial memories such as textbooks and computer banks or become part of the formal world information flow.

During the several hundred centuries of communication history before writing systems were invented, three basic communication patterns were generally, probably universally, in daily use; the first two patterns permitted the asking and answering of questions but the third usually did not. These three communication patterns may be called:

1. The two-person dialogue group or dyad.
2. The small discussion group of about seven communicators.
3. The one-to-many group, where there is one source and the many or audience might be counted in the tens, occasionally in the hundreds, seldom in the thousands, and never as today in the millions and billions.

The print and broadcast media today extend only the one-to-many pattern across time and space.

Only in the last century has the one-way, one-to-many, pattern that is built into the structures of the mass media also come to be considered as the fundamental and orienting pattern for the totality of human communication. Concurrently, and in spite of the rapid growth of the world telephone network, the billions of hours of daily conversation in dyads and small groups everywhere have often been considered in academic and policy circles as a kind of societal background noise. That narrow perspective on human communication where the "means for communication" are confused with the "mass media" has been aptly called by Jean d'Arcy, the "mass media mentality."[2]

L. S. Harms is a Professor of Communication, University of Hawaii.

Largely since 1970, breakthroughs in transceiver technologies (multi-way and interactive) have made possible dozens and perhaps hundreds of distinctively new communication services that in various ways facilitate informal conversation, dialogue, problem-solving, conferencing, consultation, negotiation and decision-making. Complex problems arise at the interface between informal conversation and the new transceiver-based communication services, and these problems often require policy solutions.

Within the broad context sketched above, it now becomes possible to state what is meant in this paper by the term *communication development.* As used here, it refers to the process of configuring communication resources into services that satisfy human communication needs; such development is understood to be guided by policy goals; policy goals are considered to be inherent in various communication rights. The central argument will be that communication resources ought to be developed to implement communication rights and satisfy communication needs and, indirectly, other basic human needs as well.

Today, the discussion of how the resources for communication in society ought to be developed is being carried out under the title of a new communication order. Because the mention of a new order immediately poses the question of in what sense the order is a *new* one, it is helpful to sketch out a sequence of communication orders, and to use those orders as a general reference framework. Such a sketch is provided in the next section. Equally, a new order raises for discussion a large number of topics, and a few of these topics are discussed further in the later sections of the paper: horizontal communication, asking questions, communication rights, and policy decisions. The paper concludes with a projection of where communication development appears to be leading.

THE EVOLUTION OF ORDERS

Whenever a new communication order appears to be taking shape, it is pertinent to ask from what this new order has emerged and toward what it can be expected to lead. Predictably, some participants in the conversations leading to a new order insist that the new order replaces not an old order, but an intolerable disorder. In a sense, this claim is to the point for a new order arises after an old order breaks apart, or deteriorates. Just as predictably, participants with vested interests in the old order argue that all that is needed is to revive and restore the old order. Typically, advocates of a new order reject the old order, or what remains of it, and stress the novel components of a new order. Subsequently, selected components of the previous order along with components from other still older orders are recombined to constitute an order that is new, but only partially so. The point is that communication orders have life spans.

Across human communication history, it is possible to discern a sequence of communication orders. Because developments occur at different times in different societies, what is presented here as a sequence would, when fully mapped out, undoubtedly appear as a vast network. At this time, for any communication order, it is possible to sort out a few of the basic assumptions that are central to the order, identify some of the revolutionary developments associated with the origin, maintenance and termination of the order, and to estimate beginning and end dates. The transition from one order to the next is accompanied by a number of conditions that redirect long term trends.

Pre-Conversation Order (4 million B.C. to 500,000 B.C.)

This long preparatory order probably resembles in societal function the babbling stage everywhere observed today in the first months of the lives of human children. During this order, the mechanisms required for conversational communication through speech developed to a functional level, particularly in the brain and larynx, and in the neural control of articulators and of associated auditory mechanisms. Pre-verbal social skills probably developed at least to the level displayed by chimpanzees today. The order would appear to be a pre-policy order.

Conversation Order (500,000 B.C. to 3,000 B.C.)

Human communication during the conversation order arose from three developments. As the size of the human brain increased and the associated articulatory and auditory mechanisms became coordinated by that brain, the basic biological conditions *sufficient* for conversational communication existed and the conditions *necessary* for our ancestors to acquire conversational communication behaviors were also met. Third, as the migration of hunters from Africa occurred between 600,000 and 400,000 B.C. (or years ago) the conversation was initiated not once but at least several times; the origins of conversation are multiple. It appears that plural origins of conversational styles are found today in human communities around the world, in what we customarily call language groups.

In this now universal order, the focus is on interaction through speech between dyads and small groups to exchange information, to cooperate, and to develop consensus. Conversation utilizes biological equipment to link two or more human brains; it is the basic means for sharing intelligence, increasing it, making it more widely useful. Conversation has been and promises to continue to be a basic means for generating new information. The conversation order has been the dominant one through almost all the whole of human communication history; further, it now provides the basic pattern for teleconferencing or, more generally, the transceiver-dependent communication services that promise to be a central feature of the new communication order. In this order, communication policy is implicit within a cultural context.

Literacy Order (3,000 B.C. to 1870 A.D.)

The literacy order shifts attention from the tongue/ear to the hand/eye channels, and constitutes a profound break from the previous conversation order. The emergence of literacy accompanies the transition in the major means of production from hunting to agriculture. Agriculture leads to organized trade, and trade to cities. Literacy has always been inseparable from cities, where it flourished first in temples and courts. For most of its history, literacy has been the skill of city-based elites. Even today, probably half of the world's adults are not functionally literate, counting among that number those who have lapsed. This order, unlike conversation, has not become a universal order, in part because the skills of literacy (reading, writing) are almost entirely acquired in institutions called schools.

Three matters are of particular importance. On the one hand, it now appears that there was a very considerable apprehension about committing to writing the large body of ordinary knowledge and oral literature that existed prior to this order. Second, most of our discussion today about literacy ignores the accomplishments of the non-literates and assumes that literacy confers only advantages to literate persons; there is little discussion of the various costs of these much praised benefits. Finally, literacy provides the basic one-way model for the subsequent mass media order. Decisions regarding the uses of literacy, from earliest times, probably provide the first instances of explicit communication policy.

Mass Media Order (1870–1970)

In this order, communication is conceived as the transmission of a message to many receivers or to an audience (much as it had been during the literacy order). For the most part, communication is nationwide in scale, and the central tasks of communication are to contribute to national development and facilitate social control. The main flows of mass mediated information are between capital cities and from capital cities to smaller communities and on to the countryside. While the importance of audience feedback is often stressed, there is very little provision for such feedback to be received and even less provision for all of the feedback which is received to be utilized. The mass media are viewed as inherently costly, complicated and complex, as requiring professional training for their effective and responsible use, and as requiring policies for control by government or business entities, or both.

New Communication Order (1970–2020)

The New communication order (or whatever title one prefers for it) embodies several assumptions about the role of communication in society. First, as in the conversation order, communication again is considered to be (in UNESCO's phrase) fundamentally interactive and participatory. Second, communication is worldscale; this is the first of the communication orders that is a genuine world order. Third, to an important extent, major communication problems are being redefined as world problems: for instance, information imbalance. The MacBride Commission legitimizes the treating of communication problems as world problems. Fourth, policy solutions developed for communication at the world level will have impacts not only on nations but also on sub-national local communities; for instance, the allocation of world spectrum on the availability of communication services in Hawaii. Fifth, communication resources can be and ought to be abundant rather than scarce in relationship to human communication needs. Summarizing, it can be said that, in this order, humankind has the right to the communication resources required to serve communication needs, especially those needs arising from interactive and participatory communication that were ignored or suppressed through much of the literacy and mass media orders.

A point must now be stressed. Perhaps as many as half of the world's adults are not functionally literate and many of these same adults have been influenced but little by any of the mass media. At the same time, these adults have maintained the interactive and participatory skills that are essential to conversation. We do not know, however, at what level the inventive and creative aspects of conversation have been maintained. In particular, are conversational societies still producing the quality of knowledge embodied in the oral literature that provided much of our secular and sacred classics?

We may now also ask whether those local cultures that have maintained a conversational order as the primary and exclusive order can leap-frog not only a literacy but also a mass media order. There is some evidence that communicators from such conversational cultures find a transceiver-based audio conference service a convivial tool for communicating across time and space, as the Peacesat Project demonstrates today in the Pacific.[3]

The sequence of orders presented here is of necessity a working formulation—subject to change, open to improvement. Its use in this context is the limited but critical one of helping to examine the important relationship between ancient conversational skills and new transceiver services.

CONDITIONS FOR A NEW ORDER

A new order develops when conditions are favorable for it to do so. Among the conditions favoring, even mandating, a new order at this time are technological breakthroughs, global interdependence and cultural diversity. To these three conditions, which are generally regarded to be of global importance, still others might be added. Further, the issues under discussion at the world level are beginning to be examined at the national or country level and, in some cases, at the local community level as well.

While only recently it would have been possible to provide a short list of significant breakthroughs in telecommunications technology, it is no longer possible. They are too numerous, too varied. But what does become apparent is that it is now possible to invent and produce almost any component of communications technology that is needed or required. Equally, it has now become possible to configure instantly the network capacity required for any communication service. The rapid production of components and the instant configuration of networks, among other developments, shift our attention to patterns of conversational interaction made possible by a given configuration of components. Thus, new ways of thinking about communication services are possible and needed.

The world communication networks for voice, video and text services that are now in place facilitate routine communication across time and space, and as a consequence increase our interdependence, our dependency, on one another. The long lines of communication that are now open can even enable us to confer with one another about how interdependent we wish to become. It is in many ways a curious question. First, the development of communication resources to meet needs and implement rights assumes that communication by various means among people who are close by or distant from one another is the purpose to be served by such resources. At the same time, it is now becoming apparent that there can be too much as well as too little of various kinds of communication. Further, we recognize that certain configurations of technology, certain kinds of services, increase dependency. It is especially important in talking of communication dependence to distinguish between two-way and one-way services, as the latter tend to accentuate dependency in many of its negative and debilitating aspects as witnessed in the later stages of the mass media order. Opportunities for modulating interdependence and dependency appear from time to time (for instance, in the periodic allocation of the radio spectrum).

Cultural pluralism is, of course, one of the most difficult of conditions to discuss fully. If one brings a worldview to the discussion, important characteristics of local cultures are often overlooked. If one attempts to view local cultures generally from the perspective of any particular local culture, a quite different bias is introduced. But if one considers cultures as collective repositories of ordinary knowledge, of tested solutions to various kinds of life problems, it follows that the sharing of such knowledge across cultural boundaries can be an important, even though at times a difficult, process. In proportion as the available communication services are two-way, such an exchange is facilitated. What becomes possible is a world-wide teledialogue or telediscussion, and we do not yet perceive clearly how that might operate and what its consequences might be.

Given the nature of conditions such as technological breakthroughs, interdependence, and pluralism, it follows that the arguments about which conditions mandate what kind of new order are likely to be basic ones. The shape of an order, how it is formed and formulated, makes a difference precisely because each order obscures some kinds of problems and makes others prominent. It is very clear that the *absence of opportunities to ask questions* was not considered a serious problem in most of the mass media order. Readership, audience size, and media effects are among the important problems of the mass media order, but of less concern in the new communication order.

Because orders are concerned, in the deepest sense, with what ought to be, they necessarily focus attention on human values. There are many values surrounding communication and these values are customarily grouped into various communication rights so that they can be documented and discussed. Importantly, a communication right constitutes a claim by someone for certain communication resources. The cost of many basic communication resources is dropping rapidly. For resources to be adequate to implement rights and meet needs, they must be configured into communication services. To guide the developmental process of configuring resources into appropriate and affordable services is the continuing task of communication policy.

Another way of viewing the conditions that mandate a new order is through the examination of communication paradigms. In the old mass media order, the central question was: Who Says What to Whom through What Channels with What Effects? The bias of this mapping question is toward the mass media; the followers of this paradigmatic map quite naturally attend to the mass media. The alternative formulation for the new communication order can be stated: Humankind has the right to the communication resources required to satisfy human communication needs. The bias of this formulation is toward interactive and participatory communication or, in a word, toward conversation. These two profoundly different views of communication are often labelled "vertical" and "horizontal." In the next section, we shall look briefly at the horizontal formulation which can be expected to constitute the dominant structure within the new order.

HORIZONTAL COMMUNICATION

Within the new communication order the horizontal structures of communication are expected to become the dominant ones, and the older vertical structures are expected to be transformed and, subsequently, assume a subdominant role. Vertical structures will not be completely replaced by horizontal ones, but a substantial restructuring of communication services is anticipated. What is forecast, then, is the emergence of an appropriate mix of affordable communication services, weighted toward the transceiver type, but also constituting a wide continuum of services from the two-way to the one-way.

There are now more than four billion human communicators on this planet, and a philosophy of horizontal communication assumes that each of these communicators has the right to communicate with any other of these communicators for any mutually agreed purpose. Nearly all such communicators have, of course, developed and maintained conversational or dialogue skills, and through these skills have built up a repertoire of ordinary knowledge which they share with one another on a daily basis through conversation or dialogue.

An important statement about the nature of horizontal communication has recently been prepared by Luis Beltran.[4] He claims that "dialogue is the axis of horizontal communication for, if genuine democratic interaction is to take place, each person should have comparable opportunities for emitting and receiving messages so as to preclude monopolization of the word through monologue. He emphasizes that from the perspective of horizontal communication it is no longer useful to distinguish between sources and receivers. All members of humankind are *communicators*.

As conceived by Beltran and others, horizontal communication requires not only opportunities for face-to-face conversation and dialogue, but also a class of communication service that extends these patterns across time and space and may be called *interpersonal telecommunication*. Such interpersonal telecommunication services, beginning with the telephone, but now expanding rapidly to include CB radio and various types of computer and audio conferencing, promise to be the prototype or reference model for horizontal communication.

What is of special interest in interpersonal telecommunication is what happens when the information or ordinary knowledge of two or more communicators is combined.[5] Often, the result is not some form of addition but rather a kind of multiplication, a synergy. Two illustrations may help to clarify the point. In binocular vision and binaural hearing not only do two eyes and two ears increase the available information, they add information of a different logical type; that is, depth perception and directional hearing. We have not during the recent century been much interested in the extraordinary dynamics of combining diverse sources of ordinary knowledge, but as the very ancient oral literature must remind us, this process can produce messages of enduring value.

As Harold Innis has recorded in some detail, when a major change occurs in either the time or space dimension of communication, major changes elsewhere in society can be expected to follow.[6] What is significant in the order that is now taking shape is that *both* time and space are being substantially altered. Telecommunication services of many types become distance insensitive. Many of the new interpersonal telecommunication services alter the basic conversational rate and become partially time insensitive, as illustrated by computer conferencing. From the perspective of horizontal communication, these alterations in time and space seem likely to become of deep significance to the role of communication in society.

IN PRAISE OF QUESTIONS

That *one cannot ask a book a question* has been evident for five thousand years. In our current quest for a new order, it is essential that we ask again about the significance of this fact if we are to avoid the most serious error of the previous literacy and mass media orders. A half century ago, in posing irreverent questions about the work ethic, Bertrand Russell wrote a provocative essay in praise of idleness. Today, as a central part of the new communication order, we need to start a long-term, worldscale dialogue in praise of questions.

In a much earlier series of dialogues, Socrates said, "I cannot help feeling, Phaedrus, that writing is unfortunately like painting; for the creations of the painter have the attitude of life, and yet if you ask them a question, they preserve a solemn silence . . ." Socrates went on to say that when you "put a question" to a written page, the author always gives one "unvarying answer."

Referring to these Socratic dialogues, Octavio Paz recently observed that "reading a book stimulates our receptive capacity and our imagination, but it sometimes neutralizes our reactions and paralyzes our critical sense. On closing the book, we cannot communicate our disagreement with the author. The book, to a certain extent, robs us of our right to answer back."[7] Paz extended these observations to broadcast television and added that "the civilizations of the future will either be a dialogue of national cultures, or there will be no civilization."

The most serious structural error embodied not only in the book but in mass media generally is that, in Paz's words, they "rob us of our right to answer back." In recent years, those in control of the mass media have been excessive in their praise of feedback and talkback and letters to the editor. But they stop short of a binding right of everyone to reply, arguing that such a right would change the nature of the media—which from the horizontal perspective is what ought to happen. Actually, the various feedback devices do little to increase the options for an audience to question and inquire. They serve mainly to increase the opportunities for control by the source.[8] That feedback should operate in this way is entirely consistent with the original concept of feedback as a means of enhancing command and control.

The inadequacy of feedback for two-way communication becomes clearer when one looks at communication from the perspective advanced by Luis Beltran. In his distinction between vertical and horizontal communication, Beltran establishes that horizontal communication structures in society facilitate dialogue while vertical ones do not. In specifying what is meant by dialogue, he cites access, interaction, and participation. He envisions dialogue as give and take, as answers and questions.

The most searching statements about dialogue probably come from Martin Buber. He claims that dialogue results only from the asking and answering of *real* questions. Further, what he calls genuine dialogue can only develop within an I-Thou relationship, a kind of human association in which the participants in a dialogue have a mutual concern for the well-being of each other.

COMMUNICATION RIGHTS

When communication comes again to be considered to be fundamentally interactive and participatory, or conversational, the communication rights that were in the past century molded to the outlook of a mass media order require to be rethought.[9] In particular, as d'Arcy and others have noted, Article 19 of the Universal Declaration of Human Rights was heavily influenced by such a mass media mentality.

As early as 1944, Jacques Maritain anticipated the emphasis on interactive communication rights.[10] He included among the basic human rights the right of every citizen to participate actively, the right of association, and the rights of investigation and discussion (as extensions of the earlier freedoms of speech and expression). The process of reshaping communication rights has continued up to the present, and has been intensified following the forecast by d'Arcy in 1969 that the rights to information proclaimed in Article 19 of the Universal Declaration of Human Rights would come to be extended into a full right to communicate.

Several component communication rights, considered at present to be of particular importance within a comprehensive right to communicate, can be set in three interrelated categories: association rights, information rights and human development rights.

Association Rights

The current insistence on interaction and participation in communication re-emphasizes the centrality of human association for the purposes of communication. Thus, a right to assemble assumes a new importance, and is extended to include a right to *assemble electronically* as by telephone and teleconference. Further, a right to discuss including a right to hear and be heard is essential, especially for a wide range of inventive and creative communication that includes verification, problem-solving, negotiation and decision-making. Add to these two rights a third associative right, the right to participate, which is taken to mean the right to participate in a wide range of societal decision-making, particularly on those matters of direct concern to the participator.

Information Rights

The next category of communication rights has in recent years attracted the most attention, in part because these information rights are proclaimed in Article 19 and in many national constitutions, and because they are of obvious importance in a mass media order where informational messages are transmitted from sources to receivers. But as Tomo Martelanc and others have argued, these rights must be active, even *interactive,* rights rather than the passive rights they appear to be in Article 19.[11] Thus, a right to *seek* information becomes a right to be informed, and a right to *impart* information becomes a right to inform.

Human Development Rights

The final category of communication rights may be called human development rights. These rights include a right to culture, a right to choose, and a right to privacy, where the right to privacy is understood to include a right not to communicate. These rights are the least established at the moment, have the briefest history, and yet are of growing importance as the capacity for communication in an interdependent world increases. Abuse of these rights leads to cultural dominance, censorship, and invasions of privacy.

What becomes evident in the consideration of various communication rights is that while each of these rights is of primary importance to some individuals, cultures, societies, and civilizations, they are not equally important to all such communicating entities. When one considers the preferences and the interactions among them, the situation is very complex. Each of these communication rights has inherent in it a number of possible policy goals.

POLICY PROCESS

To repeat, communication development is understood here to focus on the configuration of communication resources into services that meet human communication needs directly, rather than indirectly through the achievement of economic or other societal goals. In this context, policy goals are considered to be inherent in communication rights; and the standards for achievement expressed in communication rights set the criteria against which communication resources come to serve communication needs.

The policy process within the new communication order can be characterised as contextual, values-sensitive, problem-oriented and multi-method. The new order itself provides an important context for communication policy. The concern with values finds its expression in attention to a variety of communication rights. Communication problems, following the work of the MacBride Commission, are seen as world problems and are formulated as policy problems. The informational requirements for the solution of policy problems appears to require substantially different methods for acquiring and using information and knowledge than are currently available; some of the conferencing methods now being introduced appear to hold considerable promise as tools of inquiry. Thus, the policy process within the new communication order does itself present a number of challenges.

As a response to that challenge, there now appears to be developing what, with some hope, can be called a communication policy science.[12] This science will take as its central task not the refinement of theory as the discipline sciences do but rather the improvement of the process of forming and executing communication policy. Within the next decade, we shall see to what extent such a new science can indeed make a contribution to the communication policy process, and thereby to an improvement of communication in society.

TOWARD WHAT?

Within the context of a new communication order, towards what will these present and future developments lead? Toward what ought they to lead? Can these two questions be the same one?

The transformation from vertical to horizontal communication structures in society can be accompanied by a substantial increase in affordable interpersonal telecommunication services. But rather than a replacement of vertical with horizontal structures, what is anticipated is a continuum of services ranging from the wide-open two-way to the more restricted one-way. Significantly, two-way services make dialogue possible; dialogue is understood as a conversational process of asking and answering real questions. Further, formal information stores can be organized to respond to specific questions and to systematic inquiries from the widest range of communicators. As that transformation takes place, it is anticipated that we shall discover that a restoration of balance in communication flows has also been achieved.

While the restoration of balance and the achievement of equity in the availability of communication services can be seen as major accomplishments, our detailed concern with communication development can over time increase our appreciation for the significance of the long-term developmental trends that extend across communication orders. We could come to see our daily decisions and actions in the communication field as having not only immediate consequences but long term consequences as well.

An example of such a greater role toward which we might choose to develop can be taken from Lasswell's observations on the "expectation of violence."[13] He notes that inter-nation activities are often conditioned by an expectation of violence while the opposite expectation characterizes most *intra*-nation activities. By what development of communication resources might it be possible for the intra-nation expectation of being able to solve problems peaceably be extended to the world level? More broadly, how might we develop the communication resources of the world to make the "scourge of war" unthinkable? Not an easy question, but one which now can be considered.

Similar large-scale, long range questions are being posed about problems of economic and social justice problems. For instance, what mix of communication services are a pre-condition for appropriate economic development?[14] Under what pattern of equity in the availability of communication resources can social justice most fully be accomplished? And there are questions beyond these about how to prepare for future communication orders.

Most simply, within the context of a new communication order, communication development ought to lead to a world in which everyone has the right to communicate.

NOTES

1 David K. Cohen and Charles E. Lindblom, *Usable Knowledge* (New Haven: Yale University Press, 1979).

2 Jean d'Arcy, "Broadcasting in the Global Age," in *Symposium on the Cultural Role of Broadcasting* (Tokyo: Hoso-Bunka Foundation, 1979), pp. 124-30.

3 Peacesat is the acronym for the Pan Pacific Education and Communication Experiments by Satellite. Current information may be obtained from John Bystrom, Director, Peacesat Project, University of Hawaii, Honolulu, Hawaii 96822, USA.

4 Luis Ramiro Beltran, *Farewell to Aristotle: Horizontal Communication,* a paper submitted to the UNESCO International Commission for the Study of Communication Problems, 1979, p. 33.

5 Gregory Bateson, *Mind and Nature* (New York: Dutton, 1979).

6 Harold A. Innis, *Empire and Communications* (Toronto: University of Toronto Press, 1972).

7 Octavio Paz, a paper presented at the II World Encounter on Communications, Acapulco, 1979, p. 14.

8 Asok Mitra, "Development Journalism and the Right to Communicate," in L.S. Harms and Jim Richstad (eds.), *Evolving Perspectives on the Right to Communicate* (East West Communication Institute, 1977), p. 192.

9 Amadou–Mahtar M'Bow, "Communication's Decisive Role in Development," in *Communicator* (New Delhi: January 1979), p. 9.

10 Jacques Maritain, *The Rights of Man* (London: The Centenary Press, 1944).

11 Tomo Martelanc, "Forward," in L.S. Harms, Jim Richstad, and Kathleen Kie (eds.), *Right to Communicate: Collected Papers* (Honolulu: Social Science Research Institute, 1977), pp. vii–ix.

12 L.S. Harms, "An Emergent Communication Policy Science," in *Communication*, forthcoming.

13 Harold D. Lasswell, *The Signature of Power: Buildings, Communication, and Policy* (New Brunswick: Transaction Books, 1979).

14 Meheroo Jussawalla, "The Economics of Telecommunications for Development," in Dan J. Wedemeyer and David Jones (eds.), *Pacific Telecommunications Conference* (Honolulu, Social Science Research Institute, 1979), pp. 101–111.

Acknowledgments

LITERARY ACKNOWLEDGMENTS

"Here, There and Everywhere: Where Americans Get Their News" by Evans Witt, *Public Opinion,* August/September, 1983, pp. 15–22. Copyright © 1983 by American Enterprise Institute. Reprinted by permission.

"Can the Press Tell the Truth?" by Lewis H. Lapham et al. From *Harper's,* Vol. 270, No. 1616, January, 1985. Copyright © 1985 by *Harper's Magazine.* All rights reserved. Reprinted from the January issue by special permission.

"Privacy and the Press: Is Nothing Sacred?" by Nat Hentoff from *Saturday Review,* July 21, 1979, pp. 22–23. Copyright © 1979 Saturday Review magazine. Reprinted by permission.

"Readers 'in the editor's chair' squirm over ethical dilemmas" by Richard Oppel from ASNE Bulletin, October, 1984, pp. 4–8. Reprinted by permission of the American Society of Newspaper Editors and Richard Oppel.

"Editors Shouldn't Fear Ethical Thinking—They Do It Naturally All The Time" by Arthur L. Caplan from *Drawing the Line,* the American Society of Newspaper Editors, 1984. Reprinted by permission.

"Harvest of Sham" by Daniel Schorr, *Channels of Communications,* March, 1986. Copyright © 1986 by *Channels* Magazine. Reprinted by permission.

"Tube Rock: How Music Video Is Changing Music" by Richard Goldstein from *The Village Voice,* September 17, 1985, pp. 38, 42–43. Reprinted with permission of the author and the Village Voice © 1985.

From Victor Lidz, "Television and Moral Order in a Secular Age," pp. 267–270, 275–289 in *Interpreting Television: Current Research Perspectives,* edited by Willard D. Rowland, Jr. and Bruce Watkins. Copyright © 1984 by Sage Publications, Inc. Reprinted by permission of Sage Publications, Inc.

From "Understanding Television" by David Marc, *The Atlantic,* August, 1984, pp. 33–36, 41–44. Copyright © 1984 by The Atlantic Monthly Company. Reprinted by permission of the author.

"Jackpot! The Biggest, Shrewdest, Moneymakingest Little Show on Earth" by Michael Pollan, *Channels of Communications,* June 1986. Copyright © 1986 by *Channels* Magazine. Reprinted by permission.

From Robert P. Snow, "Radio: The Companion Medium," pp. 99–112, 117–119 in *Creating Media Culture,* by Robert P. Snow. Copyright © 1983 by Sage Publications, 'nc. Reprinted by permission of Sage Publications, Inc. and the author.

"Publish ads for X-movies and such?" "No" by Edward D. Miller and "Yes" by Michael Gartner from *Des Moines Sunday Register,* January 8, 1978. Reprinted by permission.